Regis College Library

W9-BTG-692

Beyond Monotheism

Beyond Monotheism is an absorbing and lyrical exploration of the possibility of a new, living theology of multiplicity that is grounded in fluidity, change, and incarnation.

Laurel Schneider takes the reader on a vivid journey from the origins of "the logic of the One"—only recently dubbed monotheism—through to the modern day, where monotheism has increasingly failed to adequately address spiritual, scientific, and ethical experiences in the changing world. In Part I, Schneider traces a trajectory from the ancient history of monotheism and multiplicity in Greece, Israel, and Africa through the Constantinian valorization of the logic of the One, to medieval and modern challenges to that logic in poetry and science. She pursues an alternative and constructive approach in Part II: a "logic of multiplicity" already resident in Christian traditions in which the complexity of life and the presence of God may be better articulated. Part III takes up the open-ended question of ethics from within that multiplicity, exploring the implications of this radical and realistic new theology for the questions that lie underneath theological construction: questions of belonging and nationalism, of the possibility of love, and of unity.

In this groundbreaking work of contemporary theology, Schneider shows that the One is not lost in divine multiplicity, and that in spite of its abstractions, divine multiplicity is realistic and worldly, impossible ultimately to abstract.

Laurel C. Schneider is Associate Professor of Theology, Ethics, and Culture at Chicago Theological Seminary and author of *Re-Imagining the Divine: Confronting the Backlash Against Feminist Theology* (1999).

Beyond Monotheism

A theology of multiplicity

Laurel C. Schneider

Regis College Library
15 ST. MARY STREET
TORONTO ONTARIO CANADA
M4Y 2R5

WITHDRAWN

Routledge
Taylor & Francis Group

LONDON AND NEW YORK

BL
221
S34
2008

First published 2008
by Routledge
2 Park Square, Milton Park, Abingdon, Oxon OX14 4RN

Simultaneously published in the USA and Canada
by Routledge
270 Madison Ave., New York, NY 100016

Routledge is an imprint of the Taylor & Francis Group, and informa business

© 2008 Laurel C. Schneider

Typeset in Sabon by
Taylor & Francis Books
Printed and bound in Great Britain by
Antony Rowe Ltd, Chippenham, Wiltshire

All rights reserved. No part of this book may be reprinted or reproduced or
utilized in any form or by any electronic, mechanical, or other means, now
known or hereafter invented, including photocopying and recording, or in
any information storage or retrieval system, without permission in writing
from the publishers.

British Library Cataloguing in Publication Data
A catalogue record for this book is available from the British Library

Library of Congress Cataloging in Publication Data
Schneider, Laurel C., 1961–
   Beyond monotheism: a theology of multiplicity / Laurel C. Schneider.
      p. cm.
   Includes bibliographical references and index.
   1. Monotheism. 2. Theology. 3. Religion. 4. Polytheism. I. Title.
   BL221.S36 2007
211'.3—dc22   2007006633

ISBN 978-0415-94190-7 (hbk)
ISBN 978-0415-94191-4 (pbk)
ISBN 978-0203-94471-4 (ebk)

To the students of Constructive Theology (TEC 305)
at Chicago Theological Seminary

Contents

Preface

Some start out
with a big story
that shrinks.
Some stories accumulate power
like a sky gathering clouds,
quietly, quietly,
till the story rains around you.

Naomi Shihab Nye[1]

When did the stories of God become a story of totality, of a closed system, of a One? To what corner of human longing does the story of the One belong? As the motors of fundamentalism in all of the religions of One God race on the fuel of battered bodies and broken hearts, the logic of the One chokes on itself like a stone in the mouth. The story of the One denies fleshiness and the stubborn shiftiness of bodies; it cannot abide ambiguities and unfinished business; it cannot speak syllables of earth. But in its failures are openings, for there are always gaps in the story of the One, fissures that widen and crumble at the edges. Through the gaps, rivers of divine faces flow, their eyes the eyes of children, hinting at depths of losses and possibilities, and of incarnate coming-to-senses. In bodies, both of the lost and of the living, multiplicity makes itself known, tumbling through the stories of the One, birthing worlds and confounding certainty at every turn. The story of the One cannot, finally, achieve the still point that it pretends to crave; the very stones cry out.[2]

This is a book about divine multiplicity. More accurately, it is a book *after* divine multiplicity in the sense of pursuit (but also in the sense of priority) of a mode of *making sense of* divinity, which is a sort of incarnation in itself. Oneness, as a basic claim about God, simply does not make sense. The world in its tenacious natality, mutability, and flesh has always exceeded and undermined oneness and totality, whether in Akhenaten's Egypt, Josiah's Israel, Constantine's Rome, or Luther's Germany. It repeatedly puts the lie to the One God's attempts at closure and control. For multiplicity, it turns out, is not just the flesh behind the mask of the

One, it is the mask and masquerade of totality as well, popping the seams of the One's oneness in every instance. Multiplicity, which is not a synonym for "many," is a preliminary gesture, an experiment in naming a logic that is supple, adaptive, and rhizomatic rather than fixed, or merely predictive. Multiplicity *turns out* the story of the One, in the paradoxical sense of (rejecting the One's totality and in the sense of producing it) This can be no either/or reduction. When the flow of multiplicity disrupts the pretensions of the One, we discover that God, so often a synonym for the One, is more and less than one, after all.

But it is true that the oneness, indivisibility, and totality of God constitute such a powerful story that no less than three world religions claim it for themselves. For over a thousand years they have fought bitterly with each other (and within themselves) over that story and for it. They have done so in part because some stories are not "just stories." A Navajo man once told Willard W. Hill, who was a guest among the people, that poverty is the lack of songs. "I have always been a poor man" he explained to Hill, "I do not know a single song."[3] This man was not spouting some romantic aphorism rich with nostalgia for a time when old men could afford to sit around on porches and swap tall tales or hum the favorite tunes from their youth. This deceptively simple description of what it meant to a traditional Navajo man to be poor is a statement at once economic, political, and metaphysical for a people whose historical sensibilities recognize the power of embodied narratives—in poetry, song, and story—to make and unmake whole worlds.

Lying behind that traditional Navajo economic observation is the assumption that songs and stories of power, which are performed narratives that involve information about the reality of things and their relations, are as valuable and potent as land and must be protected as such. This is a valuation that most Jews, Christians, and Muslims may not recognize and express with the clarity of the traditional Navajo, but the overarching value and potency to them of their stories about divine oneness is certainly evident in the long and tumultuous history of their relations with each other. That history is rife with attempts on every side to hold and defend their respective claims on the story.

The world religions of One God and the cultures that they have nurtured stand in each others' shadow, unable to divide and share a story that refuses to admit its own multiplicity and incompleteness. Despite the desperate bloodshed, or because of it, the world's monotheisms stand more and more obviously, as Kathleen Sands puts it, in the "ruins of the Absolute."[4] A question stands there also, for any who wish to ask it: What poverty comes with the ruin of the story of the Absolute One? Put another way, is oneness the only song of God?

Thankfully, it is not. Ruination and end are not the same things. The ruin of the Absolute, of the story of divine oneness is what *remains*. Every ruin demands a place in the present and is a presence.[5] Its ongoing ruin is not the end of the story of the One—far from it. It is merely the erosion of its facade of totality, which is indeed an end of the One as such. When a narrative cracks open so that its layers of contradiction and dream show like so many levels of geological shift, the story may lose its surface and line, its simplicity, its uniformity, and even its "moral." The familiar may be ruined but it is not wiped out by the depths that crack it open. The ruin of the Absolute spells the disruption of the story's conclusion, rendering it inconclusive but, as Catherine Keller suggests, that end is a beginning, an opening for the divinity that has always flowed through the cracked surface of the One.[6] The end of stasis, closure, and fixity in the ruin of the One makes possible all sorts of passages and shifts into a far more *sensible*, embodied understanding of unity, as we shall see.

The One is not lost, therefore, in multiplicity; it is just ruined in the way that stars fall, which is not falling but becoming-other in the attractional flight of planetary bodies. The ancient stories of the One God are full of just such desire, such gravitational pull toward bodies. The Divine has been there all along in the story of the One, spelling its end and beginning-again like a DNA script at the core of the living cell, like a star falling into brilliant ruin in the arms of the nearest body.

Acknowledgments

This book almost died a quiet death many times and it is only thanks to a multiplicity of friends, colleagues, and especially family members that I sit now and attempt the impossible: to acknowledge the invaluable help, direction, patience, belief, and gentle correction of others. First and foremost, I thank Kathryn Tanner, Kathleen Sands, Maaike de Haardt, and Nancy Frankenberry for their friendship throughout, for their generosity of mind, willingness to read, listen, guide, and encourage as the ideas tumbled about like stones on the beach. Catherine Keller read the entire manuscript with immense care, cheering me on and suggesting improvements precisely where they were needed. I am also unbelievably lucky to claim membership in a family of writers and teachers of writing, whose generosity of time and wisdom kept me from giving up many times. Impressive authors in their own right, Pat Schneider and Paul Schneider patiently read and reread the manuscript, including multiple versions of the most troubled and irksome sections. Their incisive editorial and poetic abilities, along with a dogged reminder that audiences also sometimes reside outside of the academy have made this a much better book. Through conversations about monotheism, covenant, and the problems of the One, my father Peter Schneider helped me to hone my reasoning as well as my passion for this project. I am rhizomatically grateful to Rebecca Schneider for teaching me about what remains and for introducing me to the writing of Gilles Deleuze and the art of Ann Hamilton. Bethany Schneider has never lost faith in me or in laughter, she introduced me to Thomas King, read Chapter 13 and saved me from some embarrassing errors as well—historical and otherwise. My family, including Kate Thomas, Nina Bramhall, Sarah Kavanagh, Megan Brown, Natty Schneider and, more than anyone else, Cindy Davenport saw me through this project in a thousand small and enormous ways. There are others who deserve acknowledgement as well as exemption from blame: Ken Stone and Timothy Sandoval assisted with Chapter 3, W. Dow Edgerton shared his love and knowledge of poetry (both silly and profound) with me and read Chapters 7 and 8, John Thiel read Chapter 7 and the faculty at Chicago Theological Seminary read an earlier version of Chapters 2 and 3 in seminar and provided

valuable comments. I am grateful to Melanie Morrison, April Allison, the
Leaven Center, and Jil Clark for providing space to think at crucial points
in the writing, and to the Vanderbilt Divinity School Antoinette Brown
Lecture committee for inviting me and giving me such a rich opportunity to test out my reading of Dante. Ellen Armour and John Thatamanil
in particular identified unintended consequences in some of my arguments
through the most pleasurable of debates, and I am in the debt of every
member of the Workgroup in Constructive Theology! Many thanks to the
students of Catherine Keller's Theory for Theology seminar at Drew University, who read the manuscript so insightfully. Thanks also belongs to
Holly Toensing for her unending friendship and assistance with my reading
of John 4; to Elena Maria Jimenez, Kunitoshi Sakai, and Adam Kotsko
for research, indexing, and bibliographic assistance; to Carolyn Benson,
Suzanne Webber and Al Miller for reading the Preface and Chapter 1 on
such short notice; to Sharon Ellis Davis, Kathryn Lyndes and Julianne
Buenting for reading Chapters 2, 3, 7, and 8 and for keeping me
accountable and well fed in the women's writing group. I would be
remiss, especially in this book that affirms multiplicity, not to acknowledge also the enduring patience and unwarranted applause granted me by
the four-leggeds in my life, especially Stoner and Emmett. Thank you one
and all.

Permissions

- Excerpt from "Telling the Story" from *Words Under the Words: Selected Poems* by Naomi Shihab Nye, copyright © 1995. Reprinted with the permission of Far Corner Books, Portland, Oregon.
- Excerpt from "I Said to Poetry" in *Horses Make a Landscape Look More Beautiful: Poems by Alice Walker,* copyright © 1984 by Alice Walker, reprinted by permission of Harcourt, Inc.
- Excerpts from *Green Grass, Running Water* by Thomas King. Copyright © 1993 by Thomas King. Reprinted by permission of Houghton Mifflin Company. All rights reserved.
- Excerpts from *The Inferno of Dante Alighieri*, translated by Ciaran Carson. Copyright © 2002 by Ciaran Carson. Reprinted by permission of Granta Books.
- "Cages" from *From Room to Room.* Copyright © 1978 by Jane Kenyon. Reprinted with the permission of Alice James Books.
- Excerpt from "Against Nature" reprinted courtesy of Daniel Halpern, founding editor of *Antaeus*, New York, NY.
- Excerpt from "The Eighth Elegy" from DUINO ELEGIES by Rainer Maria Rilke, translated by Edward Snow. Translation copyright © 2000 by Edward Snow. Reprinted by permission of North Point Press, a division of Farrar, Straus, and Giroux, LLC.

- Excerpt from "Interbeing" reprinted from *Call Me by My True Names* (1999) by Thich Nhat Hanh with permission of Parallax Press, Berkeley, California, www.parallax.org.

The author and publisher would like to thank Ann Hamilton for her kind permission to use her artwork (*aleph • video*), 1992/1993 on the book's front cover.

1 Introduction

Incarnation ... again

the whole is not given, and things are always starting up again in the middle, falling together in another, looser way ... one thus has nothing of the sense of a well-planned itinerary; on the contrary, one is taken on a sort of conceptual trip for which there pre-exists no map.

John Rajchman[1]

The logic of the One, which has governed the era of European expansion, has tendrils stretching back as far as thirty-five centuries into the reign of Akhenaten in Egypt, though it did not become dominant and flourish until much later in Persia, Israel, and Greece. The logic of the One—only very lately dubbed monotheism—has functioned powerfully on behalf of exiles and emperors alike, and it has framed a whole scientific methodology. For all of its success, however, the logic of the One simply doesn't work well enough any more to satisfy far-reaching questions about either divinity or the world. The logic of the One is not *wrong*, except, ironically, when it is taken to be the whole story. Rather than false, it is incomplete. The logic of the One (and the concept of God that falls within it) is simply *not* One. There is always less, and more, to the story.

To paraphrase Luce Irigaray's wonderfully double-edged notion, this is a book about the divinity "which is not One."[2] What is more, it is a book about divine "being" and "presence," both of which are topics that have sunk far more learned and accomplished theologians than myself. There is, however, some comfort in knowing that we need not fear sinking (or foundering, or stumbling, or falling into contradiction, or any number of like disasters that normally stump the systematic theologian). Sometimes these mishaps are the best way to move forward. As Gilles Deleuze once happily declared, "An impasse: So much the better."[3] The "ship" of theology, particularly of Christian theology, is full of holes and always has been. Sinking may be precisely the way to proceed.

The deceptively simple claim of this book is that divinity beyond the logic of the One, beyond monotheism, *occurs*. This idea of occurring divinity—divine multiplicity—sins against the ideologies of eternity and stasis required of oneness and so recognizes leaks in the Christian empire's God

Who *Is* and Ever Shall *Be*. It also sins against ideologies of linear progress, as if there is a single goal or *telos* toward which the rich manyness of the embodied cosmos must "process," in flight from itself *as it is*. Instead, the idea of occurring divinity pursues incarnation in terms of bodies (which may seem a straightforward notion but, sadly, in Christian theology it is not), and this means affirming what Marcella Althaus-Reid calls "the dissonant and multiple in theology" as much as, if not more than, the ordered and unified.[4] While not opposed to unity in a proximal sense (that would be merely a new either/or, which depends on the logic of the One) there is an epistemological challenge in this affirmation that comes directly from feminism. Not only is the question of incarnation a feminist one because it takes up the messy variability of bodies, but because, as Claire Colebrook points out, "feminism has always been more than a quibble regarding this or that value or prejudice within an otherwise sound way of thinking."[5]

What is more, this theology emerges out of a specific time and place of political uncertainty, prolonged wars with unclear rationales, and global shifts in power. Guerilla attacks by "terrorists" and massive, devastating retribution by wealthy "nations" are impossible to unravel in traditional terms of border disputes, royal lines of succession, or access to industrial wealth. The economics *and* emerging sociology of globalized capital are less and less tied to the idea of "nations," meaning that both war and peace conceived in national terms are less coherent and less effective. And theology is as mixed up in politics and the effects of global economics today as it ever has been in history. This is particularly evident in the United States and in the countries of the Middle East, all of which are intimately bound together in struggles for power that, as often as not, are framed in the languages of religious ideologies of monotheism. Theology, particularly theology emerging out of the United States, cannot avoid these struggles over the One God because it is implicated in and made complicit by the effects of American actions on the world and on ourselves.

Theologies of the One and divinity which is not One therefore occur today in the context of what Ania Loomba, Suvir Kaul, and others call the "rapidly proliferating defenses of empire (not simply de facto but de jure)."[6] Schooled in theologies of the One, we can only glimpse the divinity which is not One in retrospect or foreshadowed as the excess, temporality, and partiality of the imperial One and Same that at the same time fails at oneness, that cannot actually tolerate flesh, that suffocates in the closures of the Whole, even when it is conceived in triplicate. Only a divinity not constrained to ultimacy, eternal oneness, or numerical systems can actually *come*, can actually "dwell among us." But it is all too easy to miss such a divinity entirely, if eyes are focused only on the gilt frames of church authority. A different logic is required—perhaps an affirmative one—for following Rajchman's Deleuze "to affirm is not to assert or assume, but to lighten, to unground, to release the fresh air of other possibilities, to combat stupidity and cliché." A logic of multiplicity en route to a better theological understanding and affirmation of incarnation is what this particular search for divinity beyond the logic of the One is about.

Bread and stones: tools for the journey

I do not travel this road alone or without help. There are runes in the stones on every side, signs of ancient wisdom that exceed the totalizing drive of the One. They spill out of the unfinished and multiple biblical stories as well as the fragments and ruined returns of philosophy and poetry from the outer edges of the ancient empires of Africa, Asia, and the Mediterranean and the modern empires of Europe and the Americas. Layers of complication point to a depth that cannot be written but that funds every beginning-again. A bit breathlessly, therefore, I try to read what I can of these signs while following contemporary teachers whose own work guides them toward divinity beyond the logic of the One. I know, in other words, that a "theology of multiplicity" means nothing if it travels solo. There are strong strains here of Catherine Keller's own dive into the *Tehom* (the Deep) in search of *tehomic* divinity,[8] as there are of Marcella Althaus-Reid's search for the God made indecent by totalitarian theologies: the bacchanalian tail of the queerly migrant divine.[9] Kwok Pui-lan, Wohnee Anne Joh, James W. Perkinson and most of my students point toward divinity that does not embody or bless the powers of empire but traverses its unstable borderlines, haunted by slavery, hunted by homeland security, illegal and unassimilated—the unwhitewashed body of God.[10] There is also here A. Okechukwu Ogbonnaya's determination to hold off the curse of solitude in divinity, along with Kathryn Tanner's search for the excessive, profligate divine in love with the world.[11] Delores Williams, Ellen Armour and Sharon Welch guide me in a determination to stay accountable for the myriad privileges and recapitulations that accompany any white feminist project while Gilles Deleuze and Thomas King open pathways to a hermeneutic of empire-toppling humor, story-telling, and border-crossing joy.[12]

There are also many other teachers and guides whose ideas shape this work, at times critically and at other times constructively, because it is part of a swelling movement in theology that seeks to resist the intertwining and co-constitutive dynamics of racism, sexism, heterosexism, classism, and nationalism. These dynamics—tools of colonialism and imperial theology—do not dissipate in theologies of resistance just because they are named. Sexism, racism, classism, heterosexism, ethnocentrism, and nationalism all constitute each other in the colonial and postcolonial context and ride incognito in word choices, imagination, dream, and story; they slide into each other when pressed, and so can reinscribe themselves in even the most "liberationist" of theologies.[13] The privileges that accompany these dynamics in any of their many forms are sticky and resilient. There is no purity in resistance, including the resistances attempted in this project, which is why it travels in the company of others, critics and supporters alike. It is therefore appropriate, by way of beginning, that I follow the decidedly impure Mary Daly in seeking to pick up certain tools necessary for this work. She names them the "Courage to See" and the "Courage to Sin ... Big."[14]

Some of the resources and challenges before this project lie in the richly complicated history of Christian theology in relation to structures of empire. History is never simple, and the logic of the One has served both to shore up imperial aspirations to absolute power and, at times, to stand in judgment of those aspirations. The genealogy of monotheistic morals with regard to empire is not uniform, though the overwhelming tendencies toward totalizing claims in the religions of the One God suggest the very critique that this study undertakes. When theology provides divine orientation for empire (and what empire has not had its servant theologians?) resistance to empire also needs be in some part theological. *Empire* theology, to paraphrase Jacques Derrida, therefore constitutes a "prosthetic origin" and legitimation for both imperial rulers and citizens.[15] Access to citizenship in a nation endowed with divine right and heroic origins allows the citizens access to imperial largess and to tell their story in such a way that they forget that they were themselves once poor, once criminal, homeless, illegal, or slaves.

Deployed through the centuries since Constantine by rulers in search of a divine mirror for their totalitarian dreams of state or of church power, Christian monotheism is empire theology. I am by no means alone in this claim, nor did I come up with the idea. Early in the twentieth century Erik Peterson wrote an influential essay on the political consequences of monotheism entitled "Monotheism as a Political Problem" which many later theologians found persuasive, marking a resurgent interest both in the political consequences of monotheism and in the importance of the idea of Trinity for Christian theologians who sought to criticize the ease with which monotheistic ideas find purchase in totalitarian political regimes.[16] Among the most vigorous of contemporary theologians to take up this challenge are Leonardo Boff and Jürgen Moltmann, famous for their critiques of "monarchical monotheism" and for their interest in social concepts of the Christian doctrine of Trinity.[17]

I come to the problem of imperial *Christian* monotheism, however, not from a presupposition that Trinity should be the resolution, although some may well conclude with Boff, Moltmann, LaCugna, Tanner, Jennings, and others that it should be. Instead I come to the problem with the presupposition that incarnation, taken seriously, voids all numerical reckoning. I have therefore elected to think toward divinity in multiplicity, in which multiplicity is an ontological gesture rather than a mathematical equation and in which multiplicity indicates actual presences and relations. Multiplicity exceeds abstract principles (even attractive ones like "becoming") whenever those principles eclipse presence.

Put another way, I am attempting a logic, or posture, that resists reduction to the One *and* resists reduction to the Many while affirming a more supple and effective (rather than absolute) unity. This book is therefore not about "God or the gods," because the answer to monotheism's totalitarian limitations is not polytheism. Polytheism is monotheism's supporting cast and neither polytheism nor monotheism can attend to the uncompromising *thereness* of incarnate divinity. Incarnation is, after all, about bodies. And bodies, in their own uncompromising thereness, queerness, and susceptibility to revolt, are always a problem for abstract theologies, which function foundationally on principles that tend toward stasis. Bodies are also a recurrent problem for empires, which function on principles of progress and the abstraction of bodies into useful social categories (like legions, classes, races, and nations). To the extent that "empire" is a kind of shorthand not only for globalized consolidations of power in the hands of a few but also for the logic of the One writ large, it stands in opposition to "gospel" as a mobile and always contextualized message of good news to the poor and disenfranchised. Divine embodiment—incarnation—therefore becomes a kind of shorthand for the undoing of imperial pretensions to totality and final solutions. This is what makes incarnation the key to rethinking the logic of the One toward a Christian theology that is constituted again in relation to its understanding of God-among-us, a divine reality not only implicated in but explicated out of the very fabric of the worlds we inherit and incorporate. Incarnation in this theological sense is not just the event of a man named Jesus who is affirmed in the Nicene creed as "true God from true God made man." Incarnation is instead a basic theological posture and starting place, an orientation toward reality that, in its attention to the mutability of bodies, undoes the logic of the One and its pretensions.

Throughout Christian history, the arguments of theologians reflect, on the whole, a shared concern. They almost all endeavor to articulate understandings of the divine, a concept of which may include or even follow scripture, creed, or tradition, in light of the needs of the day. In other words, theologians everywhere are concerned to clarify how the content of theology, the λόγος (logos) about θεός (theos), has what Theodore Jennings calls a "context of plausibility" or "point of contact" in the world.[18] Theologians have always had to ask how we can speak of divine presence in such a way that its possibility is not so implausible or wholly alien as to be lost to recognition altogether. This is what sets theology apart from other kinds of modern intellectual enterprises: there is an utter investment in translating core symbols and claims of faith into contexts of plausibility that link the profundity of the symbols to the effective meaning structures of lived experiences and cultures. Theology that pretends a distance from the everyday world is both elite and irrelevant. Theology that pretends a distance from prayer is fooling itself.

So, because theology is concerned intimately with the divine,[19] and the language, ideas, and images for Christian divinity overwhelmingly have been shaped and formed out of the long process of religious sedimentation from pre-Christian to Christian sources in the ancient Near East, Africa and the Greco-Roman empire, theology must take account of its own recurring origins or suffer a true lack of profundity. Catherine Keller has made the excellent point that "theology has no choice but to return recurrently and critically to its originative discourses – unless it wants to create theology *ex nihilo*," the doctrine of which she rightly takes a dim view.[20] What is more, she clarifies, if "we do not content ourselves with an ahistorical origin, historical beginnings matter. According to the key principle of chaos theory ... beginnings repeat themselves. But always with a difference."[21]

Beginning again takes humility, and even some humor. Incarnation disallows absolutely clean beginnings and so it is also the case that a theology of multiplicity, grounded in an incarnational posture, has to tolerate some dirt and disorderly conduct. Christian theology that refuses the seductions of empire is *tehomic* theology; it recognizes its own muddy retrievals, its mistakes; it begins again in *this* time, in the "ruins of the Absolute."[22] Such theology is patient. It is not afraid to own up to its mistakes and to begin telling the story over again, in the middle of everything. Its method includes a willingness to continue to do so, to begin again, and always with a difference. This means that Christian theology in this time is historical theology to the extent that it has purchase in the given life and context of real people in real cultural circumstances, contexts that are not ever themselves pure; that have not themselves arisen *ex nihilo*.

For such historical theology, the incarnation of divinity in Jesus is not always clear in its meaning or in its genealogies. The struggle to interpret it is deeply rooted in at least three ancient cultures. First, the stories of Jesus are stories of a Jew among Jews, and a result of this fact for Christians who trace their incarnational theology to the Jesus movement is that Christian ideas of divinity are deeply shaped by the faith attributed to Jesus and by the complicated history of Jewish understandings of divinity. Second, Jesus lived in a time of profound colonial immersion in Hellenistic culture. Whether or not Jesus himself studied the Greek philosophers and listened to the Greek-educated Roman orators, the earliest framers of Christian theology did so, and so the Christian ideas of divinity are deeply shaped by the historical frame of Pythagorean and Platonic theo-philosophical thought. Third and last, although until recently it has been suppressed by racism, the development of Christian doctrine in the first centuries of the Christian era was led by Africans. This scope of early Christian imagining about divinity, forged in a rich cultural cauldron of Israelite-Persian, Greek, and African horizons of meaning, is still with us today, and so it behooves us to better understand it, even as we struggle to make sense of the divinity that comes to flesh now (and then).

In this sense theology takes seriously the loam out of which its own questions arise. For those persons raised within the cultural matrix of the fraternal trio of Judaism, Christianity, and Islam, the origins of theology lie partly, even largely, in text. Stories, poetry, exhortations, remembrances, laws, genealogies, and the occasional contradiction crowd the Jewish, Christian, and Muslim canonical and extra-canonical holy writings. In addition to the specific books called scripture, the text for theology is always the world in which those books and their stories have lived and pass on – the stories, images, rules, rhythms, and habits through which they pass and by which their meaning is shaped. This wider context of theology emerges out of and reiterates originating struggles of interpretation that echo through the written texts and through inherited practices that surround those writings, all bearing traces of those who, in their time, sought to answer the question "How does God come to us, now?"[23]

For Christians in particular, the stories of Jesus make up a principle cluster of answers to the question of divine coming. Indeed, the question Joan Osborne sings about, "What if God was one of us?" is answered both in biblical and ecclesial texts: God *was* one of us and cried as a baby, disregarded the worries of parents as a child, ate and drank heartily with friends in low places as a young adult, found a calling and some renown as a teacher and healer, suffered a high-profile and tragic execution as a man and was resurrected in a movement of liberation after his death.[24] This God who came, this incarnation, is unambiguously and palpably evocative in its presumed presence, even though the historical evidence leaves much room for the pleasure and agony of debate. Indeed, Christological theology has engendered some of the most passionate debates throughout the history of Christianity, from the earliest divisions in the Jesus movement to the Trinitarian controversies of the third and fourth centuries that resulted in the Nicene and Chalcedonian creeds. These debates continue today in contemporary arguments about the nature of Jesus' divinity, his birth, maleness, and presumed (a)sexuality, his Jewishness, political associations, and his understandings of God. The theological issue of incarnation surges through Christianity today, particularly in terms of consequences for celibacy, for leadership by women, and for the ordination of openly gay, lesbian, bisexual and transgendered people in the Church.

Divine incarnation is not, therefore, an esoteric concern of a few. The huge success of television and big-screen movies about Jesus, from Tim Rice's *Jesus Christ Superstar* (1973), *Monty Python's Life of Brian* (1979) and Martin Scorsese's film of Nikos Kazantzakis's book *The Last Temptation of Christ* (1988), to Mel Gibson's florid *Passion of the Christ* (2004) and even Ron Howard's film of Dan Brown's book *The Da Vinci Code* (2006), all speak to the fact that the stories and flesh of Jesus evoke passion and challenge among Christians as much now as they did in the third and fourth centuries. While all the rest attempt a serious treatment of the story of Jesus, *Monty Python's Life of Brian* remains one of the most brilliant satires of Christian attempts at Christology in contemporary times. A thinly disguised romp through the Christian story of Jesus in the character of another unlikely and unwitting messiah with a British accent named

"Brian," this cult classic lends a certain goofy poignancy and even tragi-comic depth to the impossible possibility of telling anything "as it really was" and thereby discerning its meaning. Through humor, it points to the very human foibles, desires, and political expectations that exist alongside faith in any theological undertaking.

Humor often comes up missing in Christian theology despite its rich and vigorous persistence in Talmudic scholarship. In addition to the relief that it brings from the weight and heft of thinking divinity, laughter also is generous in the intellectual space that it creates for uncertainty, which is necessary to a logic of multiplicity. Multiplicity cannot abide a seamless account and in this, at least, it tends toward the orthodox. Mark Jordan points out, for example, that "theology that is not written as a life told four ways already departs from the most authoritative model for Christian writing."[25] Uncertainty structures the very texts on which biblical litera-lism is built, gently slipping the rug out from under fundamentalist read-ings. This is good news for those who see room in the spaces between certainties for divinity to make itself known now and again.

Uncertainty as a mode in theology is not new. Catherine Keller points out, "theology has been growing uncertain for centuries. Therein lies its great opportunity."[26] The opportunity comes not only from the openings and shifts in the horizon of possibilities that uncertainty brings, but in the generosity toward the world that uncertainty can inspire, if the drive back to the closures of certainty is delayed.[27] Jean Baudrillard links uncertainty to the organic communality of thought: "Just as uncertainty in physics arises in the end from the fact that the object, in its turn, analyses the subject, so the uncertainty of thought comes from the fact that I am not alone in thinking the world—that the world, in its turn, thinks me."[28] Often called the "Observer Effect" in physics,[29] this aspect of "being seen" by research subjects (which is disconcerting, to be sure, for the researcher who discovers that he or she is being "watched" by the atoms she is observing) is actually funny. The humor of it lies in the toppling of the self-importance to which so many academic projects (including theology) fall prey. Humor encourages the humility of creative uncertainty because its prime target is pomposity and arrogance, attributes which Christian theo-logians too often mistake for wisdom. Humor allows insight into some of the most sensitive areas of religious faith; it often clarifies where fear lies and where cover-ups lurk. If humor departs when the divine enters, then we have to wonder if it is divinity at all that we are considering.

The divine, after all, is the grand question that fuels this project, though a successful conclusion in the sense of *closure* or *certainty* on the matter is hardly the point. For one thing, where would one begin? As there are no clean starts, so there can be no tidy finishes. There is the middle—the middle of life, the middle of the world, the middle of the story—which has the benefit of being where we are already located. And, so, diving into the middle of the question of divinity is the point of this project even though there is a masquerade of linearity to the chapters listed in the table of contents.

The chapters of Part I focus on the career of Christian monotheism from its ancestry primarily in Israel and Greece. The proximate development of one-god systems in the neighboring empires of Egypt and Persia also figure in the story of monotheism's development in Christian history and receive brief attention. The impact of the latter two on eventual Christian monotheism is less obvious because it is less direct, but their importance for filling out the ancient story of monotheism suggests further research. The pathways of theological development are seldom cut in straight lines, which makes the work of historians and textual scholars particularly challenging.

The convergence of Greek and Israelite monotheisms in the nascent Roman empire and the struggle among early Christian theologians to articulate their understanding of divine incarnation in Jesus Christ also marks a tantalizing fissure in the story of the One as it enters Christianity. An opening toward a true multiplicity appeared in the African idea of Trinity, although it quickly closed again in the change of fortunes and perspectives that followed Constantine's favor. After a brief foray into the legacy of the theological logic of One in modern science, the section ends with a dive into Hell, riding with Dante into his own poetic vision of the heart of Christian metaphysics grounded on the One. Out of that journey, we discover that divinity lies in the queer depths of Hell, the place of flesh, humor, and of God stuck in a consequence of eternity.

In my own complicated journey into this project, I sank, floundered, and began again numerous times. The hard part was not so much an exploration into monotheism's genealogy and influences on colonial Christian theology; the hard part was finding a pathway into imagining multiplicity. Dante's own despair, born out of rage at the corrupt church that would ban him from his own beloved city on pain of death by fire, led him to write the *Inferno*. It is a magnificently queer protest that, oddly enough, burst the floodgates of my own frustration with a Church and its theology that continues to burn so many of its own in a dreadful and corrupt dream of purity. Dante did not write for the imperial church of the twelfth century. Perhaps he wrote *to* it. He wrote out of a broken and exiled heart "still longing for running water" as Ivone Gebara so beautifully puts it.[30] He is a poet guide into and through the Hell of uncertainty, enabling us to see the entire structure of eternity as Hell.

Dante's *Inferno* therefore became, for me, a lyrical stepping stone toward clarity about the devastating void at the center of the logic of the One. Probably against the grain of any apologetic intention the poet had, the queer nether regions of the *Inferno* show a bacchanalian site of the very repressed multiplicity that imperial Christian metaphysics attempts to deny. The fact that he fails in the apologetic task is partly what makes his work so wonderfully rich at the same time that it stands as a reminder that any theological journey is adorned with the dusty jewels and torn fabrics of unintended consequences. Dante's conception of Hell, and indeed the very queer body of Satan, became my own surprising passage into a poetics of divinity, into the divine multiplicity that incarnation requires. The end of the critique of monotheism is the beginning of the incarnational theology that many liberationist readings of the stories of Jesus imply. In taking this route through a poetics of Hell, I finally accepted that I write this theology for exiles both within and without the Church, those who refuse the ice in which so much Christian doctrine has become mired, for whom the creeds have become bits of broken glass: beautiful still but deadly to take in. Divine multiplicity, which requires a leap into the metaphysical, emerges for me out of poetry and story. Divine multiplicity runs throughout the Bible, rich as that collection of writings is in story, song, parable, and paradox.

And so Part II begins with a meditation on story, or rather stories, that gesture toward the depth and possibility of what divine multiplicity might mean. From there, a different kind of diving expedition begins. Not a genealogy, as in our pursuit of monotheism's career, but an experimental plunge; a search for gestures and postures of a logic, or *habitus* of multiplicity.[31] The chapters of this section gather together pieces of divine multiplicity that surfaced nearby during my work. It would be foolish to suggest that the pieces make a whole. A Whole is precisely what I wish to avoid. A temporary unity, a boat with holes, is more like it. Perhaps Part II is best described as a story or, to use Rosi Braidotti's preferred term, a tracing. It does not mark a territory, or displace it, but rather gestures in a spatial way; perhaps it embarks on what Gilles Deleuze calls a line of flight.

Finally, in Part III, I take up the open-ended question of ethics from within a logic of multiplicity. Because I will emphasize Christian monotheism as a remnant of war trauma on the one hand and a tool of empire on the other, the questions of nationalism, of the possibility of love, and of unity form preliminary lines of flight into the pragmatics of this theological journey. The questions here are large, and so the chapters function more like musings—further openings, if you will, rather than conclusions. Theological construction is made up of ethical questions that lie underneath and all around it, and theologians who are drawn to the poetry and the exhilaration of casting for concepts and systems have some obligation to take up the vital questions of application and contribution to the actual well-being of people, animals, and earth. These closing questions, after all, constitute the impetus for both the critique and the construction and come before.

Divine multiplicity, I suggest in this book, is characterized by fluidity, porosity, interconnection, temporality, heterogeneity, and a-centered relation. But divine multiplicity actually flows, bodes, and bodies in spite of all of those abstractions; it is utterly *there* and so impossible to abstract, after all. It is incarnation, again. After All.

About words

"Divinity" and "the Divine" are words that, in writing, I use more often than "God." Before taking the next step, which is a dive into the story of Christian monotheism, it is important to pause for some reflection on this choice of words, not only because of their occurrence throughout this text in the occasional company of the word "God" or the "One" and so forth, but because of the larger question that looms over the whole: "Why a book on divinity at all?"

There is something about the idea of divinity, and the reality to which the word gestures, that pulls humanity, over and over again, toward itself. By this I mean that what attracts people continually to the fact-idea-suspicion-faith-experience-possibility of deep connection to a reality that far transcends whatever they create for themselves, is indeed a reality that intentionally tends toward—reaches toward—them and the world. Beyond psychology, bio-chemistry, and the social constructions of culture, the divine draws human beings out of themselves over and over again. Perhaps like the pull of chrysalis toward moth, or perhaps like the pull of moth to flame, the divine draws us to itself. What is this "Divine"? What is this widely felt experience of accompaniment and encounter with Something, that comes through the dense fabric of the world? Is it some abstract principle of reality? Is it a God? A world-soul? A Word? Ancestors? Spirit? A Being? Each of these (and countless more) is an answer that has its adherents. The record of human life on earth contains everywhere and in every period evidence of belief in some relationship to divine powers. And every culture that has made use of the invention of writing leaves its record of human attempts to make sense of these powers, to reach them in thought and language, to account for the coming of divinity into presence and meaning. From where I sit, there are no correct names for the divine. I choose to employ the names/words "divine," "divinity" and "the Divine" because they are less firmly tracked in a monotheistic groove than "God", though I sometimes use that name as well.

Names—words—are always approximations. I have written elsewhere of Christian theology's dependence on the "metaphoric exemption," which is the apophatic claim that no name, word, concept, or image captures the divine.[32] Divinity itself always exceeds and finds an exemption from the metaphors that describe it, whether the metaphor is "Father" or "Lord" or "God" or "One." The insufficiency of names does not, however, exempt us from using them. We name everything in our lives, and then some. And most of the things for which we have names, we also believe to be real, to have substance and—most of all—to exist independently of our imaginations. This is what makes a name for a thing only an approximation, a "gesture toward that which eludes its grasp."[33]

But names and metaphors for the divine make up only part of the work of theology. Theology is—mostly—predicated on belief in God, in the reality of the divine, in its existence independent of human imagining and manipulation. Furthermore, theology is dependent upon divine expression in human life, on what is typically called revelation but which I have called "experiential confession." This belief in the reality of the divine causes a fertile tension between negation and assertion, between the divinity that always eludes capture and revelation, and the divinity that enters into human life and consciousness in ways that can be experienced, witnessed, and named. As a result, I have also argued that to the extent that theology understands or believes the divine to exist beyond human imagining *and* to be active on its own behalf, we must address theologically the possibility that God also responds to human imagination and construction, comes into presence *in* those constructions, and sometimes embodies them.[34]

Certainly the question of divine reality is alive in the world today. Competing claims about God fuel, or at least legitimate, both horrendous brutality and profound acts of courage and compassion. For those who believe in or have experienced the presence of the divine, the question of divinity is less one of its existence and more one of the nature of that existence. To be sure, there are those who hold the faith that any claim of divine presence is delusion. And it is true that to speak of God, of the divine impress on human hearts, fundamentally is to assert something that is exceedingly difficult to name. Divinity is one of those unprovable but vital things, like the reality (or delusion?) of love. Still without proof, but perhaps like love, God (or more generally, the divine) is something that is nevertheless experienced, nevertheless asserted. The real presence of divinity is hoped for, sought after, renounced, feared, flirted with, despaired of, unexpectedly encountered, and embodied every day all over the world.

Put one way, as the holy source of what is and the keeper of what cannot be, divinity somehow comes, in the mesh of elements and time, through the medium of world, to human awareness and recognition. It is toward the divine that the eyes of the religious and religions turn and it is about the divine that the words of the theologians grope and stumble. It is also toward the divine that the eyes of those whose hearts have been broken—by the religious, the religions, and the theologians—turn, toward the divinity that comes anyway, even after proclamations, doctrines, and creeds have crumbled to choking dust in their throats.

Therefore to ask how the divine comes to human consciousness and recognition is really to ask many questions at once. It is a question of tradition, provoking answers embedded in the past, codified in doctrine and asserted by faith. And it is an historical question, concerning descriptions of how people over time claim to have experienced, known, or understood the divine to be in their midst. It is also a philosophical question, concerned with concepts and structures of knowledge, meaning and reality. And it is a psychological question, implicating human capacities and the sciences of perception. It is a sociological and anthropological question, concerning the psychological dimension of human awareness, but also concerning the culturally mediated, institutionally legitimated, and experientially reiterated agreements people in given societies have about what counts as real and recognizable.

Each of these disciplines asks important questions about how societies form around human beliefs in divine realities and how the human brain reacts or changes in the context of prayer. They investigate the symbols, practices, stories, and structures that indicate to people that their God (or Gods, or divine reality) is present or real. Comparative religious study, cultural anthropology, and the social sciences have all generated vital information about the landscape of religion in relation to culture, economics, history, and politics. They offer catalogues and analyses of symbols, practices, and structures that different groups have developed to express their understanding of the divine among them. But, rich as these sources are, they do not address—except descriptively—the question of divinity *itself*, of the divine that comes, sometimes directly into the human path. They describe belief, sometimes with great sensitivity and insight, but they do not attempt to articulate belief, to speak back to divinity, as it were. This is the realm of theology. Naked among those wrapped in skins of description, theology exposes more quickly than others the foolishness and obscenity of its work. It speaks of nothing but the unspeakable— nothing but barely concealed expectations, longings, loyalties, and obsessions, nothing but visions and dreams.

Theology is desire. The beauty and even endearing madness of it is that it begins with the folly of attempting to speak of the divinity itself that comes into human consciousness and recognition. Theologians not only attempt to speak of the divine that occurs—that was, is, and becomes—but to speak confessionally *toward* it. We do so in spite of our own admissions of the metaphoric exemption that insists that no language, metaphor, or symbol can even approximately express the divine in itself. We do so because of experiential confession.

The Christian experiential confession that the divine *once came*— became flesh in the first decades of the Christian era in the person of Jesus of Nazareth—means that Christian theology is based on the supposition that it starts with a certain openness toward divine coming in the world. This supposition persists, in spite of the fact that, almost immediately upon getting started, many theologians of the growing church strove to close the opening that Jesus' divinity made; they sought to minimize the fleshy implications of their own confessions of incarnation. Early Christian writers who were convinced that imperial support would advance the gospel sought to hem the incarnational opening in with strong affirmations of the absolute transcendence of divinity. But not all did so. Even as the logic of the One grew to overtake the incarnate divinity in doctrine, the practices of the people drawn into Christian faith—like the practices of people everywhere who are drawn to religions by needs of the body—brought the body back, again and again, whether in medieval plague-stricken images of a crucified Jesus, in liturgies of scent, touch, and sound, in soup kitchen communions, and in a myriad other ways. When *incarnation* figures in the basic theological premises of faith, the body's complicated implication in divinity cannot be wholly spiritualized or wholly denied. Put another way, the body—bodies—always return to disrupt theological attempts at containment. That is where a theology of multiplicity begins, again.

Part I
The logic of the One

2 Then came the word
The invention of monotheism

I have long ago made my peace with informing my students ... that ... there really are no such things as "western religions" and there never have been. It has taken me somewhat longer to wonder, if only to myself, whether the "monotheism" commonly taken to define the structure of "western religions" is a similarly vacuous concept.

Martin S. Jaffee[1]

... it's nice to talk like everybody else, to say the sun rises, when everybody knows it's only a manner of speaking.

Gilles Deleuze and Félix Guattari[2]

From its earliest beginnings, Christian theology has asserted itself as a theology of the One God proclaimed first by Israel and further revealed in Jesus. Indeed, as early as the mid-second century CE, Christian leaders debated and rejected as heresy the simplifying idea of the Marcionite Christians that the Jews worshipped a different deity than Christians. The fact of Jesus' own Jewish identity may well have facilitated the agreement by Gentiles that their Christian God was no different than that of the Jewish God. By the fourth century, in fact, the Christians officially incorporated the Torah, wisdom literature, and prophetic writings of Jewish monotheism into the biblical canon as an indispensable component of Christian scripture.[3] The gospel texts report that the central Jewish confession "Hear O Israel the Lord is our God, the Lord is One" ("*Shema Yisrael Adonai Eloheru Adonai Ehad*", from Deut. 6:4) along with the traditional Jewish ethic that love of God cannot be separated from love of neighbor formed the irreducible basis of Jesus' own understanding of his faith. Because of this, the monotheism of the first Christians cannot be counted as an entirely new revelation but as an affirmation of their Jewish roots and indebtedness to Jewish concepts of God.

But many Christians also began to distinguish themselves from Jews and Jews from Christians fairly early on, sometimes because of the claims Gentile Christians began to make about the divinity of Jesus, and sometimes because of the related issue of Gentile conversion and leadership.

Also, Christianity emerged in the form of small and sometimes quite divergent communities of converts within the context of a huge confluence of great and ancient cultures, all of which were reeling from the impact of empire, of Roman technological innovation, and of religious upheaval. As more and more people converted to the small cult of Jesus-followers, Christian advocates necessarily drew their core metaphors, images, and interpretive tools from the riches of those cultures as well as from traditional Judaism.

Because of the multicultural context of the Mediterranean basin during the years that opened what we today call the Christian era,[4] the reports of divinity and divine happenings that centered on stories of a Jewish teacher from Nazareth fit no single pre-existing interpretive frame, particularly for those listeners who were not themselves Jewish or privy to the historic or religious dimensions of Israelite conflicts with Egypt, Babylon, Persia, and Rome. Non-Jews who did not have the benefit of a Greek education tended, by virtue of widespread beliefs in dualistic realms of powerful spirits or communal realms of shape-shifting powers, to make sense of the Jesus stories in those terms, while Jewish converts attempted to incorporate the stories into the historical struggles and obligations of the Mosaic covenant with God. Upper-class Hellenized Gentiles from across the Mediterranean and North African regions likewise sought to place the Jesus story within a familiar intellectual framework; in their case it was often the eternal platonic ideals at work in the teachings and story of Jesus' resurrection.

In each case, enough people converted to faith in this god-man of Nazareth to indicate that the Jesus movement's eschatological promises of imminent good news for the poor and suffering were translatable and accessible across cultural lines, even if the "news" altered somewhat in the translations. Christian numbers grew rapidly and widely enough over the first three centuries to generate entrenched factions and conflicting interpretations. It is in such circumstances that Christian doctrines were born.

Given the polyglot nature of Palestine, Asia Minor, Africa, and the Roman Empire as a whole in the first centuries of the Christian era, any contemporary approach to the question of Christian monotheism and its origins must be necessarily complex and sensitive to the cultural differences that shaped the world at that time. This in itself makes the question of *Christian* monotheism interesting and somewhat undecidable. The historical, deeply personalistic, political covenant theology of Israel's first five millennia most certainly shaped and gave orientation to the first Christian accounts of their faith, not only because Jesus and most of his immediate followers were Jewish inheritors of that theology, but because most of the earliest Christian interpreters were also members of Jewish communities under Roman colonial rule. Also, the speculations, philosophies and political experiences of Roman Hellenism gave hefty doses of shape and content to early Christian self-understanding, particularly as Gentile converts attempted to demonstrate the viability of this culturally marginalized faith to the wealthy and powerful of the empire, especially to those who could put a stop to persecution and could fund Christian expansion. Finally, the very early conversions of African elites to the Christian movement meant that some of the first and most influential of the "Church Fathers" emerged from Carthage, Alexandria, Hippo, and Ethiopia, giving additional and distinctive shape and content to the beginnings of Christian thinking about God from cultures fed by the complex riches of the Nile.

All three of these complicated cultural contexts are significant for any serious investigation of the sources and problems of monotheism in Christian theology, and the chapters immediately following this one will take each source context up in turn. But, before we can do that, there is the issue of terminology to address. "Monotheism" itself is not an untroubled word with a serene and self-evident applicability even to those religious traditions most associated with the exclusive worship of and belief in one unique god or divine reality. Precisely because it is so widely used and so little investigated, or, as Mark Smith suggests, because "monotheism has apparently achieved a status in modern discourse that it never held in ancient Israel [or Greece, or Africa],"[5] it is good to pick the word itself up, turn it over in our hands a bit to see what strings attach to it, and so investigate both its taken-for-grantedness and its entailments.

"Monotheism" defined

Despite the great antiquity of the concept of one, universal, ruling deity, the word "monotheism", which is most often used to describe that concept, is surprisingly modern. To gauge from the history of publication, the word itself does not appear until 1680, post-dating the first appearance of the terms "polytheist" and "polytheism" by about 50 years. The Englishman Henry More apparently coined the word as a polemical tool intended not, as one might expect of that time, for direct defense of Christianity against the religions of the New World or for discrediting Jews. More published the term instead as an epithet internal to Christianity, directed against early Unitarian ideas of God–world identity. As such, the word was slow to catch on and even slower to morph into its more contemporary definition of "belief in one God."[6] In the early nineteenth century "monotheism" appears in print for only the third time, this time in reference to the persistence of the Jews to adhere "to pure Monotheism, under every persecution."[7]

The significance of the late arrival of the terms polytheism and monotheism lies both in the polemical and reductive intent of their initial usage, and in the consequent reminder that the terms themselves may be (and indeed I will argue that they are) inadequate to the task of thinking about divinity both in the ancient cultures that shaped early Christian concepts of divinity and now. Just as the equally modern words "religion" or "theology" can be problematic when applied to contexts for which those terms either have no meaning or real purchase in the language or world view of the culture to which their use is directed, "monotheism" may not in fact be the most helpful linguistic measure of either ancient or contemporary experiences and understandings of divinity.

It is striking that among biblical scholars interested in the emergence of One-God doctrines in Israel and the ancient Near East, it is only very recently that a few have begun to question the usefulness of "monotheism" or "polytheism" as descriptors of ancient systems of belief and practice. Mark S. Smith and Michael Mach, for example, both point to the relatively recent invention of the terms and argue for critical attention to the ways that their uses may invoke and deploy anachronistic concerns in biblical scholarship. In his study of Israelite worship of multiple gods in the Ugaritic texts, Smith goes so far as to suggest that the "concept of monotheism reflects our modern situation as much as the circumstances of ancient Israel or the Bible, for monotheism is largely a modern concern."[8] Mach, interested in Hellenistic influences on Jewish monotheism, emphasizes the malleable nature of the term and suggests that it always "needs qualification ... shifting socio-historical conditions will generate shifting models of so-called 'monotheism'."[9]

In general, "monotheism" has served and continues to serve two principal, related efforts in modern theology and biblical scholarship. First, it labors in the classifying and cataloguing enterprises of western social science, and, second, it has effectively served as a transport vehicle for ideologies of European cultural and religious superiority. To this latter end "monotheism," as a designation of progressive advancement, is attached to the Jewish-to-Christian trajectory of western European history, a trajectory that purportedly begins in prehistoric polytheism, advances to preliminary monotheism in Israel, and finally reaches full flower and sophistication in Christianity, all through the revelatory acts of God.

In pursuit of the first, classificatory enterprise, white European and American social scientists began in the nineteenth century to designate religions either as monotheistic or polytheistic, though some fell into the system-troubling category of "atheistic" (Confucianism, Taoism, and some other traditions of East Asia sometimes landed this designation). Today, monotheism is still "regularly used to describe a religion in which the adherents express belief in the existence of and venerate only one high god."[10] It depends upon its opposite, "polytheism", which is regularly used to describe the religion of those who "venerate a variety of important deities."[11] In recent years, however, many of the limitations of the binary distinction between monotheism and polytheism for encompassing the beliefs of the world's many spiritual practitioners have surfaced along with problems in the use of the word "religion" itself.[12]

In part, the problem of the monotheism–polytheism binary lies in the reductive character of all binary distinctions and the limitations that they place upon otherwise much more complex and shifting realities. Smith notes that it is difficult to remember that comparing ancient polytheistic religions with a monotheistic one is anachronistic, as the term 'polytheism' only has any meaning or sense because it is contrasted with monotheism. Accordingly, monotheism and polytheism in themselves hold little meaning for the ancients, apart from the identity of the deities whom they revered and served.[13]

It is not that "monotheism" or "polytheism" is without any usefulness in the work of analyzing ancient religious practices and beliefs. Rather the issue is, as Juha Pakkala suggests, that "something may be lost by using modern conceptions, and therefore we should be conscious of not forcing the conceptions."[14]

A number of scholars, such as Smith and Pakkala, point to a distinction modern biblical scholars make between "monotheism" and "monolatry", especially in reference to ancient contexts. Smith suggests, for example, that

> monotheism has usually been defined as a matter of belief in one deity whereas monolatry has been understood as a matter of practice, specifically the worship of one deity, sometimes coupled with tolerance for other peoples' worship of their deities.[15]

Monolatry, as the worship of one deity, may accompany monotheism, but it is just as likely to describe a local custom, or preference for a single god within a larger environment of many gods.[16] For scholars of ancient Israel and its neighbors in Asia Minor, monolatry is generally a more useful term than monotheism, in part because practices are easier to determine from the archeological remains than beliefs, and in part because there is virtually no evidence of monotheism—a belief in the existence of one God to the exclusion of all others—prior to the sixth century BCE.

An additional problem connected to the word "monotheism" lies in the embedded term "theism" which generally refers to the existence of a being or beings understood as divine. Derived from the Greek word for god (θεός) theism most commonly indicates conceptions or beliefs "in a person-like" god, which makes the term applicable only to those systems that allow for divinity to be understood in such a fashion.[17] While there are several local and global religious systems that can and do make sense of themselves by means of this terminology, the monotheism–polytheism divide breaks down most explicitly for those systems, like Theravada Buddhism, Taoism, or some indigenous African, Native American, or Asian religious systems, for example, that do not posit or practice the worship of separate divine beings or that incorporate ever-changing, communal manifestations of divinity that cannot be understood either in personalistic or in modern ontological terms.[18]

Even in contemporary Christian theology, theism in platonic terms of eternity and Aristotelian terms of substance is finding less and less purchase as both scientific and social-cultural knowledge about the world contribute to changing theological ideas about the god-world relationship.[19] As theologians and philosophers increasingly deconstruct theism (or perhaps re-deconstruct it, since the limitation of divinity to the category of a being has ever annoyed theologians across the whole sweep of Christian history) the category of monotheism itself begins to lose its coherence in social scientific enterprises as well as in theological ones. The work of "monotheism" as a reliable descriptor of religious belief is troubled and limited more and more by growing suspicions among religious scholars that overly simplified binary distinctions or universalized categories may cause as many problems for understanding actual religious beliefs and practices as they attempt to solve. M. L. West has rather cheekily hit the nail on the head, pointing out that the dictionary definitions of monotheism as belief in one god seem "simple and straightforward, except for the problem of what is meant by a god."[20]

The second area of difficulty for the term "monotheism" emerges from ideological roots that have not completely disappeared and so continue to shape the meaning and deployment of the concept in theology. Briefly put, "monotheism" and "polytheism" were coined in the context of anxious early modern European hegemony and colonial expansion and served the scientific efforts of Europeans and Euro-Americans to ground their assertions of religious and cultural superiority. They did this by charting monotheism as an advance over polytheism. The two terms, therefore, describe each other and have functioned in both theology and biblical scholarship as effective determinants for each other. R. Pettazoni points out that "monotheism presupposes polytheism by the very fact of denying it."[21] And Smith argues that, until very recently in biblical scholarship,

> polytheism stands out not only as the backdrop to biblical monotheism; it serves further as a negative foil to the biblical monotheism championed by [most] authors. This is apologetics, not history (or history of religions).[22]

Even more pointedly and provocatively, Smith suggests that monotheism "has served as the 'sublime idea' in western civilization in contrast to (or to avoid?) the contentious differences in actual beliefs and practices."[23] It should not be surprising that a biblical scholar concerned about the distorting lens of ideology in historical analysis would note first the problem that monotheism as a "sublime idea" can pose for objective research into the messiness and ambiguities of actual ancient practices and beliefs. But there is also the distortion that sublime ideas can effect in theology, posing problems for or overly determining the creative interpretation and transmission of doctrine both past and present. Monotheism as the "conviction," as Baruch Halperin calls it, "that only one god exists; no others need apply"[24] became, for the Enlightenment champions of European culture, a marker of evolutionary progress, a high sign of rationalism, and thereby proof positive of the superiority of those religions and cultures. Monotheism as the religious signifier of white Europe served the colonial project well, especially in terms of designating non-European, non-monotheistic peoples as backward and available for (economic) conversion.

The ideological value of the monotheism–polytheism binary in European supremacist arguments contributed to the weakening of Trinitarian thought in western Christianity, especially because of the ready association of polytheism with primitivism and even with emergent theories of racial superiority. For example, in one of the first occurrences of the term polytheism in print, a preacher, Edward Reynolds, from Northamptonshire in England wrote a tract in 1637, entitled "The Vanitie of the Creature and Vexation of the Spirit," in which he argued that the gift of Christian faith is a corrective for nature, which represents the fallen state of humanity. God's gift of the Christian faith is therefore a civilizing force, one that "saves" us in particular from polytheistic [read primitive, or non-European] nature. "There is yet a bitter root of Atheisme, and of Polutheisme [sic]" he argued, "in the minds of Men by nature."[25] This "bitter root" threatens always to reassert itself, like a choking weed. In an ideological framework such as this, so the general argument goes, only the love of the One God through the revelation of Jesus Christ can save us from the uncivilized and primitive condition of worshipping more than one god. The Christian faith, then, becomes ideologically monotheistic (regardless of its doctrinal Trinitarianism) and superior even to the rival monotheisms (Judaism and Islam) in the larger project of European cultural hegemony and colonial expansion.[26]

The polemics of monotheism came to play a crucial role as well in European and later American ideas of human progress. In 1757 David Hume, the Scottish philosopher and champion of "rational religion" argued that

> if we consider the improvement of human society from rude beginnings to a state of greater perfection, polytheism or idolatry was, and necessarily must have been, the first and most ancient of mankind."[27]

Jean-Jacques Rousseau, of course, made the link between this progressive theory of religion and the progress of humanity toward (European) knowledge explicit in his influential novel *Émile*:

> During the first ages men were frightened of everything and saw nothing dead in nature ... They thus filled the universe with gods which could be sensed. Stars, winds, mountains, rivers, trees, cities, even houses, each had its soul, its god, its life. The teraphim of Laban, the manitous of savages, the fetishes of Negroes, all the works of nature and men, were the first divinities of mortals. Polytheism was their first religion and idolatry their first form of worship. They could not recognize a single God until, as they generalized their ideas more

and more, they were in a condition to ascend to a first cause, to bring together the total system of beings under a single idea.[28]

Arguments persisted from the eighteenth century into the twentieth over which arose first in human history: monotheism or polytheism. The assumption of progression went largely unchallenged. Rousseau, of course, favored polytheism as the original religious sensibility, closer to the "natural," amoral infancy of human innocence and lack of civilization. Voltaire, on the other hand, held the position that monotheism predated polytheism, the latter representing the degeneration of humanity from its more perfect created state. Either way, the ideology of universal progress and monotheism as the rational goal or *telos* toward which human progress aims remained strong, deeply influencing the development of the social sciences and of liberal theology.[29]

In biblical scholarship, those scholars most invested in the progressive, ideological weight of European culture made evolutionary arguments for monotheism, marshaling evidence gathered from archeology to support the premise that it emerged "through several natural stages of evolution toward increased intellectual sophistication until they attained monotheism and an ethical view of reality."[30] With some variance in the particular pathways that they thought this evolutionary process followed, for example from fetishism to polytheism and finally to monotheism (Auguste Comte), or from animism through polytheism to monotheism (E. B. Tyler), or from polytheism through henotheism to monotheism (J. Wellhausen), the point of monotheism's superiority remained. And so, whatever the classification of the stages, Hume, Rousseau, and their ilk characterized in the eighteenth century what would be "a ruling notion in Old Testament Studies" from the nineteenth through the mid-twentieth centuries, namely the status of something called monotheism and its relationship to western cultural and intellectual supremacy.[31]

A similar evolutionary progressivism took hold of theology as well. Following Hegel, in 1897 Ernst Troeltsch gave impetus to the liberal adoption of this progressive ideology by developing strong arguments for the historical nature of religion in general. The idea of liberal progressivism opened up theological discourse to the possibility of real engagement with culture and with creative possibilities for contextual interpretation such as eventually took place in the Social Gospel movement and later in various liberation and feminist theologies. But this move also relied heavily on the notion that rational Christian monotheism, itself a progressive improvement over other religious forms, reveals the progressive nature of all doctrine. It stands to reason from this vantage point that doctrine itself should progress as well. The assumption that Troeltsch made is that theology will advance ever closer toward connection to the one "Divine Being" as its "future goal." In so doing he also identified Christianity as the key to that progress, based on its logic of oneness (with no apparent recognition of similar claims made by other religions, such as Islam):

[Christianity] is the only religion to claim an absolute and unconditional universality; to have produced out of itself a philosophy of history linking the beginning, the center, and the end of human history; and to recognize in this history a coherent and unique reality promoting unconditionally worthwhile goals. Above all, Christianity does not simply assert its universal validity but derives it from an inner necessity in the being of God: creating the world out of love, the Creator *must* lead creatures out of the world, out of illusion, out of guilt and discouragement, back to the Divine Being.[32]

The confidence that there is an inner necessity in the being of God that orients the world *universally* to the divine presupposes the very kind of rationalistic monotheism that seems to have fueled European confidence in the universality of its science, its culture, and its wisdom. Combine this ideological premise with Cartesian and Newtonian arguments for a unified cosmos rationally ordered by first principles (hence the *uni* in universe), monotheism indeed became the sublime idea of western culture and has functioned as such into the present.

Given the troublesome character of its social scientific and ideological entailments, it is appropriate to ask whether monotheism is even a term we should use when undertaking the constructive work of thinking about divinity past and present, and in particular for thinking about divine incarnation, or God beyond the logic of the One. As we shall see shortly, monotheism is not a term of overwhelming value for understanding the roots of the One-God doctrine in Judaism or for understanding the Hebrew, Hellenic, and African cultural confluences in early Christian thought. As Pakkala reminds us, "monotheism and polytheism are only generalizations. Religious concepts of the ancients cannot be reduced to any modern category."[33] Indeed, monotheism as such has never really existed anywhere except in ideology, and so can only function polemically.

To add further provocation to the problematics of the term "monotheism" itself, there is Jürgen Moltmann's support for the theory for monotheism-as-ideology in his argument that theological ideas of divinity are also always political constructs, always entailing with them concepts of αρχη (arche) or rule. In the case of monotheism it is not only the "worship of a single, unique God," Moltmann suggests, "but also always the recognition of this God's single and unique universal monarchy. There is no monotheism without theocracy."[34] The dimension of monarchy and political rule is without a doubt deeply embedded in early Christian formulations of concepts of God and, as we shall see, gives impetus and shape to the innovation of Trinitarian thought as well.

If Moltmann is correct (I am persuaded that at least in this point he is), the term "monotheism" has wielded significant power in modernity, both as a sublime idea to which all rational roads purportedly lead, and as a foil for white Euro-American supremacy "under God." The contemporary clash of exclusivist monotheisms—Christian, Muslim, and Jewish—or rather the clash of nations and movements deeply shaped by monotheistic claims, sharply illustrate the very current proximity (and vulnerability) of the monotheistic sublime idea to ideological battles for ideological and economic supremacy and for political legitimacy and control. The logic of the One is powerful and it is not extricable from monarchical and supremacist entailments. Christian monotheism may run aground at last because it is ultimately an empty concept in itself, apart from these entailments. This means that a long-term question for Christians will be whether the Trinity, with all of its complicit impulses toward the One in church history and doctrine, really succeeds in overcoming the hegemonic ideology and monarchical emptiness of monotheism, or whether it simply dresses the emperor up, "new clothes" in triplicate.[35]

To look at these questions en route to a more *tehomic* concept of divine multiplicity, we will look at three significant inheritances that flow through Christian imagining about divinity. First there is the emergence of the Yahweh-alone movement in pre-Christian Judaism, then the monistic framework of Hellenic philosophy in pre-Christian Greece, and finally the triune logic of early African Christianity. All of these ancestral forces shape the origins and energies of Christian theology and play a continuing role in tracing the horizon of possibilities for imagining divinity in reference to Christian tradition. Metaphorically speaking, these three great cultural traditions form principal aspects of the geology that underlies, supports, and limits the terrain on which Christian descendants now stand. Indeed, understanding the basic character of the ground is really very important to the work of construction or of reconstruction, as any architect or builder will tell you.

The term "monotheism" arose in modernity for some specific scholarly, religious, and political purposes, most of which have to do with securing the dominance of One-God belief systems in a world of difference. It remains a useful term, short-hand for the ideology of oneness that grew up out of the context of empire in post-exilic Israel, imperial Greece, and imperial Rome. Monotheism in this sense is the religious—or better yet, the ideological—aspect of a larger cultural framework that I call the logic of the One. And so, as a *theological* term, it is insufficient and misleading. It does not refer in any helpful way to divinity. But as a sociological and political term, that refers to what Ruggieri calls "self-interest with a justificatory veneer"[36] for the religious logic of the One, it has its uses and I will not throw it out completely, at least not yet.

3 "No god but me"
The roots of monotheism in Israel

I am the Lord your God, who brought you out of the land of Egypt, out of the house of slavery; you shall have no other gods before me.

Exodus 20:2[1]

I am the Lord, your Redeemer, who made all things, who alone stretched out the heavens, who by myself spread out the earth ... who says of Cyrus, "He is my shepherd, and he shall carry out all my purpose."

Isaiah 44:24–8

The emergence of monotheism in ancient Israel has long been a subject of some contention in biblical scholarship. A variety of theories shaped by a variety of scholarly, cultural, and religious investments attempt to explain its origins, many of them only thinly disguising an eagerness that Israel be the first locus of revelation for the oneness of divinity. For some modern scholars of the nineteenth century in particular, the concern has to do with shoring up the position of western culture through a progressive model of monotheistic development toward modern scientific theories of a unified cosmos. For others, the concern is more pietistic, centered on belief that the revelation of divine oneness and unity is a distinguishing mark and so a special revelation of Judaism (or, by extension, Islam or Christianity). For example, in the mid-twentieth century William Albright argued for a "Mosaic revolution" that rejected a gradual development and located the emergence of Israelite monotheism instead in a particular transforming, exodus "moment," giving weight to the idea that Israel's monotheistic claims were both unprecedented and unique in the ancient world.[2]

The revelatory status of the One-God claim is primary for all three religions associated with Israel, first codified in the form of the seventh century Jewish Deuteronomic Shema Yisrael ("Hear O Israel, the Lord your God, the Lord is One")[3] and later in the form of the fourth century Christian Nicene Creed ("We believe in one God the Father Almighty"),[4] and still later in the ninth century Muslim Shahadah ("There is no God except God").[5] It is probably for this reason that Baruch Halperin suggests that "among the questions relating to Israel's religious odyssey that of the origin of monotheism is intellectually and theologically primary."[6]

While the blatantly Eurocentric view of monotheistic origins has, for the most part, lost credibility among contemporary biblical scholars, the emergence of a strong One-God doctrine in Israel remains important enough to generate ongoing study and debate. This has meant in some cases that the evolutionary arguments are rendered into less parochial, more nuanced, and culturally relative terms, and that pietistic arguments for Mosaic revolution and revelation are cast more carefully in social scientific terms. It has become increasingly clear, for example, that the influence of neighboring cultures, such as those of Egypt, Assyria, and Persia, must be more seriously taken into account as the evidence of integration and acculturation in the formation of a distinct Israelite identity and world-view accumulates.

In general, there is too much evidence of complexity and multiplicity in the divine sphere for most of Israel's history prior to the long years of siege by Assyria and Babylon that ended in Babylonian captivity in the early sixth century BCE to support theories of monotheism as the dominant religious view before then. Robert Gnuse points out that

> the new models [of scholarship] describe Israelite religious development as a slower movement toward the distinctive monotheistic ideas found in the Hebrew Bible, and their final precipitation in the literary texts occurred much later than previously assumed."[7]

This means that doctrinal views that emphasize Israelite uniqueness in the larger ancient Near Eastern "polytheistic" world cannot be accepted at face value. The Israelites were not the first or only ones in the region to develop strong One-God doctrines, but in the context of prolonged assault by Assyria in the sixth century and by the end of the Babylonian exile in 539 BCE they had had in fact begun to adopt an exclusive One-God idea that is dramatically and poetically declared throughout Second Isaiah.[8]

Many aspects of the development of Jewish monotheism are important for understanding the complex history of Israel and of Judaism both then and now, as the lively state of scholarly debate attests. But, as Michael Mach notes, "it is of importance that those biblical texts that are normally granted some kind of monotheistic world view or else contribute to main changes in Jewish 'theo-logy' are connected with the crisis of the Babylonian exile."[9] It is fairly clear that before the early seventh century, the religious cultures of Israel and Judah both tolerated the existence of a multitude of local deities sometimes collected under the plural titles of *Elohim* or *Adonai,* or sometimes merely acknowledged as lesser members of the gods ruled by Yahweh.[10]

It is, however, too simple to place the emergence of exclusive monotheism in Israel solely on the Babylonian exile. The expulsion of lesser gods among the Jews began a century earlier during the reign of King Josiah, usually dated from 640–609 BCE. The Deuteronomic reform that Josiah initiated under the looming threat and power of the Assyrian empire laid the groundwork not only for a theology that more tightly linked the kingdoms of Judah and Israel to each other through the sharing of exclusive worship of one deity, but it laid the groundwork for consolidated power as well.[11] With Assyria tottering dangerously to one side, and Babylonia beginning to rise on another, Josiah pursued theocracy as a way of holding together his own somewhat fragmented people in a kingdom that, he hoped, would manage to stay afloat through the titanic clashes of empire all around. But, of course, the consolidated Israel could not finally fend Babylon off, and in three sweeps between 597 and 537 BCE when Cyrus II of Persia brought the Babylonian empire to its knees, thousands of Jewish leaders, scholars, land-holders and priests were forced into exile. The sojourn in Babylon lasted long enough to raise up several generations who did not know Israel at all.

In exile, the theological challenges to remain Jewish and yet to survive in a new land were immense. It is a testament to the poets, philosophers, and priests that they did so. The pathos and beauty of Second Isaiah, whose first words are "Comfort, O Comfort my people, says your God," is filled with lament, outrage, strutting determination, and pleading hope that speak clearly through the twenty-five centuries that separate the exiles from today. It is here also that the unifying exclusivity remembered from Josiah's reign and the monolatrous claims of earlier centuries begin to narrow into monotheism.

Before dealing directly with the sharpened One-God ideology that emerges out of exile in the Second Temple period beginning with Second Isaiah, let us step back a bit and look at the larger historical context out of which this monotheism came and which made its emergence possible. While later to form than previously believed, a dogmatic One-God doctrine did become distinctively established in Israel in the early seventh to sixth centuries, and it did not emerge *ex nihilo*. The late political context of clashing empires and superpower violence are the forces that most influence the exclusive and dogmatic dimensions of Israel's One-God claims, but it is important to recognize that more ancient hints and variations of One-God worship and thinking did exist in the cultures from which the Jews eventually stepped and differentiated themselves. Halperin argues, for example, that Israel probably had a place among a number of "Hebrew successor-states to the Egyptian empire in Asia, all of which crystallized at the close of the Bronze Age along the major trade routes from Mesopotamia to Egypt [and which] appear uniformly to have devoted themselves to the worship of the national god."[12]

Certainly One-God philosophies did not constitute new news to the Egyptians nor, therefore, presumably, to the subject cultures that they ruled along the Nile.[13] Indeed, numerous scholars have made the case against granting an overly exceptional character to biblical monotheism, especially when the whole complexity of religious belief and worship is taken into account. As early as the fourteenth century BCE the Egyptians were experimenting with a dogmatic One-God theology under Akhenaten, while over a millennium later in sixth century BCE Babylon (the century of exilic Jewish presence there), Nabonidus focused the imperial cult on his own deity. Likewise in Persia during its colonial rule of Israel, followers of Zoroaster and subjects of Cyrus II claimed Ahura-Mazda to be the sole, cosmic God.[14] The cross-fertilization of these theologies is likely, particularly given the intimacy between them in imperial conquest. It is also good to remember, however, that all of these so-called "monotheistic" traditions maintained their complement of "subordinate immortals" in the forms of saints, angels, demons, or devils. "Monotheism, in short, as the modern monotheist imagines it, was neither original to nor practiced in the historical Israel of the Bible."[15]

What is more, because of its ancient non-monotheistic complexity, many now argue that Israelite religion and belief cannot be understood apart from pre-Israelite Canaanite worship and practices that involved many deities. Evidence against a sudden conquest of Canaan has mounted in recent decades and so, consequently, has the importance of Canaanite culture for understanding the development of Israelite religion, especially in the connections between El, Baal, and Asherah, all Canaanitic deities who become related in various ways to Yahweh.[16]

"[M]onotheism," as Mark Smith puts it, "was hardly a feature of Israel's earliest history."[17] And it is clear that the process of its eventual development was not entirely unique to Israel either. M. L. West notes that "monotheism may seem a stark antithesis to polytheism, but there was no abrupt leap from the one to the other."[18] The biblical texts are filled with references not only to the existence of other gods and to Israelite tolerance of them, but also to indications that faithfulness to the God of Abraham did not require the denial of the existence of others' gods. Rachel's theft and protection of her father Laban's household gods en route to the mythic establishment of Israel (Genesis 31:19) is one example of this, as are scattered references to the Queen of Heaven. Psalm 82 depicts Yahweh judging the various gods in their assembly, and Psalm 29 calls upon the gods to praise Yahweh.[19] What is more, "according to Deuteronomy 32 and much other biblical thought, each people had been allotted its own god as Israel had been allotted YHWH (Deut. 32: 8–9; cf. Micah 4:5)."[20] Even the first of the Ten Commandments listed in Exodus 20:2 and Deuteronomy 5:7 is ambiguous in this respect, instructing the Israelites to have no other gods *before* Yahweh but not necessarily informing them that no other gods in fact exist.

> What has struck the biblical scholars about the pre-Deuteronomistic literature was the fact that there was no real polemic against the existence of other gods ... Even one of the major passages in Deuteronomy itself (4:19–20) seems to imply that the heavenly bodies are a legitimate

object of worship for the non-Israelite, though the same chapter provides the denial of other gods (vv. 35–9).[21]

Monotheism as the notion that the God of Israel alone is *real*, that no other deity or divine reality even exists, was fairly clearly not a part of Israelite thinking until quite late, and then in relation to rather desperate circumstances of exilic differentiation. The concept of an only god rather than a top god, and practices supporting it, had to be developed, to find a footing and become legitimate, at least among the religious leaders of Israel. For the millennium or so before that happened, even the name of the Israelite's deity isn't settled, indicating a gradual convergence of multiple gods and their names as the social, political, and cultural entity of Israel emerged out of a multiplicity of peoples, experiences, stories, and gods. In fact Yahweh, a German-to-English adaptation of the unpronounceable Hebrew consonants JWHW, or more properly in Hebrew יהוה, is according to Thomas Thompson

> a very specific deity, probably originating in the Shasu regions of Seir or Edom. Certainly Judah of the 8–6th centuries and Samaria of the 9–7th centuries maintained Yahweh among their dominant deities, along with El, Baal, Anat, Asherah and others. However, there were many Yahwehs … That some in Judah saw his consort as Asherah is hardly any longer debatable, but that he was sole god of Jerusalem or of the state of Judah seems unlikely. One should no more identify the many Yahwehs than the various Baals (with whom Yahweh is identified) or Els (of which the biblical tradition is replete).[22]

Because, as Smith points out, "Yahweh's qualities were often expressed in terms largely shaped by the characteristics of other deities belonging to ancient Israel's heritage that Israel rejected in the course of time,"[23] the condensation of these divinities into a single, universal deity served some purpose in the formation of Israel's identity. While piety may require some to assert that a strict monotheism was part of God's communication from the very start (the problem lying in typically faulty reception on the part of human beings) the development of the idea of one deity alone was clearly not crucial to the humans involved until quite late in the story, at which point the socio-political dimension becomes quite compelling.

Israel's eventual development of a strong, even intolerant monotheism by the time that Second Isaiah was written (ca. 540–520 BCE) is unquestioned.[24] What is interesting is that it developed so strongly then, with clear polemics against other gods and against multiplicities of gods. Israelite identity, in this period, became associated ineradicably with One-God worship practices. Fidelity and infidelity also became a standard metaphor and currency in Israelite identity, a move that continues to reverberate two and a half millennia later. The ongoing contributions of scholars like

Smith, Mach, Halperin, Assmann, and others demonstrate that the emergence of strong monotheism in Israel was both complex and multifaceted, but the significance of Israel's political crises in the formation of what Pakkala calls "intolerant monolatry" cannot be underestimated in the challenge of thinking responsibly about monotheism's entailments in theology today. That is, the millennium stretching back from the Romans' final destruction of the temple in Jerusalem in 70 CE could be seen as one of almost unceasing threat to Jewish identity. From the beginning of the monarchy around 1000 BCE, its almost immediate division into dual kingdoms in 926, and then an 800-year state of siege and colonial domination by a succession of superpowers cannot be insignificant when we think about relationship of context to theological imagination.

It is in the middle of that millennium during a time when, Smith suggests, "nothing seemed possibly good for the Judean elite held in captivity in Babylon" that the poetry of Second Isaiah brilliantly turns the rhetoric of political defeat into cosmic victory, "doing a new thing" in the land. The imagery and language of the defeated kingdom is not lost but is converted into the language of victorious divinity. The ruler of Israel is clearly no longer a human king, and no longer a parochial deity, tied to one land or one people. No, Smith suggests, the genius of this period is the transformation of the political downfall of Israel into the political ascendancy of Israel's God: the warrior-king and creator are melded, and in so doing "'Second Isaiah' addresses the issue of loss of land and king. Yahweh is [now] not just the god of Israel (both as land and people) but of all lands and nations."[25]

> For thus says the Lord, the King of Israel, and his Redeemer, the Lord of hosts; I am the first and I am the last; besides me there is no god. Who is like me? Let them proclaim it, let them declare and set it forth before me ...
>
> Isaiah 44:6–8

> For thus says the Lord, who created the heavens (he is God!), who formed the earth and made it (he established it; he did not create it a chaos, he formed it to be inhabited!): I am the Lord, and there is no other ...
>
> Isaiah 45:18

> He says, "It is too light a thing that you should be my servant to raise up the tribes of Jacob and to restore the survivors of Israel; I will give you as a light to the nations, that my salvation may reach to the end of the earth.
>
> Isaiah 49:6

The hitherto local god of a small, defeated people declares himself ruler of the universe, having used the Babylonian Cyrus as his tool, having included the exile of the Israelites in his plan, making all of the suffering and struggle no longer reflect defeat but victory. And, most of all, the voice of God in Second Isaiah confounds all other powers and divinities by declaring them not subordinate but non-existent. This is no longer monolatry, the mere worship of one god only (without having to deny the existence of others elsewhere), but it is monotheism, a philosophical claim of one god alone, unique and triumphant.

Smith's theory that Israel's eventual One-God doctrine is the result of convergence and differentiation is persuasive. The complicated historical evidence best supports the theory that diverse peoples and their deities came together over a long period of time and in the process of merging their increasingly shared ancestral stories also differentiated themselves as a people from others. The world is not without many examples of this kind of phenomenon where communal identity among different groups is slowly forged over time, pressed down and mingled, the stories and ancestors (and divinities) merged. Convergence yields a new identity, one that becomes distinct on its own and so requires a process of differentiation from others. Perhaps this latter aspect even entails a hint of aggression, or of defensiveness, in the face of other, more established identities. Convergence and differentiation, of course, are never fully complete as the biblical texts demonstrate over and over. This theory is persuasive in relation to Israel's religious development largely because it accommodates so much of the ambiguity and tantalizing remnants that pervade the historical record. In fact it finds in the very inconsistencies throughout that record a persistence of pre-exilic multiplicity and complexity of both humans and of divinity that, while repressed in post-exilic doctrines of monotheism, still exert influence over time.

It is important to remember that the "monotheism" that is forged out of the millennia of Israelite convergence and differentiation is not itself monolithic or always consistent. The different circumstances of Jews after the exile and throughout the Second Temple period (from ca. 520 BCE to 70 CE) meant that monotheism played different roles in the religious and political rhetoric of the still-colonized people. Mach identifies three distinct types of exclusive monotheism that influenced this later period, all of which reflect political anxiety in the face of continued and changing external threats to Jewish identity. The first type of exclusive monotheism is contained in the polemic against other peoples, nations, and cultures found throughout the Babylonian exile period. With the physical center of worship gone, the political and religious leaders in captivity far away, and the conquering powers ever present, such polemic makes sense as part of an attempt to keep the exiles, and perhaps particularly their children, from giving up and taking on the identity of their captors. The struggle is perhaps not all that different from that of people today in fragile cultural environments who seek to resist the forces of global capitalism and "Americanization" that draw so many of their children away.

A second form of exclusive monotheism that became important in the post-exilic period in particular, Mach argues, was one that actually sought connection with the colonizing culture. In many ways, the Persians may have been smarter in their colonial practices than the Babylonians whom they defeated. Their victory over Babylon resulted in a kind of freedom for the captive Judeans, many of whom returned to Jerusalem to begin, with Persian colonial help, to rebuild the Temple. The Persians were, in other words, more soft-gloved than the Babylonians, communicating some degree of respect for the native religion and practices of the Jewish people. This made polemics against them less effective. The beginnings of Hellenistic culture in Greece certainly began to enter into Jewish intellectual life during this time, and some speculate as well that Persian Zoroastrianism, a non-Hebraic form of One-God belief, was attractive to upper-class Jews. Mach suggests that in this context a new form of exclusive monotheism emerged which added philosophical depth to Jewish notions of Yahweh's sole dominance. It came out of an identification some Jewish religious leaders began to have with the elite of Hellenistic culture (about which I will say more in the next two chapters).[26]

Where we might think of the first form of monotheism as a kind of exclusivism based on ethnic or national distinctions between gods (Yahweh against all others), this second form excludes on the basis of social class (the universal properties of Yahweh's divine nature, which he shares with the Persian One-God Ahura-Mazda, sets the One-God of Israel apart from more parochial and less philosophically advanced conceptions). In this form, "those who do not belong to that cultural stratum will be defined as 'others', and their worship will be open to mockery."[27] Again, a contemporary analogy might be those individuals from threatened traditional cultures who pursue advanced study in the universities of Europe and the United States and find among the intellectual elites of those cultures a conceptual affinity with their own such that they begin to see themselves as members of a transnational elite who do not need to return home or who no longer feel at home except among fellow graduates.

Thirdly, Mach suggests, "Jewish 'monotheism' had to realize that the Jewish nation in itself is split, yet, still opposes 'others.'"[28] The nation of Israel, divided in itself between those in exile and those left behind, between north and south, and between diasporic communities had to develop a means of accommodation to the divisions, or possibly die through amputation. Exile had forced a profound question of divine nature on the Jews. The idea of a cosmic god, able to transcend national boundaries was difficult to understand. For example, even though he proclaims "there is no God in all the earth except in Israel" the sixth-century Aramaean commander Naaman carries bags of Israelite soil on two mules with him back to Damascus so that he might worship Yahweh even there.[29] A cosmic concept of God that he could affirm intellectually was inaccessible to him on a practical level (or inaccessible to those he commanded). The deity attached to land still made more sense, and so the land had to travel with the commander if he and his soldiers were to continue to practice their faith, to be "heard" by their God.

A monotheism that transcends time and space but that binds a people as a people regardless of time and space took time to catch on but eventually made possible the retention of a distinctively Jewish identity in the face of relentless assault. The people had to learn that the God of Israel no longer bound them through the presence of ark or temple or even land, but through act and obedience. A cosmic deity, they discovered, can transcend divisions and even splits in the nation and still be God. Even more important, however, in being One, that deity can continue to bind the nation and keep its identity intact despite its military or political devastation. It is both the cosmic scale (the universality) and the disavowal of all other gods (the exclusivity) of Yahweh's emergent oneness that made this transcendent identity possible for Israel. The transcendence of the One-God freed the people's identity from the limitations of geographic space or from narrow and fragile national boundaries, all of which had been shattered by the exile and continued to be threatened by superpower empires on every side.

For the sixth-century Jews, squeezed between the crumbling Babylonian empire, the du jour Persian empire, and the volatile Greeks soon to coalesce under Alexander, the possibility of a transcendent deity that could rule even over a scattered and exiled nation became more and more attractive and meaningful, as the vicissitudes and traumas of imperial violence forced a choice between the tradition of a god of the land whose might had once overcome the Pharaoh's armies (but now seemed unable to smite the Babylonians), and a cosmic god of the displaced, whose might made use of those armies for purposes far removed from land and temple. Faith in the cosmic One-God required a different practice of worship, which gradually became tied more to acts (of fidelity and obedience, for example) than to genealogy or temple, though memory of the god of the land never disappeared. In this huge conceptual and practical shift on the part of the Jewish people, Yahweh made the political shift from genealogical patriarch to national warrior king to cosmic emperor. These all were shifts that carried fundamental implications for the political, social, and religious identity of the people.

Prior to the Babylonian exile, the political gamble of nationhood and monarchy certainly required of the Israelites a capacity to interpret themselves to themselves and to the world as a unified and strong entity protected by a unified and strong divinity lest they be mistaken on the imperial shuffleboard for a puck rather than a player. No one doubts that the resulting, long experience of foreign assaults, warfare, and finally of Babylonian exile gave energy to the Yahweh-alone movement, which also caused the Israelite identity to sharpen.

All of these and more lead up to the poetry and polemics of Second Isaiah, in which we can glimpse the distinctive monotheism of Israel being hammered out. Monarchy, siege and exile, especially instigated by neigh-boring superpowers, coupled with the challenges of always-uncertain national identity seem to have enough to do with monotheism's formation in early Israel that the resulting One-God doctrine carries with it through the millennia a residual and persistent anxiety of political rule. The Dur-kheimian theory that communal or national identity is always borne by the gods certainly fits here.[30] They serve as emblems of that identity in their military protective roles and in their capacity as keepers (and authors) of the people's stories of origin.

The traumatic dimensions of Israel's emergence as a nation are reflected in the deeply defensive aspects of its developing monotheism. "We may deduce," Mach suggests, "that the sharp polemic against foreign gods has its roots in a social-historical situation where Israel is not really sure of its own religious-political identity."[31] Certainly the monotheism that emerged out of the political disaster of exile is the warrior king and cosmic creator all in one. And although Israel and Judah's combined contribution to the contemporary monotheisms of Judaism, Christianity and Islam is complex and ever-changing, in much of Christian theology at least, it is the imagi-native strength, the poetry, and the mythic power exemplified in these beautiful and desperate sixth-century writings from "the banks of Babylon" that resonate through the centuries and that have entrained so much theo-logical thinking about the One-God.

The exclusive or strong monotheism that came to full flower in Israel during the second temple period served to orient Jews more clearly and deliberately both as Jews and as victors in what could otherwise have been a culturally and religiously devastating set of circumstances. The clarity that the writers of post-exilic Isaiah and Jeremiah possessed concerning the universal dominion and cosmic supremacy of their One-God was, as many biblical scholars have argued, the result of a long and gradual development out of a much more complex socio-religious past. The fact that such a clear monotheistic doctrine emerged at all is interesting and important from a variety of angles that are both academic and religious. The fact that Jewish monotheism came to fruition when it did, and under the circum-stances that it did, makes it particularly interesting and relevant for the project at hand.

Virtually no one seems to disagree that the context of Babylonian exile was profoundly significant to this development. Jewish religious leaders in exile, who were struggling to keep together their powerful understanding of God's care for and connection to the Jews against multigenerational evidence of social, political, and cultural loss and confusion, realized that the cosmic unity and supremacy of God made Israel's political defeat irre-levant at worst or instructive at best. "Even the nations are like a drop from a bucket," the exilic Isaiah poet writes, "and are accounted as dust on the scales; see, he takes up the isles like fine dust."[32] This constructive theological turn frees God from the constraints of place, whether in ark, temple, mountain, or land, and proclaims God founder and governor of every place, even Babylon—or Persia. This theological move, or realization, set Israel's theocracy up to become Judaism, by freeing its God from the sacral necessity of temple or land, to be as ubiquitous as life itself, and as mobile as a Torah scroll.

The link that scholars like Smith, Halperin, and others have made between the exile in Babylon and the clarification of divine singularity, unity, and cosmic transcendence in the case of Israel suggests strongly that the theological imagination is always responding to the question of divine presence, interest, and legitimacy in social and political affairs. What can a priestly theologian do when virtually all of the popular beliefs (and even traditional wisdom) about what God ought to be and do seem contradicted by present conditions? For the Israelites in exile, the apparent defeat of the ethno-political deity through the defeat of the *ethnos* and *polis* probably meant one of three things: either their God was dead, or he was not powerful enough to keep his promises, or the people had misunderstood his true nature to begin with. The Jewish teachers in exile and under colonial rule decided for the third option, arguing for a "new song."[33] They reaffirmed the shaken, apparently defeated *ethnos* and *polis* by claiming it to be other than that which lay in ruins. Their God transcended the local in every way, did not reside in human-made dwellings, and so could not be defeated by foreign armies or the destruction of a temple.

Forged in a context of profound political and religious uncertainty, the blossoming identity of the God of Judaism as a deity without borders or limits meant for the buffeted Jews a transcendent foundation that could endure the confusion and relentless cultural assault of colonialism, even after the emperor Cyrus defeated the Babylonians and allowed both the return of the Jews to Israel and the rebuilding of the temple in Jerusalem. The Jewish concept of One-God, built on more ancient and familiar assertions of Yahweh's superiority and strength as warrior-king, apparently merged with divine creation traditions to yield the absolute, cosmic transcendence of God that *negated* all other divine realities. This ultimate notion, long a known possibility in Egyptian religions, was also familiar to the other ancient Near Eastern contexts that probably contributed to the development of post-exilic Jewish monotheism, not least of whom were the Persians, the very people who had "liberated" the Jews from Babylon into a less repressive rule. And at only a slightly greater distance, the busy Nile corridor ferried a wide range of African cosmologies northward, many of which supported unified ultimate divine principles that would have added to the general legitimacy of the notion of a single divine canopy under which *all* of the strange and alien peoples belonged.

While the assault of more than a half millennium of war, exile, and colonization is clearly not the whole story of monotheism's emergence in Israel, its importance is unmistakable in setting the conditions that made *exclusive* monotheism both intelligible and persuasive, particularly when what was at stake was cultural survival. When the apparent choice in the face of overwhelming odds is death or change, hindsight suggests that change is the choice to make. When a local deity cannot survive the conditions that war and cultural assault impose, that choice also is usually the same. What is remarkable is that most deities die because (for many reasons beyond their control) they cannot change. In the case of Israel, the very human, expedient need was for the familiar and local warrior-king-patriarch protector and progenitor to merge into and with the more cosmic, abstract, and unfamiliar (and unnameable) source of all things, a single God now not only of the Israelites but of all the distant and unfamiliar peoples. It is this move (or recognition), grounded in cultural trauma and in the genius that necessity births, that reverberates through Christian monotheism and continues to help in shaping its concepts of the divine.

4 End of the many

The roots of monotheism in Greek philosophy

The Pythagoreans ... hold that the elements of number are the even and the odd, and that of these the latter is limited, and the former unlimited; and that the One proceeds from both of these (for it is both even and odd), and number from the One; and that the whole heaven, as has been said, is numbers.

Aristotle[1]

It also lies in the very nature of the [Greek philosophical] enterprise that one tries to explain the world in terms of as few principles as possible.

Michael Frede[2]

The story of Israel's slow and sometimes traumatized movement toward a doctrine of monotheism is not the only source for eventual Christian development of the One-God idea. Nor is that history the only source for later Jewish or Muslim developments of the idea. In fact, although Jesus and his immediate followers were almost all Jews, and it is said of Jesus that he was well-schooled in the Torah and prophets, and Paul (as Saul) was well-known as a learned Jewish leader, there is another tradition strongly at work in the beginnings of Christian monotheism that cannot be separated from it or, for that matter, from the Judaism of first century Palestine. That tradition is Greek philosophy, a tradition whose principle concerns for logical coherence and abstract ideals were well integrated into the dispersed intellectual circles of the Mediterranean world by the time of Jesus' life and death.

In the five centuries between the return of the Jewish leadership to Israel from exile in Babylonia and the reported birth of Jesus in Nazareth, the Persian empire with its sophisticated Zoroastrian monotheism gradually gave way to Greek rule and cultural ascendency, an ascendancy most commonly associated with the warrior emperor Alexander, tutored by Aristotle, whose final victory over the Persians at the battle of Issus ushered in the Hellenistic age. Of course, by the time that Jesus was born, Greek rule had given way to Roman, but not before the largely anti-intellectual, militaristic Romans absorbed much of the Greek language, ideas, and theological interests. Given the power of the Greek heritage in the Roman empire and the heavy influence Greek philosophy had begun to have on

Jewish thought, it is not outside of the ballpark to suggest that, by virtue of the success of Alexander's empire in laying an essentially Greek foundation for the education of upper-class males throughout the region, their own philosophical notions of divinity and their own brand of monotheism were as deeply stamped on the early Christian theological imagination as those of the Second Temple poets. To be sure, later Christian associations of God with Greek ideals of immutability, purity, and the intelligible realm of spirit and mind are as inextricably woven into the theological fabric of Christian thought as are the more personalistic notions of father, warrior king, judge, and protector so foundational to ancient Jewish imagination. Therefore, just as it is important to avoid casting overly Christianized ideas of God backward in the attempt to understand the impulses at work in the emergence of Jewish monotheism, it is important to look also at the ways in which the notion of oneness became such a basic part of Greek thought long before the Christians arrived on the scene.

For social or political minds tempted to find causation where there may only be correlation, it is a tantalizing coincidence that, at roughly the same time that the Jewish leaders were in exile and faced with a most profound turning point in their theological understanding of the God of Abraham and Moses, another impulse toward monotheism was taking shape in Greece. Here is the tempting similarity: in both contexts war and the changing sweep of empires made hash of former theological systems that had legitimated former social and political arrangements (and, in the continuous feedback loop of theology and politics, the breakdown of social and political arrangements further eroded the legitimacy of former theological systems). In both contexts political life had become intolerably inconstant with consequent deep wobbles in the cultural traditions that gave meaning to the whole fabric of life. In both contexts the local gods were proving impotent against invasion and conquest. In both contexts, at roughly the same time, political trauma correlates with theological innovation toward ideas of cosmic divine unity.

Unlike the Jews in exile, however, the Greeks did not begin with a roughly coherent ethnic deity whose power, legitimacy, and location was threatened by forced separation. For them, the issue was more one of diminishing legitimacy and coherence among the family of gods who, above the banners of rival armies, increasingly competed and clashed across the volatile Greek world. It wasn't the grand drama of exile but the ongoing petty plays of local city-states at war with one another under a confusing and apparently often changing array of local gods who themselves seemed to swing between allegiances according to the fortunes of local warlords. Their sixth-century situations were not entirely the same, nor were the theological solutions that Jewish and Greek elites contemplated. Forced exile on the one hand and prolonged civil war on the other can engender different traumas and (still flirting with causation) engender different innovations in the theological realm. Intriguing similarities exist here, particularly from the vantage point of theological hindsight. From out of the multicultural broth of imperial expansion, both the Jewish elite in exile and Greeks in the conquered Asia Minor territories sought to resolve the question of divine plausibility in the face of violent political and cultural flux by contemplating a divine One beyond and apart from the smoke and stench of defeat.

Like all people, the ancient Greeks were a complicated mix of contradictory characteristics, which they generously passed on to their Roman conquerors. On the one hand, Greek popular religion thrived on the messy soap operas clogging the divine airwaves and so tolerated high levels of inconsistency and even of contradiction in the identities, stories, and capacities of the gods. On the other hand, Greek intellectual life became increasingly obsessed with coherence and demanded that "the truth" tolerate no contradiction or inconsistency whatsoever.[3] This seems to have resulted in a growing secularization in upper-class public and intellectual affairs, or at least an increasingly nominal cultic dimension where gods were invoked more or less out of habit, or for the purposes of public display.

This emergent Greek focus on theory and coherence could have been in part the result of the feuding city-states, where competition between local communities and petty rulers was played out in actual warfare, but was also channeled into less violent forms of dispute between scholars (not to mention the narrative dramas of jealous rages and covert alliances among the entailed gods). In any case, local deities kept proliferating as the Greek world expanded through commerce and relentless warfare, and the divine life depicted by the epic poets seemed increasingly to confuse matters. For example, in a later polemic against Greek religion, the early Christian apologist Theophilus gives some indication of the potential for religious confusion across the Greco-Roman world, albeit from a prejudiced perspective:

> I shall inquire of you, O man, how many kinds of Zeus there are. First there is Zeus called Olympian, and there are Zeus Latiaris and Zeus Kassios and Zeus Keraunios and Zeus Propator and Zeus Pannychios and Zeus Poliouchos and Zeus Capitolinus. Zeus the child of Kronos, who was king of the Cretans, has a tomb on Crete; the rest of them were probably not considered worth burying.[4]

But like the processes in Israel whereby the many Yahwehs coalesced eventually into one, there is some evidence that the same might have occurred in Greece had circumstances been different. For example, in a fragment of Aeschylus' *The Daughters of Helios,* one of the characters grants a kind of inclusive unity to Zeus, saying "Zeus is air, Zeus is earth, Zeus is sky, Zeus is the universe and all that lies beyond."[5] But for reasons that far exceed the capacity of this project to explore, it seems that the Greek pantheon for the most part did not follow the route of other ancient gods in response to the multicultural confusions of war and empire. Rather than coalesce gradually into a religion of one divine rule under a single deity whose biography vacuumed up the traces of the many, Greek (and Roman) religions remained a diffuse and complicated array of divine clans and identities scattered about the shifting empire. Perhaps this happened because the philosophers had already begun to argue for a different framework altogether, one that did not depend upon gods and their personalities at all, but on abstract, unifying principles as true divinity.

It is therefore curious to note that, while a sixth or fifth century BCE exilic Israelite poet in despair in Babylon (or remembering despair in Babylon) was writing constructive theological poems concerning the One-God, a similar move toward absoluteness and divine unity was happening in Greece. It is hard to imagine it a complete coincidence that both developments occur in roughly the same period at different ends of the same imperial world. In the sixth and fifth centuries BCE, great Jewish exilic theologians lifted the formerly local, monolatrous concepts of God, who demanded their strict allegiance *over* all other gods, to a monotheistic level, that of the One-God who exists alone in all the cosmos. And, at the same time, several important teachers in Greece began to doubt the soundness of their traditional ideas about divinity and started to pursue mathematical and other abstract notions as an antidote to the inconstant and unreliable realm of gods.

Just as the historical facts around the writers of Second Isaiah, Jeremiah, and the other early Second Temple writers are shadowy and incomplete, there is little solid knowledge about their contemporaries in Greece. Three men, each reputedly born within the lifetime of the others, stand in the murky foliage of the beginnings of Greek philosophy, casting partial shadows out toward us. The first, a man named Thales, was probably born in the seventh century BCE in Asia Minor (now Turkey) and he is credited with being the first known Greek philosopher and mathematician. Nearly a millennium later in the mid-fifth century CE, one of the last major Greek philosophers named Proclus wrote that Thales studied geometry in Egypt, which enabled him to bring spatial mathematics into Greece.[6] None of his writings survive, and so it is impossible to say much with certainty except that his name is invoked over and over in ancient texts as a founder of *theoria,* which led to the peculiarly Greek form of thinking about reality through abstraction. The Roman historian Plutarch writes that "Thales alone had raised philosophy above mere practice into speculation."[7]

Why is this an important originating moment for Christian monotheism? The massive cultural river we can call Greek philosophy and its impact on Christian thought can in one sense be traced back to the trickle that begins in the seventh and sixth centuries BCE when the notion that reality may be best understood through abstract ideas and especially through mathematical grids begins in Greece. Thales is simply one who stands at the very trickley beginning, possibly bringing what was already a venerable tradition of speculation in Egypt into a new context, one that would for a huge number of complex political, military, economic, and social reasons become a conduit and justification for eventual imperial domination. But that is still far in the future. For the moment, let us stay with the trickle and examine what substance it will give to the flood.

During Thales' lifetime, another native of the conquered territories in Asia Minor named Pythagoras came on the scene and helped to further the growth of Greek speculation. What little we know of this reputed mystic and mathematical philosopher is that he was born and probably raised in Samos on the western coast of Asia Minor under the violent rule of the tyrant Polycrates, who often switched alliances as armed conflicts persistently arose or passed through. According to Iamblichus (writing three hundred years later), as a young man Pythagoras met the older Thales, who recommended that he travel to Egypt, both to get away from the parochialism of the Greek city-states at war and to study the great African philosophies of Egypt as Thales himself had done.[8] Whether he did so or not is not known. What is known is that he founded a school under his name in 530 BCE in Croton (what is now southern Italy) that became famous both for its scientific development of mathematics and for its mystical-cosmic associations with numbers. It is not insignificant that the number one, for the Pythagoreans, was touted as the number of reason itself, and that in geometry they saw the number one as the generator of all dimensions.[9]

We cannot know what attracted Pythagoras the man to the simplicity of numbers, to their quietness and imperviousness to change. What made him (or more likely what is known as the Pythagorean school) associate these cool, unarmed, and yet untouchable things with ultimate reality is a matter of speculation, but it is not hard to imagine that part of the answer might be found in the ravages and traumas of petty wars, even pettier gods, and opportunistic tyrants. The beauty and simplicity of numerical relations and their unchangeable truth (two plus three will always equal five, regardless of which tyrant is in power) offer a tantalizing possibility if those very qualities of immutability and simplicity are somehow evidence of eternity and the divine. When political trauma seems endless, the abstract world is solace, is it not?

Finally, the third of the shadowy early Greek contributors to philosophy was Xenophanes, a respected teacher from the Greek colony of Colophon. He was born in the late sixth century, and his extant writings are only fragments, but they appear repeatedly in the writings of later Greek, Roman, and even later Christian authors who attest to his fame and importance in the emergence of Greek intellectualism.[10] A significant part of Xenophanes' contribution to what would eventually become uniquely Greek thought was his initiation of a sustained critique of the Greek pantheon. He argued ultimately for a philosophical concept of divine reality that is immutable and so indivisible, and he may have been the first Greek to attempt a systematic approach to constructing a concept of God.[11]

He did so because he was unimpressed by the antics of the gods, particularly as Homer and Hesiod had popularized them. Like others of the ancient philosophers, he recognized the importance of these poets in shaping Greek understandings of divinity and it concerned him that narratives of such fickle gods should influence the understanding and morals of so many. Following Xenophanes, Plato later expressed dismay that Homer seemed to function as "educator of all Hellas."[12] The argument is not very far removed from contemporary academicians and parents who complain bitterly that Hollywood, "reality" television, or the story technicians of Sega and Atari seem to be the educators of all the world. For his part, Xenophanes attacked the theology at work in the Homeric epics on the basis of its social and political ramifications: "Homer and Hesiod have attributed to the gods all sorts of things which are matters of reproach and censure among men," he argued, "theft, adultery, and mutual deceit."[13] As a consequence of these poets' popularity and influence, the gods of popular Greek religion were not, he claimed, worthy of emulation, something for which Xenophanes apparently believed that gods exist in the first place.

It is clear that Xenophanes' arguments for religious reform were politically minded, focused on the impact of theology on the social realm. Morally debased depictions of the gods were responsible, he claimed, for the morally debased and confused nature of society.[14] What a curiously modern, sociological argument this is: human ideas of divinity reflect back on and influence the shape of social and political life itself (or perhaps we should say, instead, what a curiously ancient and Greek-influenced set of assumptions is stamped on modern sociology of religion). Through the medium of ridicule, Xenophanes hoped to point out that the fairly obvious similarity between the many gods and the humans who worshipped them indicated fabrication and projection on the part of the worshippers:

> But if horses or oxen or lions had hands or could draw with their hands and accomplish such works as men, horses would draw the figures of the gods as similar to horses, and the oxen as similar to oxen, and they would make the bodies of the sort which each of them had (fragment 15). Ethiopians say that their gods are snub-nosed and black; Thracians that theirs are blue eyed and red haired (fragment 16).[15]

An argument such as this is not really so far removed from Paul Tillich's claim in his systematic theology that references to God as king indicate the royalty of God, but at the same time imply the divinity of human kings.[16] Nor is it that far removed from the most contemporary critiques of ideas of God that seem to lend support to social structures of oppression by presenting the *face* of the oppressors, such as James Baldwin's conclusion that "God—and I felt this even then, so long ago—is white."[17] And Mary Daly reflects this surprisingly ancient insight in her own notorious adage that "if God is male, then the male is God."[18]

For Xenophanes, social reformation in tumultuous sixth-century Greece started with reformation of the divine realm (or reformation of our thoughts about it). How, he must have wondered, can human improvement occur when the gods misbehave so badly and seem to sanction and deify the most base characteristics, like greed and deceit? Again, the contemporary resonance of this argument is striking, as if he is laying the groundwork for various forms of critical constructive theology that ponder the parochial interests, for example, of those European and American theologians more than twenty centuries later, who imagine God in their own images. But in fact it is unlikely that Xenophanes was thinking along the lines of metaphorical theology two and a half thousand years ago. As all that actually remain of his writing on divine matters are disconnected sentences, what they really only indicate is an opposition to the popular depiction of gods as human, and a philosophical interest in the nature and place of divinity in the order and generation of things.

Xenophanes seems fully to accept the general cultural assumption that the realm of heaven is an eternal one in which no change occurs. Even the Homeric tales assume Mount Olympus to have unchanging sunlight and pure, ethereal air that never dims. The Homeric gods who cannot seem to keep from tripping over themselves constitute the theological error according to Xenophanes, not the notion that something of divinity is unchanging and indivisible. For divinity to bear responsibility for heaven, for its creation and for creation of the eternal cosmos (including the earth) "God" can be nothing like the flighty, passionate, divisible, inconstant and fickle human and so can be nothing like the gods of Greece and Rome. To approach understanding of the divine, he says, one must "deal neither with the battles of Titans nor Giants nor Centaurs, fictions of old."[19]

The answer to the problem of divine pettiness and misbehavior was, for Xenophanes at least, a characterization of the human as flawed by inconstancy and of the divine as perfected by immutability. Like his contemporary Pythagoras, he began to argue that the answer lay in a more abstract and, most important here, a more *coherent* conception of the divine realm. True divinity, Xenophanes seems to imply, does not occur in human form, or in any imaginable form. Instead:

One god is greatest among gods and men, not at all like mortals in body or in thought (fragment 23).
Whole he sees, whole he thinks, and whole he hears (fragment 24).
But completely without toil he shakes [moves] all things by the thought of his mind (fragment 25).
Always he abides in the same place, not moving at all, nor is it seemly for him to travel to different places at different times (fragment 26).
For all *things* are from the earth and to the earth all things come in the end [my emphasis] (fragment 27).[20]

Living in a chaotic world of recurrent violence, petty wars, and always colliding stories about gods, it makes sense that a move to the abstract, to a realm completely removed from the "sound and fury" of unreliable human affairs was both attractive and persuasive. When even good people seem to fall into corruption, to betray neighbors for greed or out of fear, to change allegiances with the tides of fortune, to value sporting champions over teachers and moral leaders (one of Xenophanes' pet peeves), to vote with an eye only for one's own well-being, and when the *gods* seem to do the same, there is little of value left in the divine–human relationship. The gods, Xenophanes argued, must represent the very structure of things— they must be about what exists truly, not about what is false, misleading, or parochial. And what exists truly, *must not move about,* for moving about (now here, now there) is the first indication of inconstancy. And inconstancy is the result of change. So it follows that, to be true, a thing cannot change. Here the logic of Greek philosophical theology, and the curious stamp that it will make on Christian ideas of God, emerges.

And so, what begins in Greece in the sixth century BCE is a process of philosophical reflection on the *nature* of divinity and cosmos that deliberately eschews the anthropomorphism so persistent in popular religions everywhere. Starting with the Pythagoreans and Xenophanes, the emergent Greek philosophical tradition sought clarity and coherence in the structure of things. Narratives and stories became gradually less compelling than arguments and frameworks. The followers of these Greek teachers began especially to favor notions of divinity that were holistic, unmoving and abstract. From a vantage point of two and a half millennia later, it seems almost inevitable that such reflection would lead the Greeks ultimately to reduce the gods to God, and even God to a principle, or an idea. They sought, in the immutable nature that they ascribed to the divine, a necessary simplicity that leads logically to the requirement that divinity ultimately be uniquely One. Thales, Pythagoras, and Xenophanes stand behind this move, and together they laid the groundwork for their monumental successors, Plato and Aristotle, to bring this idea fully to fruition, just as Greek society stretched to its own broadest reach across the ancient Near East.

Plato's devotion to One

A few words about Plato and his student Aristotle, giants of the fourth and third centuries BCE, are not nearly enough to plumb the reach of their influence on later Christian concepts of divine oneness. Just their more or less direct influence on major Christian theologians like Tertullian, Origen, the Cappadocians, Plotinus, Augustine, Thomas Aquinas, and the Scholastics is enough for endless study, not to mention their direct influence on Alexander the Great, whose own global aspirations for empire would provide a template for later Christian expansion. Together, these two monumental Greek thinkers make a claim on the present through the waves of influence their writings exerted and still exert in philosophy, science, and theology. Even a glance in their direction, however, can't help but snare centuries of debate among scholars about the meaning of their writings and the nature of their contributions. It is a conundrum: how to say enough to move forward; not so little that the gloss is ridiculous or so much that the salient points are suffocated. With the risk of unsupportable gloss ever at hand, a running jump will have to do for the present. We will try at least to identify what it is that made *Greek* ideas of divine oneness distinct so that we can better understand the peculiar influence of Greek thought in early Christian theology, an evolution that gave early Christians a platform from which to argue with the educated elites across the Roman empire. We know that the platform they built was successful; enough of the elites of Hellenism did convert to open a route to eventual Christian empire which they legitimated through hybrid notions of monotheistic supremacy.

Despite the founding importance of earlier philosophers like Pythagoras, Plato is the one who provided a conceptual means for later Christians to follow the Christ in an educated, "Greek way." Born into Athenian privilege in 429 BCE in the midst of the Peloponnesian War, Plato is possibly the single most significant contributor to the Greek monotheistic project. It is impossible to know what direct influence Athens and its troubles had on him during his formative years, but it is possible that the effects of plague in the city at his birth, warfare throughout his boyhood and youth, revolt when he was 17, and surrender to Sparta when he was 25 contributed to his own search for absolute answers and to his famous dismay over the fact of change in the physical realm. He was fully taken up by Pythagorean mathematical theories, both in the mystical sense that linked the stars with an eternal calculus of musical notes and in the scientific sense that saw mathematics as the underlying framework for existence itself. It seems that, like Pythagoras, Plato found in the reliable realm of numerical schemes a relief and beauty unavailable in the world around him.

It is sometimes difficult for moderns to remember that the ancients had no genetic science with which to discern the biological and material relations between living things. Plato took up the Pythagorean supposition that numerical relations (measure, distance, motion, and so forth) could provide answers to questions about the nature and relations of things. With Pythagoras, he believed that numbers, while not physical, also do not change over time. The ideas of "one," "two," "three," and so forth would always be the same, regardless of context. He also shared the Pythagorean interest in the number one, fascinated by its simplicity and apparent self-sufficiency. In his late dialogue *Timaeus,* Plato discusses the perfection of One and imagines it as a sphere: inviolate; without beginning or end; the shape of unchanging perfection; divinity. The Pythagoreans argued that the *truth* of numbers and of their relation to each other is unassailable. One plus one *is* two, *always*. Ten *is* larger than nine, *always*. And so forth. While they largely remained focused on mathematics, the Pythagorean insight into the unassailable truth and permanence of numbers, Plato decided, was really ontology; it was the unassailable truth and permanence of *reality*.

But before getting into the content of the ideas that Platonic philosophy contributed to Christian theology, it may help to remember what energized these Greek thinkers in such abstract directions. Plato and others had come to distrust the explanatory power of narrative stories that involved human-like actions on the part of gods. The "old fictions" as Xenophanes called them, had grown shaky, and the emergent Greek philosophy pointed away from stories per se (not realizing, perhaps, that math is a kind of story, too) toward principles, frameworks, laws, and ideas, *all* of which can be put to the test again and again. Stories of the gods, after all, like those of the Homeric epics or of Moses on Mount Sinai had to be taken on faith just like the promises of every new conqueror. After so many generations of war, such faith was exhausted among the Greek philosophers. They sought something more reliable, more resilient against the vagaries of politics, something that transcended human tyrants and emperors. And rather than a tale of Zeus' or Hera's ascent to the absolute pinnacle of transcendent power over all of the peoples of the earth (for even this, as Xenophanes had argued, was marred by human likeness), they soared past the idea of One-God to the principle of existence upon which the One-God depended. They aimed for the pure and soothing realm of uncontested essence, the eternal quiet of numbers. They were after a unifying and single realm of Thought itself, residing in the sphere of the logic of One.

Ironically, Plato was perhaps the greatest storyteller of all the philosophers. He inherited his fellows' exhaustion with the stories of gods who look and, more to the point, act like the mean-spirited, chest-thumping political leaders all around him. Through the academy that he founded in Athens and the writings that he produced, Plato sought ground on which he could stand and make solid claims about right and wrong, law, happiness, and the meaning of life without having to slip back into unsupportable "fictions" about the gods. The very idea that truth, happiness, the good, and so forth are not favors doled out at the whim of capricious deity was the central tenet of Plato's neo-Pythagorean/neo-Xenophanean school. Through dramatic renderings of dialogues conducted by his murdered teacher Socrates, Plato rolled out a systematic method of critique of any truth claim that rests solely on authoritarian grounds. Gods and emperors no longer control the truth, according to Socrates/Plato, instead truth is always and eternally available to anyone with the stamina and courage to pursue it. Through Socrates, Plato stresses over and over again that the only things worth knowing are true things, and true things bring happiness because they are unchanging, and utterly reliable.

There is a rampant hope resident in the Platonic school, a hope for access to what is really real and, what is more, to a truth that will not crumble, fade away, or be sold to the highest bidder. By proposing an ontology of stasis, Plato sought to locate the *real* and *true* existence of the world in a realm in which change, decay, time, and fortune cannot alter it or take it away. Truth, therefore, requires immutability. So, the simplest test of what is true is the test of whether it changes. Building on the Pythagorean mathematical foundation, Plato and some of his followers linked truth with change in a negative relation so that what is really real, really true therefore cannot change. While temporary existence may participate in reality, its participation is partial and so does not constitute fully real being.

According to this reasoning, since all bodies undergo change (even stone, even molecules), what is really true about them therefore cannot be their bodies—there must be something else that constitutes the absolute and reliable truth about any given thing. For Plato, that something was the disembodied idea, or ideal form of a thing. Christians later picked this up in a dualistic distinction between soul and body. It is self-evident to all that bodies decay and even disappear completely, but Platonic thought offers a powerful antidote. Not only can the soul, posited by classical Christian theologians as a kind of eternal entity, disengage from and survive the body, but being bodiless and ideal it constitutes the essential truth and fundamental reality of a person. It is not a large leap from this theory of eternal, immutable souls to an eternal, immutable God (and vice versa), necessarily separate from body and world in order to constitute the true reality of its existence.

This is where Plato unwittingly made his most significant contribution to the development of the monotheistic idea in Christian thought centuries later. He developed this ontology of stasis almost as a side note in his discourses on love, creation, happiness, and the state as a way, perhaps, of working out the meaning of life in a world that executed its wisest man, Socrates. Influenced by Xenophanes' claim that the false gods look and act just like the people who worship them, Plato sought a foundation for understanding a divine center of the cosmos that did not sway and shift with the caprices of politics and peoples. In a world of apparently unrelenting violence and loss, he sought unchanging truth that plagues, rogues, armored legions and corrupt governors could not kill, steal, defeat, or purchase.

The Platonic requirement that truth be immutable requires only a few assumptions, assumptions that many today are still quite willing to accept. If like Plato one accepts, for example, the assumption that what is real is also true, the category of truth must be clarified. That which is true, he argued, cannot be false at any point in time, otherwise which version is true? And this is the second assumption, namely, that truth requires stability over time and place. It follows easily from these two assumptions that *that which is most real cannot change.* Or, what changes is not real, because it is not always true. And so only ideas (not physical things, like bodies) are real.

The logic of this becomes clearer in an example. Human bodies undergo massive amounts of change over a quite short period of time, including passing into and out of existence as human bodies. They alter almost completely in form and size in a few short years. I have heard it said that every cell in the human body is replaced over the course of each period of seven years throughout life. This stunning amount of change begs the question of the *real* person: *which* body is the real me? The pre-fertilized egg and sperm? The baby? The child? The adolescent? The adult? The octogenarian? The scattered ashes? The projections and memories of others? "Well," you might say, "all of these things together are the *real* you. Any one of them alone is incomplete, not the real you." And so right there the cluster of cells and limbs that I carelessly call my body, in order to be real (to be *me*, that is), the real me is abstracted to some idea or disembodied *form* of me—it is an ideal that all of the multiple versions from year to year, moment to moment somehow approximate but that none fully achieves. *This* body, right here, right now, is therefore much like a shadow of the real thing, dependent on the real thing, but at some distance from it.[21] The real body, according to Plato, cannot suffer decay or change, otherwise it violates the basic Platonic criterion for being true. The real body, therefore, cannot be a physical body, since change is what they do. This became the heart of what came to be known as Greek idealism, or Plato's theory of forms. The unchanging "form" of any physical thing, the idea of it, is what is real about it.

Greek monotheism (or what some might more properly call monism) came to full expression in this philosophical concern with a reality that transcends the sensible and chaotic world. From the requirement of immutability for truth the indivisibility of truth easily follows. In other words, truth is undivided against itself and so contains no multiplicity. In his *Metaphysics*, Plato's most famous student Aristotle interprets his teacher as having proposed "a One and an infinite dyad as ultimate principles."[22] The One, Aristotle argued, creates order, form, and limit onto the otherwise meaningless and formless manyness (the "Great-and-small"). While the One is not apparently prior to the infinite dyad in Aristotle's interpretation, it is certainly superior and so provides the basis for any claims about divinity or the "Prime Mover." "This type of dualism," John Kenney argues, "seems to have occupied Plato's students in the Old Academy."[23]

The doctrine of truth that led Plato to a theory of reality based outside of the material world provided answers to huge questions about the meaning and value of existence in the midst of a world where good people like Socrates are destroyed and where the destroyers of good people suffer no harm. To declare the material world a chimera neatly voids any claim it can have on the meaning and purpose of existence. True existence lies elsewhere. To say that this theory influenced the early Christian theologians is hardly strong enough. In the four hundred or so years between the life of Plato and that of Paul, variations on the Platonic doctrine of forms found their way into many corollary schools of thought, from the Stoics and Epicureans to the Gnostics, and so thrived among educated Gentiles and Jews even after the Greeks fell to the Romans. While the influence of Hellenistic ideas on Jesus and the men and women who counted among his immediate disciples is hard to determine, there are clear traces of Greek-influenced education throughout the New Testament writings, particularly in the Gospel of John and in the writings of Paul.

Aristotle's pragmatic One

Although Plato's own student Aristotle rejected the counter-intuitive, strict formalism made famous in Plato's *Republic* (Aristotle reports that Plato called him "the Foal" for the animal's habit of taking sustenance and then kicking its mother[24]), he may have ensured its overall success in later Hellenistic thought by making the doctrine more pragmatically accessible to common sense. Indeed, Aristotle was fundamentally concerned with the practical application of Plato's ideas in the unsettled world around him, especially in the realm of ethics and governance. In the *Physics,* he insists on the reality of material things, but retains the Platonic forms as an aspect of reality (rather than the whole of reality) in such a way that enables him to continue to associate divinity more with that realm than with the material. The result is a kind of idealism grounded in pragmatism. His acceptance of the Pythagorean, Platonic notion of divine oneness mixed liberally with ideals for natural governance led, in the case of his own most famous student Alexander, to a semi-divine imperial vision of total rule on earth.

Aristotle made Plato's ideas more pragmatic and accessible by disrupting the sharp dichotomy that his teacher had drawn between the material and the ideal. He did so by focusing on cause and motion. All things, he argued, move or rest (are caused) by virtue of their physical matter and the stamp of their eternal form. A person, for example, is caused by flesh and bones, but also by a specific and categorical shape. In addition to these two factors, however, all things have a prior cause, meaning a genealogy of effects, and here the analysis not only of physical change but of social and political change comes in. "The person who advises an action," he writes, "is a cause of the action; the father is the cause of his child; and in general, what produces is the cause of what is changed." Finally, he argues, each thing is put into motion or brought to rest by its own inherent purpose, its aim, and fulfillment. This last "cause" became Aristotle's contribution to religious cosmology and empire, in the immediate sense that Alexander found a fundamental rationale for his imperial designs (a fulfillment of divine purpose) and later Christians found a fundamental rationale for Christian rule and natural (divine) law.[25]

In adapting Plato's dualistic scheme into a more pragmatic and powerful empiricism, Aristotle did not argue with the Platonic identification of the number one as a principle of order in the cosmos. In fact, he made the logic of the One less mystical and more compelling. Where Plato's scheme solved the problem of change in the world by denying its ultimate reality, Aristotle refused to let either the world or the Pythagorean value of simplicity and eternity go. As a consequence, he put the two together and posited instead the idea that *motion* is *eternal*. But he realized that "eternity" is incompatible with change and bodies do change, so he concluded that "eternal motion" must be without body. Following the Pythagoreans, he also concluded that eternal motion itself, while the cause of all things, cannot itself move and so cannot itself be multiple in any way. It is without division, One, unmoved, a "Prime Mover."[26] (This vision of eternal motion so inspired medieval Christian theology that Thomas Aquinas wrote the *Summa Theologica* based on it, and it inspired Dante's own vision of a serene and eternally rotating heaven—*Paradiso*.)

The logic of the One was therefore deeply rooted in Hellenic thought by the time that Rome notched its first victories over the Greeks in 196 BCE. In fact, the fame of Plato's Academy and the success of Alexander the Great had ensured that Neoplatonism become the standard of education throughout the Alexandrian empire. As Rome's armies advanced on the city-states of Hellas, Roman orators and public leaders like Marcus Tullius Cicero (106–43 BCE) realized that military might alone would not build an empire to replace Alexander's. With no epic poets, no philosophers, and even no vocabulary like the Greeks, Cicero and a few of his contemporaries (such as Publius Vergilius Maro or Virgil) busily set about translating and co-opting the stories and ideas of Homer, Pythagoras, Plato, Aristotle, and other Greeks into Roman stories and ideas. In so doing, they provided a ready-made cultural and intellectual base to the emergent Roman empire along with a vastly expanded vocabulary in Latin.[27] The fact that Greek philosophy, now firmly rooted in the logic of the One, became Roman philosophy, or that Roman philosophy was Hellenic before it even began, is no surprise. Nor is it any surprise that the Romans became the champions of imperial imagination, carrying forward the Pythagorean and Platonic mission to unify the world and so rule it.

The One, immutable, indivisible, disembodied, perfect, and eternal: these were the characteristics of Greek theological imagining that stretched across six centuries to the first Christian converts. How these monistic notions combine with that of a God-become-a-Jewish-man *and* with the One God of his tradition is the challenge that Christians faced and still face. Incarnation changes everything.

5 "I am because we are"

The roots of multiplicity in Africa

I am dedicated to the ideal of Ujamaa because it invites all [people], in a down to earth practical way, to imitate the life of the Trinity which is a life of sharing.

Bishop Christopher Mwoleka[1]

Theologians and other exponents of rational arguments commonly make a few bad mistakes.

Eric Osborn[2]

Despite the relative modernity of the term, monotheism as a doctrine of one cosmic principle or a summary statement of faith in a solitary God emerged independently in the two ancient cultures of Israel and Greece some twenty-five centuries ago. Although they largely generated their ideas of cosmic oneness independently of one another, the wisdom of the Hebrew and Greek philosopher-theologians was destined to converge in the Roman empire. As we have already seen, over the course of the five hundred years leading up to the start of the Christian era, Greek thinkers gradually developed the notion of cosmic unity in terms of eternal principles of mathematics and the perfection of unchanging ideas (represented by the number one) as an antidote to the evident susceptibility of the gods to political manipulation. And, in the same period, Israelite thinkers also responded to the utter devastation that the Babylonians had wrought on their sacred kingdom by developing a strong and universal concept of one God alone who created the cosmos, governed its history, and so engineered and transcended the apparent defeats of the Israelite people. Both cases exemplify brilliant theological construction, accomplished under the pressure, or perhaps as a result of the pressure, of changed and changing circumstances. Both ideas of powerful theological oneness—monotheism and monism—came out of cultural defeat and war trauma. They bore ever after the marks of disassociation from worldly uncertainty and change.

By the start of the Christian era both Israel and Greece were (again) colonies, thrown together this time under Roman rule. Although the Romans despised the conquered Greeks, their own lack of educational traditions and even of rudimentary philosophical or political vocabulary meant that they turned to the wisdom and scholarship of the former Greek empire for the tools with which they built a distinctively Roman culture. Clothed in a jump-started Latin language and helped along by Roman scholars such as Cicero, Virgil, and Seneca who were trained in Greek literature, Greek ideas soon shaped the substance of Roman culture.[3] By the start of the Christian era Jewish scholarship also reflected strong Greek influences. Young Jewish men with the means to study, like Saul/Paul of Tarsus or Philo of Alexandria, regularly supplemented Torah instruction with Greek and Latin language and rhetoric. It was typical for them to read the pre-Socratics (Pythagoras, most notably) along with the Socratic academicians like Plato and Aristotle. Jewish thought in this period retained its strong monotheism expressed in patriarchal and covenantal terms, but began to add more noticeably Greek ideas of forms and mathematics, at least among the urban scholars.

Philo of Alexandria is a prime example of the Hellenization of Jewish and nascent Christian thought. He was 20 years old when the Christian era began with Jesus' birth and in his seventy years he self-consciously brought together both Jewish and Greek strands of thought in his writing. His work is critical for any discussion of early Christian thought because, despite the fact that he never intended to encourage Christian theology, his writings influenced Christian writers throughout the first three centuries of the Christian era.[4] A member of the Jewish upper class that benefited from Roman rule (his nephew Tiberius Julius Alexander played an important role in the Roman suppression of the Jewish revolt in 66–70 CE),[5] Philo's fusing of Greek and Jewish thought crystallized the monotheism of Jewish belief in terms of Hellenistic concerns about order, rule, and empire, a combination that the Christian apologists found perfectly reasonable and useful in their own development of a political model for Christian authority. Erik Petersen

> has shown that it was the doctrine of the universal monarchy of the one God which molded Philo's Hellenistic re-formation of Jewish belief: 'The God of the Jews was fused with the monarchical concept of Greek philosophy.'[6]

As a member of the Stoic school, Philo was unabashedly Hellenized, referring to Plato as "most holy Plato."[7] On the other hand, he asserted Jewish theology and history as superior and prior to that of the Greeks, claiming that Moses was the teacher of Pythagoras, thereby representing the "summit of philosophy."[8] Early Hellenistic Christian writers such as Clement of Alexandria, Justin Martyr, Tertullian, and Origen, it seems, all paid Philo more heed than did their Jewish counterparts. He modeled a mode of connecting the Jewish personalistic beliefs in an anthropomorphic God—a deity who speaks, acts, and makes covenants—to the a-personalistic theories of perfection, oneness, and stasis of the Greek philosophers. This fusing of Jewish monotheism and Greek monism into a sort of Hellenized theology aided the ideas of early Christian thinkers, who were struggling hard to understand divinity as eternally one in relation to the Jewish Jesus of Nazareth. An "ally of the Roman aristocracy,"[9] Philo's Jewishness was a convenience for his Christian followers several centuries later who found themselves at last in the light of Roman imperial favor. Under Constantine's "Christian" rule, they would use his apologetic blending of Greek and Jewish thought to legitimize and shape a new Roman Christianity.

Long before Constantine plucked the Christians out of obscurity and demanded a marketable theology from them, the earliest communities organized themselves principally around the stories and sayings of Jesus, which as stories and sayings offered little philosophical or theological clarity about the nature and scope of divinity itself. The earliest New Testament writings are therefore ambiguous about Jesus' divinity. For example, at the Pentecost feast in Jerusalem a short time after the execution of Jesus, Peter declares to the startled crowd that

> this Jesus God raised up, and of that we are all witnesses. Being therefore exalted at the right hand of God, and having received from the Father the promise of the Holy Spirit, he has poured out this which you see and hear.
>
> Acts 2:32–3

Although scholarly debate continues over the understandings these earliest writings contain regarding the nature of Jesus' divinity (does "exalted" mean "divine," for example, or simply "honored"?) it was not long before the Christian writers made explicit their conviction that Jesus was/is God, not simply a prophet honored by God.

When the Jesus movement survived its first generation and began to grow into a network of increasingly multicultural communities, the Christians responded to the challenge of evangelism in the Hellenistic environment by paying more attention to strong claims of Jesus' divinity. Jesus was, they increasingly affirmed, the Christ (a *Greek* translation, not coincidentally, of the Hebrew term "Messiah"), miraculously risen from the dead, the "Son of God" and, in a blatant co-option of Hellenistic Stoic philosophy, the divine "Logos." The hymnic first lines of the later Gospel of John represent an excellent example of the clarification, at least in the largely Gentile Johannine community, that "this Jesus," exalted by God in the resurrection, is intricately bound up in communion with God, if not one with God:

> In the beginning was the Word [Logos], and the Word was with God, and the Word was God. He was in the beginning with God; all things were made through him, and without him was not anything made that was made. In him was life, and the life was the light of men. The light

shines in the darkness, and the darkness has not overcome it. ... And the Word became flesh and lived among us, and we have seen his glory, the glory as of a father's only son, full of grace and truth.

John 1:1–14

While the three earlier synoptic gospels are very vague about Jesus' divinity, they are not vague about his status as the long-awaited Messiah. For the most part, in Matthew, Mark, and Luke, the question of Jesus' identity is a major narrative tension, leading always to his eventual disclosure as the "Christ, the Son of the Blessed One" (cf. Mark 14:61). In these gospel writings, Jesus himself regularly refers to God as "my Father" or "the Lord."[10] While the first title is not as typical of Jewish liturgy and teaching as the second, it is nevertheless consistent with Jewish scriptures that understand the familial relationship of God with the people to resemble that of a patriarch to his clan.

But neither Jews nor Greeks schooled by the Socratics were fully prepared to interpret the Christians' claim of Jesus' *individual* sonship literally. Except for the purposes of civic pomp and circumstance, educated Hellenistic Gentiles had largely dispensed with the pantheon that cavorted sexually with humans (though "mystery cults" thrived on just such divine–human claims throughout the less-educated Gentile world of the early Christian era). And, particularly after his execution, the majority of Jews saw no evidence beyond his followers' own affirmations to justify acceptance of Jesus as the Messiah/Christ or, for that matter, as in any way divine like God. After all, Rome still ruled with an iron fist and Jesus had been unable to save even himself. For most Jews of the time, exclusive monotheism, born out of the trauma of exile and flourishing under the strain of colonization and apocalyptic imagining, made it imperative that they reject the emerging Christian affirmation of Jesus' divinity. At the same time, for most Hellenized Gentiles the idea of absolute oneness in the cosmic order born out of the trauma of imperial collapse and the evident ineffectiveness of the Greek gods also made it imperative that they reject the emerging Christian affirmation of Jesus' divinity. For the Jews, any claims of Jesus' divinity challenged the iconoclastic singularity of God and for Hellenized Gentiles, any claims of Jesus' divinity smacked of superstition and personalistic deity.

Given the intensity of the struggle with this issue in the second and third centuries of the Christian era, it remains a curious node of interest for scholars that the synoptic gospel writers seem relatively unconcerned about the conundrum of Jesus' divinity in the context of strong monotheism. It is possible that this is because those writings were composed so early in the years after Jesus' death, and the first communities that kept the stories and wrote them down did not see (or need to see) Jesus as *divine* in quite the way that later Christians came to do. The meanings of the fatherhood of God and the sonship of Jesus were apparently self-evident enough to the members of those communities that their writers felt no pressure to explain what Jesus meant when he called God Father, or they did not see Jesus as divine in any way that required explanation.[11]

This self-evidence is not as true of the later gospel of John in which the divinity of Jesus is made much more explicit. As New Testament scholar Gerd Theissen notes:

> freedom from any tension between monotheism and Christology is characteristic of the first generation of primitive Christianity. Certainly through Paul we hear a good deal about controversies with Jews and Jewish Christians over questions of law. But nowhere do we hear of controversies over a "high Christology" and a threat to monotheism from it as we do later in the Gospel of John.[12]

The Johannine writer seems to have been very much aware of a need to explain both the fatherhood of God and the sonship of Jesus in divine terms. For example, in the eighth chapter of the gospel Jesus accuses the scholarly Pharisees of missing the connection between himself and God: "You know neither me nor my Father; if you knew me, you would know my Father also" (8:19). Similarly, just after proclaiming himself the "way, the truth, and the life" in the fourteenth chapter, Jesus says to Thomas "If you know me, you will know my Father also. From now on you do know him and have seen him" (14:7). The Johannine writer admonishes the Jewish scholars for missing Jesus' true identity with God, and reassures uncertain or wavering followers of Jesus that it is indeed God with whom they have been dealing in Jesus. Presumably such reassurance would not have been necessary if the divinity of Jesus were not in question.

It is clear from the texts that, by the time the Johannine gospel was written down, the coherence of both Jewish and Greek monotheism in Christian worship among Jewish and Gentile converts had begun to erode, or at least to raise enough questions that for the first time the church leaders needed to put into writing explicit claims regarding the nature of the man Jesus and his relationship to the One God that he was accustomed to calling his father; the man whom Christians had begun, according to their hymns, to worship and call Lord (cf. Philippians 2:10ff.).

The principle of One that had come fundamentally to shape both Jewish and Greco-Roman world views meant that growing Christian claims for Jesus' divinity presented immediate challenges to both kinds of (educated) converts. And so, while conflict over monotheism is not readily evident in the New Testament texts beyond an apparent need on the part of later canonical writers to begin to make explicit the divinity of Jesus, storms were brewing on the horizon that erupted into full view among Christians by the early third century. The growth of Christianity in that time made such conflict inevitable, particularly as the older communities maintained a strong One-God principle while others—like those Gnostic communities that ascribed to "docetism" (from the Greek δοκέω, to seem)—began to elevate Christology to the point that they denied the bodily existence of Jesus altogether.

Theissen suggests that explicit references to Second Isaiah in texts like the Philippians hymn (2:6ff.) mean that the emergent canonical Christologies exalted Jesus to a godlike status not "as an attack on the monotheistic conviction but as a fulfillment of the expectation of a [Jewish] belief in the one and only god which will establish itself over all the world."[13] This may explain the success of Christian evangelism among some Jewish communities. But as different Christian groups succeeded in attracting converts, especially among wealthier and more Hellenized Gentiles, the question of the united nature of Jesus with God grew more pressing. The familial metaphors of father and son made less sense, theologically, to that crowd. Indeed, it smacked of the very polytheistic "superstition" that neo-Pythagorean and Platonic teaching particularly warned against.

Pythagorean thought generally equated oneness with perfection, eternity, and stasis. The incarnation of divinity in Jesus claimed by Christians could only make sense to those schooled in this thinking if the perfect oneness of divinity was in no way disturbed by change, subtraction, or multiplication, even in a genealogical sense. Aristotle had already made clear in his influential *Metaphysics* that the creator, that he calls the Prime Mover, moves (thus constituting creation) but is unmoved in itself. This Prime Mover "is immovable, is one both in formula and in number, and therefore also is that which is eternally and continuously in motion. Therefore," Aristotle concludes, "there is only one heaven."[14] This kind of presupposition among the Hellenistic elite is summed up in the popular adage from the *Iliad* (which Aristotle also quotes in the *Metaphysics*): "The rule of the many is not good; let one alone rule." The lordship of Jesus in light of the Hellenistic requirement for a perfect unity of God seemed to contradict this most basic cultural presupposition. The idea of incarnation therefore became a volatile issue among Christians, as the movement grew and gained purchase in the increasingly Greek-educated world, a world that more and more cynically worshipped a pantheon of deities out of civic habit but *believed* in the Pythagorean dream of a cosmic, spherical, perfect One.

The cosmic oneness of divinity, inherited from strong Jewish and Greek (and even some Egyptian) monotheistic orientations, does not easily square with the idea that a living, breathing man can be God. James Davila asks "[How] did the man Jesus come to be worshipped as a divine being by communities who nevertheless regarded themselves as monotheists?"[15] Or, as William Rusch puts it more finely,

> how is the church, in an intellectually satisfying manner, to integrate the doctrine of the one God, Father and Creator, inherited from the Old Testament and Judaism [and, I am arguing, Greece and even

Egypt] with the revelation that this God had disclosed himself uniquely in Jesus and had given the Holy Spirit to the church?[16]

Some early Christian communities attempted to resolve the conundrum by positing the existence of several deities, resolutions which had the advantage of satisfying the contradiction of Jesus' divinity in a monotheistic frame by bursting the monotheistic frame altogether. Such resolutions also often squared comfortably with the inherited world views of those converts unfamiliar with Judaism on the one hand, and not yet schooled in Greco-Roman philosophy on the other. There is evidence to suggest that the Jesus movement found purchase in the less-educated classes in and around Jerusalem and Asia Minor, groups typically less bothered by philosophical conundrums or the niceties of theological distinctions.[17] If so, there is little reason from a sociological perspective to think that the very first generations of converts would have seen it necessary to deny the separate divinity of Jesus and his God.

It was not until conversions began to include the likes of Justin Martyr, Clement of Alexandria, Tatian and Theophilus of Antioch in the second century CE—all men of Greek schooling and all eager to explain their Christian faith to others of their class and schooling—that the question of Jesus' divinity in the context of strong monotheism required "apology," or explanation. These "Apologists," as they are known by scholars, began the effort to dispel the confusions that Christian claims already were arousing: to assert the oneness of God *and* the divinity of Jesus. Rusch notes that their works "divulge the lack of a technical vocabulary sufficient to describe the eternal plurality within the Godhead," but that they knew the task that lay ahead; "these authors did apprehend the distinctions."[18]

The so-called Apologists were not the only ones attempting to use philosophy and history to clear the air about Jesus' divinity in the context of monotheism. Gnostic, Manichean and other Docetic efforts to split God into light (good) and dark (bad) as well as Marcionite efforts to split the divine into the God of the Jews and the God of the Christians also took hold in some communities. But the presuppositional strength of the One-God principle among the Christians of Jewish and Hellenistic heritage throughout the Mediterranean, Aegean, and North African lands seems to have guaranteed the eventual dominance of monotheism in emergent Christian theology. Certainly, as the Christians added to their ranks philosophers and writers of wit and talent, schooled in Greek and Roman thought, the idea of God took on more and more Pythagorean notions of the One: eternity, stasis, and simplicity. Following Peterson, Moltmann notes that

> from the time of the Christian apologists onwards, Christians won over the educated in the Roman Empire by proclaiming the one God: "ΕΙΣ ΘΕΩΣ." It was the acceptance of philosophical monotheism and

the idea of the universal monarchy of the one God that made Christianity a "world religion," and that got over Christianity's appearance of being a Jewish messianic sect, or a private religion."[19]

And so, despite some exceptions and increasingly bitter debate, the question among Christians was not primarily whether they were monotheists or not in their worship of the Christ: they understood themselves to be so. The question centered on the divinity of Jesus in light of that prior oneness. As Geffré and Jossua note, it has been "the historical task of Christians to prove in practice as in theory that the basic dogmas of the Incarnation ... do not compromise the divine oneness in any way."[20] The Christians did so by assertion, at first in hymnody and worship (as is reflected in the first verses of the Gospel of John, or Philippians 2) and later with more prolonged philosophical disputation as the effort to clarify led only to greater complexity.

Richard Bauckham suggests that the difficulty of squaring incarnation with monotheism meant that, from the start,

> [the] decisive step of including Jesus in the unique identity of God was not a step that could be facilitated by prior, less radical steps. It was a step which, whenever it was taken, had to be taken simply for its own sake, and *de novo*. It does not become any more intelligible by being placed at the end of a long process of Christological development.[21]

Bauckham goes on to argue that the theological innovation of the divinity of Jesus should therefore be placed very early in the movement, which also means placing it early in the New Testament writings. Either way, early or late, the inclusion of Jesus in the identity of the One God posed a challenge for the first Christian leaders, those who wished to make the Christian faith intelligible or, failing that, to make it compelling to themselves and to others steeped in monotheistic world views.

The African moment

"In the year 213 of the Christian era, a Latin-speaking African composed a treatise in which he set forth his understanding of the doctrine of the Trinity."[22] His name was Quintus Septimus Florens Tertullianus or "Tertullian" to the more prosaic modern scholar. "A man of keen and violent disposition (*'acris et vehementis ingenii'*),"[23] he strove to bring understanding and clarity regarding the Christian claims about divinity to the Hellenized world. He lived in Carthage, best described as a richly Creole port city on the North African coast, underlaid by the resilient independence of Beduin cultures and shot through with millennia of imperial overlay from Persia, Egypt, Greece, Nubia, and cultures further up the Nile in Africa. This multicultural city was a fertile port not only for traders of goods but of ideas, and became an important space of literary production for the African framers of Christian theology, most notable among whom are Tertullian, Cyprian, and Augustine. Complex in real life and exoticized in fiction (it is the site of Dido's epic grief) a social history of Carthage specifically in relation to the intellectual development of Christianity could certainly shed light on the ways in which its native Christian sons have contributed both to anti-imperialist impulses and to imperial drives in nascent Christian thought through the first five centuries of the Christian era.

By the beginning of the third century CE, the various Christian communities scattered across the Mediterranean basin and North Africa had matured into multigenerational practices, habits, and disagreements about their relationship with the God of Abraham and Jesus his divine son. As the Roman empire promised both greater threat to the still-persecuted Christians but also the possibility of greater success in conversion (and so progress toward the eschatological promise of the kingdom of God), the problem of resolving the increasingly bitter disputes about the divinity of Jesus and oneness of God became more and more important to the Christian leaders in Rome, Jerusalem, and elsewhere. Born in 155 CE to a military father, little is known about Tertullian's early life except that he received an excellent education in Greek, studied jurisprudence, and converted to Christianity in his forties. He was renowned for his scholarly wit and independence, and his relationship with the growing Christian center in Rome was often combative, particularly later on in his life as he resisted efforts by the northerners to stamp out ecstatic practices in worship. This alone speaks loudly to the Creole dimensions of his own identity; he was Hellenistic by education which encouraged skepticism about emotional practices and divine interventions, but he was Carthaginian by birth and culture, which meant that such skepticism was tempered by the riches of other cultures and practices.[24] His writings betray a shaping of imperial impress without full accommodation. In an anachronistic sense, Tertullian makes an interesting subject for study through a postcolonial lens. His extant writings mimic and foreshadow what will become the Roman imperial theology, even as they also reveal the failure of its desire for a logic of One. Tertullian created an opening in Christian theology (an opening, of course, that already existed) for multiplicity.

The treatise that he composed in 213 was a polemic against a certain "Praxeas"[25] who taught that God is a perfect monad and so contains no essential distinction; "Father" and "Son," Praxeas argued, are exactly the same. But for Tertullian, the crucifixion *is* a distinction between Father and Son, a distinction that preserves the absolute rule of the Father, but allows the suffering and death of the Son to be real nonetheless. The cross, Tertullian clearly saw (as did many Christians who would come to be labeled heretics for attempting to exempt God from any association with Jesus' suffering), forces the issue of God's relationship to Jesus. This relationship between the "Father" and the "Son", if the divinity of the "Son" is to be affirmed, necessitates a theory of incarnation, which in turn necessitates a third term relating the cosmic Father to the localized Son, the three of which Tertullian dubbed "Trinity:"

> ... οἰκονομίας *sacramentum quae unitatem in trinitatem disponit, tres dirigens patrem et filium et spiritum, tres autem non statu sed gradu, nec substantia sed forma, nec potestate sed specie, unius autem substantiae et unius status et unius potestatis, quia unus dues ex quo et gradus isti et formae et species in nominee patris et filii et spiritus sancti deputantur. Quomodo numerum sine divisione patiuntur procedentes tractatus demonstrabunt.*
>
> ... that mysterious economy which distributes unity into trinity, setting forth father and son and spirit as three, three however not in quality but in sequence, not in substance but in aspect, not in power but in manifestation, yet of one substance and one quality and one power, seeing it is one god from whom those sequences and aspects and manifestations are reckoned out in the name of the father and the son and the holy spirit. How they admit of plurality without division the discussion will show as it proceeds.[26]

Tertullian understood the intellectual stumbling block that Jesus' divinity posed to monotheists who believed that the essence of God is neither divisible nor changeable. "The simple people" (by which he insists he does not mean "the thoughtless and ignorant") "claim that the plurality and ordinance of trinity is a division of unity" and so, Tertullian argues, they miss the point that "a unity which derives from itself a trinity is not destroyed but administered by it."[27] It made sense to Tertullian to speak of this plural administration of divinity in the world in prosaic terms that could work analogically for his listeners. Like the apologists, he employed political language, calling the tripartite activity of God an "economy" to focus the plurality of the divine on its functionality, making sense therefore of eschatological Christian claims that God became human to save the world. The rhetorical purpose of this kind of argument is that, by way of political analogy, Tertullian sought to address all of the objections to Jesus' humanity *and* to Jesus' divinity together in such a way that those who insisted on absolute singularity in the divine and those who insisted on Jesus' divinity would be satisfied.

One thing about these first generations of Hellenized theology that is significant for the future of Christian ideas of divinity is that, a mere 120 years or so after the execution of Jesus, the theological construction of Christian understandings of God had begun to move squarely into the realm of political analogy. By this I do not mean that political analogies between God and empire did not already exist, they certainly did in all of the cultures that made up the ancient Near East, including Israel, Egypt, Greece, and Rome. Evans argues that the term "monarchy" was "introduced into Christian theology by the apologists as a protest against polytheism."[28] While this claim may technically be true in terms of the existence of monarchical allusions in New Testament writings, the apologists by no means introduced the idea to Christians. Monarchical images of divinity had long been taken for granted by most of the people in the empire.

Indeed, for virtually all of the cultures bound by imperial Rome, the idea of monarchy itself was both political and religious, making monotheism a powerful ideological force in favor of rulers who aspired to absolute power. Both ancient and contemporary theocratic notions at the start of the Christian era made the correspondence of divine rule with political rule a commonplace assumption throughout the region, and had done so for millennia.[29] But curiously, from the record of his sayings it is not at all clear what Jesus or the first generations of Jesus' followers thought about analogies between divinity and imperial might. Allusions to the political situation of the Jews do exist in the texts, one example being the demoniac called "Legion" in Mark 5:9,[30] but the synoptic gospels most often record domestic and pastoral analogies for the divine–human relation: grieving fathers and prodigal sons; women and lost coins; sheep and diligent shepherds rather than rulers and subjects.[31] By the time that Tertullian constructs his argument and introduces the term "trinity" to Christian theology, however, such ambiguity about the significance of political thinking in relation to Christian theology has all but disappeared. Christians turned their analogical attention to politics in earnest, indicating a developing interest in Rome's governance among Christians.[32]

Moltmann claims that the apologists of the first three centuries of the Christian era shared a preference for the Roman empire because among them "the idea of theocracy was very much alive."[33] This view makes sense in light of Tertullian's argument for the trinity, at least if his consistent references to politics and illustrations from imperial rule derive from rhetorical responsiveness to his audience's concerns. Tertullian's argument for a unified concept of God is strenuous, but he insists that the concept of God contains within it an essential plurality. To accomplish this argument and to counter what would have been widespread repetitions of Aristotle's critique of the rule of the many, he deftly makes use of common monarchical allusions. For example, Tertullian writes that

> no kingdom is in such a sense one man's own, in such a sense single, in such a sense a monarchy, as not to be administered also through those other closely related persons whom it has proved for itself as officers: and if moreover he whose the monarchy is has a son, it is not *ipso facto* divided, does not cease to be a monarchy.[34]

He scoffs at those who think that plurality in the "economy" of rule (meaning its distribution and effect) is a diminishment of power or even of unity in the ruler or in the empire. "Do you account provinces and family connections and officials and the very forces and the whole trappings of empire to be the overthrow of it? You are wrong if you do."[35]

Tertullian was a man of his time and place. The Roman empire was itself in a process of political change that in another few generations would eventuate in the absolute consolidation of imperial powers in one man, Constantine. But although he utilizes imperial images readily, Tertullian appears to be concerned less about consolidating divine power than explaining that plurality in the divine nature in no way diminishes its power. Nor, he declares, does the notion of essential plurality diminish the ability of the Christian God to claim universal and unifying status. Famous for his rhetorical skill, Tertullian's approach to the theological construction he named "Trinity" has the ring of someone who sees something clearly that he cannot believe is not obvious to others. It is as if he is saying "Look, this is common sense!" Even more than the political imagery that he uses, it is statements like "yet the shoot is not shut off from the root nor the river from the spring nor the beam from the sun, any more than the Word is shut off from god" that speak of a deeper heritage revealing itself through Tertullian's theological innovation, one in which communality is— at the level of the taken-for-granted—understood to be ontologically prior to and embedded in individuality:

> Therefore according to the precedent of these examples I profess that I say that God and his Word, the Father and the Son, are distinct: for the root and the shoot are two things, but conjoined; and the spring and the river are two manifestations, but undivided; and the sun and its beam are two aspects, but they cohere. *Everything that proceeds from something must of necessity be another beside that from which it proceeds, but it is not for that reason separated from it* [my emphasis].[36]

Quintus S. F. Tertullianus, the man who responded to growing confusion about the oneness of God with a recognition of the inner multiplicity of all things from weeds to suns, was African. He was raised in the rich cultural repository that the northerly flowing Nile—economic and cultural channel for nearly all of Africa—made of the North African coast. This latter fact may well turn out to be the single most important reason that Christianity contains within its own ancient heritage an opening beyond the dualistic one–many divide toward ontological multiplicity. And the ascendancy of Roman imperial demands for absolute rule in empire and in church may be the single most important reason that this opening was for the most part suppressed, particularly in the Latin west.

The opening to more fluid ontological multiplicity does exist in the history of Christian thought, however, and we can trace the leak at least in part to Tertullian and his conceptual offering of the trinity. He was a complicated man, never completely happy with the directions that Christian theology was moving in the main. He despised episcopal authority;

fiercely defended the "Montanist heresy" (a strain of Christian belief and expression that encouraged ecstatic expression and direct encounters with the Holy Spirit); he was increasingly bitter and, perhaps not coincidentally, his writings on women are deplorable and vitriolic. But as a contributor to the emergence of Christian doctrine regarding the relationship of Jesus to God, Tertullian is an undisputed theological genius. He is also an inheritor of African social world views that would have traveled north with merchants into Carthage via the powerful empires of Nubia and Egypt for thousands of years, world views in which oneness is unintelligible outside of communality; in which matrices of belonging are more essential or primary than separable individuality.[37] John Mbiti has summed up this insight common to many African cultures with the famous aphorism that one might see as a correction to Descartes: "'I am because we are, and since we are, therefore I am,' or in its populist version, 'I belong, therefore I am.'"[38]

The most cogent argument thus far for a revision of the racist tendency to discount specifically African influences on Tertullian and other African Church Fathers—and thus on the sources of Christian theology—comes from A. Okechukwu Ogbonnaya.[39] He argues for a new focus on the importance of what Mika Vähäkangas and Raymond Mosha refer to as the African "general idea of communality,"[40] particularly in thinking about Tertullian's development of a relational understanding of the Father, Son, and Holy Spirit. Although the record of Christian historical studies out of Europe and the United States over the past three hundred years is a litany of efforts to discount Africa as a source for Christian theological innovation, the reasons for doing so are no longer persuasive (if they ever were), nor are they interesting.

There is no historical evidence or reason except blatant racism to discount the influence of deeply held communal ideas about divinity on a man raised fully in the path of trade routes from those cultures that explicitly held such beliefs. Illustrations of the kind of unscholarly denial of African influences on Christian origins are easy to locate in any collection of Tertullian translations, as they are in treatments of other Church Fathers of African descent such as Augustine, Athanasius, Clement, Cyril, Origen, and so forth. Ernest Evans, a primary translator of Tertullian into English, takes pains in his 1948 introduction to *Adversus Praxean Liber* to excise the man from his context by rehearsing the colonial privilege of redrawing geographic lines of meaning. This means that even though he grants to Tertullian the appellation "African" he takes care to define the name such that most of the continent and its cultures is left out. Evans claims that the "designation Africa is applied in its ancient sense, denoting the provinces now called Tunisia, Tripolitania, Algeria, and Morocco, but excluding Egypt and Libya which in language and in general interest were more closely related to the Levant than to the West."[41] He collapses the term "Africa" into a tiny strip at the northernmost edge of the continent, to preserve from Tertullian any hint of sub-Saharan or Nile-based cultural influence.

There is nothing historically valid, or anthropologically sound in such reasoning. A simple look at a map of the African continent, particularly noting the direction of flow of the Nile, puts the lie to this kind of racist fretting about Christian origins. What is particularly convoluted about Evans's version is that, like Augustine after him, Tertullian himself was from Carthage, a city located in the area now known as Libya. And so, even though Evans calls Tertullian an African and then carefully draws the lines of Africa to avoid the bulk of its cultures and peoples, according to Evans' own script Carthage does not even lie in Africa but in "the Levant," another colonial designation intended to claim the cultural heritage of northern Africa for Europe. Perhaps the hoped-for dissolution of academic white supremacy will eventually result from the poor scholarship its claims require.

African Christian scholarship today is yielding results that may lead to much richer readings of African foundations in Christian theology. As Ogbonnaya's research suggests, to exempt from Tertullian the context of his world and the pervasiveness of communal ontologies in sub-Saharan, West African, and Egyptian African cultures and then to explain the development of his particularly organic understanding of Christian divinity without that influence is bizarre. Although as Ngong suggests, some of Ogbonnaya's positive assertions of *direct* Egyptian Trinitarian influence on Tertullian's construction of the Trinity may need further grounding and development[42] (and although contemporary African Christian communities are often hostile to orthodox Trinitarian thought)[43] he is nevertheless persuasive in his point that the innovation of "trinity" makes the most sense in terms of African cultural presuppositions of communal (which is not to say polytheistic) divinity in general. Ogbonnaya calls this divine communality "communotheism," suggesting that

> Tertullian's historical-cultural situation allowed him to develop a particular conception of the Divine as community—one which enhances ontological equality, personal distinctiveness within the Divine, and a functional subordination among the persons of the Trinity that is temporal rather than ontological.[44]

The value of this reading of Tertullian goes beyond its long-overdue correction of racist exclusions of African influence in Christian origins, although that alone is monumental. To read Tertullian as African lifts up those aspects of his argument that tilt away from the closures required by strict monotheism in favor of relationality *in* divinity that cannot be reduced to numbers or to absolutes. Such a reading suggests leaks in the otherwise unrelenting logic of the One, even in the earliest moments of Christian doctrinal formulation. The sharing of substance for which Tertullian argues in *Adversus Praxean* stands against the monotheism–polytheism divide, for it is neither monotheistic nor polytheistic. Ogbonnaya's "communotheism" may be a good alternative. It is a multiplicity that cannot be reduced to the One, nor can it be divided into separate ones, or the many. The singularity of the Persons of the Trinity are made possible by their ontological sociality, their belonging. Each is because they are. Each *belongs*, and therefore *is*.

Tertullian's argument for a fundamental communality in the divine resists reduction to cosmic monotheism and so resists disassociation from the sometimes disappointing world. He refuses to cede the incarnation entirely to platonic ideals and thereby deny the bodiliness of God. "For who will deny that God is body," he demands, "although God is a Spirit? (John 4:24). For spirit is body, of its own kind, in its own form."[45] The body of God in Jesus and in Holy Spirit is not a problem for Tertullian, both because God is body and because the unity of the divine is in no way compromised by its fundamentally communal, embodied nature. "Communality, relationality, and fundamental interconnection underlie the African mode of seeing and being in the world," Ogbonnaya writes, and there is no reason to think that Tertullian would not have shared, at least in a broader cultural sense, in this mode of seeing and being.[46]

The Christian empire

> We have received from Divine Providence the supreme favor of being relieved from all error.
>
> Emperor Constantine[47]

Regardless of Tertullian's passionate and expressive arguments for it, the idea of trinity proved to be a stumbling block for Christians throughout Christian history because the underlying monotheism was never actually challenged. Even Tertullian knew that, in dealing with Hellenistic cultures bred on Pythagoras, his claims for "tres personae – una substantia" or three persons in one substance required mental acrobatics, especially when speaking of the substance of Jesus' humanity in relation to the substance of his divinity. In his arguments against Marcion, for example, he is both witty and deft in relation to the question of Jesus' body, acknowledging that Christian faith in the divinity *and* humanity of Christ is a kind of foolishness out of which even he cannot argue his way but which he, like Paul, embraces as *divine* foolishness.[48] As Osborn notes, "Tertullian quite properly does not so much solve the problem as elucidate it."[49]

Persistent confusions about the trinitarian nature of the Christians' god ignited full-blown warfare in later generations when the emperor Constantine insisted upon a single, coherent set of Christian beliefs for the now-Christian empire. Despite the emperor's directives, the conciliar creeds, and subsequent centuries of theological explication clarity about the trinity within the frame of monotheism eluded and continues to elude most Christians. "I remember how confused church members often were around the concept of the Trinity," the former pastor of a community church wrote. "They struggled with holding on to God's unity while affirming multiple expressions of God's divinity."[50]

The conundrum of trinitarian thought in Christian history may, in part, result from what Theodore Jennings calls its "erosion and decomposition towards a concentration upon the monotheism and monism from which it, in part, derived."[51] While the record of Christianity's evolution into an imperial religion of state shows clear evidence of a shift away from the multiplicity implied in the earliest formulations, the problem may be less one of erosion and more one of stunted growth. As Catherine Mowry LaCugna points out, "the doctrine of the Trinity was no sooner formulated than Christian theology moved away from it."[52] Even the Cappadocian theologians in the east, who dismissed platonic ideas of stasis in favor of energeia (energies) or relational personhood in the trinity could not stem the tide of political reductions of God to a divine monarch. Indeed, from the beginning, Tertullian, Hippolytus, Irenaeus, and the apologists before them infused their language about the triune God with imperial references, which could only serve to offer up this new understanding of divinity to political justifications of monarchical authority. In turn, the imperial understanding rebounded on ecclesial practices and theological imaginings.

Ogbonnaya and others rightly point to the African heritage of communality latent in the notion of trinity itself, and particularly to the ways that Tertullian develops the concept, but like all of the Church Fathers he was schooled as well in the Hellenistic principles of simplicity, eternity, and absolute unity. He introduced Latin to the Christian writings, and was known for his grasp of the Greek classics. Tertullian was a product of the empire in which he was raised. He claims a plurality in divinity, but a closed plurality.

Like his contemporaries, Tertullian makes use of political images to explain his theology, and both the inherent monotheism pervading Christian ideas and the emergent trinitarianism were ripe for imperial picking in justification not only of monarchical monotheism but of the late Roman empire, "the first totalitarian state in history."[53] As Guiseppe Ruggieri suggests, even after Constantine's consolidation of power and after

> the orthodox definition of the dogma of the Trinity, the links between the Church and the Roman Empire did not come to an end, particularly in the East. And the history of the Byzantine Empire includes the famous acclamation of Herclius and Tiberius as co-rulers with Constantine IV Pogontus: 'We believe in the Trinity: we here crown the three.'[54]

In the ecclesial realm, Ignatius of Antioch explicitly linked the idea of one God to a hierarchy of authority in the church in the formation of the episcopate. What is more, he justified solitary ecclesial governance on the argument that bishops represent Christ who represents God, and so: one God—one Christ—one bishop—one church.[55] And the first Christian emperor, Constantine, made use of Christianity's monotheistic roots and its doctrinal infancy as well as its missionary impulses to further the plans of empire.

> The emperor Constantine inherited a throne to which, it was claimed, the whole world was subject, and he chose a religion whose founder had bidden his disciples, "go, make disciples of all nations." During the thirty-one years during which he ruled either parts or, from 324 CE until his death in 334, the whole of the Roman Empire, Constantine strove to fuse a revived empire's imperial impetus with the Church's missionary monotheism ... [T]he full implications of the first Christian emperor's position are best brought out by the assault he planned on late antiquity's other superpower, Sasanian Iran.[56]

The opening toward multiplicity in the divine that the idea of trinity represents in Christian theology was almost immediately narrowed by ecclesial and political pressures such as these. Constantine in fact needed a religious system that would not oppose his own political aspirations. There is a great deal of debate among historians about his supposed conversion en route to battle against one of his rivals for sole power over the empire and his subsequent choice of Christianity to be the religion of the empire. What is not disputed, however, is his understanding of the importance of religion in empire, his calculated rise to power, and his success in abolishing the system of shared governance. The synchronicity of several things is very significant for the fate of trinitarian openness in Christian concepts of divinity: Constantine's brutal, if brilliant, rise to absolute monarchy and his desire to have a state religion that reflected that political arrangement; the resulting sudden turn-around in Christian fortunes; and the still nascent development of incarnational theology.

The trinity as a real multiplicity that could not be reduced to the monarchical One or opposed to the worldly many was probably doomed by the convergence of these events. There is a striking irony here, as Andrew Alföldi points out. The Diocletian Tetrarchy under which Constantine was raised, in which the rule of the Roman Empire was shared between two Caesars and two Augustii,

> required four divine patrons for the four rulers ... [T]he unity of the Empire, on the other hand, led inevitably to the belief that a single divine power must watch over the single earthly ruler."[57]

Constantine set his sights early on the goal of sharing power with no one and in 312, after killing the last of his co-rulers in the imperial Tetrarchy, became both the first Christian emperor and the first absolute and sole monarch of the Roman empire. Immediately the Christians began to favor their benefactor with theology of absolute monarchy, thereby continuing in analogical form the Roman practice of divinizing the emperor.

> [J]ustification of this political choice in favor of the Roman empire ran as follows: The polytheism of the heathen is idolatry. The multiplicity of the nations (which is bound up with polytheism, because polytheism is its justification) is the reason for the continuing unrest in the world. Christian monotheism is in a position to overcome heathen polytheism. Belief in the one God brings peace, so to speak, in the diverse and competitive world of the gods.[58]

Eusebius, "court theologian" to Constantine, worked especially hard to describe the absolute rule that Constantine had fashioned for himself as a reflection of Christian divinity. To begin with, he declared that the empire could only have resulted from divine providence (a circular argument, to be sure, though a familiar one). Also, God had deemed the unification of the nations under one ruler necessary to ease the proclamation of the Gospel. He went on to point out that this unification also reduced the likelihood of war, thereby bringing about the eschatological peace promised by the scriptures. Finally, according to Eusebius, the one ruler on earth corresponds to the one God ruling in heaven, which removes from polytheism its very basis in existence.[59]

The explicit rejection of multiplicity in divinity here is the work of a servant theologian eager to please his master, but it reflected the majority of Christian theological approaches to the question of God once the rule of empire was within Christian grasp. The "Trinity" served imperial purposes so long as it did not analogically contradict the imperial rule. In the case of Byzantium, it even served to justify a tripartite rule, as the acclamation of Herclius, Tiberius and Constantine IV demonstrates. The triune God therefore could not imply plurality in agency or rule (economy). The emperor Constantine was fine with the trinity, so long as it never contradicted the One and, by extension, his own supreme authority.

Even Augustine, who by the time he wrote *City of God* was deeply critical of the empire, started with the One God and so configured trinity in conformity with absolute oneness, rather than the other way around.[60] Also an African from Carthage, Augustine had long been drawn to the binary clarity of the Manicheans who divided reality into absolute categories of good and bad, corresponding to spirit and flesh, and light and dark. He sought an understanding of the trinity that would help to explain an eternal relation between "Father" and "Son" without making the relation vulnerable to the rampant weaknesses of the flesh which, like other Christians of his time, he also associated with heathenism and polytheism.

To get at the mystery of the trinity, Augustine first suggested a relational analogy of lovers: "You see the Trinity when you see the eternal love, for the three are the one loving, the beloved, and their love."[61] But, as LaCugna points out, he soon discarded that analogy in favor of one that could more easily be contained in an image of the One, namely, the mind. Despite its enduring popularity (and, quite interestingly, he did not delete it from his text) the analogy of lovers suggests an opening to the world, especially if the expression of love is understood bodily, and communally. "Lovers" is a more open and relational analogy than the individual mind ever could be and it is the analogy to which contemporary theologians are now increasingly returning. It is more like Tertullian's images of the root and plant, and the sun and its rays. Understood both bodily and communally, lovers and beloved(s) resist the stasis of the One, as Kathryn Tanner's recent work on economies of plenitude suggests.[62]

On the other hand, Augustine's own preferred analogy of mind (understood as the mind, the mind's knowledge of itself and the mind's love for itself)[63] emphasizes individual agency, relegating multiplicity to the structure of the inner life of the One. By focusing on the oneness of divine being in the cosmos, and relegating the trinity to the mysterious composition of the inner being of the divine, Augustine effectively and perhaps unwittingly accomplished a new binary in divinity, this time between "inner" and "outer" rather than between light and dark, spirit and flesh, or old and new as the Gnostic, Manichean, and Marcionite heresies all had tried to do.

Like Tertullian, Augustine attempted to articulate an essentially organic rendering of the trinity. But he individualized it, suggesting that the human soul is drawn to God because, as mind, it individually represents the image of God. The trinity is thereby expressed internally or "intramentally" rather than socially or communally.[64] By likening it to the individual human mind, Augustine's trinity ends up collapsing the three into the one, and so serves the One in theological imagining, rather than clarifying the multiplicity at work in divinity.

Augustine's stature in the history of Latin Christianity meant that his own preference for the individual rendering of trinity profoundly influenced the stunting of communal possibilities in trinitarian thought. Even though "the psychological triads serve a modest role in Augustine's overall *intellectus fidei* of the Trinity, they were adopted and made central to subsequent Latin tradition."[65] This means, as Moltmann, Jennings, and others have pointed out, that what came to be the Christian Trinity could not sustain the communality originally given it against the pressure to accommodate it to the hierarchical rules of empire and of imperial church. Nor could it sustain that openness to world implied in Tertullian's organic images against the pressure to maintain individual agency (such as the mind) that can dissociate itself from the disappointments and traumas of life on earth.

As a doctrine of God, therefore, the Christian Trinity fell into incoherence in the context of imperial demands for a theology of absolute rule and a

Hellenistic cultural presupposition of the perfection of stasis. "Trinity" does make best sense in the light of common African cultural presuppositions that understand organic communality to be ontologically prior to individuality. To be alone, the Akan claim, is to be cursed—why would any religion curse its own God with monotheism?[66] It is the primal sociality of the trinity that scholars like Ogbonnaya suggest can be traced through Tertullian to African ontological presuppositions that make "belonging" a prerequisite for existence. But it is precisely the communal category with its possibilities for a more dynamic multiplicity that were quickly downplayed for the sake of ecclesial and imperial hierarchies of order. The logic of the One that dominated imperial Roman theology relied more and more heavily on the assumption that stasis and perfection are synonyms, which meant that, over time, the imperial Christian theologians picked up the threads of Greek anxieties about change more than they picked up the threads of African anxieties about isolation. Increasingly, they did not hear, or see, in the ancient stories rich aspects of flow, partiality, or change in the nature of the divine. Over time, they consolidated the idea of Trinity into a self-enclosed One, rejecting organic multiplicity or "communotheism" as an ontological posture for imagining divinity and the world in Christian terms until the church creeds and hymns took the logic of the One to be synonymous with the Divine. This astounding consolidation of divinity with stasis in the logic of the One robbed any talk about incarnation of depth. Indeed the logic of the One "dried out" Christian theology, desiccating its possibilities for expressing divinity in more fluid and changing ontological terms.[67]

Eminently useful in the administration of imperial power, the logic of the One survived the fall of the Roman Empire, the splintering of the Greek and Roman Churches, and the convulsions of the Reformations. The Westminster Confession is just one influential example of this logic expressed in Christian theological terms. Written and adopted by the Puritan clergy in England in 1647, the confession became the basis of Scottish and English resistance to Catholicism, and so shaped the theological expectations of Puritan colonists, who set out to found new societies across what would become the British Empire:

> There is but one only, living, and true God, who is infinite in being and perfection, a most pure spirit, invisible, without body, parts, or passions; immutable, immense, eternal, incomprehensible, almighty, most wise, most holy, most free, most absolute; working all things according to the counsel of His own immutable and most righteous will, for His own glory; most loving, gracious, merciful, long-suffering, abundant in goodness and truth, forgiving iniquity, transgression, and sin; the rewarder of them that diligently seek Him; and withal, most just, and terrible in His judgments, hating all sin, and who will by no means clear the guilty.

... He is alone the fountain of all being, of whom, through whom, and to whom are all things; and has most sovereign dominion over them, to do by them, for them, or upon them whatsoever Himself pleases ...

In the unity of the Godhead there be three Persons of one substance, power, and eternity. God the Father, God the Son, and God the Holy Ghost. The Father is of none, neither begotten nor proceeding; the Son is eternally begotten of the Father, the Holy Ghost eternally proceeding from the Father and the Son.[68]

By the mid-seventeenth century Christian theology, steeped long enough in an imperial emphasis on the One, held virtually no question of the dominance of the logic of the One in its various claims regarding God, Christ, church, and world. Having settled over centuries into a kind of Christian cultural assumption, the logic of the One governed more than church doctrine and theological education. The first scientists of modernity were schooled in this theology; indeed, many were priests and teachers in the medieval universities founded by Christian communities. As we shall see in the next chapter, the logic of the One, with its demands for truths that do not change, comes to full flower in modern science where it meets its own limits (not for the first time, but perhaps at last most dramatically) in terms of its own failures to *be* One.

6 Monotheism, western science, and the theory of everything

For I am not so much in love with my conclusions as not to weigh what others will think about them, and although I know that the meditations of a philosopher are far removed from the judgment of the laity, because his endeavor is to seek out the truth in all things, so far as this is permitted by God to the human reason, I still believe that one must avoid theories altogether foreign to orthodoxy.

Nicholas Copernicus[1]

they had to misapprehend the nature of the knower; they had to deny the role of the impulses in knowledge; and quite generally they had to conceive of reason as a completely free and spontaneous activity. They shut their eyes to the fact they, too, had arrived at their propositions through opposition to common sense, or owing to a desire for tranquility, for sole possession, or for dominion.

Friedrich Nietzsche[2]

The logic of the One is dualistic, demanding a process of reasoning that absolutely and certainly separates truth from falsehood, just as it demands that God be clearly and absolutely distinguished from not-God. It should be no surprise therefore that scientific reasoning, pulled like a brilliant thread from the fabric of monotheistic teaching and learning, makes this same demand, although its orthodoxies lie more in method than in conclusions. The very point of early modern scientific reasoning was to pursue the "truth" by separating fact from fiction, an estrangement that relied on the prior assumption that the two are separable. While the logic of the One abides the notion of inclusive truth, meaning that different *perceptions* of truth can be accommodated, truth "itself"—that to which the perceptions presumably point—primly draws its veil of isolation and purity when brazen fiction or falsehood saunter by. The problem with this binary structure of exclusion is that it serves the orthodoxy to which Copernicus was willing to bow more than the common sense which Nietzsche lamented. So-called true things are after all always promiscuously involved with the so-called false, just as "good prose is written only face to face with poetry: all of its attractions depend on the way in which poetry is continually avoided and contradicted."[3]

The science that evolved in Europe late in the seventeenth and eighteenth centuries and that gave birth to the modern technological and scientific world grew out of Christian political and ecclesial struggles for dominance in the new worlds over which they fought and from which they sought to gain imperial advantage. How the complex of economic interests, religious interests, scientific innovations, and ideologies of dominance converged to set up the colonialism that would later dominate Christian expansion is more than this study can explain, although those forces also supported the growth and consolidation of the logic of the One in the passage of Christian theology from the early medieval context of Europe to the early modern context of European expansion across the globe. What is vital for this deconstruction of the logic of the One in pursuit of a postcolonial constructive theology of multiplicity is examination of the power of that logic to break its bounds within the Roman and Eastern churches and to shape the emergent "secular" endeavors of modern science, endeavors that largely shape academic discourses and investigations today.

Of course, any analysis of the European "scientific revolution" that exposes its conceptual ties to monotheism sins against the received wisdom of that revolution as a "pure" revolt against theology and its intellectual constraints. However, the logic of the One does frame the horizons of science that came to fruition out of the European scientific movements of the seventeenth and eighteenth centuries. It is significant that some experimental scientists, along with some experimental theologians, are now beginning to resist the constraining logic of the One in their attempts to overcome its biases toward simplicity and binary thought. In so doing, the lines between fact and fiction, truth and falsehood, proof and faith blur and allow for cross-pollination. They also grant brief glimpses into other realms ungoverned by reduction to true/false binaries. For theologians who seek pathways toward multiplicity, some reckoning with the scientific power of the logic of the One is necessary lest it be mistaken only for an ecclesial constraint.

Pilgrim's progress: the monotheistic basis of modern science

The logic of the One, cemented in Constantinian Christian theological reasoning, gradually became the foundation for knowledge in the empires governed by the Holy Roman and Eastern Orthodox churches. Over the centuries of medieval church rule, truth claims kept slipping in blood and the excesses of papal designs on power, but although the empires of Christendom stumbled and frayed, the logic that had grounded their orthodoxies took on a life of its own, eventually erupting in Europe in the seventeenth and eighteenth centuries in the "scientific revolution." The theological claim of a single ruling deity had not only provided Constantine with a rationale for the consolidation of shared Roman governance into an absolute and solitary ruler over an empire that was symbolically envisioned as

universal, but it outlasted the Roman empire to take root and flourish in
the post-imperial emergent European imagination. This is in part because
the Roman church had assumed the shape, scope, and governance of the
Roman empire even as the latter dissolved, carrying on its essentially
monotheistic idea through consolidation of church doctrines and ecclesial
power under an ideology of oneness.

Although the impact of the logic of the One may have taken its most
subtle and effective turn when it shaped the ground rules for what would
become modern science, it is important to remember that this metaphysical
theme of monotheism (or "monotonotheism," as Nietzsche wittily dubbed
it)[4] which links the idea of a universal, unchanging God to a single creation
ruled by universal, unchanging laws and the dream of a single all-powerful
temporal government, did not travel a smooth and unbroken course in
Christian (or Jewish or Muslim) history. As we have already seen, the complexity, contradiction, and openness of the Bible on the topic of monotheism helped to ensure all along a persistence of minority theological and
devotional traditions throughout Christianity's long development, diversi-
fication, and expansion. There have always been themes that run counter
to a metaphysics of divine oneness at play among Christians, however mar-
ginal or temporary they may have become in relation to the emergent modern
Church, particularly in Europe. The hagiography of eastern Christian communities, the perennial and resilient infusion of African and other ancient
indigenous philosophies, ontologies, and possibilities for divine multiplicity
into Christian worship and theology (wherever Christian missionaries or
soldiers have gone in Africa, Europe, the Americas, or Asia), as well as
persistent Christian musings on the trinity and incarnation, mean that the
career of monotheism in Christian theology has never been assured, despite
its ability to dominate the received theological texts of Christian tradition.

Nevertheless, as the various early Christianities grew and spread, adapting themselves into ever more distant cultural frames, the theme of a
single, unchanging divinity continued to dominate church theology, especially in its evangelical and missiological emphases. What is more, the
scholastic projects of the medieval church largely succeeded in joining the
ideological analogy of the One ruling patriarchal deity in heaven with an
idea of eschatological unity for creation—an ideological union resulting in
an equally ideological concept of a single reality, a monocosmos, if you
will. Thomas Aquinas argued, as one of the principle points of his massive
Summa Theologica, that the goal and purpose of *all* of creation is its destiny of unification under God.[5] The idea of a unified creation under one
God was not new to Scholastics like Thomas, of course—we have already
discussed its ancient resonances in Israel, Greece, Persia, and Egypt. What
is important for the story of monotheism as an ideology of reality in the
emergent European church is that its greatest scholars effectively melded
the idea of a solitary divine reality with the idea of a single physical universe
in the form of church doctrine and set this idea against falsehood or heresy.

True existence, or the eternal reality of God, became for the theologians an abstract unity of all things in which there can be no division or disagreement. Even the dialectical style of Thomas Aquinas' constructions, carried forward through his own reading of the Greeks, reinforced the assumption that disagreement is ultimately the result of error in fact or argumentation: error that he believed reason and faith can eliminate.

A serious challenge to this scholarly reduction of "truth" to the "One" was that the world—ancient, medieval, and early modern—was never experienced by its inhabitants "on the ground" as essentially one, or unified. The gap between day-to-day life in an empire (be it *Pax Romana* or *Ecclesia Romana*), made up of so many different peoples, languages, and cultures, and the idea of that same empire as a divinely ordered unity was enormous. It was precisely that gap that made the cultivation and maintenance of an ideology of oneness so important to its rulers: daily experiences of difference could easily fracture the political and religious order unless a strong vaccination or antidote of an ideological vision of unity could prevail. But Thomas Aquinas argued strongly for a new theological attention to the world and its manyness: he was confident that such attention and study would reveal what the ancient Greek philosopher Aristotle had said it would reveal: a single Prime Mover both behind and before the ever-changing world. For Thomas, this meant that the world itself could serve as revelatory text of the one, unchanging God of all Creation.

By the time of the Reformations and the resultant weakening of Rome's religious authority, more than a millennium of Christian theo-political rule had made the religious and ontological claim of a single, unchanging divine order a basic cultural assumption throughout the upper classes across Europe, Asia Minor, and North Africa. And though one might expect the division of the church to result in a parallel dilution of the monotheistic underpinnings of the old order, the opposite was the case. Out of the battle fatigue wrought by centuries of church corruption, plague, and years of bitter bloodshed over Christian fanaticism and factionalism, Christian monotheism indirectly received a huge shot in the arm, culturally speaking, thanks to several aspects of the Protestant critique of Roman authority.

Led by Martin Luther, Jean Calvin, and Ulrich Zwingli, European Protestantism not only spawned a new vitality in religious fervor but the Protestants' emphasis on the authority of Bible over Church also encouraged a new literacy so that common folk could actually consult the Bible in support of their individualistic piety. Over time, this emergent emphasis on direct access to the divine source opened the door among both Protestants and post-Reformation Catholics to skepticism about ecclesially received truths. This meant that the splintering of the churches only reinforced the oneness of truth because it essentially lay outside of the all-too-human church, rather than the other way around. Modern science was born in the minds of priests and theological scholars drunk on the possibilities of "going to the evidence" for God's truth—about everything.

Their avowals of skepticism about received truth did not, however, prevent the early modern "scientists," most of whom were theologically trained, from employing what we have already seen was the equally received truth of metaphysical oneness as a guide in their quest for knowledge. Nearly two millennia of Jewish, Christian, and Muslim cultural saturation in the idea of metaphysical Oneness did not simply go away when Francis Bacon, René Descartes, Isaac Newton, and others sought a means for attaining knowledge that was not dependent on church authority. The early modern European philosophers made their forays into a new science based on empirical observation and mathematical logic, a method that grew directly out of the neo-Pythagorean and Aristotelian framework that itself had informed the very church doctrine the early scientists were hoping to evade.

The first bold "princes of Reason" expected to find a unifying order in their explorations of nature, and so, naturally, they did find it. From Ibn Sinna, Bacon, and Descartes to Galileo and Newton, it is quite clear that no other alternative to a monocosmic idea was seriously considered. Even Descartes' *Meditations on First Philosophy*, in which he posited the famous line "cogito ergo sum" (I think, therefore I am), explored the possibility of a different kind of universe under the rule of an evil genius as a rhetorical device only.[6] And Bacon railed against the power of preconception to rule the mind, but even he did not imagine the extent to which logical frameworks are themselves produced within imaginative horizons shaped by culture and religion.

The work of the dominant culture on the horizons of human imagining—in this case late Roman and Reformed Christianity—is readily apparent in the early modern philosophers' search for a "new science" that they believed would free humanity from the control of knowledge by a relatively few (easily corrupted) clerics. Today, from our post-Freud and Foucault perspectives, it is difficult to miss the underground workings of the theological assertion of the One on the very structure of inquiry in the wholly "secular" endeavor of science. Sir Isaac Newton's mathematically derived *universal* laws, for example, were not solely the result of unbiased observation. They fit well into his own preconceived acceptance of a "single" creation and answered questions that the "discovery" of the New World and another hemisphere recently had raised about the unity of creation. For Newton and the other early modern innovators of western science, the eternity and essential stasis of the universal physical laws provided intellectual breathing room and respite from the constraining trappings of Christian theism but enabled them to stay snugly within the fold of what they could affirm to be an essentially Christian monocosmos.

In some cases the early modern scientists may have held back their inquiries because, as the experience of Galileo Galilei showed, they had reason to fear the very real power of suspicious clerics. Or they may have quite honestly not thought to question the basic theological assumption of cosmic unification. But their motives are more or less irrelevant—the fact is that they did not fundamentally question the metaphysical assertion of Oneness, derived from the religion that saturated their culture from cradle to grave. Quite the opposite, they adopted this faith as a basic principle of "post-religion" science. The fact that the search for a single, unifying theory of everything still dominates the imagination of some of the greatest minds in theoretical physics is an indication that the theological assumption of oneness is alive and well even in contemporary science. This is so despite a common popular acceptance that Newton and his colleagues mark the break of modernity (in the form of scientific reasoning) with religious reasoning and faith, at least as far as explanations for the observable universe are concerned.

The intellectual dilemma of the logic of the One: truth in a false opposition

From the seventeenth century onward, the European marriage of religio-political claims of metaphysical oneness to an emergent empirical science founded on mechanical assumptions of universal laws further deepened the western cultural assumption that all of reality is encompassed in and reducible to an as-yet not fully revealed unified system—an intrinsic One. At the same time, however, this powerfully imagined metaphysical unity and oneness at the heart of western cultural and scientific imagination has also resulted in a deep conceptual split, requiring a division of all of existence into the "real" and the "not real." The proposition of metaphysical oneness as a basis for truth brooks no contradiction. In a monocosmic system, that which is true (meaning that which has passed sufficient tests of universality and sameness to qualify as "true") constructs by implication a vast realm of falsehood against which it stands and whose claims to truth it rejects.

In theology, the more radical and exclusive forms of monotheism make this logic very plain and easy to spot. Exclusive monotheism *demands* the denial of all but the One God. There is no other God but the One God, in other words, and so all other appearances of or claims about divinity are deemed false. Any logical or perceived contradiction to the existence and supremacy of the One eternal God implies the presence of a falsehood (a heresy) or an error in perception. This either/or reality structure is brittle and absolute. It requires a great deal of apology, defense, and reinforcement to survive.

The dualistic logic of true against false is not restricted to the rigid forms of exclusive monotheism, however. Even a more adaptive, inclusive monotheism that accepts and subsumes all differences within itself depends on the conceptual split that oneness creates. Inclusive monotheism requires a kind of denial of "real" differences between things in its assertion that all differences are ultimately insubstantial; the perception of differences may be valid perhaps, but each perceived difference (in religion or in reality claims in general) are nevertheless bits and pieces of a larger unity, a larger whole that may or may not be accessible to human comprehension. When combined with monotheism's typical corollary of unchanging eternity, inclusive oneness, like exclusive oneness, is a denial of difference in ultimate terms; rather than rejecting differences by expulsion, it rejects them by dissolving all differences in a mystical, overarching One.[7]

The reality claim of oneness that undergirds monotheistic religion and culture therefore serves to reduce, by virtue of the imperatives of the number one, the messy complexity and manyness that everyday experience implies. Everyday experience requires some kind of frame precisely because it is messy and complex. There is no known culture and language that does not, on some level, provide a limiting and rationalizing frame for otherwise random experience.[8] For all of reality to be "One," or subsumed in a One, however, means that *all* discontinuities, aberrations, and complexity must at some point disappear.

Oneness as an exclusive or inclusive reality claim therefore induces a certain kind of anxiety (though assuredly more for the exclusive than the inclusive sorts): How do the manyness, ambiguity, and changeability of everyday experience actually fit into an ultimate frame of One? If *all* of reality must fit the laws of the One God and/or the laws of the One Nature, then those things that confound either or both present problems for faith. And, indeed, they do, over and over again. "True" and "false" in Christian monotheism and in western science become terribly important distinctions in all aspects of life because the true and the real cannot contradict each other. As Socrates argues through Plato's pen, the true and the real are the same.[9] What a burden this places on the ambiguities of sensory existence! The ideology of oneness demands, in both systems of thought (scientific and monotheistic), that what is true, conflated with what is real, and what is false, conflated with what is unreal, cannot ultimately coexist, even though distinguishing true from false and real from unreal is sometimes next to impossible.

The funny thing is, ambiguity between true and false doggedly persists in modern scientific methodology despite its larger cultural context of a presupposed logic of One. In the world of empirical exploration where "laws" are hypotheses, "facts" are provisional. They can be overturned by new experiences hitherto unexpected. This was Francis Bacon's point in the early seventeenth century about proofs; he argued that they only apply to the past.[10] Stephen Hawking puts it this way: "No matter how many times the results of experiments agree with some theory, you can never be sure that the next time the result will not contradict the theory."[11] Modern science as a *methodology* is therefore much more flexible and open to multiplicity than it is as a defense of *truth*. It is only in the realm of ideology that boundaries between true and false cannot be permeable, regardless of the offense such ambiguity might give to some scientific believers in a monocosmos or to some religious believers in monotheism. In fact, the persistence of ambiguity in empirical approaches to knowledge has inspired a number of thematic responses, all of which attempt to accommodate recurring ambiguity between "true" and "false" within the logic of the One.

For example, the logic of the One can tolerate ambiguity between true and false through a kind of scientific eschatology of ignorance. "We don't know *yet*" is a response that is sometimes applied to factual uncertainty or apparent contradiction. The *truth* of the matter may not be fully formed for the present or even accessible through current instruments of observation. What *is* known of the matter is distorted by ignorance, but through diligence and study, and perhaps improved capacities for close observation, the truth will be revealed eventually. This deferral of truth to the future makes a place for ambiguity or outright contradiction in the present. Not surprisingly, it also mirrors a typical Christian conception of sin and eschatological hope, wherein the taint of "wrong" and "false" within the "right" and "true" is a sign of corruption that will be undone—eventually— in the work of redemption.

In order to maintain strong lines between "true" and "false," the logic of the One in both science and theology also relegates ambiguity to the realm of myth and art, where the blurred boundaries between true and false in experience are domesticated under the condition of "fiction." These relegations defer ambiguity away from the present: to an eschatological future of full knowledge on the one hand and to a mythical past of memory or a fictional "never was" on the other. "The earth is flat," for example, falls into the latter category. It was presumed true, but upon better observation became a fiction that was then presumed never to have been true, regardless of the lives and exploits its adherents had once pursued on the assumption of its truth. Both claims—flat earth and round earth—cannot be "true" or "real" in a logic of the One (understood scientifically *or* theologically) and so any ambiguity that persists (if any persists at all) between a flat and a round earth falls into the realm of myth, fiction, and error. In other words, my own experience of the world as generally flat is an error in perception rather than an ambiguity in truth, according to a strict logic of the One. And this is why the logic of the One is a problem for science, because it functions as an ideology that in fact disallows the actual ambiguities of experience to occasionally contradict oneness. The present, on which the empirical method relies, cannot be present when truth is assumed to be One, precisely because the present is rife with regular ambiguities: flat surfaces that are also round, truths that are also false, rights that are also wrong, visions that are also bodies, particles that are also waves, minutes that are also lifetimes, and so on. The logic of the One states that, from a distance, all contradictions fall away—the earth becomes obviously round. But *privileging* the perspective of distance—near or far—is precisely what the empirical method attempts not to do, lest what Bacon famously called the "idols of the mind" take hold.[12]

A deceptively simple example is dreaming (and, interestingly enough, it is the example of dreaming that confounded Descartes). Dreams can seem so "real" that they cause the dreamer's legs to twitch in the motion of running, or they can cause the dreamer to speak or even to scream words aloud, to physically respond to a dream lover, or to break out in sweat from dreamed exertion or fear. Are these physical effects "real" and the dream "just" imagined? Many native North and South American cultures claim that dreams carry all the reality of the physical world: they are experiences of worlds that exist in reality alongside or in some other place than the world we experience in waking (accessible through dream passage). For a traditional Iroquois, for example, discounting the reality of that other world or those worlds is about as intelligent as discounting the reality of a truck hurtling down the highway in your lane (which is not to say that, even in those cultures that take dreaming this seriously, dreams do not still need to be interpreted).[13] But then, traditional Iroquois and Algonquin cultures never made monocosmic or monotheistic claims and so were never forced to relegate the multiple truths they experienced, waking and sleeping, entirely to fiction or ignorance. A more supple posture toward the world is possible when the world does not—always—have to behave.

The long-term effects of the monocosmic and monotheistic models in European imaginings have been profound. The logic of One in science translates into the methodological rules of simplicity and non-contradiction, both of which function as faith claims, and both of which have been crucial to the huge successes in modern scientific research. These rules function as faith claims not only because they reflect the deep cultural roots of Christian monotheism out of which the modern scientific methodology grew, but also because of their many successes in providing meaningful explanation and successful experimentation. Faith in science is no different than faith elsewhere: it lasts as long as it works and as long as it is useful.

Simplicity

The principle of parsimony, popularly known as Occam's razor, insists that, in a situation of more than one plausible explanation for any phenomenon, the simpler one is better. "It is vain," William of Occam wrote, "to do with more what can be done with less."[14] As a working principle for scientific exploration, this has meant that unless the evidence absolutely requires it, simpler explanations are preferred to complex ones. In the very first of his "Rules of Reasoning in Philosophy," published as part of a larger work entitled *Principia*, Isaac Newton declares that scientists should "admit no more causes of natural things than such as are both true and sufficient to explain their appearances."[15] Stephen Hawking, a contemporary physicist who has made famous the search for a single Theory of Everything (TOE), repeats this rule in his discussion of the emergence of quantum physics in the twentieth century:

We could still imagine that there is a set of laws that determines events completely for some supernatural being, who could observe the present state of the universe without disturbing it. However, such models of the universe are not of much interest to us mortals. It seems better to employ the principle known as Occam's razor and cut out all the features of the theory that cannot be observed.[16]

Modern science has been able to advance at awe-inspiring rates in no small part because of the economy that the principle of simplicity affords. Occam's razor is, however, a tool and not a truth.[17] And the question grows, as the mechanical model of Newtonian science begins to falter in the face of relativity and quantum possibilities, whether the razor cuts more than it should, *sine necessitate*. But that question is, if the pun can be pardoned, currently at the cutting edge in science and not in its received doctrines. Particles and waves are the building blocks of atoms which in turn make up more complex matter. The principle of simplicity is a bedrock article of faith in a reality that can be described by the simplifying concept of a single, cosmic text: a "uni-verse." As such, it is therefore also "true."

The equation here between science and religion is not a dismissal of science's real material and ideological contributions to human life on the planet. All systems of belief must "pay their way" with discernible benefits and "real" answers to pressing questions of life. Until (and if) the reductive razor of simplicity fails enough times to raise suspicion among its adherents, or until enough edges of the real and the supposedly unreal refuse to stay separated, or until (and if) enough scientists begin to see dreams, desire, allegory, and vision in their facts, the followers of Europe's scientific revolution will continue to put their faith in simplicity that is based on an ontological whole, a functional One that binds and grants coherence to the many and the complex. As long as it works.

Non-contradiction

Even more integral to the scientific method than Occam's razor is the principle of non-contradiction. Put simply, this is the deep faith, grounded in Newtonian universalism, that truth is solid and ultimately unassailable. That which is true cannot also be false. The problem is, of course, that contradiction persists in human experiences. A short route takes longer than a long route. Ugly is beautiful. Death is birth, and vice versa. A shaman becomes a beaver for a while. A recently deceased person shows up and speaks to the living. A particle is a wave. And so on, and so on. What is contradicted here is the singularity and inelasticity of truth. In the face of such a requirement, the occurrence of contradiction is rampant.

There are several strategies that modern people tend to deploy for coping with recalcitrant contradiction or betrayal of simplicity. The most explicit and stiff strategy is the accusation of outright falsehood, lying, or other forms of denial. The map-maker erred. The mirror lied. The watch stopped. The kindness was a ruse. The shaman lied. The living dreamed. The instrument failed. In other words, there is no contradiction, just lies and falsehoods. Two other, related strategies focus more specifically on contradiction as a problem in the perceiver. They are: error in knowledge and error in judgment.

Error in knowledge

The first strategy for coping with apparent elasticity in truth—error in knowledge—asserts that in a situation of contradiction some piece of knowledge is unavailable or incorrect, resulting in a situation of contradictory conclusions. Better research, leading to improved information or knowledge, should expose the error, eliminate the contradiction, and so restore an unfractured conclusion. For example, one could say that the reason that highly intelligent people assert that God exists and other equally intelligent people assert that God does not exist represents a contradiction founded on error in knowledge. Neither side *knows* enough to convince the other side. The evidence for divine existence that convinces some can be explained otherwise, and so is not persuasive to all. And evidence against divine existence does not disprove divine existence altogether and so is also unconvincing. As an error, or gap, in knowledge, then we can presume that once science, or philosophy (or even God!) provides the missing *information* that is persuasive to all, then the contradiction will be resolved and (here is the assumption at work) *one* side will be proven "right."

This strategy that focuses on explaining apparent contradictions as an error or gap in knowledge has been extremely helpful in the evolution of modern rationality and its science, providing a powerful method for experimentation that, for the most part, really works. If I compute the balance column in my checkbook twice and I get two different sums, it is a fair bet that I have made an error in addition or subtraction somewhere along that dreary path. Or, if I bake a birthday cake in Boston and do it again with the same recipe and ingredients in Denver but get two dramatically different results, I may not have *known* that the difference in altitude can affect baking. Filling that gap in my knowledge can make all the difference in the result, resolve the apparent contradiction between two otherwise identical processes, and show that, as Star Trek's Dr. Spock would say, "There is a logical explanation." No contradiction here, just a gap in knowledge.

Error in judgment

The second strategy in dealing with contradiction—error in judgment—asserts that, again, there is no actual contradiction in truth or reality but rather mistakes in perspective. From the proper vantage point, contradictions cease to be contradictory as the apparently opposing elements or conclusions resolve into complementary parts of a larger coherence, a larger non-contradictory One. This option is often invoked, for example, to explain what appear to be hopelessly contradictory claims between religions. Are Allah, Krishna, Ahura Mazda, Esaugeta Emissee, the Virgin of Guadalupe, Ogun, and Yahweh the same? It all depends on perspective. From the vantage point of devotion, the differences may seem important enough to take up arms.

From the proper distance, at least according to the "error in judgment" strategy, all different religions represent paths *to the same,* and the differences ultimately resolve into sameness, at the proper distance. To be converted to the One in this inclusive sense is not to deny the validity of the many, it is simply to deny their manyness in any absolute sense (regardless of what believers may themselves actually think or believe). There is a spatial implication to inclusive Oneness: step back far enough, and you can see the coherent whole. But there can also be a temporal implication: hang around long enough, and over time you will understand the sameness that is the true nature of all difference.[18]

In physics, this strategy has been put to use with some success to explain apparently contradictory behavior at the heart of atoms. Earlier research had neatly sewn up the structure of matter in observable atomic bits called protons, neutrons, and electrons. However, throughout the twentieth century, the evidence was not entirely adding up. There seemed to be even smaller bits at work (some of which came to be known as "quarks"), but under laboratory conditions these smaller bits exhibit a contradiction that excited the eschatological hopes of scientists and their funders whenever faced with an investigable dilemma: these quarks behaved both as particles and as waves, disrupting one of the accepted either/or rules that governed research in physics up to that point.

This contradiction appeared to be the result of an error in perspective: researchers began to find that the *relation* of the observer to the observed makes a difference in the behavior of the observed—the quark appears to behave differently if it is being watched—suggesting to those scientists who seek unified explanations that they had not yet located the proper vantage point from which to determine what really is going on at the heart of matter. In other words, the apparently contradictory results *must* point to some deeper or more encompassing not-yet-revealed truth about atomic structure such that the quarks, behaving strangely according to "known" laws, could be explained (rendering them non-contradictory) by a deeper theory of "true" atomic structure and dynamics.

From the proper vantage point, the particle-wave supposed contradiction must reveal itself to be a necessary non-contradictory aspect of a deeper, coherent and unified structure. The fact that that deeper structure is still elusive both in space and time *and* that quarks seem to multiply and shift doesn't matter: the logic of oneness requires the existence of a unified deeper structure, and so it will be found, even if the provocatively named quarks located thus far (Up, Down, Strange, Charm, Bottom, and, finally, Top) continue to multiply. That is the teleological faith of modern science, anyway. The contradictory results, which indicate either a falsehood or a different logic that abides contradiction, become instead equally true proximal supports for a more ultimate truth. Their difference, being proximal, is eliminated in the more ultimate oneness that sweeps them up into its resolution.

The dualism of One

Ontology that is shaped by the logic of the One has a number of important characteristics that are worth reviewing, all of which in becoming imprinted on the Christian imagination also shape the cultural and scientific imaginations of the world dominated by Christianity. First, the logic of the One is dualistic. In order to account for difference, change, and ambiguity that continually recurs, reality within the horizon of the One necessarily falls into the true (real) and false (unreal) in order to support the singularity of reality. This leads as well to a splitting of the empirical from the intuitive. That which is real is confined to the tests of empirical observation and repeatability. The strange, the fleeting, the anomalous, the felt—the unverifiable, in other words—become "real" in their effects only or they are deferred altogether.

For example, A. I. Hallowell, a Euro-American anthropologist living among the Great Lakes Ojibwa in the mid-twentieth century, heard a number of important stories of the people that involved rocks engaged in animate interaction with various ancestors at critical moments in their history. Looking for a principle, or rule regarding the living and non-living, he asked the elder with whom he conversed if the stories about the rock that took initiative and intervened in their affairs meant that all rocks are alive. Hallowell has reported that the old man looked at him with some pity when he answered "No, of course not." But then the elder added, "But *some* are."[19]

The implication Hallowell received from this exchange was that his own thinking was not supple enough to understand what to the Ojibwe was self-evident, if unverifiable by western scientific standards. Of course rocks are not alive. But *some* are. The evidence lies in experience unencumbered by too many shutters. Ontology shaped by the logic of the One, in order to derive universal principles, must shutter anomalous experience, or else look for a universal law that will accommodate it. The truth that some rocks are alive fails the test of universality altogether and so must be relegated to the realm of collective imagining or creative story-telling. The aliveness of rocks becomes thereby a fiction and the experience of living rocks adheres to the dualistically understood category of "culture" (relative truth, or fiction) rather than "science" (universal truth, or reality).[20]

If I am depressed by a dream, or change my life on the basis of words delivered by a rock, tree, or cloud, ontology shaped by the logic of One can only accept the "reality" of such things in terms of the verifiable, which in these cases is the effect on my behavior, particularly if that behavior is consistent enough to sustain observation over time. The most that a modern imagination within the logic horizon of the One can do in the face of such things is to suggest that even delusions and hallucinations can have the "effect of truth."[21] A rock does not actually have to speak, or an actual dream realm exist, for the imagination to construe a trick of light and sound, or a fictional story woven in dream *as* real. There is a lot going for this argument. No one can deny that human beings are very capable of self- and other-delusion, alone or in groups. They can kill themselves or others, or do an endless number of dramatic things as the verifiable effects of unverifiable experiences. But it is also the case that those cultural traditions that do not participate in the logic of oneness and so maintain a more supple posture toward anomaly and flux in experience also have systems for adjudicating delusory or falsifying behavior as well. The modern tests of western science by no means sum up the possibilities for determining and dealing effectively with pathology.

The point here is that inspiration's attachment to reality is in no way guaranteed in any cultural system, at least if the long records of human history are taken into account. It is, however, a curious simplification of the dualism of true/false indicated by the logic of the One to suggest that that which cannot be verified by empirical observation or by the test of universality therefore exists only either in the realm of ideas (imagination, hallucination, dream, speculation, hypothesis) or in the realm of the "not yet verified." While indispensable as a standard for empirical science, and notwithstanding the enormous advantage and real successes that this dualism has achieved in modern science, technology, and the "soft" sciences of psychology and sociology, the true/false dichotomy also establishes limits to the social and religious imagination and sense of the queer possibilities for existence. And perhaps it limits access to divinity.

When a true/false dualism is rigidly enforced (rocks are either sentient or they are not, God either exists or does not), existence is normatively reduced to the verifiable. Put most simply, if no one can verify it, it does not exist. Without the possibility of ontological both-and answers, of shape-shifting, time interconnection, and other forms of ontological multiplicity, there is only being within the horizon of the same, of the One. So many non-European cultures like the Ojibwe that are open to many other possibilities for existence make the finality of true-or-false a non sequitur, a bit of nonsense.

The failure of One

A second characteristic of ontology that is shaped by the logic of the One is that it is reductive, meaning that existence itself must conform to a single explanation, or understanding. The rule of Occam's razor and the related quest for a single theory of everything have a resonance in the deepest heart of Pythagoras' mystical infatuation with the number one and in Christian notions of a singular, unchanging God. It is possible that the imaginative overlap of a single created cosmos knit together by discernibly universal laws under a single divine principle succeeds in science even more effectively than in religion because scientific exploration roots the concept of oneness in the self-referencing rules of simplicity and non-contradiction. The scientific faith in reductive simplicity and non-contradiction, which refers to a dogmatically affirmed cosmos, causes science to appear as if faith has little or nothing to do with the question of reality, especially when the scientist's own religious faith, say, grounded in monotheism, undergirds the oneness of the cosmos. As Gleiser notes, "Platonism echoes strongly in the offices of theoretical physicists, especially those preoccupied with questions of cosmic origin. Stephen Hawking has equated understanding the origin of the universe to knowing 'the mind of God.'"[22]

Simplicity, in theology and in society, is an economy of identity. Sameness becomes the basis for establishing real from unreal. Something is "real" if it is the "same as" (not anomalous or strange to) the known. And, so, the reducibility of reality to simplicity, or oneness, effects a negation of difference as a basic tenet of reality itself. Otherness, especially otherness that cannot be somehow resolved into a recognizable frame of the One, indicates, as we've already discussed, an error in knowledge or in judgment precisely because fundamental *otherness is not real*. Or, we should say, fundamental otherness cannot be real in a uni-verse.

If ontology is built on a reductive basis, then there should be no surprise when philosophers become obsessed with the question of otherness. If to *be* is to *be the same*, then *to be other* is a frightful loss of existence (remember the dualism—if to be the same is to be, then it must follow that to be other is to not-be). It is only within the logic of the One that the category of Other can come to hold such negative power, such fascination, horror, or attraction. Jacques Lacan certainly understood this in his development of the concept of phallogocentrism, in which the One (as Father, as Logos) attempts to blot out all but itself, thereby granting to the Other (as the feminine, the body, or anything that resists the logic of oneness) the status of "lack" or negation. This neo-Freudian reduction of otherness, its feminization and its rendering as the negative space within which the positive substance of reality—the One—can express itself exposes the failure of phallogocentrism to achieve oneness.[23] Luce Irigaray in particular has attempted to move past this logic, actually to *think* the other as other, to imagine a logic not bound to this uni-verse. She suggests we do so by "thinking the body" since, despite everything we try to do to control, repress, deny, or compress them, bodies do prosaically tend to resist oneness.[24]

The dualistic concept of and fascination with the Other that cannot be grasped in thought (this Other often depicted among the philosophers as

Woman) makes sense only within the logic of the One. It is easy to get stuck attempting to articulate this supposed Other *as other*, and forget that within a different logic, a resistant logic of "becoming," perhaps,[25] or a fluid logic of multiplicity, there is no One against which the Other is projected as grotesque nemesis. The Other is neither projected nor negated by the One in a more shifty ontology of multiplicity. Even more reassuring, the One is not negated by its contradictions. They simply *are*. What is the Other unmoored from its master One? An unruly cacophony of anomalies? A fertile depth? A swamp of unknowing? An unending matrix of possibility and so a multitude of answers? This is the fear, isn't it?

The horizon of One precludes real difference by virtue either of exclusion through the true/false dichotomy or by virtue of transcendent inclusion in a larger or deeper singularity that enfolds all difference into itself. Inclusive understandings of contradiction that insist on singular truths binding all differences together in some explanatory "end" presuppose a negation of difference or otherness at truth's own limits. And so, either way, Oneness is by necessity divided in itself between true and false and between real and unreal. If the contradictory realities stand even as an eschatological possibility, then the One is dismantled—and it is this that most deeply challenges the core points of faith in western science and Christian imagining.

What will happen to the horizon of Christian thought if the One—even as an eschatological hope that disciplines the many in the now—is not one? What if we see that the One is, paradoxically, constructed by its own exclusions of external and internal contradiction, and this exclusive move *itself* divides the One? We could say, then, that the One never *really* was one by virtue of its necessary exclusions—the One by itself is in fact the only impossibility, both now *and* then. Indeed, it is this claim that will carry us at last off the deep end (which is where we want to go after all) into the overdue realm of imagining divine multiplicity. But, in the meantime, which is the mean time of imperial Christian metaphysics, the One which is not one nevertheless asserts itself at the cognitive center of modernity, shaping the presuppositions of both theological and scientific hopes. The logic of the One dominates modern thinking about "the real" against the always recurring multiplicity at the heart of what could be and sometimes even has been (and I dare say should be) Christian religious imagining.

The ontological horizon of Christian Oneness funds a deep cultural anxiety about identity, sameness, origins and pedigree/roots. The One that denies its own constitutive multiplicity also denies and suppresses hybridity or contradiction. It is a reductive Theory of Everything, a TOE out of water that is unconnected to any feet; it is not fluid or supple, not mutable, partial, or temporary. It is unchangeable, just as it has made truth unchangeable. The genealogical trace of this reduction runs through the Constantinian doctrinal consolidation, the medieval scholastics' stratification and legalization of eternity, the early modern scientists' conflation of nature, law, and stasis into contemporary scientific strivings after a Theory of Everything. Each move relies entirely on a logic of oneness that betrays the actuality of incommensurate experiences and of bodies in all of their irreducible *thereness*. In other words, the logic of the One betrays the empirical method. It is a fundament *that had to be made* for imperial consolidation and "westward expansion." It is an ontology of ice, whose fluid dynamics we have forgotten even exist.

7 When hell freezes over

There are three elements which either alone, or combined with others, summon images of the uncivilized, the savage, and the sexual deviant body alike. These elements are vulgarity, horror, and impunity. To reflect on them is to reflect on the constitution of exclusion in theology in the double sense of formation by exclusion and of the legal body of moral allowances allocated to people in a particular historical setting.

Marcella Althaus-Reid[1]

I know some people died of their tragic story.

Bighorse[2]

Somewhere along the long road of its intellectual history Christian metaphysics got stuck in the ontological ice of monotheism and has not been able to thaw itself out sufficiently to re-enter the world and make sense to everyday people. To call it ontological ice is, of course, to say something else as well. Ice is water—the solution necessary for life—a richly malleable substance, infinitely shape-shifty when it is warm and especially when it is hot. Ice is water appearing to be still. We might say, for metaphoric purposes, that ice aspires to stasis. It does so via the absence of warmth. What a lovely metaphor this is for the problem of the One in Christian theology! It is lovely because the problem of the One in Christian theology could be viewed, from a certain poetic and allegorical angle, as a problem of too little warmth.

In my reading of the complex history of monotheism in the west, I have pointed to its emergence in association with times of deep communal threat, of loss, and of cultural shifting. One way to tell the story is that, at many points along the way, divinity that was poured out like a libation for a people battered by change, war, and uncertainty, became a prisoner of the people's fear. They attempted to freeze the divine in crystalline structures of mathematics or in the gilt armor of warrior kings to reassure themselves of its allegiance and presence, to keep it from soaking into the ground, or from rising up in a vapor; and *eo ipso* to keep divinity—and themselves—from ever changing again. The people became afraid of the waters of life, pretending that the ice that had been their living, changing divinity was not wet, not fertile, not changing, and finally not even God. The Divine to them became Something Else; it floated up into a more dry, faraway place. But despite such disassociative fears, the waters off of the Deep End remained, and so became a repository of the people's repressed terror of change; no longer did they think of the fluid depths as the very substance of divinity. To control their fears, to hide from life lived in the midst of sometimes cruel change and flux, they froze the Deep. They trapped their fear of change and with it their lives. They became very, very cold, and wondered why they could never quench their thirst.

That is one story. Here is another. The place is Italy, the time around the year 1300 CE. An educated, middle-aged man was exiled from his native city-state of Florence, having ended up on the wrong side of the Guelph/Ghibelline power struggles there. While in Rome on diplomatic business for his White Guelph clan and constituents, he learned that the pope had secretly conspired with the Black Guelphs and Ghibellines to kill or exile his kindred. In this Hatfield/McCoy-like drama, the man also learned that if he *ever* returned home to Florence, he would be burned to death alive— *igne comburetur sic quod morietur.*[3] So rather than meet that painful fate, he wandered the length and breadth of the Italian-speaking countryside, mourned his lost city and family, and wrote about Hell. Of course, once he had done so (like Milton three hundred years later), he felt obliged to write about Purgatory and Heaven, too. But any reader of Dante Alighieri's tripartite *La Divina Comedia* can see that it was neither the regimented logic of Purgatory nor the serene choruses of Heaven that got his creative genius for verse going.

Whether approached as populist criticism of a corrupt government and church or as indigenous art, whether a theological vision or as the first blockbuster hit of the Italian *hoi polloi* (Dante wrote in Italian, the cadence and language of the street and countryside, not in Latin, the language of the church and its doctors) the *Inferno* is a rich, robust, and bawdy read. In addition, the poem offers one angry and broken-hearted man's vision of the deepest heart of Hell that, beyond explicit (and satisfyingly vivid) excoriations of the medieval church's hypocrisy and corruption, paints a striking and provocative picture of the limits of the church's metaphysics.

The *Inferno* begins in the middle of Dante's life, in the middle of a wood, in the middle of the world. The poet awakes on the road to the realization that he is lost:

> Half-way through the story of my life
> I came to in a gloomy wood[4]

This opening is not unlike the many creation stories of Native North America that begin more or less in the middle, quite simply, with the words

"There was a village," or "Hare [Trickster] was on his way to a village."[5] There is no obsession here with absolute beginnings and endings, even though Dante's vision can be read as a specifically Christian metaphysical imagining of hopes, fears, and ends. *La Divina Comedia* is concerned, from the very first stanza of the *Inferno,* with being in the middle, faced with complexity and the multiplicity of options that characterize even the meanest life. The three parts of the trilogy form an allegory of relational consequences—a geography and ontology of human enmeshment in world, bodies, relations, and divinity (both monstrous and tame).

Dante relates his attempts to climb out of the dark valley in which he first finds himself, only to find that his way is blocked by various monstrous animals. He is rescued, however, by the appearance of the long-dead pagan poet Virgil, who informs Dante that the only way out of his current fix—the only way to find his way—is through Hell itself. Virgil declares to Dante's delight that he, Dante's own favorite poet, will escort the Florentine exile there, "where you'll hear the shrieks, unqualified / by hope, of those who suffer so much pain, / each wishes he died a second time."[6] Dante has "awoken" into a realm of ghosts, spirits, and animal servants, assuring his listeners that he is as incredulous as they, but insisting thereby on the veracity of his tale. He has, one could say, removed the blinders on his mundane life and glimpses, through the porosity of dream, vision, and the poet's pen a closely abutting world of difference. This is a non-reductive awakening to difference that Voltaire, Bacon, and the princes of colonial Reason would thoroughly have rejected. It is not, however, an awakening that would startle the majority of the peoples of the earth whose primary point of reference is not the narrow vision of western empiricism. As Calvin Martin pointedly asks in his own study of the brittle inadequacy of modernity's metaphysics, "whose *reason* is it, after all, that moves the Spirit of the Earth in its errands?"[7]

The medieval man Dante, not yet entirely forbidden to view the world through the rich membranes of dream and vision, insists that his story is "true" not because it is reasonable and plausible, but precisely because it is so hard to believe—no one could make this stuff up, he seems to be saying. Nearly a thousand years before, Tertullian declared, of the divine body of Christ, "I believe because it is absurd" for much the same purpose.[8] Of course, from the latter ends of a jaded modernity, we see a clever literary device here, one employed by many of the best writers of fiction who know how to manipulate by appearing to share their readers' own incredulity, thereby injecting a pleasurable uncertainty about the author's own view of the matter. Recently, Dan Brown turned a similar trick in the frontal matter of his runaway bestseller *The Da Vinci Code,* inserting a fictional note from a fictional "expert" that authenticates certain "facts" of his story, principally by identifying the fictional aspect of others.[9] It is a clever device, to be sure. Like Dante, Brown also wishes his audience to understand his story to be "true," but in Brown's case "truth" (or better yet, uncertainty about it) is an entertainment device that banks on an audience schooled in rigid distinctions between "truth" and "falsehood." Brown shows his readers that he knows the difference by exposing *some* of the parts of his own story as made up, and thereby he strengthens the distinction between "fact" and "fiction" while adding for some a pleasurable moment of uncertainty about the rest of the story.

Such games with fact and fiction are only possible in a milieu that draws impermeable distinctions between the two. Dante did not live with the benefit of Newtonian mechanics or a fully realized scientific ontology of oneness. We might say that his world was in fact closer to the outer edges of our own, where the fluidities and surprises of quantum mechanics are being explored, where reductive, ontological oneness is coming under question. For him, the fabric holding the realm of potentiality within the realm of actuality, the realm of sleep within the realm of waking, the realm of story within the realm of fact, had not yet been fully rent. The story of his journey, he tells us, is true because it is so fabulous. He expects doubt, but is writing centuries before the faith of western science established its dogmas and lists of heresies. Dante enlists the credulity of his audience by sharing their incredulity. It may also be the case that the quality of fable suggests, in the *Inferno* especially, a truth that is very hard to accept. Throughout the world, fables and parables have often borne the most startling and dangerous messages, wrapped in cloaks of poetry, art, and story-telling. In the case of Dante's inferno, the difficult truth lies quite literally in the center of Hell, namely, that *the metaphysics of absolute and eternal stasis on which the monotheistic doctrine of God is founded, is a lie.*

From Dante's gates of Hell, where the weak-willed and undecided are condemned to flit about in eager crowds chasing meaningless banners, from the descending rings of imagined horror, from the excrement-filled swimming pits, the glued lovers and the shape-shifters, to the deepest core where Satan is fixed in exile, Dante's vision is much more than a ribald catalog of retribution for particular wrongs (though it is that, as well). Despite their groans and tears, there is an unmistakeable humor and lilt to the damned—while they must suffer to satisfy the vengeful imagination of the living—they create a kind of community of excess within which there are certain taboo pleasures. From pit to pit and punishment to punishment, the damned indulge, at times almost like masochists in an S&M scene, in obedience, subterfuge, gossip or complaint. They interact, jibe, change form, deceive, and, to put it simply, seem to get by with what little they have. If this is Hell, then Hell is life itself in all of the myriad ways that human beings are caught up in and maintain webs and pits of greed, need, guilty pleasure, and excess.

Granted, nobody seems to be having *fun* in Dante's *Inferno* (except perhaps for the demonic keepers), but the torments of the damned seem less cruel, allegorically speaking, than merely consequential: the people throughout the *Inferno* are simply experiencing the consequences of choices they have made. This is what gives the journey its pleasure: many of the pits entail the intimate consequences one might secretly wish on rude neighbors, bad bosses, co-workers, ex-lovers or the occasional cardinal and pope. It is a fantasy of consequence, less along the lines of Eliza Doolittle's rageful vision of a royal firing squad that takes out Professor Higgins, and more along the lines of "be careful what you wish for." In some cases the damned receive the very thing they sought in life, but in spades. This seems to be a vision of intimately embodied consequence. What *is* unspeakably cruel, however, is the unendingness of the consequence. Indeed, the theme of eternity is the only truly horrifying dimension of Dante's journey through Hell. Here is a poem that in its fantasy of retribution indulges in an almost juvenile body-humor. Like the hugely popular television series CSI, it trades in the queerly attractive recoil of each bodily transgression. But the *Inferno* contains at its heart a real horror: the metaphysical overlay of eternity.

From his very first steps, Dante reveals to us the horror that is Hell's banal eternity. As Virgil guides Dante from the gloomy wood to Hell's entrance, they pass under a gate engraved with the famous words:

> Before me there was nothing made to be,
> except eternity; eternal I endure;
> all hope abandon, ye who go through me.[10]

This is a remarkable theological claim: *nothing* but eternity itself (God, presumably) existed before Hell and its gates. Eternity created Hell first, out of itself, perhaps because Hell is all that Eternity *can* create. Eternity is, by definition, devoid of change and so it is devoid of the punctuations in sameness that temporality bestows on the living with such generosity. The shock here is that Hell only really becomes the site of evil in its eternity, at which point it becomes indistinguishable from Heaven. The *Inferno*, in Dante's vision, is mostly an excess of life, qualities under control in *Purgatorio* and distinctly missing in *Paradiso*.

What is more, it is reasonable to wonder about the very meaning of such eternities, as Sartre does in his own reflection on Hell in *No Exit*. Kierkegaard notes in his own critique of things eternal that "[e]xistence without motion is unthinkable, and motion is unthinkable *sub specie aeterni*."[11] The eternal and change (motion) are absolutely incompatible. So from the very first lines, Dante leads us into a remarkable realization: eternity created Hell first because that is what eternity *is*. What a marvelously queer exposé and condemnation all at once of the deadly canker at the heart of Christian metaphysics! The deadly canker, the *ontos* of Hell, is stasis, which is Eternity, which is God.

From infernal pit to pit, round and round toward the center, Dante treats us, however, to a carnival of bodily excess. We meet those who in life sought illicit love, those who lied, those who pilfered, those who did not meet their debts, and those whose souls live in hell but whose bodies still walk around in life. Each suffers a "poetic" justice and is pitiful, comic, and human. Toward the end of his journey through this Vaudeville of human consequence, after a narrow escape from the pit of excrement, close encounters with body snatchers, and various other funhouse delights (many of which could, from a certain allegorical angle, describe a day in the life of active toddlers) the fires die out, giving way at the very center to a vast, still lake of ice. Who knew? A snowball does stand a very good chance in Hell. The most damned of the damned lie frozen in the deepest pit with Satan himself mired at their center, the only movement a slow fanning of his massive, frigid wings.

It is this eternal deepfreeze regulated by Satan's wings that Dante offers out of the riches of his medieval dream-vision, constituting for him the true meaning of damnation. The worst fate, beyond which no greater punishment can be imagined, is the absence of movement, of warmth, and of change. It is not stench and heat, putrification, entanglement, complaint, tears, or wasp-stings. It is not endless labor or being upended in a hole and having one's feet set on fire. It is not even walking ever forward while looking ever back. No, far worse than a body that experiences pain, remorse, or change is what lies at the center of Hell. The eight circles, from the gate to the penultimate pits of Malebolge are mere (okay, big) messes of consequence. But Hell itself really begins when the two traveling poets see their own breath, as their own warmth is sucked out of them.

Dante reserves this place of ice for betrayers who, in his own partisan grief, he can never imagine forgiving. Whether or not the frozen lake of the deepest pit of Hell is the proper place for those who betray fundamental trusts is an interesting question, but at issue here is less the matter of *who* is frozen into that lake and more the vivid image of the ice itself as supreme punishment. The chill of the place comes through the verse, "a lake so cold it was not wet, but looked like glass instead" in which the bodies of the most damned are locked:

> so were these wretched ghosts embedded in
> the ice, blue to the gills; and like a crowd
> of storks, they clacked their teeth. With icy grin
>
> each set of features desperately was bowed;
> each mouth bore witness to the cold; each pair
> of eyes was damp with gloomy, inner cloud.[12]

At the outer edge of the lake, as their tears freeze in their eyes, the damned still gibe, however. They confide, bellow in anger, and insult one another with wit. They are cold, they are stuck in the ice up to their lips, but they are still full of life. And that makes this scene at the edge of the lake not quite the horror it is perhaps meant to describe. Anyone who has lived through a northern winter has experienced at one time or another the kind of bitter cold that causes the body to become "numb in thought and deed."[13] In one sense, as elsewhere in the *Inferno,* the Hell depicted here in the final circle cannot be the elements, for they are experienced elsewhere. Even a Florentine, who may only have experienced bitter cold through the stories of northern travelers, knows that if Hell is the cold (or the excrement, or the fires, or the hot sands, or the wind) then Hell is everywhere on earth.

As in the first eight circles, the real difference here, of course, is not the elements but unchanging eternity that traps them. And because the poet paints a vivid picture, the stillness at the center of the lake confirms it. As Virgil leads Dante across the lake (occasionally treading on an unsuspecting head) the chill deepens and the stillness grows; there is no more banter or complaint from the damned. Dante himself becomes so cold he cannot tell if he is dead or alive. The damned here are completely covered up in the ice:

> At last I'd reached that place that terrified
> me then, and makes me shudder still to write,
> where souls lay every which way, clarified
>
> as straw in glass: some upside down, some right
> side up, or this one angled, that one flat,
> another face to feet like bow bent tight.[14]

Their every motion is now stilled, and so they are the essence of eternity. Or, to put it another way, eternity is the essence of damnation. True hell, this means, is stasis. And in Dante's rendering of the Christian metaphysical story, the ice of Hell is the fundament upon which the eternity that Heaven claims for itself is built.

Or so it would seem. Remarkably, Dante "discovers that" this most hellish place of enforced stillness in Hell *isn't.* It is a trick of *motion,* of the cooling action of Satan's massive wings. The ice is not in fact integral to the place, but it is the product of continuous effort on the part of the so-called Prince of the prisoners. What is more, it is literally through the body of the devil that the two travelers find their way to Heaven. What a queer vision! Hell is, for the most part, a hot, smelly, messy place. It is every bit the *body* in motion or in labor. But Satan, the keeper and prime penitent of Hell, himself supposedly a prisoner, is frozen in the center of a lake of ice he himself chills. Satan manufactures the allegory of eternity at the center of the ninth circle upon which, Dante is about to discover, the structure of earth and heaven rest. Presumably, therefore, Dante unwittingly reveals to us that that the most basic tenet of Hell and Heaven, namely eternity (namely God), is not in fact eternal. There is *machina* in the *Deus.*

In the beginning, Virgil brings Dante to Hell in order to help him get out of the woods and on the right path in his life (remember, he starts out having lost his way). Why is this trip to Hell necessary? The answer is not obvious, at least not until we get to the end of the *Inferno* and ride on Virgil's shoulders down and apparently *into* the hairy, bound body of "*the former Beautiful Aristocrat*," a name that Dante might well have applied nostalgically to his own, lost, Florentine self.[15] After scrambling across the heads and faces of the frozen damned to the mired torso of Satan himself, Virgil leads Dante literally *down* the chest and thigh of the giant body of the monstrous angel in order to climb *up* at the groin into heaven's light:

> he lighted on the shaggy carapace;
> then down from tuft to tuft he climbed, between
> the matted hair and frozen interface.
>
> When he had reached the lower mezzanine
> of where the hip meets upper thigh, my guide,
> performing a most difficult routine,
>
> head over heels revolved, then occupied
> himself in starting to ascend the hair,
> hell-bent, it seemed to me, on going Hellside.[16]

Dante is confused. No wonder. Having climbed down and now ascending, he finds himself turned upside down, looking "*beyond a rounded opening, of store on store of things of Heavenly delight.*"[17] Just what this rounded opening is in Satan's body is not entirely clear, but there are only so many holes in the body "where hip meets thigh". At its own infernal "end," we find out that Hell is a kind of vaginal or anal passage to Heaven, meaning that the journey into Satan's pubic region has resulted in something unexpected and overturning. Heaven lies in the body of Satan. Once they invert themselves at the pivot of hip and thigh (becoming inverts?) they are also, provocatively, upside-down on Satan. Instead of looking up to see the three-headed torso towering over them, now Dante looks up to see the equally massive feet of the angel "pointing straight at me." No rustic troubadour could possibly mistake the sexual connotations that this image conveys. Dante, however, also has a cosmic point to make in this inversion and so demands an explanation of Virgil:

> "Where is the ice? And how come the Afreet
> is upside down? And how has time so whirled
> along, that night so rapidly retreats?"
>
> And he: "Your problem is, your mind has walled
> you in: you think you're where I caught the hair
> of that vile worm that penetrates the world.
>
> As long as I descended, so you were:
> but when I turned myself, you turned the pier
> on which depends all weight from everywhere ..."[18]

The stunning assertion here is that Satan is the foundation of the universe. His position is pivotal not only as an axis in the world, but the hairy place where hip meets thigh is apparently the point upon which the edifices of Purgatory and Heaven—the whole realm and creation of God—are built.

What are we, theologically, to make of this? First, there is the matter of the "pier on which depends all weight from everywhere." What kind of God builds an "everywhere" (including, presumably, the everywhere of Heaven) that depends on, well, *the devil*? Not to mention the devil's groin? And then what kind of God gives the devil, a most unreliable monster we're made to believe, the "job" of keeping that pier firm and solid enough to hold all of that heavenly delight *up* (hence the ice)? One begins to wonder, very queerly indeed, just who these two characters, God and Satan, are and by what machinations they engineer such a going down on the One who holds the whole structure together. What masquerade may be playing here, what drag is vamping? If there is someone at the center of it all, someone holding it all up, someone working to keep the foundation (or whatever that bodily pivot point really is) firm so the stars can spin—well, meta-physically speaking, is not that someone God?

Second, and related to the first point, there is the marvelously provoca-tive way that Dante places entry into the realm of so-called Heavenly delight right into the shorts of the naughtiest angel. He approaches heaven ultimately through the bawd of the *body*. That alone should make us wonder about the God in this most metaphysically Christian of stories. After scrambling about in "the hair of the vile worm that penetrates the world," the two poets look through the "rounded opening" at "store upon store of heavenly delight." There is, in the body of God's reviled Other, a rounded opening through which one may glimpse heaven. This suggests that Satan is the closeted, transversible, sexual *body of God*, the opening, the vagina, the key to Heaven. Satan, here, by god, is God.

Of course, *La Divina Comedia* is just a medieval story. But it is a story built on a theological imagination that shows up still in the language of Christian piety. Its images still fund the metaphysics that run throughout modern Christian worship and imagination. It is also however, a wonder-fully queer story. It reflects the metaphysical claims of the Christian church up to and beyond the thirteenth century but throws those metaphysical claims into some very real question. What is this ice at the center of Hell? As we have noted, ice is water pretending to be still, and water is the most enduring and vivid image of fertility, change, and possibility.

It is here that Dante's story manifests, whether he meant it to or not, a profound critique of the metaphysics of Christian monotheism. Satan becomes God. Indeed, it cannot be otherwise because as Augustine argued so forcefully centuries earlier, in the logic of the One, God can have no Other, no contradiction and so, presumably, no Satan as the Other of God. This is the principle of non-contradiction at work in the heavenly logic of monothe-ism. The Hell, Satanic figure, and multitude of the damned that Christians have imagined as the container for their fears of real life and messy consequence in fact reveal a repressed face of Heaven, of God, and of the blessed.

Queer theory via Foucault offers a helpful view of this: the repressed Other is not a byproduct of the dominant Same but produces it. The repressed Other is *needed* by the dominant Same. Eve Kosofsky Sedgwick writes, for example, that the homosexual closet is not really about homosexuals at all but heterosexuality. The closet produces heterosexuality in that it makes heterosexuality normative, enables heterosexuals to pretend that they alone exist. The closet is a function of the myth of heterosexuality's monolithic claim to normalcy.[19] An outcome of Dante's *Inferno,* which is a riff on medieval scholastic theology, is that Satan is not just a product of God. God is Satan, who is the repressed body, mess, and worldliness of divinity.

Perhaps, therefore, the bodies of the damned, who are enmeshed in a vast humor of consequence in Hell, are not the *opposite* of the blessed saints sipping their nectar in Heaven, but they are the saints themselves. The *Inferno* is the closet of *Paradiso*; Hell and even Purgatory are the indispensable containers of the repressed fluidity and ambiguity of Heaven, the very repression of which makes Heaven's monolithic claim to superiority possible. *Paridiso,* Dante's vision of Heaven that inspired millions of Christians in the centuries after him, is a very sterile place. But the *Inferno* reveals to us that the purity of the saints depends upon repression and removal of all excess. And, as in all things, it is the excess that defines the remainder.

The singularity of divinity in monotheism is sustained in this cosmic medieval allegory by the symmetry of Satan-on-ice and God moored at Heaven's celestial pinnacle. Dante therefore neatly deals with the perennial Christian theological problem that the figure of evil presents to the doctrine of a single god by making the icy pit a mirror of heaven and also the closest spot in Hell to Heaven. Virgil guides Dante all the way through Hell because the only way out is not out at all, but in. There is no "out" from Hell, and who would want an out? The body is messy and constrained by consequence, but at least it is alive. Satan's own nether region is indeed the link to "everything."

The ice of Hell, in other words, is a reflection of the pure stasis of Heaven. Heaven and Hell are One or, as Christine Uberti suggests, they "have the same address".[20] Within the imaginative horizon of Oneness, one of the deeper truths in this vision is that Hell really has no opposite; its opposite is its same. Satan himself offers the travelers passage (he is the Way?) toward heaven. But in the three-tiered universe of classical Christian imagining, you don't just "get" to Heaven, a destination built on the repudiation of bodily consequence. Because you are born in a body, especially if you are born into the wrong body, or at the wrong time or in the wrong place, getting to the Christian Heaven requires the hard work of leaving one's body—and the world—behind.

Purgatorio, at least according to Dante, is the disciplinary site of bodily renunciation required for entrance into Heaven's blessed stasis. It is a realm of the not-quite saved/same. It is very nearly a proto-Reformed vision in its serious regimentation of effort, investment, payment, and progress. Like the eight circles of the *Inferno, Purgatorio* is a tale of consequence, but this time with heavy doses of class aspiration and fantasies of progress. Seen through the lens of late global capitalism and postcolonialism, *Purgatorio* is a Protestant work-dream transposed onto the bodies of the not-good-enough, whose self-denial and enslavement feed a fantasy of eventual advancement. It is the fantasy that insufficient birth into bodies of the socially damned can, with proper obeisance and many lifetimes of humiliation, be overcome. Entrance to the golden realms of the saved is attainable for those aspirants in Purgatory because, the Church teaches, untamed and untamable bodies are dispensable. Bodies are the problem, not the eternal sameness that the ice of Hell and the crystal of Heaven represent.

In Dante's regimented *Purgatorio,* the darkness, stench, and chaoid[21] shiftiness of nomadic bodies are under the disciplined tutelage of civilization, entrained toward the goal of ultimate renunciation of change and of world. They are, as Gilles Deleuze would say, "arborized," in training for the strictly plotted garden of *Paradiso.* All eyes of these hopeful liminoids are focused upward, chained to the promise of eventual release from the labor of repentance for having been born. Like all heavy laborers in the cruel fantasy of merit capitalism, they dream of an end to their labor and believe it possible because they accept the lie that merit and not raced, sexed bodies are the determinants of their plight. But do they know they dream of ice?

Once through Purgatory, Dante is dazzled by the gated community of Heaven, before which Virgil must leave him, being a pagan and so not included on the guest list. His unrequited Florentine love, Beatrice, therefore escorts him in. He quickly shows us that *Paradiso* is as frozen in its bright circles of light as Satan is in ice. The saved have their appointed spots, like members of a Big Ten marching band, from which they have no desire anymore to deviate (except, apparently, to escort the occasional visitor such as Dante). The whole of Paradise forms a lovely, glimmering rosette. The groaning, sweating machinery of Hell and the bureaucratic regiments of Purgatory that keep the crystal polished and the light bulbs changed are kept completely out of sight.

Dante was an avid reader of Thomas Aquinas, for whom the metaphor of a great chain of being leads inexorably and sedately upward through levels of sanctification (and increasing disembodiment) to the pure light of God. After writing his monumental *Summa Theologica,* Thomas is said to have had a vision of God at the end of his life that caused him to declare that everything he had written was straw and he would write no more.[22] Perhaps this famous story was on Dante's mind when he faced the challenge of describing God at the pinnacle of Paradise. Certainly the closer he comes to that point in *Paradiso*, Dante loses words. He says that the vision leaves him speechless. It is also possible that a virtuoso of words can be robbed of words by unimaginable beauty. But there is another possibility, which seems more likely given his increasingly rote descriptions of the tiers of heaven that lead up to his final failure of speech. Dante becomes so bored of Heaven that he can find no more words to describe the sameness of the place and its serene residents. He is a master story-teller, *but here there is nothing, really, to tell.*

No splashing about in muck, no pleasure in pain or complaint, no shape-shifting, no giants, no Virgil—and so, one can only imagine, no poetry—in *this* beatific Hell of a Heaven of eternal sameness. Difference is relegated to the interstitial realms of almost-Hell in the first circles of the *Inferno* and almost-Heaven in the workrooms of *Purgatorio*, where the demons cavort and the desperate labor in their denial. Without excrement, effort, blood, noise, upside-down church officials, the challenge of escape, or the pull of desire there can also be no life, and certainly no humor. Is it any wonder that it was the many chambers of Dante's idea of Hell that most attracted readers through the centuries? There in the messiness of bodies pressed into and changing into one another we recognize ourselves, perhaps even with a certain queer pleasure. It is the *Inferno* that made Dante famous in his own time, and it is the *Inferno* that continues to do so.

I have suggested that Hell is Heaven's closet. There is a funny thing about queer closets. They sometimes explode and, in so doing, dismantle the whole house by exposing the lies upon which it is built. One lie that the exploded closet usually exposes is the one that "normal" and "abnormal" can somehow separate themselves, or that the so-called "abnormal" can even be eliminated. This is the myth of sameness, or of oneness, at its most violent. Absolute repression of the uncontrollable excess of bodies of difference, whether of race, class, sex, gender, shape, ability, or desires, is a labor toward sameness, toward the frozen plots of Heaven's garden, made by the fallen angel's dream of eternity.

At its heart, monotheism demands an ontological stasis that cannot tolerate excess, difference, or deviation. And because sameness simply cannot be achieved in the transient shiftiness of an embodied world, the god of Oneness has to freeze the core, trap the excess into a facade of stasis. But the frozen closet of Satan's Hell is about to explode, or maybe shift shape. The ice at the core of Hell, mirrored in the serene rose of Heaven, is both a metaphor for the disease of stasis at the core of Christian metaphysics (and theology) and a dismantling of it at the same time. Ice is not a permanent condition and that is the joke of Hell's eternity. *Ice can melt.* The stasis of ice is a partiality: it can morph into the very shape-shifting fluidity and flux (the non-eternity) that it appears to repress. Indeed, Dante seems to be aware of this when he describes the massive wings on Satan's back that, in a slow fanning motion, keep the damned frozen. Presumably, if Satan would still his wings, Hell would melt and there would be no center or root left, only a many chambered nautilus of naughty life flowing in the fertile fluids and fire of the living.

Why doesn't Dante's Satan let the ice melt? Perhaps he cannot do so and keep up the facade of his difference from the god of Oneness. Perhaps, as mirror and repressed same/shame of the god of Oneness, he motors the very structure that keeps the facade of Eternity from slipping, the waters of life from thawing. The satanic snowball melting in Hell might cause Heaven's blushing rose rouge to sweat and run, revealing the Vaudeville just under the surface of high art. Without a solid base in Hell to hold up the scaffolding of Heaven, the ascending seats of celestial light might slip and tilt into one another, snapping an angelic wing or two. The beatific smiles of the blessed might become strained as their disavowed secret pleasures tumble up and out of a closet stuffed too full of life. The smell of thawed meat drifts in under the tape-loop of harp sonatas, which begin to sound just a bit juke-jointish.

A theology and ontology fixed in ice is a theology of Oneness that is under constant pressure to keep the not-Oneness of living safely packaged in the freezer. Otherwise, all Hell breaks loose.

The way out is through: tehomic thaws

As Dante hesitates in the first Canto of the *Inferno,* caught in the valley of his mid-life crisis by merciless animal defenders who keep him from pursuing any obvious way up and out, the poet Virgil tells him quite simply that the only way out is counter-intuitive, the way back to his own life is through Hell. Virgil's advice is well-taken. At the center of Hell Dante inadvertently (is it inadvertent?) exposes the lie of traditional Christian metaphysics: eternity runs on a motor, a cooling system of satanic wings. Heaven is founded on this lie, as is the figurehead God who sits at Heaven's pinnacle, like the great and terrible head of Oz.

So the question that this great allegorical poem poses to us now is this: How can we find our way past the vicious lies that the god of Oneness has placed in our path, just like the snarling beasts who keep Dante trapped in his "depression deep"? How can the waters of Hell free divinity from *our* labor of illusion that it must never change? Perhaps we should pay more attention to the ice. All of the expulsions necessary for Christian theology to maintain its imperial hold on the bodies of women, slaves, barbarians, and laborers collect around Hell's deepest pit of water. Milton did not miss this association, cinematically beginning his own poetic vision of *Paradise Lost* with the fallen angels stunned on the surface of the waters of the deep. The way out of the lie of stasis may be in Hell. That is where the waters of creation are, after all.

And so the heart of Hell, the broken-hearted medieval poet tells us, is a frozen lake. And this isn't just any lake. It is the water of bodies, the perfect salt solution for the support of life; it is a lake of tears. The slightly salty water of weeping, which is the very same salinity of the earth's oceans, is a very good place to begin to make the case for a less frightened, less certain, and more generous approach to ontology than Christian theology has typically taken. This is a trip through the Hell of the god of Oneness, but that big God's credibility isn't what it was, because we've glimpsed the motor of His ontological folly. Satan's facade, thanks to Dante, has slipped, showing the desperate machinations of a very small god, a very large fear, a very mean spirit of illusionary control over bodies, hopes, and life itself. Maybe this dream place of bodily consequence isn't Hell, after all. What if we were to realize that the ice of Hell is melting, and the waters are rising? Are we prepared for a different story and, consequently, a different ontology?

Part II

Toward divine multiplicity

8 Starting the story again

The way to learn stories is to listen.

Laura Tohe[1]

"Let me ask you," said Poetry.
"When you pray, what do you think
you'll see?"
Poetry had me.

Alice Walker[2]

Stories, words, and images change with experience. Those that do not change gradually lose their grasp on meaning, as fewer and fewer experiences find expression in them. The threads of connection between words, images, stories, experience, and meaning are therefore tangled and dense. The story of the three-tiered universe, fleshed into image by poets like Dante and artists like Botticelli and Michelangelo, is an example of the fluidity and vulnerability stories have in relation to experience. Ever since 1608, when Hans Lipperhey first applied for a patent from the Dutch government for an invention called a telescope, descriptions of reality that depend on the architecture of a realm of God above the clouds and a realm of Satan below the crust of the earth have eroded, despite the cinematic appeal of such a vivid and simple cosmic and ethical scheme. Under the weight of quantum physics and historical criticism, the center of the story of the three-tiered cosmos, occupied by a fallen angel embedded in an ice floe of his own making, does not hold. But what stories of power are able to take its place and hold the ever more vast heavens and earths? Does not science tell stories (offer hypotheses) *in order to* test and undo them? Is it not better, therefore, to dispense with stories altogether, to seek facts without the distractions of narratives that are conditioned by context, by the very temporality of location?

If it is possible to possess truth without a context-rooted story, then perhaps these questions would succeed in guiding contemporary theology through the seas of modern and postmodern skepticisms. The evidence suggests, however, that truth is constituted in story, even in the hypothetical stories that scientists tell in order to make coherent their findings and to guide their investigations.[3] This means that whatever human beings strive to call truth is inaccessible to human life except fleshed in folds of language, culture, and interpretation. The co-constitution of truth with time, place, and culture does not discredit the truth as such (though such co-constitution does make any single truth very difficult to assert across all time and space, except hypothetically). Instead, it makes the vitality of stories—myth, if you will—less easy to dismiss when pursuing truth. This is nowhere more obvious than in theology, where the inseparability of stories in all of their fluidity and occasional inscrutability form the frame around the very things that theologians seek to say are true of divinity and reality.

This is not to say, however, that theology always recognizes the inseparability of story from its attempts to make truth-claims. Beginning with Aquinas, but accelerated in the philosophical systems of Kant and Hegel, theologians of the past three centuries like Friedrich Schleiermacher, David Hume, Ernst Troeltsch, Ludwig Feuerbach, Paul Tillich, Pope John, Karl Rahner, and others strove to argue for theological claims in an intellectual environment increasingly shaped by scientific premises of objectivity. Rudolph Bultmann, a mid-twentieth century New Testament scholar, is a prime example of one whose goal was to strengthen modern Christian faith by relieving it of its thick involvement with fiction. He sought to separate the density, malleability and contextuality of stories from enduring (and presumably universal) theological truths. In his influential essay *Jesus Christ and Mythology* Bultmann suggests, for example, that the ancient images of "Satan and the evil spirits" are mythical, meaning that they give shape to intangible truths like a sheet thrown over an invisible man: "myths give to the transcendent reality an immanent, this-worldly objectivity."[4]

Bultmann argues for an existentialist reading of the mythical images that run throughout the biblical texts such as heaven, hell, Satan and the demons that structure and people the imagination of New Testament writers. The images prevalent in Dante's Middle Ages functioned also in early Christianity and up through the late medieval world because they referred to generally accepted scientific, earth-centered accounts of the structure of the world and heavens. But, Bultmann argues, although those images no longer wield persuasive power in modern scientific reasoning about the cosmos, they also bespoke in their time—and presumably can illuminate in ours—a real human depth of experience and need for meaning. The science and its picture of the cosmos may have changed dramatically since the first fifteen centuries of the Christian era, but the existential depth and need still remains. As he points out, "for scientific thinking to speak of 'above' and 'below' in the universe has lost all meaning, but the idea of the transcendence of God and of evil is still significant."[5]

Confident in the powers of modern rationality to express scriptural truths despite vast changes in the worlds of the biblical writers and our own, Bultmann advocates a theological process of "demythologization." This is a kind of peeling away of the mythical story from an underlying existential or psychological truth that, he claims, the myth originally labored to express. Even Dante's Satan in all of his excessive monstrosity can be rationalized thus into

> a deep insight, namely, the insight that evil is not only to be found here and there in the world, but that all particular evils make up one single power which in the last analysis grows from the very actions of men, which form an atmosphere, a spiritual tradition, which overwhelms every man.[6]

Leaving aside for the moment the typically modern concern with reductive theories evident in this last statement, Bultmann's demythologization of the core scriptural stories has taken hold among scholars in the twentieth and twenty-first centuries for precisely the reasons that he names, summed up in the claim that "we no longer think mythologically."[7] Without mythological *thinking,* moderns like Bultmann struggle to separate fact from fiction and so either dispose of the myth altogether or assume that the myth is a covering for something else: a something else (like a psychological need, for example) that conforms to the modern world view and so is itself more *real* than the story and characters that enclose it. Thus Bultmann "saves" the myth and the scriptures for moderns as a sort of curious or ornate box that can hold timeless truths. Do not throw the myth (the scripture) out, he says. It *bears* truth even if its dressing is out of date or strains credulity.

Largely in agreement with Bultmann, but realizing a hubris latent in his confidence in rationality and perhaps suspecting an error in his attempts to split the meaning of myths from their form, Edward Farley has gestured, cautiously, toward a correction. He points out that theologians today typically avoid describing God, the world, and the cosmos with the mythical flourishes that more ancient writers employed. But we are still lured, eschatologically lured even, by certain "deep symbols" that "have the power to summon and constrain."[8] He suggests that such deep symbols exist in every culture, characterized by "words of power," meaning that they are "enchanted." What curious language this "enchantment" is for theology! Farley knows that he is bucking a several-centuries-old trend and "many things" he claims, "prompt us to resist such a notion":

> Our left-brain tendencies, urged on by a world-view of quantification and inclined toward clarity, data, and objective explanation, can find no room for enchantment. Did we not get rid of enchantment when civilization and its sciences displaced magic and mythopoetic thinking? And did not the Reformation erase the last vestige of that thinking when it swept Catholic sacramentalism from Protestant churches?[9]

Bultmann and Farley are surely correct in their claim that mythology is utterly connected to human concerns for powerful intangibles like love, belonging, orientation, fear, goodness, evil, and hope. But Bultmann's attempt to separate story from truth (in order to match the scientific logic of the One which we have seen also separates fact from fiction) has had a desiccating effect on theology. Indeed, what truths does theology possess without the poetics and tangled density of stories? Bultmann misses the mark, as Farley begins to suggest, when he assumes that human under-standing of deep, intangible truths can be surgically removed from the myth or enchantment that not only bears, but *produces*, or *builds* those deepest truths. Story and meaning coincide and co-constitute truth, and separation is neither possible nor productive of anything but sterile narra-tions and even emptier theories that, in the end, are attached only to nothing.

This is not to say that demythologization as a part of biblical scholarship and theological reflection is a bad thing and should be eradicated. Indeed, as a tool of metaphoric exemption it has contributed mightily to liberation efforts (especially in terms of sexism and racism), and functions well to remind students of scripture and theology of the cultural parameters of meaning, especially when some seek to impose oppressive meanings on others.[10] The point here is not to set up a kind of "either/or" and in so doing reinscribe the logic that we are trying to rethink. Bultmann himself suspected that stories—what he called myths—would always return, and certainly not every theologian committed to scholarly engagement with critical historical analysis has sought to divest theology and truth of their flesh of myth.[11] A tension, resident always in theology when it seeks to account for its claims in terms of contemporary plausibility, is evident today between modern skepticisms about myth and more or less post-modern and postcolonial skepticisms about the possibility or even desir-ability of transcending myth. The partiality, communality, and utter contextuality of stories—whether from the Bible or from the barber shop (or both)—are making a comeback in the work of theology, not as pro-blems to be overcome, but as critical openings and ends in themselves.[12]

The notorious failures of theology to meet the demands of scientific reason therefore provide an opening, not only for Christian theology, but for multifarious contemporary human strivings after divinity. Despite cen-turies of attempting to squeeze into a modernized frame of what Farley calls "quantification and objective explanation"—resulting in a kind of theological anorexia—the attempt to structure theology in terms of the logic of the One ultimately fails, for it is in the realm of theology that fact and fiction still cling together with some tenacity and inseparability. In Christian theology this is particularly vivid.[13] Fully divine, fully human. Crucified God. Creator, sustainer, lure, future. Child in a manger. Tongue of fire. Scourge of oppressors. Liberator. Dark night. Broken bread and cup of wine. Stories build, and they unbuild. Enchanted stories, stories of power,

scriptural stories, medicine stories, powerful stories, do not simply transport truth or existential reality. They also create and uncreate it.

There is a swirl of mist and enchantment that clings particularly to the
Biblical stories of creation, of exodus, and of Jesus, even though the idea,
particularly of divine incarnation as Christians have tended to tell it, may
be as hard to believe in modern terms as Dante's dark wood of snarling
beasts, or his conversations with Virgil. And so those who claim a point of
access to the divine in the Bible must work to account for the nature of
that divinity in some way that resonates in the world that we experience in
everyday life, and to make sense of human life and spirituality in light of
that resonance. This making sense is an ontological task. Early medieval
Christian theology possesses a rich ontology of multiple realms that offered
itself up to the poets and storytellers. In turn, the poets and storytellers
gave the Christian world a wealth of enduring images and ways of entering
the spiritual reality that the theologians sought to articulate.

Once upon a time, poets told stories and theologians explained the stories. Once upon a time, theologians explained their own dreams and visions,
and poets gave them wings. Poet and theologian sometimes were (and can
be again) closely related, at times the same person even. Although for most
people the static ontologies of early and medieval Christendom can no
longer sustain credulity, they have not yet been poetically supplanted and
so retain a hold on many who seek divinity in the Christian stories. It is
therefore past time for theologians, storytellers, and poets to listen again to
each other and inspire one another. The disenchantment that the logic of
the One now requires along with various estrangements between belief,
imagination, story, and credibility in the telling of Christian theology have
weakened theology, particularly those theologies that have turned away
from poetry, tears, laughter, and deep (or tall) tales.

Making tracks: methodology for multiplicity

Dante Alighieri of Florence gave the medieval European world and its
descendants a cinematic story that projects a rich panorama of images for
the Christian metaphysics of stasis that he drew from Aquinas, who drew
it from Aristotle. As we have seen, his tale also provides us today with a
wily foreknowledge of the watery instability of that stasis. *La Divina
Comedia* is a story crafted out of a particular time and place, reflecting the
anxieties, hopes, faith, and humor of that time and place. Most of all, it
reflects the edifice of medieval Christian belief in a three-storey universe
and the masquerade required for One God to hold it all together. Perhaps
Dante intended the very critique that I have argued is present in his tale,
though it is more likely that he merely intended an excoriation of the corrupt church through a rich rendering of its own ontological–ethical structure of the cosmos. But the story gets away from him, as all powerful
stories do. From the vantage point of the depths, from a *tehomic* sensibility,

the ice gives him away. Ontologies of the One, even in the hands of their devotees, betray a slippery multiplicity. The Christian God of Eternal Stasis is not dead, He never was.

Cracks in the surfaces of the Neoplatonic, diamantine foundation of stillness upon which Christian metaphysics have been built open up many possibilities for theologians to think pointedly toward a more organic and relational foundation for understanding divinity although in so doing we cannot dispense entirely with the recuperative risks of ontological talk. *Ontos* always brings us back to attempted stories of a Whole, but that is a problem, paradoxically, only if we insist that the Whole has to be whole, without holes (a point that will appear in more detail in Chapter 11). Catherine Keller challenges us to pay attention to the watery depths that already characterize the Biblical story of creation, to delve into those waters of the Deep, the *Tehom*, perhaps to find out what we can say *from there* about divinity, incarnation, Spirit, ourselves, and our place in the flow of things. Surely the deep is a time and place, still, of as much ontological possibility as it is of enchantment and power.

A constructive—poetic, philosophical, theological—journey away from ice and the *ontos* of eternity is a necessary first step, if indeed we wish to move beyond the metaphysics of stasis and the drive for certainty that have constrained Christian theology for so long. Dante's cartoonish image of a crystalline heaven made possible by a groaning, writhing underworld held together by a masquerading god-on-ice is, however, valuable to remember. It limns the contours of Christian imagination through the centuries and it continues to describe what many devoted people in the monotheistic traditions believe or suspect to be the case about the world, God, heaven, and hell.[14] We cannot forget this poetic and symbolic story (and others like it) largely because theology will say nothing if it does not resonate with the actual imaginative substructure of the culture that produces it. To be helpful and effective in articulations of faith, theology that speaks to the "deep symbols" embedded in the cultural language of an era is theology that has a voice, a story to tell. Dante succeeded in enfleshing the theology of the medieval Roman church fathers because he brilliantly and vividly illustrated what he and his cultural contemporaries already believed to be true about their experiences of the world and its realms of shadow, life, and death. Everyone knew what he was describing, even if some of the details, like the ice or Satan's role in holding everything up, melt under the light of too much scrutiny.

And so theology needs the storyteller's genius for traipsing past the guarded gates of social, political, or theological doctrine to what images and beliefs actually own the grounds. Unconcerned about the modernist separation of fact from fiction, the poet and storyteller can sometimes more directly, effectively, and artfully expose lies and fabrications on which the dominant institutions, cultures, classes, races, genders, religious authorities, nations sometimes rely for their power. If Dante intended us to shudder at the pits of *Malebolge*, and long for the unchanging spheres of *Paradiso*, he also could not help but show us the Dr. Seuss-like edifice of Christian metaphysics in which Eternity is a clumsy fabrication that exacts—and has indeed exacted—a horrifying cost on bodies (of people and of water). Good storytellers seem effortlessly to make their tales do multiple duty this way. They provide a narrative that always offers more than the sum of the events. Like the Babylonian stories of Tiamat and Marduk, the African accounts of Ogun, Hare, and Isis, the many tales of Jesus, the Buddha, the Prophet, the Underground Railroad, the white whale, the murdered martyr, and on and on, there is—always—something more going on to be gleaned from the good (or should I say honest?) storyteller's story. This is one of the things that make stories so rich, philosophically speaking, and that make good stories philosophically interesting. It is also what makes the art and ritual of retelling them so important. A good story told only once is a prelude without the song.

Contemporary constructive theology has become adept at the apophatic work of criticism, which is an important adjunct to storytelling in our time (criticism being one of the ways that we moderns tell stories, in fact). But constructive theologians have also become too timid in our obligation to gesture positively, kataphatically, beyond criticism to what "is" and what "should be." We are painfully aware of the many ways that certainty in the hands of the righteous powerful has historically meant hard(er) times for the outsider or oppressed. There is much yet to be dismantled, which is not to say that the desire to imagine divinity in positive terms is absent from contemporary theology, though it is often in conscious retreat. Sallie McFague's emphasis on metaphors,[15] for example, has helped a whole generation of contemporary theologians to claim positive images more or less "safely," meaning that the gap between metaphoric image and the reality that it seeks to describe is large enough to disclaim any ontological reference. As in Bultmann's scheme, the existential "meaning" of the metaphor or poetry disassociates the image from the divine, banking still on a scientific separation of language from that which it invokes.

Constructive theologians are rightfully cautious about making positive claims about God, Spirit, or revelation lest affirmation be co-opted for nefarious purposes. Too much theology has been thus used. And so, more confident today in criticism than in affirmation, theology faces the challenge of connecting ancient stories and traditions to the lived present and future hope in more than negative fashion. But given the work of process theologians such as Catherine Keller, and liberation philosophers and theologians such as Ivone Gebara, Barbara Holmes, Luce Irigaray and Mary Daly, there is the possibility of a thaw in Christian metaphysics along with openings for courageous re-imagining. What is more, poetry, tough thinking, and the ontological suspicions of those unafraid of bodies or of change are tools available for navigating pathways clear through the (master's) house of eternity, exchanging the dominology of One for the return of the complex or, as Keller puts it, exchanging the elementary for the elemental.[16] In short, theology that refuses the separation of myth or poetry from an ontological engagement with divinity is now poised to do three vital and important things. It can become concerned with its own poverty of storytelling about divinity in the world today. It can seek to inspire courage in those who would tell new or retell old tales of divine flux, fertility, multiplicity, and depth. Finally, in order to do this, theologians can begin—again—to *think* a metaphysics of flux and multiplicity that, enfolded in the complexities of story and language, articulates a more plausible and energizing framework than the three-storey universe. Only then can theology speak words of power, by beginning, again, to connect ancient and contemporary stories of divinity to the shifty world we actually inhabit.

Before drawing out the possible contours of a more supple and mature metaphysics for Christian theology, it is good to keep in mind some guiding, or corrective, norms, each of which implies its own set of tests or questions that theologians can ask of our work. First, we are after theological claims that can be accountable and responsive to the inevitability of our own mistakes in judgment. A reasonable question to pose to any contemporary theology goes as follows: Does the work possess sufficient humility and humor to allow for error and correction? If not, it is already lost in a greedy clutch at certainty and liable needlessly to be a menace to others. This means that "systematics" when applied to theology will look less and less like a sealed structure and more like an evolving and open-ended process.

Second, a theology in search of a more supple and mature metaphysics is curious and open to the alleys and back roads of contemporary existence in which divine presence and life occurs without permission or without respect for doctrinal requirements. This means that doctrines become dialogue partners, rather than adjudicators, of human experiences of divine presence and life. Most contemporary constructive theologians already do this, holding in tension the rich traditions with the challenges of lived experience.

Third, there are a variety of context-driven questions that can help to clarify whether the theological concepts with which one is working assist or hinder apprehension of divinity in particular communities. Among such questions, for example, are the following: How do the theological concepts under consideration help to identify actual points of access to divinity in this time and place? What norms reside in the theological concepts under consideration that will help a given community to discern what is true in the stories of power that it tells? How can this theology help, with some philosophical rigor and some poetic grace, to point out not only what is destructive (through criticisms, for example, of the Christian metaphysics of stasis that pervade and shackle Christian doctrine, liturgy, and communion) but also honestly, courageously, and humbly to name what the community

believes and claims to be divine life and presence? And where are the
openings, the fissures, the spaces of revision and postures of change that
allow this theology to live and breathe?

These normative guides and questions speak to the *spiritual quest* of
theology, to borrow a phrase from popular culture. Theology is just a
mind-game if it is not passionately engaged in questions of depth and
meaning for actual people in actual circumstances of complexity in life. All
of the faith systems of the world (including atheistic systems) exhibit concern with questions of meaning, purpose, ethics, and cosmic orientation.
Farley calls this apparently universal phenomenon the human "passion for
the real," a commonly felt need to grasp onto reality itself, however differently reality may be conceived across cultural systems.[17]

If, for Christians, part of this grasping onto reality has to do with
restoring a metaphysical understanding of incarnate divinity, the task is
made easier by doctrinal claims for fully human divinity in Jesus the historical, Jewish man. And it is made easier by doctrinal claims for a trinitarian Spirit that flows throughout creation and is at times embodied in the
gathered community of worshippers. But the task is also made exceedingly
difficult for Christians by doctrinal claims that limit the incarnation of the
divine to a single human being, and that limit the Spirit to disembodied
ecstasies or to carefully controlled substances of sacrament or liturgy. The
spiritual quest of theology—to articulate the old stories today in ways that
help people to experience and to be open to the creating, loving, and
evolving divinity that flows in the world (that is, the world's flow)—makes
it clear that *Christians have not gotten our own story quite right.*

There is good news in the fact that part of getting it "right" lies not in
getting it right in any absolute or final sense (*that* would be a reduction to
certainty), but rather that getting it "right" lies in a suppleness of posture
toward truth and toward the stories that give themselves to be told, again.
Getting out of the ice on this quest for a poetic metaphysics of multiplicity
and flux is going to require some tools that may be rusty with disuse:
humility, humor, doggedness, and a willingness to start over, again and
again. Although the Christian claim of incarnation has ever gestured
toward these tools, theologians everywhere have an unfortunate tendency
to absolve the obvious from contemplation. Indeed, Nietzsche makes a
good point when he claims that theologians suffer from the malady of self-
importance and forget the utter necessity of laughter for clearing the cob-
webs of solipsistic self-justification.

By way of antidote and beginning-again, Catherine Keller has suggested
that we turn to the Deep. I agree. The *Tehom* of Genesis 1:2, ever giving
birth to new life and new reality, ever folding in and pulling down, ever
enveloping and ever pushing out, is a fully orthodox concept of the Divine
that lacks nothing but our ability or willingness to tell the stories about it
that will help us to stop resisting the life we have been given, to stop
freezing the truths that flow through us, to stop dying before our time. In

her brilliant commentary on this jewel of a verse, Keller suggests that the long history of Christian theology exhibits a tension between what she calls "tehomophobic" (literally, fear of the deep) and "tehomophilic" impulses. The waters of the deep, fluid and rich with becoming, cause the "founding certainties" of "the Roman sense of order," especially its sere metaphysics of One, to tremble.[18] Stories that gesture toward change, relativity, and interconnection as the substance of existence may not only help us rediscover the presence of God but thereby reorder our daily lives, our values, and our priorities in community, politics, and religion. Going off the deep end, however, is frightening if you are not used to it, or if you are used to believing that the place you are standing is not already moving.

As Keller is careful to point out, *Tehom* is not just a synonym for water. Water, however, embodies some of the qualities of flux, indeterminacy, and potentiality that have historically been ascribed to the chaotic deep of Genesis 1. Prosaic, everyday water may therefore be just the substance we need to begin again to think ontologically about the divine. Certainly Keller's study of tehomic potentiality and watery depth in scripture, Kabbalah, theology, and literature suggests this: "creation takes place *within* a fluid interdimensionality."[19] This means, she concludes, that the Christian doctrine of *creatio ex nihilo* (creation out of nothing) is itself ungrounded in scripture and unwarranted in faith. She argues that

> The Bible knows only of the divine formation of the world out of a chaotic something: not *creation ex nihilo*, but *ex nihilo nihil fit* ('from nothing comes nothing'), the common sense of the ancient world.[20]

The chaotic something, the deep, has traditionally been characterized in terms of fluidity, like a vast ocean of potentiality and flux, and also vilified as the root and source of evil. Keller points to the doctrine of *ex nihilo* as a core doctrine aimed against the birthing powers and fertile blood of women and so against both femaleness and bodiliness in dominant Christian theology. The space, she argues, between tehomophobia and gynophobia is very slight.

So let us begin there. Let rich and complex fluids swirl into this again-beginning for theology-in-thaw. Shifting matter of the Deep. Shaper, destroyer, and redistributor of land. Source and surface of the divine face. Without absolute beginning or absolute end, water flows through bodies, giving them substance and presence. Close to 50 percent of the substance of human bodies is water. The percentage is even higher among plants. And individual cells in humans and other animals are often over 80 percent water.[21] Without the fluid properties of water and oil that plump cells and shape flesh, we all blow into dust. Life is, quite literally, fluid.

With that in mind, it makes sense that an ontology of stasis too long attributed to divinity does not match—or grace—the ontology of *life* that is characterized by multiplicity and flux. And so the next task is to think more precisely about what the characteristics of a tehomophilic metaphysics might be. This means imagining a theological posture (with sea legs!)[22] from which Christian theology can once again find incarnate intimacy, solidarity, and hope of divinity. Perhaps a metaphysical skeleton is even possible (a frame, posture, map, dialect, story), on whose bones the flesh of ethics and hope in a world of flux and change may occur. Following hard on the heels of Dante's vision of ice at the heart of Christian metaphysics, two very different stories may help to launch us, suggesting not so much a way out of the ice or an eschatological escape from the waters frozen deep in the cosmic body of Christ, but a way *into* them, not to eliminate those frozen depths but to change their temperature, to suggest a thaw, and so a flow, and so a flood. Put another way, this is not a flight from the story of the One but a more careful listening to the multiplicity it reveals. A story from the Gospel of John in the Christian scriptures, and a story from a North American storyteller named Thomas King lead the way. Not surprisingly, both tell of water.

A jug of water: John 4:7–29

> τὸ ὕδωρ ὁ δώσω αὐτῶ γενήσεται ἐν αὐτῶ πηγή ὕδατος αλλομένον εἰς ζωήν αἰώνιον.
>
> The water that I give will become in them a spring of water, rushing into the life that is God.
>
> The Gospel according to John 4:14b[23]

The seventh verse of the fourth chapter of the Gospel according to John opens at an ancient well in Samaria—Jacob's, we are told—where Jesus has apparently stopped to rest. He has sent his disciples on into the town to purchase food, and is alone. A local woman comes up, water jar in hand, to draw from the well. The writer of the gospel says that Jesus demands a drink from her. She doesn't comply, or rather we are told that she questions his motives: what is a *Jewish* man doing, asking a *Samaritan* woman for a drink?[24] They begin to argue about water.

The Greek word for water that the Johannine writer uses in Jesus' debate with this unnamed woman is ὕδωρ (hūdor). This word traces itself in Greek literature to things of the ocean, and to the idea of deluge.[25] Poor people living in the arid regions of the Mediterranean basin were fully conscious of the power that water had over their living and dying. Wells were core economic and political symbols not only carrying immediate power and wealth, but indicating the capacity of a people to live in the present and to continue into the future—in essence to have ζωήν αἰώνιον (zōèyn aiōnion), life to come. Water is a word with immediate power, especially when it is scarce and one is thirsty.

The Samaritan woman whom Jesus meets at the lip of the deep well in John 4:14 is momentarily in charge of the situation due to her possession of the means to draw water and his apparent lack of a jug. She challenges the Jew on his willingness to drink from the ethnically suspect cup of an outsider. Though he has demanded a drink from her, Jesus responds by dismissing her water, telling her that he possesses even better water than she, and, had she known, she would have been asking *him* for a drink of his ὕδωρ ζωή (*hūdor zoë*), "water of life" or "water alive." When she expresses quite reasonable skepticism (could the storyteller be implying that they enjoy this bit of sparring?) Jesus becomes even more declarative. The water that he gives, he announces to the woman, is *zoë*, it is alive. The implication, of course, is that her well water is not alive. Regardless of Christian tendencies over the years to abstract the living water that Jesus refers to from anything that is actually *wet*, there is another, equally plausible way to understand it. "Living water" commonly refers to water that moves, water that cannot become brackish or sour. Such a phrase is still used among those who make their living with boats. It means that the water is not still, but running; it is a river, an ocean, endlessly flowing and returning. The water that Jesus boasts of is living in that it will support life. Can the woman be so sure that her ancient well water can do the same?

The phrase ζωήν αἰώνιον (*zōèyn aiōnion*) that Jesus then uses to describe what comes of his water is literally translatable as "life continuous" or "life to come," though it is usually translated in Christian Bibles as "eternal life." In Christian writings of this period, however, *zōèyn aiōnion* is also a cipher for God.[26] Jesus asserts that the living water he *would* have given the woman had she thought to ask (despite his obvious thirst for *her* water and his lack of dipper) is actually life continuous, or God, and he further boasts that any who drink of his water will never thirst again. Now it seems fairly clear that the gospel writer is indulging here in metaphor. Being quite a practical woman, or angry, or a joker, or being made to miss the point so that the storyteller can have Jesus correct her and so instruct us, the Samaritan calls Jesus' bluff (if it is a bluff) telling him to give her this living water. If nothing else, she says, it should relieve her of the hot and tedious trip to the well every day.

Whether or not the Johannine storyteller intended Jesus to use the adjective αἰώνιον (*aiōnion*) literally to mean a continuous supply of water for the woman's jug (like the European folk tale of the pot that unendingly made porridge for the poor woodsman's family), we are not told. We are told, however, that Jesus responds by telling her a few details about herself en route to telling her more about himself. He tells her that she has been married five times and currently lives, unmarried, with a man. What is more, he instructs her that God is spirit and truth and must be worshipped as such. Finally, apparently leaving all metaphor aside (or is he?), he tells her that he is the Messiah. Perhaps distracted from her banter by his knowledge of her many failed marriages, *this* last piece of information she appears not to question.

Remembering that all stories have multiple layers, it is interesting to note that the Johannine writer (or Jesus) did not *need* to go from *hūdor* (water) to *hūdor zoë* (water alive) to *zōèyn aiōnion* (life continuous), in order to equate "life continuous" with "God." As I have noted, both terms (life and continuousness) appear without fanfare elsewhere in early Christian writings as references for God. The rhetorical wit and poetry of the progression is, however, wonderful. The Johannine writer is apparently executing here a play on words, depending on the second century Hellenized listener to make the common association of *zōèyn aiōnion*, life continuous, with "God." But, still, the storyteller uses water to get us to God, telling us that it is water Jesus brings, water that will become *in those* who receive it a rushing spring of the very life of God. Fifty percent water. A rushing divine spring.[27]

Why the gospel writer places Jesus' *first* self-proclamation as the Messiah at a historic well in Samaria, directed to a woman of low social and religious status, is a matter of extensive and rich scholarly speculation. Few scholars, however, pay much attention to the water itself, beyond the well's economic and political placement. The important moment of Jesus' self-acknowledgement of his divine calling takes place away from his homeland, in the context of a foreign community's prized source of life and support of livelihood: its water.[28] A woman whose marital status means that she should have been declared unclean is the recipient of this news. Jesus declares his water to be better than hers. We don't know if she ever agrees to *that*, but she does become convinced that he is who he says he is, the Messiah, and rushes off to tell her community of him: a first apostle.

When one pays attention to the water itself, this story lends itself to all sorts of ambiguities. Does this unnamed woman's acceptance of Jesus' claim to be the Messiah, translated through his offer of life continuous, mean that this is a story of an arid spirituality trumping the earthy wetness of actual water? Remember that he does catechize her regarding the nature of God as "spirit and truth" which neither he nor the Johannine writer probably confused with water. On the other hand, he speaks of his gift in a watery way: he will give the gift that will become a spring in those who accept it, welling or gushing up into the life to come, into God. Do we hear the story, again, from a tehomophilic or tehomophobic posture?

Tehomophobic readings indeed emphasize a gnostic, or stoic, or Manichean separation of the spiritual from the earthy-wet, thereby attempting to freeze the *hūdor zoë* around the torso of *zōèyn aiōnion*. But the liveliness of the banter that persists in this ancient scrap of text between a hot and thirsty Jewish man and a tired Samaritan woman leaks a little, as do all good stories. We don't know if she ever pulled up water and handed him a drink, but we are explicitly told that the woman leaves her water jug behind when she returns to town to tell what she has learned. Having received the peculiar water that Jesus promised, is it possible that she is freed of earth, never needing to drink a drop or trudge heavy laden to the well again? Although this is a logical conclusion for a tehomophobic reading that refuses divinity to the water itself, it does not account for Jesus' own thirst for *her* water, nor does it account for the jug that she leaves behind.

It is unlikely that her encounter with the self-proclaimed Messiah freed this woman of her trips to the well and we are not told that this is what happened. It is also unlikely that Jesus needed no drink of her water that day or that he did not thirst again many times, even up to his death. To make his encounters with drink *all* allegorical simply requires too much Docetic twisting and turning of interpretation in favor of a disembodied divinity. We cannot know for what purpose the woman whom Jesus met that day left her water jug with him at the well. It is reasonable to imagine that she forgot it, but then the story and storyteller is likely to have done so, too. Like the water itself, the woman's jug is easily overlooked, but there it is, still taking up space and time in the story. Among the possibilities, it seems most interesting to imagine that she left it for a reason, though that reason is not clear to us across so many years and with so few of her words. Perhaps she left it out of politeness and generosity, in the end leaving him an abundance of the drink of earth that he had demanded at the start.

Such imagining leads to the thought that there is instruction going on on all sides of this wonderfully ambiguous story. A woman stands in the gap between a new Messiah who claims to possess a mysterious spring of wisdom about a God of spirit and truth and the deeply pooled ancestral water that keeps the flesh of the world from drying up and blowing away. Her gesture of the earthen jug may be a gentle correction, or instruction, to him in thanks both for the rich banter and for the teaching he has given her. He has taught her something of his God. And she has taught him, with her own body of water, that his God may be spirit and truth indeed, but without her, without the water of earth, they are both *nihil*, nothing. What is a theology of "spirit and truth" that also learns to be a spring, a *body of water?*

Beginning . . . again: Thomas King's *Green Grass, Running Water*

Sixteen or seventeen centuries after the Johannine writers wrote down this story of divinity at the edge of a dusty well in Samaria, Thomas King offers us another story of divinity at the edge of a huge dam in the Province of Alberta, Canada. King is an American writer and teacher of mixed Cherokee, German, and Greek descent, from whose 1993 novel *Green Grass, Running Water* the *Tehom* beckons, offering again the storyteller's way into the ongoing flow of divinity that tells the world into being. Like Dante and the gospel writer, King knows how to tell a story that lives in the juncture between laughter and tears. It is a consummately North American story, rooted in the oral rhythms and hybrid imaginations of Native and immigrant peoples in Canada and the US. It is a joke. It is a song. It is an enactment of judgment and forgiveness. It is a story of water.

The majority of native cultures of North America, like many cultures across the world, tell stories of divinity that involve multiple perspectives, and most grant to the realm of the divine, or spirit, a "trickster" dimension.[29] This means that even in the most sober and serious of stories of divine power there is room for disturbance, error, and humor. Indeed, in most of the northern woodland and plains cultures of the Americas, both error and humor appear to be critical to the very occurrence of the world, to its creation and sustenance. King's story is no different. Four old Indians of ambiguous age have disappeared from a mental hospital. The hospital cleaning woman Babo Jones isn't worried; they've done this before. The hospital director is worried because, although he knows that when they have done this before they have come back of their own accord ("they like it here," Babo tells the director), he suspects a correlation between many of their disappearances in the past and major events like fires, floods, and earthquakes. He decides to set out after them and takes Babo with him because she seems to understand them. At the same time, four 30-something Indians, born on the same reserve in Canada, are adrift in their modern lives, each slowly drying up with despair (not unlike Dante at the start of his story, in the middle of his life). Latisha, divorced from the man who had beaten her, runs a café on the reserve that panders to tourists. Her brother Lionel works a dead-end job at a television store in town and dreams of being John Wayne. Charlie, whose father played the doomed Indian in countless Hollywood movies from the 1940s and 50s, works a high-paying job in Edmonton. Alberta, a professor in Calgary, is half-heartedly dating both Lionel and Charlie. Although it is Sundance season, it is Lionel's 40th birthday that has the four of them converging on the reserve again.

As King's story begins, the old Indians (women, according to Babo; men according to the hospital director), who call themselves The Lone Ranger, Ishmael, Hawkeye, and Robinson Crusoe, claim that they have to begin their journey to the reserve the correct way because they are setting out to redress a wrong in the lives of the four young people, to fix the story, if you will. As with all of the eastern woodland traditions of North America and the Jewish and Christian traditions, they weave the world with story, and they begin their story with water.

The status and power of the four old ones is ambiguous; if they do not have the former, they certainly seem to have the latter. Their names on the hospital charts are Mr. Black, Mr. Red, Mr. White and Mr. Blue, the colors of the four sacred directions, according to numerous plains tribes. But their identities are shifty; pinning *them* down is clearly not what is important, rather it is the story they tell that matters, literally in this case. They are worried about the people, the land, and the state of the story, and they remind each other (and the trickster Coyote, who hangs around but never listens) that big fixes can result in even bigger messes. This means that the old ones correct each other and start over a number of times before they even begin. Making mistakes seems to be an integral part of the divine process, and starting over, we begin to learn from this story, is not a bad thing.

Like Dante in his time, King offers in our time a poetic vision of metaphysics, but this time it is the metaphysics of shift and tide through which divinity (never alone, always revising) flows. Nothing is lost, though nothing stays the same. Coyote is always present (is he Trickster? Dionysius? God-in-drag-as-Satan? Jesus? Our own ego selves? The world?). Like the trickster figure of so many Native American cultures, he is always making the mistakes that end up making us who we are. King tells his story by weaving many stories together, consciously linking the biblical narratives of creation to the eastern woodland earth diver narratives of creation, hinting at a changing story that is all at once ancient, contemporary, and hybrid. But watch out, the story matters and, as Ishmael reminds the Lone Ranger, it is best not to make mistakes with it.[30] But of course they (we) do make mistakes with the stories, and so the story—and the world—changes, and changes us, in unexpected ways. Divinity, from the standpoint of this kind of sensibility, has quite literally nothing to do with stasis and everything to do with ebb, flow, space, and time.

King's story also reveals that no divine movement happens without wading in and trying again. No divine creation happens without help, without a group effort. "You can't tell the story alone," Hawkeye cautions. Even the narrator gets involved, offering to begin the story (which is the book, the journey, the ritual, and the medicine) with the earth diver narrative of creation typical of the eastern woodland traditions. The narrator's attempt ends up reflecting not only an ancient story of Native America, but gestures humorously, through Coyote, toward the Bible and modern life, which also tells and so embodies the experience of the people. And like most Native American creation accounts, the story begins in the middle of something. In this case, First Woman is walking around telling everyone in the Sky World to "straighten up" and to "mind your relations." She is so busy looking for "things that are bent and need fixing" that she doesn't watch where she is going, and she falls off of the edge of the Sky World. "Oh, oh, First Woman says, looks like a new adventure. And she is right." Far down below, in the Water World, ducks see her falling and fly up to catch her. They put her on the back of grandmother Turtle who has surfaced to see what the fuss is about, and together they dive for mud to make land.

> That's a pretty good trick, says Old Coyote, who comes floating by on that air mattress. Maybe I can help.
> Straighten up, says First Woman.
> Mind your relations, says grandmother Turtle.
> So that mud gets big and beautiful all around.

That is beautiful, says Old Coyote, but what we really need is a garden.[31]

A lesson that runs through King's narrative is that one of the first and most necessary ingredients in revisioning serious and significant theological problems is a leavening of humor. The hybrid Americans, living off of the generosity and strong back of Grandmother Turtle, also have stories of a garden and of exile. For any American of dubious descent like myself (and we all, everywhere, are dubiously descended, which is funny in itself), the Coyote, Hare, Spider, and other creator/trickster accounts of the coming-to-be of things from across a wide diversity of Native American traditions offer themselves as gifts of wisdom. They leaven certainty while gesturing toward interconnection and the resiliency of relation. They remind us in the guise of deep and tall tales that any theological enterprise that makes claims to certainty about what is really real or that paints the "big picture" of divinity and cosmos, is itself laughable and should laugh at itself even as it spreads color on canvas.

King employs Coyote for this purpose in what appears to be his preface to the novel. "In the beginning," he tells us, "there was nothing. Just the water." And so, already, nothing is, of course, not *nothing*. Then we find out that Coyote is there in the beginning too, asleep and dreaming. Nothing, water, Coyote. It is enough for a beginning. The narrator immediately warns us that "[w]hen that Coyote dreams, anything can happen." And indeed something does happen. One of Coyote's dreams "gets loose and runs around. Makes a lot of noise." And that Coyote Dream proceeds to make the mistake that Coyote himself always makes (that humans so often make, that Christian theology has made): he gets greedy:

> Hooray, says that silly Dream, Coyote dream. I'm in charge of the world. And then that Dream sees all that water.
> Oh, oh, says that noisy Dream. This is all wrong. Is that water we see? that silly Dream says to those dream eyes.
> It's water, all right, says those Dream Eyes.
> That Coyote Dream makes many sad noises, and those noises are loud and those noises wake up Coyote.

Coyote then demands to know who is making all the noise. The narrator tells him that it is his own noisy dream. "It thinks it is in charge of the world." The Dream loudly confirms this, and then demands to know who Coyote is, wanting to know (in Coyote's own typically self-important fashion) if Coyote is someone important. Coyote tells his unruly dream not only that he, Coyote, is Coyote, but that he is very smart. Coyote's dream (being of course just like Coyote in temperament) therefore claims to be Coyote too. Coyote tells the dream no, it cannot be Coyote too, but offers it the option of being a dog. After haggling about the smarts of dogs, the

Coyote Dream agrees. In its eagerness, though, the dream gets confused and becomes a "Contrary", switching "dog" around to "god." The narrator senses trouble. Soon the backward dog—or god—demands more:

> But why am I a little god? shouts that god.
> "Not so loud," says Coyote. "You're hurting my ears."
> I don't want to be a little god, says that god. I want to be a big god!
> "What a noise," says Coyote. "This dog has no manners."
> *Big one!*
> "Okay, okay," says Coyote. "Just stop shouting."
> There, says that G O D. That's better.
> "Now you've done it," I says.
> "Everything's under control," says Coyote. "Don't panic."
> Where did all that water come from? shouts that G O D.
> "Take it easy," says Coyote. "Sit down. Relax. Watch some television."
> But there is water everywhere, says that G O D.
> "Hmmmm," says Coyote. "So there is."[32]

One thing that the traditional elders of many nations in the Americas agree on is that stories do far more than describe and entertain. Stories themselves have lives and creative agency. Stories, told in the right season and in a good mind, build and unbuild the world. Time collapses and reconfigures in the context of the stories we tell. A story may begin with "once upon a time" or "in the beginning" or "I'll tell you what happened" but the apparent past tense is dissolved in the solution of its telling, in the sideways and forward sway of the telling, in the story's story. Time is spatial in stories because stories form geometries of meaning in space, in the orientation *toward* that "takes place" in the story, in the story's telling, and in the story of the story's telling.

Because of the spatial "taking place" of stories—their capacity to shift the light and the room and to irrevocably alter the landscape—storytellers must take care to tell their stories in a good season. Honest stories have power and sway, which, once told, are *never* under the control of the storyteller. This is in part because storytellers also become the story, and stories change the world. Just think of Moses and his stories and the stories of Moses. Or think of Jesus and his stories and the stories of Jesus. Think of Harriet Tubman and her stories and the stories of Harriet Tubman. *These are not "just stories," I can tell you.* Think of Newton. Or Constantine. Or Hitler. Or Gandhi. Or forget famous people and the stories of what they did that continue to make and unmake us. Think of other stories that have made and unmade the world. Think of gold in the New World. Or think of Jerusalem. Think of the story of Eden. Or of the Big Bang. Think of the story of America (that's a good one!). We and our stories make and unmake the world. And, sometimes, our stories are a noisy Coyote Dream shouting and insisting that they are important and in charge of everything.

Barry Lopez tells of an anthropologist who began to "listen to a wealth of Indian stories, ... [he] studied them, dreamed them, told them, taught them" and so became incapable of talking *about* them. Scheduled to give a paper at an academic conference, he listened to the papers being delivered before his and he found them "more than dull: they're dead. They're about anthropological Indians, not the *real people* ... whom he knew from the stories ingrained in the soil and from the wind that breathed into his soul." He ended up not reading from his paper at all. Instead he tried to tell a story, "to express the stark poetic anguish of the nineteenth century in the memory of these northern buffalo hunters, when the world of spirit was coming apart." The scholars could not really hear him.

> The applause was respectful, thin, distracted. As he stepped away from the podium he realized it was perhaps foolish to have accepted the invitation. He could no longer make a final point. He had long ago lost touch with the definitive, the awful distance of reason. He wanted to go back to the podium. You can only tell the story as it was given to you, he wanted to say. Do not lie. Do not make it up.[33]

Stories—the ones that get loose, build, and unbuild worlds—are the real concern of theology precisely because they express the motility of creation. The story/stories of God are told everywhere. They lean, sway, and take place. Stories of God will continue to do so. The question for the story-tellers and theologians is not whether stories of divinity can be told, but whether they are truthful, and in season. It is for this reason that Ishmael tells the Lone Ranger that although mistakes are a part of the journey, it is "[b]est not to make them with stories."[34]

King's *Green Grass, Running Water* is a story that reflects in its own way the hybridity, the interdependent, fluid, and non-static ontology of the world that we actually experience and that our sciences begin increasingly to affirm. It describes a divine reality that is tied to stories, to interaction, and to interrelation. Like most people in the world today, the four young Indians of King's narrative live in multiple worlds, their futures tied to many places, pasts and interweaving traditions, cultures, and identities. An old uncle of theirs, who left the reserve as a young man to study in Toronto and whose life in the city made returning home inexplicably difficult, finally returns when both the lover who kept him away, and the mother who wanted his return, die. He takes up residence in the empty house of his childhood which stands in the sluice-path of a massive new dam, with his body continuing his mother's refusal to allow water access to the Edmonton-based power company. He is old now, and makes coffee for the dam supervisor, who ritually visits him every morning to try and talk him into leaving.

Water is both the physical and the spiritual currency of power in King's poetic narrative, as it is the harbinger of change, destruction, connection, and new life. As the old Indians travel, the rain comes and there is water everywhere in the story, welling up and leaking out all over. The water creates a pressure for reconnection that none of the people can fully withstand because they are already connected, already linked in multiple ways to the story of convergence that King relates. They chafe as they begin to rehydrate; even their clothes do not fit some of them any more. If it is true that old wineskins cannot hold new wine, here we have some new fermentation without foreknowledge. This is a story of everyday people who do not know that they are in the midst of a fertile, powerful, destructive restoration. They do not know that they are the restoration. No one is dry by the end, and no one is entirely whole.

Perhaps one of the greatest theological gifts in this story is its own lively admission of error. Every story that sets out to fix something also makes some mistakes, and this is particularly true of sacred stories. *Nothing*, however, is lost (in both senses of the phrase.) As *Green Grass, Running Water* draws to a close, Ishmael says, "Wait a minute. Before we begin, did anyone offer an apology?"[35] Apology, laughter, and beginning again. What gracious norms to adopt for theology.

Water runs through these two stories. Thawed, living water. In both cases traditions are in conflict; they bump up against each other, resist each other, offer the hospitality of drink to each other. In both cases, divinity is not something outside of the story, speaking through it, nor is it unambiguously one thing in the story. Water is there, change is there, conflict is there, partiality is there, all of which mean that bodies are there. If anything in these stories indicates a thaw in the ice of Christian metaphysics, it is these elements. Metaphysics tends to imply closure, or totality—another kind of One—in the history of Christian thought. Must it continue to do so? Are there metaphysical gestures that take wing in the metaphor of water, the immanence of change, the productivity of conflict and the motion of partiality, that fly into view in these stories and others like them? There are many texts and traditions embedded even in the most closed systems of divine oneness that suggest such possibilities, that gesture toward more *tehomic* accounts of divine reality. They do not have to be invented out of whole cloth though they do have to be imagined, to be allowed to speak, to tell stories.

9 Thinking being? Or why we need ontology . . . again

From our own experiences we know that reality is not a seamless whole. Multiple realities rise, recede, and eclipse on our cognitive horizons as subuniverses that we inhabit from time to time.

Barbara Holmes[1]

Hers are contradictory words, somewhat mad from the standpoint of reason, inaudible for whoever listens to them with ready-made grids, with a fully elaborated code in hand.

Luce Irigaray[2]

If the Christian imperial dream of eternity, which it has equated with God, is really the suppression of life (as Nietzsche and Daly suspected) and of divinity, then what becomes of the Christian story of God? Hell's weight of horror turns out to be merely the story of bodies, "testimonies" as Althaus-Reid suggests, "of real lives in rebellions made of love, pleasure and suffering."[3] The imperial Christian dream of eternity, which is actually a story of Hell turned upside down, tries to condemn bodies that have failed to stop being bodies; that have failed to stop changing, feeling, longing, and indulging in gravitational contact. This makes "Hell," as I have argued, the makeshift closet of the imperial God, stuffed with the improper, bodily reality that is the cosmos itself. All of which suggests that the *divinity* that Christians occasionally glimpse in the Incarnation is not to be in any way throned in the eternal, bodiless death of Heaven but—so loving the world—fleshed in the space/time of shifty becoming. It takes courage to see this, against the wisdom of logic of the One, and it takes a certain courage to sin, in looking to Hell for the divine. The God which is not One is, as Irigaray suggests, unintelligible within a phallic frame of oneness.[4] Even to talk of an "outside" of the One is to stay within its frame. There are other logics, however (at least that is the suspicion and hope upon which this whole project is based), other logics that do not deny the One, but are not bound by it, either. Divinity imagined within and through frames that are otherwise to the phallogocentrism of the One requires thought that is also somehow Other wise.

This brings us directly to the challenge of *thought*. To think a non-static basis for reality *en route* to a thawed and living sense of incarnate divinity is no small task given the power and duration of the logic of the One in the religious and scientific stories of Christian imperial expansion thus far. How to begin even approaching a logic of multiplicity without slipping always back into the logic of the One? As Gilles Deleuze and Félix Guattari point out,

> to attain the multiple, one must have a method that effectively con-structs it: no typographical cleverness, no lexical agility, no blending or creation of words, no syntactical boldness, can substitute for it.[5]

While syntactical boldness and the creation of words may indeed be just what are needed, Deleuze and Guattari's point is that this thinking is a challenge that cannot rely solely on verbal acrobatics.

I have already argued for a fact–fiction intercourse that poetry, myth, and story embody, but there is the additional, drier task of schematizing and provisionally naming some of the characteristics of divine multiplicity that emerge from that exchange. There are tactics required in *thinking* toward a logic of multiplicity. The approach cannot be brittle or dogmatic; we need to tolerate some contradiction en route, or else we have not opened any new doors and simply revolve still around the One. This sug-gests a supple posture and a generosity of imagination as there will be slippage in and out of oneness, in and out of the logic that made this very inquiry both necessary and possible.

Before setting off, however, it is good to pause here at a preliminary fork in the road. The fork is a decision: to take up the relatively unpopular question of ontology or attempt to side-step it. I choose to take it up. After several years of side-stepping and stalling, I have come to the conclusion that imagining multiplicity *beyond* the One–Many dichotomous divide is an ontological task and so requires an ontological approach. Forks in roads are just that, however. They are only labeled "right" and "wrong" when reputations and certainties are at stake, neither of which apply here. But perhaps the fork is deceptive. To deny the challenge of ontology in pursuit of a logic of multiplicity does not eliminate ontological presupposi-tions; it just sends those presuppositions underground. And the ontological presuppositions generated out of a very long period of domination by the logic of the One in theology, science, and the empires they have built make *thinking* a logic of multiplicity nearly impossible even when the language or task of "ontology" is denied. I therefore pause here, briefly, to make clear the reasons that I take an ontological approach to theology, at least when taking up the question of divine multiplicity.

In western philosophy, the study of the problem of being, or ontology (from *ontos* and *logos* in the Greek) developed in terms of the question of what, exactly, constitutes existence (for example, is the world a random aggregation of matter; is it a disembodied system of ideas somehow imprinted on matter; is it all in our heads—a web of delusions?). This problem may seem ridiculously esoteric and, in a sense, it is—or it can be. Very often in philosophy texts ontology has taken the form of a pursuit of abstract and categorical equations for an accounting of reality and what can be known of it. Questions of reality, being, or ontology, however, have generally fallen out of favor among most theologians, and so I must give an account for the foolishness of taking them up here. Quite simply, if all accounting for divinity is summed up by linguistics and metaphor then we must assume that the divine itself is subaltern; it cannot speak, so to speak, its reality is wholly inaccessible to the master tongues. The divine cannot meaningfully interrupt enough to get a word—or a Word?—in edgewise. And further we must assume that the divine itself (that "in itself" being the point of obsessive impossibility for Western thought) can thereby have no actual presence in human life, cannot show up, ask for a drink, and say something revealing, maybe something that makes a difference. Of course *God* can do this, the theologians argue. We simply cannot *account* for God's showing up, ontologically, without somehow reducing the divine to a system, a project, a thing, a less-than-God. And of course they are right. But refusing to take up the question of divine reality in an ontological sense leaves the old ontological structures in place. Linguistics and the metaphoric exemption attempt simply to skirt around them. But *reality* in its most integrated sense of ethical orientation in the physical and social world is, at heart, what Christian theology attempts to articulate. Canonical scripture is one guide to that reality. It is made up of many stories embedded in a complicated set of texts, communities, and traditions that have been handed down through the millennia. Regardless of the anachronisms and errors regarding the physical and social world that these ancient texts, stories, and traditions contain, Christians can still turn to them, maintaining that therein is a wisdom that we need for understanding reality and our place in it. There is also culture and the generations of social wisdom laid down like sedimented layers of bedrock, compressed into customs, daily habits, and norms that guide us to reality. And there is the constant touch of the physical world itself—or rather the ever-changing worlds that we attempt to understand and name with physics, culture, geography, story, language, and memory.

While philosophy, biology, literary studies, or other scholarly and rhetorical fields may be able to dispense with one or more sides of the tripartite equation of scripture, culture, and world in their explorations, all are indispensable for theology. The fact that the "reality" of divinity always eludes full capture in thought, language, and symbol does not negate the nearly paradoxical circumstance of the divinity that confronts human experience on a daily basis, demanding recognition and interpretation. Neither does the fact that human knowing is fleshed out on all sides by tissues of culture, narrative, history, and biology negate the human longing for understanding of that which seems to surpass the very limits that hold us, which bears fragments of news from other territories of being.

The very notion of limit begs trespass, even though one thing that can be said about human being and knowing is that it has limits. And, yet, something within or without human being and knowing is not entirely bounded by those limits, and traverses them occasionally with ease. Holy Spirit, Ancestor, Earth Energy, Soul, Mind, Presence, Other, God—does the name really matter for ontology? The *arrival* of such into human experience and awareness is an embarrassment to those who would reduce reality to grammar or to physics, just as it is a threat to those who would keep the divine safely ensconced elsewhere. To account for the coming of God in ontological terms is risky business but, if there is to be any worldly basis for proclaiming a god-dimension that is narratively characterized by the freedom to arrive, to encounter, and even from time to time to incarnately *be-with*, it is the fundamental human passion for the real that demands an attempt at accounting for such a reality, a reality that can accomplish such astounding things.

Academic studies in ontology, especially if they remain abstract and overindulge in technical jargon, can make tooth drilling seem appealing. But ontology itself—the burrowing question of what is "real"—cannot be exterminated by obfuscation or pedantic writing. Indeed, it is alive and well in politics and art, in spiritual writings, editorial pages, and courtrooms. Regardless of ambivalence among theologians, interest in—perhaps even ultimate concern for—what is real pervades contemporary globalized American culture, evident in the huge popularity of movies like *The Matrix, Sixth Sense, Contact, I ♡ Huckabees, Babel* or *Crash*. Long-running television series that take on esoteric themes, like *The Twilight Zone, The X Files,* or the many generations of *Star Trek* also indicate a wider concern with questions of reality, as does the poetry of many popular songs. Bird York's song *In The Deep* is a good example, as is Jason Mraz's *The Remedy,* Mos Def's *Life is Real,* John Mayer's *No Such Thing,* TLC's *Chasing Waterfalls,* REM's *Losing My Religion,* and The Indigo Girls' *Galileo.* These multimedia philosophical reflections on the nature of reality (not to mention any number of novels, or examples of visual arts, or legislative deliberations) suggest only the smallest beginning to what could be a very long syllabus of popular study in contemporary expressions of ontological concern.[6]

Ontological assumptions are asserted all of the time, they are just not always recognized as such. It is probably very difficult to put one's finger down at any point on a human historical timeline and avoid ontological contests that mattered very much to the people in that time, whose answers affected (and in some cases continue to affect) cultural and ethical patterns today. For example, the ontological issues of "world" and of "human being" loomed large in the centuries of early modernity, as European colonization reterritorialized much of the globe. Answers to the ontological questions of world and of human had long-reaching implications for colonized and colonizer, depending on who was asking and who possessed the power to enforce their answer. A group of hunters from West Africa, betrayed and sold into the Euro-American slave trade, would have answered the question of their own humanity very differently from those who sought to extinguish that humanity in chattel slavery. It was how European financiers (and consumers of sugar and cotton products) and white American slavers and planters colluded in answering the ontological question of African humanity that kept slavery in business for so long, engraving the modern social, economic, and political world with habituations and institutions of racism that still yield color hierarchies across the globe. And it was how thousands of African-born and African-descended slaves and children of slaves insisted on answering the ontological question of their own humanity that kept them alive, that eventually ended legalized slavery, and that will—some day—end its spawn of race hierarchies.

There are implications in ontology, therefore, of value, power, and pragmatic concern. What constitutes life such that rules about the living can be applied? And what constitutes "the real" such that social navigation through experiences can be accomplished? Pragmatically speaking, these are questions of agreement, since answers to the question of what is "real" mean very little if none agree. This is where poets, story-tellers, and singers come in. A shared story enables a shared vision of reality—especially if the story gives some account of a community's origin and purpose. But the fact is that answers (and agreement about answers) to ontological questions are not always self-evident—perhaps even seldom so—and so the philosophical task of ontology never fully goes away. Narrative traditions cannot hold the real in an unchanging textual format forever. Translation gets increasingly difficult. Indeed, that is why truly oral cultures have such resilient narratives: not having been written down, they can respond to the world in which they come to be, again.

The reason that the challenge of ontology persists in every generation is because of the ways that social, political, and economic powers wield answers to questions of being in any age. The humanity of Africans sold in chattel slavery is only one example. Social, political, religious, and economic power struggles over ontological questions are evident just under the surface of contemporary debates, for example, about reproduction and euthanasia, school or prison design, definitions of family, citizenship, war, torture, slavery, childhood, ownership, and identity. *What is real? Who are we, really?* These are among a multitude of questions of being and reality that philosophers in every culture and in every age must attempt to answer, in analytic texts, in art, in poetry, in story, on legislative floors, and in theology.

By virtue of academic constraints and requirements of employment, full-time philosophers and theologians whose medium is the academic textbook often forget to contextualize the question of being, to place it within the very real experienced realms of human life where answers are contested daily, and matter very much. By the same token, many people from non-academic walks of life forget that even the most obtuse philosophy or theology concerns itself with the questions of existence that affect and shape daily life. The imperatives of lived experience need the nuances of careful reflection, but the critical arts of academic inquiry have no purchase on meaning without some explicit connection to the lived issues at stake.

If ontology is so vital to contemporary life, why is it out of favor among contemporary theologians? Why do so many theologians shy away from the words "being" or "is"? Of course, part of the reason for this aversion to ontology is centuries' old: the medieval theologians like Thomas Aquinas failed on the one hand to prove the existence of God through cosmological arguments and more modern theologians like Friedrich Schleiermacher failed on the other hand to prove the existence of God through subjective arguments. Discussions of divine existence became, by the late twentieth century, something of an embarrassment to theologians both within and outside of fundamentalist circles. Quite reasonably, theology turned to textual and narrative analysis, to existentialism and the riches of psychology and sociology to investigate ways of interpreting doctrine and scripture in contemporary terms, presuming the existence of God but bracketing any investigation of divine being itself.

Second, theologians found reason to avoid ontology because of growing sensitivity to the multiplicity of cultures and therefore to multiple, sometimes contradictory claims regarding the real. Many became fully persuaded that Christian theology has contributed far too much suffering in the past through its absolutist and universalist claims about reality, claims that turned out to be thinly masked Eurocentric and patriarchal views of reality. James Cone declared that "God is Black," Mary Daly and Rosemary Radford Ruether declared the self-interest at work for patriarchy and for global imperialism in God's maleness, William R. Jones declared that God is a white racist, and Alice Walker pointed out that the whiteness of God was also male, starting a flood of critiques of traditional Christian claims about Christian divinity. These critiques only strengthened growing theological suspicions of ontology and its tendencies toward totalizing claims tainting it with imperialistic intent. Better to avoid ontological discussions altogether.

Third, shifts in biblical studies and in philosophy to linguistic hermeneutics and semiotics as a mode of thinking about differences in perception provided many theologians with an "out" from the philosophical and political problematics of ontology. Heidegger's attempt at an ontology without divinity meant that his coined conjunction "onto-theology" became a refrain of self-loathing among the more philosophically minded of theologians. A "God Without Being" or a theology without God has seemed to be the very thing that theology has needed to pull itself out of the swamp of *ontos*, a swamp that somehow froze around all possible conceptions of the divine. How could it not? Even those theologians in full revolt against any conflation of ontology with theology still presumed, for the most part, that divinity and oneness are the same.

These three accounts of theological allergy to ontology are over-simplified, but illustrative. Indeed, ever since the Reformers reacted against priestly corruption by asserting not only that priests may not act "for God" in administering indulgences but that all of the sacraments of blessing (baptism, communion, ordination, and so forth) are *symbolic* rather than effective, the move away from ontological claims for divine presence as a means of reducing dominant claims to power has been afoot. What is more, "God" did become an embarrassment to philosophical theology, there is no doubt about that. Twentieth-century struggles to account for divinity in ways that would avoid the traps set by the tyranny of the One have succeeded in making possible the arguments and questions that animate this book. Bit by bit and in a myriad different ways, for a long time theologians have been prying open doors to new connective possibilities for theology. From Tillich's hermeneutical ontology to Altizer's Nietzschean death of God, to Daly's Verb of Verbs, to Cone's Black God, to Althaus-Reid's indecent God, Tanner's voluptuous God and finally to Keller's depth of God, *tehomic* fissures have opened all across the doctrines of Christianity, allowing multiplicity to shimmer into focus under and in the tattering shroud of the One.

The grand, even grandiose task of theology is that it somehow takes stock of the God-dimension—the divinity—in the life, time, and circumstances in which theologians find themselves. And, despite very reasonable fears of failure or ridicule, there is an unavoidably ontic dimension to this taking stock, even if the theologian says that the God-dimension "is" inexpressible, or "is" borne by tradition and narrative, "is" summed up in the commandment to love one's neighbor, or even if there "is" no God-dimension at all. All of these claims (and thousands more) involve ontic presumptions insofar as they attempt to make plausible the reality of divinity in the world—whether based on cosmological, narrative/cultural, existential, or social grounds. There is a metaphysical *there* implied in every theological undertaking (including, I am saying, those undertakings that explicitly attempt to disavow metaphysics or take an agnostic position toward it). It is possible to dismiss the plausibility of a being wandering around on clouds. That dismissal is relatively easy. But it is not possible to engage in theology with any seriousness and also avoid making *any* claims or gestures toward some concept of what is "real."

Theological ontology that is rooted in lived religion seeks to bring an understanding of reality at its most extreme limits into narrative focus and comprehension, through story, ritual, and song. It concerns the big picture of origins, orientation, and ends that come into question for real people in situations of real uncertainty. Ultimate meaning—sometimes figured in terms of divinity or cosmology—is often the embedded question for anyone who wonders about the "place" of his or her own life in "the scheme of things."

For some, the question of divinity sits quietly camouflaged as an answer given by pastors, temple elders, scriptures, parents, biology class, philosophy, habit. "God is," or "God isn't," so the answer goes. The question of divinity masquerades at times as an answer, until the question behind the answer has occasion to arise. On those occasions, the God of doctrine may stumble on the unbearable intimacy of suffering. The hard won no-God of the most rigorous and certain atheism may shimmer into something—*just there*—in an act of revolutionary generosity, in a glint of red on a green leaf, or in the stillness within a Kyrie. The question of divinity does not go away either for those who daily ask or for those who consider themselves, most of the time, to be certain.

It is not uncommon for ontological questions to surface when crisis hits. A friend from New York said to me not long after the trauma of the attacks on the World Trade Center in 2001,

> In the aftermath of all of that horror, as I scooped the ash of neighbors off of my window sill, I realized how fragile my life is, and that gave me a glimpse into the reality of the world.

Another friend, present at the birth of her adopted son, wrote to me that

> the world shifted into focus in those hours, in the blood and mess and noise. I knew then that he's always been here, I've always been here, his birth mother's always been here. We're always changing, pushed by the uterine muscle of the world into some form or another, drawing a new, noisy breath, leaving the warmth of something familiar, waking up. For the first time, I knew something of God then. But everything I'd been taught about God doesn't fit anymore. I've felt God's hot breath, and don't have anywhere to go with that. Can you help?

Divinity, in the form of question, ripples on the surface of countless raw moments, when life leaves the living, or pushes its way in, drawing back the curtain on every uncertainty about what really *is* and what *matters*. Not long ago, after emphysema and lung cancer resulted in a breathing tube that kept my only maternal uncle barely alive and possibly unconscious, my family decided together, heartbroken, that he should be allowed to die. The doctor told us that when he removed the tube, my uncle would live only for about ten minutes, and probably not be conscious. Along with his fourteen grown foster children we clustered around his hospital bed, quiet, stunned by the enormity of the moment. As the uneven line of his heart faded on the monitor, someone started singing "Amazing Grace" and we sang until he was gone:

> Twas Grace that taught my heart to fear,
> and Grace my fear relieved.
> How precious did that Grace appear,
> the hour I first believed.

Why "Amazing Grace"? Why this assertion of benevolence in the face of the vast unknown into which our uncle was slipping, like a seal into the night-time ocean? There were any number of songs that we could have sung to bid farewell to our funny, irreverent, wounded, and generous uncle, father, husband, brother. Any number of poems, crass jokes, or Eugene V. Debs speeches recited. Perhaps silence itself would have sufficed. I am struck by the fact that that song, which lays claim to divinity in spite of it all, is the one that we found ourselves singing, humming, and weeping over as the heart monitor slowly smoothed itself down. Somebody laid claim to an *ontos* of Grace as death's door opened in our midst and, softly, shut again.

Ontology is not a fusty matter for the bookish. It is a matter of import for everyone who lives—and dies. The questions, answers, songs, and stories that rise up in response to moments of raw intensity reveal much about what ontological map lies under the surface of everyday life. Although, contrary to aphoristic wisdom, atheists do persist in foxholes, it is no mystery that times of great danger, hope, death, birth and uncertainty can pull back the covers on whatever ontological questions may have dozed through the routines of less fragile times. The point is, for most people in most places, ontological questions persist, embedded in the cultural fabric of every time and place. Artists, storytellers, poets, and musicians are the most abundant source of articulation of these questions, but theologians also seek a kind of accounting for the way things are and for the changes that the world continually seems to undergo. *Ontos* is the object, in other words, of the deepest human questions. This is why the ontic has always taken up residence in stories of worldly beginnings and endings, of creation and future, why it takes on the valence of divinity and becomes the stories of gods. And gods, we might go so far as to say, are *ontos* always becoming, clothed now and then in the flames of our passion for the real. Tillich was right that art carries the heartbeat of this passion and is so often thereby a conduit of the divine, which *he* called "Being-Itself."

Even systematic thinkers disdainful of the necessary acrobatics and whimsy of ontological art depend upon its labor. They become artists without really meaning to whenever they fish for thought, letting the thin line of imagination loose, casting it out to see what just might be beyond the blankets of light, beyond the symmetry of the usual equations. Perhaps they even indulge in a fancy that the line might go far and deep enough to brush along something large and momentous, impossible to draw in or hold, a monstrous edge of possibility, a black hole, a whale of a displacement. And should the line catch—send back along its slender length a tremor from the abysmal edge—do not all of the neat and systemic anchors of doctrine suddenly lurch and move as if they were creatures suddenly wakened, and does not thought itself then stumble, losing its footing and then its feet, shifting shape and direction like the startled school of fish it seems to have become? When the fisher becomes the fished, thinker becomes the thing thought, do not the certainties of doctrine tend to tatter and disperse? And is it not the secret hope in all philosophy and theology that they will? Is this not the same hope children have of glimpsing great monsters of their dreams?

Theological ontology, at its best, is this kind of adventure. I am after a theological ontology that, as Deleuze suggests, makes a "looser kind of sense," that is "closer to life itself." This is no arithmetic of minutiae. The gods and their claims upon us, which name the start, expression, reach, and edge of all things, are constituted by stories rather than formulae. They frame the knowable and the unknowable more effectively and expansively because stories open out, limn, and gesture rather than enclose. There is usually room in the truest stories for contradiction, pause, and the anticipation of monsters. But Christian theology has too often betrayed its ontological art in a quest for the solitary confinement of maximum security. As a result, ontological claims themselves become caricatures of the very being that they seek to find.

And so it is no wonder that ontology has fallen out of favor among the more adventurous and artistic of theologians. The theological account of being became, in the history of European-centered thought at least, a brittle equation rather than a supple story. It became an equation of limits—what *is* over against and excluding what *isn't*—instead of a story of passages, of leavings and arrivings, of sex with gods (and monsters), of what *is* and what *isn't* exchanging glances and green cards, of deceptive edges and attractional orbits. This is a lush way of saying that ontology, to the extent that it represents a problem in theology, has largely been reduced over time by iconoclastic theologians and philosophers to arithmetic in the most prosaic sense of the word. The substance of reality "itself," a Theory of Everything, an equation for chaos, is the distorted, bound, growth of the idea of monotheism. It holds that reality does not shift, slip, approximate, or contradict. The arithmetical view of being is a presupposition of absolute stillness at the center of the story, not the heartbeat, flame, contraction or gush. It is a presupposition of Law, not Myth. It is citizen Greek, not shepherdess Greek.

The fact is that while all of the reasons for becoming suspicious of ontological arguments for divinity are well-founded, all are also dependent on the assumption that such arguments must result in corroboration of oneness in the divine. That may well be true, but it is also the case as we have seen that even One never achieves oneness, and that changes everything, ontologically speaking. Ontology therefore is precisely the place where we might begin to navigate past the imaginative limitations that the doctrine of One has placed on theology. Oneness, rooted in a psychology of scarcity and an ontology of stasis, is unable to allow for the multiplication of dimensions and intersections necessary even to imagine a single loaf of bread and a single fish feeding four or five thousand hungry souls.[7] Deleuze holds one of the keys to the ontological challenge of theology in a logic of multiplicity. Rather than tracing the ontic signifier "Is," I follow Deleuze in a more fluid direction toward the multiplying, connective "And."[8] In this way, multiplicity is not the opposite of oneness, just as water is not the opposite of ice. Multiplicity is limitation *and* possibility co-constituted, not opposed. It is creativity *made possible* by disability.[9] It is shape-shifting, abundance, finitude, *tehom*, and story. There are ways to *think* this way, if at times only through poetry. There are ways to allow for possibilities for being that disobey the logic of the One, that exceed the demands of "either/or" thought.

10 Thinking multiplicity

Do I contradict myself?
Very well then I contradict myself,
(I am large, I contain multitudes.)

Walt Whitman[1]

And the body, what about the body?

Jane Kenyon[2]

Ontology framed by the logic of totality, or the One, long ago become for theology a dead-end. This is because the One—whether system, thing, tradition, or God—always fails to be one. It is from this dead-end that "the death of God" was (correctly) trumpeted. But I have already argued that the dead-end of ontology framed by the logic of the One need not be a dead-end for all ontological or theological thought. Nor is it necessarily the case that a passion for reality is finished off along with God by the failures of the logic of the One demanded by monotheism. The One–Many divide, necessitated by the logic of the One and by the demands of the One God, is a masquerade, a projection out of the fluidity and flux of divine creation. The One, and the One–Many divide that produces it, has mesmerized and split monotheists who must look to the abstraction of certainty: to a Heaven purified of Hell, to a conclusive end to the story of being instead of its always-beginning—again. If ontology is to serve theology beyond the logic of the One, it clearly calls for a logic of multiplicity that, in shaping new ontological claims, cannot fully escape the risks of totalization. Ontology does not, in other words, ever entirely avoid gestures toward oneness, but when pursued with "a logic" of multiplicity such oneness is perforated and exposed as not-One. This is something of a paradox: I am arguing that, in order to undo the One, ontological creativity is necessary, but ontology consorts intimately with dreams of totality which reinscribe the One all over again.[3] But right here lies the distinction upon which I am staking this ontological journey: there is a real difference between the logic of the One that ever hides the totalizing drive of ontology and a logic of multiplicity that ever seeks to expose it. Any effort to annihilate the One only feeds the logic of the former. This means that some sort of being-with oneness is required of any logic of multiplicity. *Absolute* disavowal of oneness is not the goal, but rather a more mature (and skeptical) intimacy with it, as we shall see in the final chapter.

A logic of multiplicity is therefore not *the* logic of multiplicity because it is necessarily provisional and partial. A logic of multiplicity that is a thinking-toward divinity demands that we take the notion of incarnation much, much more seriously than Christian theologians since Pelagius and until Ruether have been wont to do. Most of Christian theology has fallen into more or less of a Docetic groove, unwilling to grant to divinity the freedom to incarnate except in one "conclusive" time and place in the person of Jesus. Following the early ecumenical councils' insistence on the uniqueness of Jesus' divinity, most Christological formulations throughout Christendom tend narrowly to conceive the richness and openness of what it means to *be* bodied in the person of Jesus, and then for the sake of proclaiming his divinity.

Indeed, the Hellenistic themes of divine eternity and impassibility carried over fully into early Christian battles over Christology. The incarnation was, as we saw in Chapter Five, a profound problem for these Christians largely because of their own inheritance of the logic of the One that could brook no internal contradiction. They were obliged to declare the incarnation of God in Jesus a divine miracle and a mystery precisely because, in the dualistic logic of the One, divinity as spirit and world as body are conceptualized in opposition to each other, at times in order to define one another by way of exclusion. For that reason, incarnation has remained a challenge for Christian theology, meaning that the "in-" has held place of privilege over the "carnation", usually in order to keep ecclesial control over the actual and actualizing multiplicity of bodies.

Since the emergence of process theology, and of feminist and other liberation theologies in the latter half of the twentieth century, however, the body has begun to return to theology. The close (and explicitly derogatory) association of woman with matter and earth in the hierarchical chain of being throughout the history of Christian theology certainly made the question of the status of the body and earth a natural target for nascent feminist theologies.[4] Although the doctrine of the incarnation emphasizes a male divinity in the person of Jesus, some feminists saw right away that the rupture of divinity into *any* body in Christian theology could represent a fissure in the otherwise full exclusion of the female from concepts of God. Grace Jantzen points out, for example, (quoting Irigaray) that

> if Jesus is taken as in traditional Christendom as unique, then he "truly does represent the realization of the Patriarchy, the appearance of the father's and the Father's power" and feminists should have nothing to do with him. But if he was partial, then his incarnation leaves room for other incarnations, other trinities, other sexualities.[5]

Regardless of insights such as this, most feminist theologians have constrained themselves within a monotheistic logic, causing them to stumble against the carefully controlled embodiment of divinity in the man Jesus on the one hand, and, on the other, against the doctrine of monotheism that forces them to continue to split the evident manyness of bodies from the oneness of the divine. Consequently, many feminist theologies spiritualize Christology in order to speak beyond male particularity and so diffuse the very embodiment they sought to celebrate.[6]

Likewise, some black, Latin American and Asian liberation theologians have labored to restore body to divinity, insisting upon a Christology in particular that emphasizes divine solidarity with the poor and oppressed, especially with those enslaved, oppressed, tortured, and executed. But even here the notion of divine fleshiness tends to be narrow or strongly spiritualized, usually restricted to the experience of suffering. Liberation theologians are quite cautious about incarnation otherwise.[7] There are many good reasons for this, not the least of which is the overwhelming fact of suffering among the oppressed, a persistent reality that imperial theologies tend to dismiss either as the plan of God or as the result of oppressed peoples' own sin. But the relative quiet among liberation theologies regarding incarnation in larger terms of creation, abundance, or pleasure *as a critique of imperial theology* is only slowly beginning to change, not surprisingly, by women such as Ivone Gebara, Marcella Althaus-Reid, Karen Baker-Fletcher, and Wohnee Anne Joh.[8]

Process theology represents another important move to restore embodiment to theology, this time through a mechanics of evolutionary change in which divinity is conceived as accompanying the "particularities of the actual world" without becoming conflated with it.[9] Process theologians accomplish this distinction between body and divinity through the "en" of "panentheism" which also allows, in Whitehead's thought at least, for plurality in divine expression in "the multiplicity of the primordial character."[10] Process theology has been the first to take seriously the limitations that ontologies of stasis place upon divinity, recognizing the significance of incarnation from an ontological vantage point. The very concepts that irrigate this project come in no small portion from this rich source, especially the emphasis on concretion, change, and "fluency."

But Whiteheadian process thought still tends to stop short of a logic of multiplicity. When it does so, process theology cannot (actually) achieve the more promising, if more radical, possibilities of imagining *divine* incarnation or divine *multiplicity* except in terms of accompaniment, primordiality, or finality, each of which abstracts divinity more than I believe necessary (although not less than is necessary for the logic of the One). Process notions of bodies and worlds do cast divinity (and worlds) into the evolutionary motion of always becoming, or "concretion," which is a marked improvement over earlier, more static concepts. However, divinity conceived as a primordial principle or a completion—even as a transcendent lure—can easily remain aloof to what makes particular bodies particular, namely their utter unrepeatability. With this avoidance of particularity by virtue of a summation of all particularities, the logic of the One remains intact and satisfied, if somewhat humbled. This is a far subtler satisfaction than other theological attempts at incarnation that also remain wedded to oneness. The logic of the One is not essential to process thought (as, for example, the most recent work of process theologian Roland Faber attests) but it does recur in Whitehead's insistence that what makes God *God* is the totality that "he" represents in his accompaniment of the world and all of its particularities:

> He is the beginning and the end. He is not the beginning in the sense of being in the past of all members. He is the presupposed actuality of conceptual operation in unison of becoming with every other creative act. Thus by reason of the relativity of all things, there is a reaction of the world on God. The completion of God's nature into a fullness of physical feeling is derived from the objectification of the world in God. He shares with every new creation its actual world; and the con-crescent creature is objectified in God as a novel element in God's objectification of that actual world. This prehension into God of each creature is directed with the subjective aim, and clothed with the sub-jective form, wholly derivative from his all-inclusive primordial valua-tion. God's conceptual nature is unchanged, by reason of its final completeness.[11]

The logic of the One is a resilient framework in traditional Christian theology, but it is also to date largely uninvestigated. As process and liberation theol-ogies begin to take multiplicity up as a fundamental issue in their work to re-imagine embodiment and concretion, there is no telling where and when divinity will erupt into theological focus. In part, this is because the matter of bodies is particularly acute in Christian thought, wherein the assertion that God-became-flesh occurs over and over again, even though the gap between doctrinal claims of incarnation and actual bodies in the world remains wide. This gap is a theological error that strips Christian theology of its greatest and most distinctive contribution to religious wisdom. The astounding news of *ethical* incarnation, "God with us," of good news for the poor *by way of enfleshment*, is nearly lost in the carefully controlled doctrinal insistence of closure on the topic of incarnation. I follow Cathe-rine Keller's process thought in another direction: "*Always* already taking body," she writes, "creation opens up the concept of the incarnation beyond its singularity [my emphasis]."[12] Indeed, as Spinoza noted five centuries ago in his own argument against the superiority of mind over body, "no one has hitherto determined what the body is capable of."[13] Incarnation, God-with-us, is a most profound theory of revelation and of responsibility. It is incarnation that beckons now, from beyond the limits of the One.

Literally meaning "in the flesh," incarnation is *about* bodies and so already cannot be reduced to oneness without withdrawing, again, from actual bodies in their necessary particularity. The challenge of thinking multiplicity is therefore, in part, one of thinking bodies against abstraction, against universals and generalizations. But this is surely an impossibility. The demand itself is incoherent, because language requires generalization, as does thought. Even to say "a logic of multiplicity" implies a reductive move, an abstract and generalizing shift away from the inescapable manyness of particular bodies. "I am trying to think the multiple as such," Michael Serres writes early on in his reflection on time.[14] But the multiple *as such,* at least for those of us raised on modern idealist configurations of reality, is contradictory and so nearly impossible to think within the horizon of the One, except as a reduction to "the many" which props up "the One." As Rosi Braidotti notes, "the mental habits of linearity and objectivity persist in their hegemonic hold over our thinking."[15] Serres explains the difficulty for modern Europeans and Americans in terms of our historic fascination with ones that "only a unity seems rational to us":

> We want a principle, a system, an integration, and we want elements, atoms, numbers. We want them, and we make them. A single God, and identifiable individuals. The aggregate as such is not a well-formed object; it seems irrational to us. The arithmetic of whole numbers remains a secret foundation of our understanding; we're all Pythagoreans. We think only in monadologies.[16]

But, if Braidotti is right (and I think that she is) that "the only constant at the dawn of the third millennium is change,"[17] then the point of seeking a logic of multiplicity is not to locate a universal and final closure for thought that will always and everywhere successfully resist reduction (this itself would be *too* contradictory, would it not?). The mode of thinking multiplicity cannot be some kind of equation *ad absurdam* that captures (or finishes off) "the multiple" or "multiplicity" per se. No, it is not "the many" that I am after when I invoke the term "multiplicity", but a mode, something more like a posture or even an idiomatic dialect that, in its very partiality, locality, and equivocity, alters the frequency of the One–Many divide in high philosophy, linearity, and objectivity.

It bears repeating here that "multiplicity" is not the same as "the many." It does not refer to a pile of many separable units, many "ones," and so it is not opposed to the One or to ones. "The multiple" (it is ironic how the English language seems to want to make it into a singularity), or "multiplicity," results when things—ones—so *constitute* each another that they come to exist (in part, of course) *because of* one another. Essential separation becomes incoherence. So does essential wholeness, or oneness. The whole is constituted by its parts but, then, the parts are also constituted by their participation in the whole. As Jean Luc Nancy points out, the Latin "*plus* is comparable to *multus*. It is not 'numerous'; it is 'more.'"[18] Multiplicity is what happens when something is more than the sum of its parts but also, by virtue of its necessary participation as a part of other somethings, is not itself therefore completely whole. The multiple is therefore more but also less than whole, or One. And of course, as we have seen, the One fails to be only one, over and over again. Nancy puts it this way:

> The One as purely one is less than one; it cannot be, be put in place, or counted. One as properly one is always more than one. It is an excess of unity; it is one-with-one, where its Being itself is co-present.[19]

This is a mathematical statement, but it is also a qualitative one. Mathematically, "one" is a relational number. It is fully dependent on its relation to and distinction from all other numbers (two, three, and so forth). One has no actual meaning without at least one other. The One comes into being in relation to Other/s, or not-ones. This is the conundrum of the One: why it cannot get away from the One–Many divide, even when it is conceived not as a simple one, but as a totality. Nancy's point is that a "pure" One is impossible because as such it implies no other, no relation. And so the pure One is less than one because it "cannot be ... counted" since counting requires the defining company of others. This is the mathematical contradiction of the One.

At the same time, as Nancy suggests, there is a qualitative contradiction in the One which comes from its more-ness, its excess of totality that results from its necessary coming into being in relation. One way to think of this is through Thich Nhat Han's famous parable of a piece of paper. Pointing to a chair, or to a desk, or even to a sheet of paper, he asks "What *is* this?" After receiving the ready answer "a chair", "a desk", or "a piece of paper", he says, "That is the name, but what *is* it?" Gradually, his listeners begin to list the component parts of a sheet of paper, desk, or chair: wood pulp, water, chemicals, and so forth. He encourages them to continue, "And what are *those?*" Wood pulp is the tree, which in turn is the sap, the rain, the nutrient minerals, and the wind. And the rain, nutrient minerals, and wind are, eventually, the cosmos. His listeners learn, finally, that the paper *is* everything because it can be separated from nothing. "If you are a poet," he points out in *The Heart of Understanding*, "you will see clearly that there is a cloud floating in this piece of paper."[20]

Because the paper, desk, chair, contain the cosmos and cannot be separated from any part of the cosmos except through conceptual violence and a falsification of the "interbeing" of the object, as an entity any object is also *empty;* it is no-thing. Each object is an excess of totality; it is so much more than one that it evacuates the One completely into emptiness.[21] This reminder from Buddhist philosophy is that a logic of One need not only lead to a substantive metaphysics of one God, as it has done in the monotheistic west. It can also lead to an evacuation of that metaphysics in another kind of totality: emptiness. Both are founded on a logic of unicity; both expound truth as reductive to a single claim or as expansive to a totality: a Theory of Everything.

What is going on with contemporary European philosophers of multiplicity, however, is somewhat different than either traditional claims to the One or to Buddhist claims to emptiness. Jean-Luc Nancy, focusing on the impossibility of totality (substantive or empty), describes pure multiplicity as the "One-minus". Gilles Deleuze likewise calls it the "less than totality, or (n-1)." And Alain Badiou characterizes multiplicity as "without-one."[22] All three are attempting to think multiplicity beyond the One–Many divide by exposing the mathematical (logical/nominal) and spatial (relational) interdependence—or compromise—of the One with its others. There is also an interdependence, or compromise, of the One and its others in terms of time. This is the issue of stasis and change. One can only remain One if no change (time) fractures it. In time, the One is without oneness. It is, as Badiou suggests, "without one." One then and One now can only remain one if there *is* no then and now. From this it is easy to see why the negation of time in eternity became such a firmly rooted doctrinal assertion about God in Christian philosophical theology.

It is one thing to see that the One–Many divide is a projection of the logic of the One. It is another thing entirely to imagine *thought* in some other dimension. Can we imagine multiplicity as a mode that opens a possibility for thought beyond the One–Many divide? We must try, at least, to begin. Again. Any other option, it seems to me, will keep us slipping back into the groove of opposition to the One, which thereby reinscribes the One–Many divide and its conclusive logic. This is no small task, although the circumstances in which we find ourselves now may demand it. Rosi Braidotti agrees. New modes of thinking that better reflect actual embodied complexity require monumental effort, she claims, because "we live in permanent processes of transition, hybridization, and nomadization, and these in-between states and stages defy the established modes of theoretical representation."[23]

The closer we look at life as we actually live it, at relationships, bodies, nations, and scriptures, wholeness flickers in and out like a hologram. It collapses into incoherence; or rather it expands porously into something both more and less, as Nancy suggests. It expands into a *moreless*.[24] Thought like this requires sea-legs. It must find its rest not in the land-locked stability of conclusions but in the rhythms of Aionian motion, in the flow continuous. This exercise is not, therefore, about a search for some kind of "pure" multiple, or a "pure" multiplicity precisely because that effort remains fully within the mode of the One–Many divide, requiring an aim and a dialect of reduction and abstraction. Alain Badiou has already made this point. "Pure multiplicity," he argues (against Heidegger and Deleuze), is fundamentally platonic. It is ideal and mathematical because only mathematics can make a multiplicity without imposing an interpretation (a unity) upon it.[25] Unfortunately, in his excellent criticism, especially of Deleuze's claims to a fully immanent philosophy, Badiou is conflating multiplicity with the many and so makes his point still from within the logic of the One–Many divide. His use of the word "pure" here may be the signal of that entrapment. It may also be that the word "multiplicity" is itself too deeply tied to the mathematics of the One–Many divide (which is, in part, Badiou's point) to allow us to use it to move into what Braidotti calls a more nomadic mode.[26]

It is entirely possible that Deleuze is right and there is no *ontological* "logic of multiplicity" that is readily available to philosophy or to theology as they have constructed themselves, steeped as both disciplines are in modes of thought that require reduction and simplification, that frown upon contradiction, and that valorize the universal.[27] But an ontological logic of multiplicity may be available both to philosophers and theologians if they are willing to do three things: to dispense with Eurocentric requirements for European precedent in argument (already I am advocating a departure from accepted understandings of the terms of logic!); to risk meaningful contradiction; and finally, to consider with Miguel de Beistegui the possibility that "the ontology of the multiple can only be locally circumscribed."[28]

All of these steps may well make my use of the word "logic" incoherent. I wonder increasingly if this is so, and begin to suspect that a localizing term like "idiom" or "dialect" would be better than "logic." At the moment, however, I am not willing to cede "logic" entirely to the trajectory of the One–Many divide. But we shall see about that. First, if a logic or even a dialect of multiplicity is possible for the sake of imagining incarnation that actually has purchase in the world/s we now inhabit (to imagine God more queerly, as Marcella Althus-Reid argues), then I say that theologians must get over our terror not only of nomadic trespass into the impurities of body-thought, but must get over our terror of ontology.

As I discussed in the last chapter, theological ontology has generally fallen out of favor due to the persuasiveness of postmodern critiques of grand, meta-narratives regarding being and the association of such narratives with the theological. This association can be seen clearly, for example, in the characterization of Badiou's project as "a genuinely metaphysical attempt to free thought from the double horizon of unicity (whereby it posits itself as ontology) and transcendence (whereby it is theology)."[29] *Any* claim for totality, unicity, and the like is conflated, as a result, with the theological. And the more suspicious postmodern philosophy becomes of meta-narratives, the more "the theological" comes into question. Rightly so. Ever since Kierkegaard railed against "system" thinking that he claimed would tame God, and Nietzsche taunted the self-importance of German idealism that presumed its "metaphysics" were not in fact produced by its own politics, theology's ontological claims have been implicated in the corruption of empire. Indeed, in the early twentieth century, Martin Heidegger's interest in ontology was focused on saving it from theology, to posit a philosophy of being that would meet Nietzsche's deep critique of the theo-political trajectory in western thought. Consequently, theological attempts since the early twentieth century have sought to avoid Heidegger's epithet of "onto-theology" either by sidestepping questions of divine being alto-gether, or by casting it in phenomenological or existential terms.[30]

Heidegger's forays into an alternative ontology that sought to do away with static metaphysical structures in favor of eventful states of "becoming" opened doors for later philosophers, and even the occasional theologian, to follow. Heidegger correctly saw theology, Christian theology in particular, as a buttress for metaphysical systems of platonic stasis that cannot abide immanence or always-passing-away of actuality. His own efforts to resist what he called "onto-theology" have deeply influenced later theological efforts, to the point that theologians who take up ontology in explicitly theological ways risk pity from their peers, if not a fear of return to the grandiosity and violence so indicative of religious metaphysical claims about God's "Being" over against the world of difference.

It should therefore not be surprising that in some quarters, especially among the hybrid intelligentsia of postcolonial Europe, more philosophers than theologians have begun to play with ideas of "multiplicity," processive "becoming" and non-processive "becoming" as possible corrections to the closures (and anti-democratic dimensions) of ideas of the One.[31] Indeed, one could even suggest that, thanks to a few of the brighter philosophical lights clustered particularly around the universities of France over the last fifty years, "multiplicity" has become something of a fashion among con-tinental philosophers: Rosi Braidotti (*Metamorphoses*), Luce Irigaray (*This Sex Which is Not One*), Jacques Derrida (*Monolingualism of the Other*), Gilles Deleuze (*A Thousand Plateaus*), Jean Luc Nancy (*Being Singular Plural*), Alain Badiou (*Being and Event*) and Jean Baudrillard (*Impossible Exchange*) to name only a few of the more recent European efforts in the direction of thinking multiplicity as a way out of the "onto-theological" morass that Heidegger so provocatively had diagnosed.

Meanwhile, from other, non-European directions, less plodding modes of thinking multiplicity—not tied, in other words, to the heavy genealogi-cal constraints of dialecticism that burden European thought—come con-cepts of fluidity, disorientation, change, presence, and shape-shifting that may go much further than the philosophers in *thinking* multiplicity beyond the One–Many divide. Thomas King's *Green Grass, Running Water* is only one example of this. Others include the Uncle Remus cycle of stories, Ana Castillo's *So Far From God,* Leslie Marmon Silko's *Ceremony,* Calvin Luther Martin's *The Way of Human Being,* not to mention the poets, song-writers, and visual artists whose *thinking* is not tied down to the logic of One that exacts an "is" or "is not" upon every expression.

Some might say, with good reason, that the tellers of parables have never lost sight of multiplicity and becoming as modes of thought. It is just that their ranks have been thinned by monotheistic evangelism, colonizers' guns, and the unification of global capital (not necessarily in that order), all of which depend upon the dualistic logic of the One–Many divide for success. And philosophers have begun to see dull poverty of imagination, if not a masquerade of control, at the dualistic true/false center/mirror of the One. Can the center of the Logos-logic of the One actually be empty? Or is it a closet? A messy, ugly divinity self-mired in an ice of stasis, masquerading in repression as the opposite of itself (God), in order that disappointment, grief, and rage (at the cost of excessive pleasure, exultation, and gratification) be contained and disciplined by an ethereal image of purity and sameness projected elsewhere? This kind of possibility certainly fits with the philosophical trajectory from Nietzsche and Freud through Lacan, Foucault, Kristeva, and Irigaray.

Where the philosophers influenced by Lacan's neo-Freudianism see the logic of the One in dualistically powered, historically contingent terms of control and excess, subjection, and abjection, one and other, non-European-minded thinkers tend to see the logic of the One in less dialectically framed terms. The Logos-logic of the One looks more like an elaborate, violent farce. The tragedy of the story of the Logos-logical One, whether in terms of cosmic theological oneness or in terms of global capitalism, is the violence, death, and extinction it wreaks on the small, the supple, and the local. If it did not hurt so much to laugh, it would be funny; a Big Joke of self-importance—call it shock and awe—that *will* eventually collapse on itself. Trickster is always trying to project (him)self into grandiose postures; always attempting control; and thereby *always* making a fool of himself even as he changes the world in his greedy, but creative, folly. The question from this perspective is less "Can the abject become subject?" or "Can the subaltern speak?" and more, at least from the perspective of Native American poetry and story-telling, something like the laughter that puffed-up pride—no matter how big it has become—cannot abide. As Calvin Martin notes,

> people who can define themselves as cardinal points, primary colors, segments of the day, the seasons, even the journey of life itself—people such as this are clearly engaging a reality different from the usual western points of reference.[32]

While philosophers from indigenous traditions in the Americas (among other Others) have never started from the Logos-logic of the One and so retain a supple posture of reasoning that might be called "multiplicity," it is significant that the Logos-logic of the One is beginning to trip on itself so much so that even European philosophers who insist upon European precedent for every claim they make have taken note. As I have already noted, at least since Nietzsche, European philosophers have suspected grandiose metaphysical narratives of evacuating ontology of its capacity to describe anything but pure (projected) ideals that serve particular political ends. The projected ideal loudly declaimed *as truth* certainly goes further back than the hapless wizard of Oz, and further back than the Dantean vamp of a God on ice. "Need we recall Plato's repressive decision," Jason Barker notes, "to expel the poets from the Republic, since their art allegedly dealt with appearances and not truth, as evidence of the *violence* of metaphysics?"[33] But even Plato is late on the scene of such metanarrative declamation and cannot be made to shoulder all of the weight of it, given the importance of the earlier Pythagoreans in their turn.

Although it is important to remember the antiquity of the issue of the One–Many, same–other divide, there are a number of global intellectual developments over the last two hundred years that can also give account, in part, for the emergence of more recent philosophical interest in multiplicity as a logic that confounds the Logos-logic of the One. First, physicists and other physical scientists have continued to develop strange new theories that cast doubt on the reducibility of things to atomic structures or to mechanical processes. Einstein's theory of relativity (with its possibilities of multiple, concurrent and contradictory universes,) Gödel's theory of incompleteness, and their progeny in quantum physics have thrown all sorts of philosophies based on unified systems into question.

Second, the gradual—and often painful—shaking off of colonial rule by peoples all over the earth has suggested to philosophy that *European* knowledge, particularly in its long Pythagorean passion for reductive oneness, is still inadequate to the task of thinking about reality in this world. *Difference* and local, embodied wisdom have become crucial and sometimes strident notions for many artists, poets, and philosophers, particularly for those whose own experiences of colonialism and global capitalism accentuate the flattening demand of *sameness* that European and American colonial powers have attempted to stamp on the cultural surface of others. Indeed, the energy and work of this book is hugely indebted to this particular, on-going shake-up. Multiplicity as a *logic* that confounds the One–Many divide follows from local and postcolonial art and thought in the form of attention to the persistent wisdom of resurgent indigenous sciences that never had to deny multiplicity in reality to begin with. Multiplicity, as a logic resistant to the One–Many divide, is a challenge to think "after" the dominance of European thought, which is a challenge to think "after" oneness as a principle norm.

Third, the development of existentialism and phenomenology since the late nineteenth century in Europe and North America have contributed to philosophical interest in multiplicity by rejecting the possibility of systemic, objective knowledge. Existentialism is a broad-brush name for a general philosophical reaction against the possibility of reason to fully articulate (and systematize) human experience in ideal or objective categories. Likewise, phenomenology is a broad-brush name for philosophical attempts to acknowledge the profound limits of human reason fully to grasp objective reality in itself, without letting go of the evidence of *perceived* objective reality dished up in the events—or phenomena—of daily life. Both schools of thought assert a non-reductive *more* to being and existing than what can be conceived, imagined, or put into logical systems. In their separate countries, Nietzsche and Kierkegaard each raged against the complacent but dominant tendencies of nineteenth-century German philosophy and theology to accommodate the unutterable and unsystematizable uniqueness of actual experience to codes, laws, and bourgeois moralities. They charged that there is something absolutely irreducible and excessive to each life, and so to the world, that evades and even resists order. It is a something that "occurs" and "becomes" and so eludes capture in static catalogs of being. Existence is event, they charged, not *thing*. And so, interested in the utter uniqueness and singularity of each moment—each experience, each life, each world—existentialist and phenomenological philosophies are also consumed by loss, mesmerized by the constant passing away of absolutely unique singularities and by what Jean Baudrillard calls "the impossible exchange" of *any* thing for another.[34] As the poet Rainer Maria Rilke wrote at the conclusion of his remarkable Eighth Elegy near the end of his life, "*so leben wir und nehmen immer Abschied*" ("and so we live, forever taking leave").[35] Multiplicity, as the simultaneity and presence of unique becomings and passings away, becomes thereby an intriguing—and necessary—lure for the philosopher willing to let go of the comfort of ideal resolutions.

Black, postcolonial, and white feminist psychoanalytic attention to dark-skinned and female bodies as sites of suppressed (dangerous) knowledge and wisdom are a fourth source for philosophy's new-found interest in multiplicity. Actual bodies, especially those that deviate from or are deficient in relation to the northern European norm of colonial domination suggest "ways of knowing" that exceed the acceptable "logocentric" (or "phallogocentric" as some suggest) modes resulting from the long-standing white men's club of western philosophy. Until very recently, most white feminists mistakenly accepted the race–gender divide in their work, assuming that the categories of "gender," "race," "nation," and "class" do not construct and contain each other in colonial and postcolonial reasoning. Nevertheless, even assuming that "woman" transcends categories of "white" and, say, "French," the logic of the One–Many divide took a heavy hit when white, French, psychoanalytic philosopher Luce Irigaray pointed out that "woman," as the "sex which is not one" threw into possibility an immanent logic, resident in the female body, that fully confounds the One.

The challenge of embodied thought, issuing not only from white feminists in the European and American academy but from Asian, African, African American and Native American thinkers intent on resisting colonial and globalized versions of Euro-American idealism, leads those same thinkers, and any others who take up the challenge of "thinking the body," to multiplicity as a question and as a possibility. Through the centuries,

Christian teaching has been particularly unkind to notions of female intelligence, dedicated to rationalizing the subjugation of all women's bodies (and so their brains, too) under the control of men. But Christians have by no means been the only ones to so treat women, nor have women's bodies been the only ones to be so vilified.

However, with a few notable exceptions, white feminists have thus far largely focused attention on the link between Christian rationales for the subjugation of women's bodies and the larger pathological drive in historically European thought that seeks absolutely to divide bodies from mind and spirit.[36] At the same time, postcolonial feminist philosophers and Womanist theologians have tended consistently to focus on the subjugation of non-white bodies through colonialism and slavery, more fully exposing thereby the racialized variables at work in European and American philosophical hesitation over bodies.[37] Thanks to the growing intersection of black feminist, postcolonial, white feminist and queer attention to the historic policing and violent normalizing of bodies and their mess, modern notions of race, sex, gender, and class are only beginning to reveal deeply *co-constitutive* roots in the material interests of Europe and white America's colonizing drives.[38] Only a logic of multiplicity can "make sense" (even a "looser sense") of such co-constitution.

All of these intellectual moves toward thinking multiplicity through actual bodies raises the question: What does "embodied thought" mean? Thought that actually "has body" must be structurally and substantively different than thought forged through the centuries in opposition to bodies. As I have already indicated, the effort of *thinking* the body, as some feminist and postmodern philosophers attempt to do, leads inexorably to the question of multiplicity *as a mode of thought*. Ideas formed in opposition to the actuality of bodies are formed that way precisely so that they can do the work of generalizing. Bodies themselves cannot be generalized. Or rather, what is generalizable about bodies is not the body/entity itself. For example, the last two sentences are generalizations *about* bodies but, because of that, the sentences are not bodies but rather abstractions *from* bodies. One can think of a disembodied category of dog, or arm, or stick, and so forth, but insofar as those categories remain general, they have no body and cannot "speak" or "show" on their own terms. To *bodily think* a dog or arm or stick is on some level to forego the generality and attend to the irreducibility and presence of that which I am calling dog, arm, or stick. It is for this reason that Badiou argues that multiplicity is necessarily only possible to think in terms of the local. To attend to bodies, as much of feminist, liberationist, and Womanist thought insists that we must do, is to beg the question of multiplicity precisely because it is to take up bodies themselves, rather than unifying ideas about them. As Claire Colebrook suggests, it "might be time to think of the body in its various distributions. This would not mean offering a ... theory of the body, but would *look at the body to think differently* [my emphasis]."[39]

Multiplicity, thought through bodies, indeed demands a different kind of thinking than the generalities that categorical ideas allow because bodies always fail in the end to *be* general. A logic of multiplicity, we can say therefore, has body. Multiplicity-thinking is, in part, a local body-dialect. But even something we might call "body-thought", helpful as it may be in pointing us toward a logic of multiplicity, is not free of abstraction. I point this out lest we fall again into the trap of either/or thinking, that embodied thought must therefore resist all abstraction, must pursue some nostalgic "pure" immanence. The multiplicity logic that I am after is not purely anything. It is a hybrid of bodies in motion, of localities shifting. Catherine Keller says it better than anyone:

> we theologize beginning or begin to theologize from a fluent multi-dimensionality. That depth of beginning cross-cuts in theory the "chaotic variability" of a proliferating matrix of tehomic icons: *difference*, creativity, trace, Khora, infinity, *complicatio*, multiplicity, the heterogenous dimension. As *dimensionality* rather than as *a* dimension, the depth enfolds an infinity of virtual finitudes: the creations, the creatures.[40]

All of this is why I suggest that multi-dimensionality is not an end, but it is a posture with sea-legs. There is something of yoga in this effort. Yoga, one of the most embodied practices of breath-centered body-contemplation, names its postures and motions just as it aims *through* them toward body-presence, a kind of body-thoughtfulness. There is pragmatic abstraction in Yoga just as there is irreducible body-presence. Abstraction—here what I am calling a logic—is only a problem when it forgets its own partiality, when it ceases serving proximal purposes. So, too, oneness or unicity is only a problem when it forgets its also-already equivocity. What is most challenging about this effort is that Christian systematic theology is so deeply wedded to abstractions as ultimate ends (to purity of thought and devotion, in other words) that it is always tempting, like a favorite drink offered to an alcoholic, to slip into the either/or logic that so possesses us. It is a kind of madness, after so much critique of abstraction, and of oneness, to take up the risk of naming—of proximally unifying even—a logic of multiplicity in the interest of leaning *into* or *toward* a more full mindfulness of divine presence/s in our midst, *into* or *toward* becoming incarnate. But that is just what we must do: attempt to name the postures, the idioms, of multiplicity. We do not seek purity of thought, or a mathematics of manyness.

Perhaps the idea of parable will help here. Many of the parables that the gospel writers attribute to Jesus begin with "The kingdom of heaven is like this." The richness of the stories that follow—a woman searching for a lost coin, a father grieving over an errant son, a potent mustard seed, lilies whose excessive blooming does not depend on consideration, an excessively generous employer—offer likenesses to what Jesus calls heaven. They are stories and images that confound any attempt at reduction or systematization.[41]

Let me be bold, then, and suggest that a glimpse of some kind of heavenly bodiliness, thawed, deep, and flowing right out of the stories of Jesus, may look something like children, something like an overstuffed closet, something like an underground, and lilies, something like gravity, a cup of water, belonging, the generosity of dead flesh, and surprise; and something like Coyote in the garden of Eden, something like being given six months to live, a flow of blood, and touch. If such are glimpses of Heaven rather than the trauma-founded Hell of Heaven's pristine eternity, then it seems that we can also be bold in imagining what divine multiplicity, understood ontologically, is *like* parabolically as well. Divinity may not only be *like* but may *be* these things in a different ontology of fluid multiplicity. How do we know? We know because we have begun to assume the posture of open-handedness and open-endedness that a logic of multiplicity engenders. We know because we are gradually becoming fluent in an ontological dialect of fluidity, porosity, a-centered relation, nomadic generativity, promiscuous love, and impossible exchange, to name just a few, for starters. These are the kind of ontological notions that recognize the fertile incompleteness in theological reflection, that find rich beginnings-again in old biblical texts, that never tire of the ancient stories, tragic-and-comic, of seekers after divinity. These are some proximal marks of divine multiplicity. Let us now turn to those marks in more detail.

11 Divine multiplicity . . .

Instead of considering it—as you always do—a sign of death, can you not hear some summons to life in that something which melts within you?

Luce Irigaray[1]

Out of earth comes water; out of water, soul.

Heraclitus[2]

This quest to imagine divinity in more richly present terms than the logic of the One has ever afforded has brought us to the nitty-gritty: to the proposition-making center of the project. Here we attempt to "speak in stones" which means weaving together the necessary skepticism of the metaphoric exemption with the equally necessary claim-staking description of experiential confession. The metaphoric exemption demands caution whenever we attempt to say anything direct or descriptive of God while experiential confession demands that we say something specific and fleshy about the incarnate divinity embedded in Christian stories of faith. Porous exchange between skepticism and affirmation—between words and stones and stories and bodies—leads to divine multiplicity.

In *Re-Imagining the Divine*, I argued strenuously for a methodology in constructive theology that takes both metaphoric exemption and experiential confession utterly seriously as counter-balancing correctives in theological construction.[3] It is good to remember that thought alone cannot encompass the divine in reality, just as how-to manuals cannot, in the end, achieve alone the ends that they illustrate. This is the metaphoric exemption: *everything we think or say, teach or proclaim, believe or catechize, is not God, not the Deep, not multiplicity, not enough.* Everything, "Ground of Being," "Tehom," "God," "Dear Lord and Father of Mankind," "Logos," "One," "Divine Multiplicity," misses the mark in some way. All are incomplete; each is a metaphor. And, yet, something that so many call *God* comes. Divinity responds and shifts into shape, is born under stars of longing, is washed in rivers of connection, touches a wounded body here, a shredded heart there, walks, thirsts, and learns, rises up, is broken like bread, slips through the open door of death, returns. What are we to do with this God, these Gods, who come? The metaphoric exemption, I have argued, is a step toward multiplicity because it refuses, finally, to say. It refuses dogmatism and militates against the hubris of canonical control. It reminds us of our place in the vast flux of what is. It is the metaphoric exemption that reminds us that we, theologians and dreamers of God, are not God just because we are a noisy dream of God. But the metaphoric exemption alone cannot abide the *thereness* of Gods who come: the intimacy and reality of them.

And, so, the metaphoric exemption is only part of the story. Experiential confession is also, at the very same time, true as flesh. We cannot *know* the depth of the divine that comes, we cannot ever grasp it. And yet we are met on the dusty road by divinity itself, prosaic and thirsty, and may even come to know that we have met God. How can this be so? How can God—"that than which nothing greater can be conceived" as Anselm so grandly phrased it in the twelfth century—be *here*, intimate and dismissible as the touch of fog, poor and prosaic enough to mistake for a city gardener in a cemetery? How can human beings come theologically to understand this apparent contradiction?

As I suggested in the introduction to this book, it is this question that exposes the metaphoric limitations of the logic of the One. At the same time, the Christian claim of incarnation goes to far greater depths than the architects of Christian empire could allow. There is really no contradiction between God and gardener, not if divinity is freed from the conceptual constraints of Pythagorean stasis, shored up by patriarchal exclusivity. There is no contradiction, in other words, if we can imagine God to be big enough to break the laws of the theologians, to incarnate *freely*, to respond, again and again, in the flesh of the world. And so, what are the characteristics of such divinity, if not the traditional negative exile of infinity, otherness, stasis, and absolute oneness? With the proper caution of the metaphoric exemption, we cannot declare a thing but, with the urgency of experiential confession, we can gesture, take up a swimmer's posture of buoyancy and openness, begin the story ... again. It is experiences and stories of the world and cosmos itself, of star showers, wind, rain, rock, life, and death that give clues to the divinity that comes, creates, and dares trespass on the theologians' negations with its buoyant "nevertheless." What follows are therefore positive gestures that dare an ontological brush stroke of kataphasis, a limning of advent.

Postures of fluidity and fluency

Divine multiplicity is first and foremost characterized by fluidity which means it is characterized by change. The story of the unnamed woman who leaves her well-water vessel for Jesus at Jacob's well and the story of rising waters that accompany the four Old Ones in *Green Grass, Running Water* certainly suggest fluidity both in terms of actual water and in terms of a deep, flowing, earthy truth about closures that are openings, endings that are beginnings.

The fluidity that elementally, tehomically, persists in desert wells, in ice, in roving rhizomes, and even in stones is inexorable and powerful. It cannot, in the end, be dammed or damned; the waters always return but with a difference. And when they do, Coyote, that pagan poet, is usually somewhere in the background, maybe getting ready to speak a few syllables of stony earth, maybe quietly masquerading as an almost forgotten water jug.

It falls to reason that a logic of multiplicity that is a posture or a dialect (rather than a pronouncement or a specific content) is fundamentally fluid, fluent, or supple. In turn, such suppleness implies a deferral, a difference that cannot resolve questions of "is" or "isn't" in any absolute sense, including the is-ness or isn't-ness of God. From within a posture of multiplicity, any theory that attempts closure on the story of reality, or that attempts to theorize a totality—even if that totality is called God—is inane. It is as if asserting that the grammar of a local dialect is the rule of speech everywhere. Just because a local dialect is not spoken or intelligible everywhere does not mean that it is not true or intelligible when and where there is someone to hear and respond to it. This is the issue at the heart of divine multiplicity. Can Christian theology weave together the necessary skepticism of the metaphoric exemption with the equally necessary chaos of experiential confessions of divine presence and in so doing release its dogmatics of divine otherness into a promiscuity of response and embodiment in the ever changing dialects of reality? Might divinity be responsive like an idiom, specific and local like a dialect? Might theology thereby articulate localized concepts, language, and practices of faith that assume postures of fluency rather than mastery? Or will the jealous, Constantinian desire to secure the presence and meaning of the divine in a universal dialect of reality foreclose any real ability, in the end, for theology to hear and respond to divine comings-among-us?

Fluency in the literal sense of language is not a bad analogy for what I am trying to say about divine multiplicity as elemental fluidity. It exposes a difference between a foreclosing mastery of *ontos* rooted in stasis, and a supple posture required for *thinking* divine multiplicity. Becoming fluent enough in a new language to fully participate in normal conversation is quite a different—and more difficult—task than the more preliminary one of mastering correct grammar, pronunciation and vocabulary. Even native speakers, masters of their own language, are always still becoming-fluent. There is no final attainment of fluency as there might be of grammatical mastery. Becoming-fluent requires an "ear" for the language. This implies a certain openness to gaps between words, the porous nature of language even as it is coming into speech. Listening en route to becoming-fluent is a learning to hear differently that goes far beyond one-for-one vocabulary comparison or obedience to grammatical rules. And fluency requires attention to more than spoken languages as body gestures and contexts figure in as well. Good translators seldom rely on mere mastery. We might call becoming-fluent a posture of attention, a willingness to enter into a flow of language that is ever shifting, diving into language without much of a net, without mechanical or predictable outcomes. Anyone who has sought such conversational fluency in a new language knows that entering such a stream takes the courage of fools and the generosity of listeners.

Becoming-fluent in a language usually happens in surprising ways, and those who insist on didactic or mechanical methods of learning language seldom do become fluent enough to get a joke or hear the multiple levels of a story. And those who insist on language as a content that can be encompassed in knowledge, rather than a mode, also have less chance at becoming fluent. They do not risk the flow of language because they are too frightened to give up a posture of certainty that puts its faith in the laws of grammar. But who among native speakers ever consistently follow grammatical rules? Native speakers break the rules of their own languages often *in order to communicate,* rather than in a failure of communication. Language is alive and always under revision as it rolls around the wet tongues and lips of human speech. Fluency is never complete or total, but is instead made possible by the malleability and porosity of language, for fluency is a posture of engagement and contribution rather than a data set.

That is why the logic of multiplicity—and so divinity ontologically approached by that logic—is fluid and unable to aspire to a reductive "theory of everything." It is a mode toward fluency, a lens through which we might better understand our own relationship to divinity that comes among us to be divine, to be real. Divine multiplicity is a serious, mature, tehomic theory of incarnation that is also a way of knowing, or what Marcella Althaus-Reid might call a "contextual epistemology."[4] A certain maturity, a dispensing with nostalgic rules and comforting narratives of control, is required to assume a posture of multiplicity that might glimpse through the masquerade of icy doctrinal foundations a divine incarnation, god-beginning-to-be-with-us ... again.

Maturity in theology is no small challenge. Immanuel Levinas argued, in his reflections on Judaism after the Holocaust, that he had become interested only in a Judaism for adults; a faith that does not pander to the immature psychological needs of children to be assured that their guardians will keep all harm at bay.[5] With the twentieth century a close and stark reminder of the failure of that kind of God to keep faith with that kind of demand, Levinas concluded that faith could only be possible in the face (literally) of fragility. Such faith meets no developmental needs for security or comfort. It has grown up or is, always, growing up.

Growing up is not a linear process, and all too often "grown-up" refers to a bourgeois conformity rather than wisdom or maturity. It might be more helpful to use the lens of queer theory as Kathryn Bond Stockton does, and talk of "growing sideways," to avoid the illusion of untangled progress.[6] Or we might do better to understand "grown" from a Womanist perspective. One of the classic definitions of a Womanist from Alice Walker's famous litany is that a Womanist is a Black woman who is "grown," meaning, in essence, that she faces the world as it is without cowering, without acquiescing to the white fantasy that she submit or disappear.[7] She has learned the hard way not to expect protection. With one eye on her people and one on the North Star, she lets go of neither. "Grown" in Walker's sense is, unlike for Levinas, about claiming a presence in a world that would deny it rather than facing up to the failures of the fantasy God who was supposed to protect and avenge. Both arguments for maturity have something to do with the virtue of taking responsibility for the riskiness and ambiguity of being in a terribly big world that has proven itself over and over again to be unreliable in the matter of the protection of Jews or of Black women. For Levinas, this growing up means a recognition at last that God cannot be the mighty fortress. For Walker, it means the ability a Black woman must have to "love herself, regardless" and not waiting for external approval. For both, the actual world in all of its ambiguity, change, betrayal, and abundance calls for another logic, one that need not skip over tremendous losses but carries the lost in its flow, a logic that is not frozen in fantasies of absolute power or absolute nihilism.

If a principle mark of divine multiplicity is the fluidity of the Deep, then theologians of the Deep must be willing to dispense with the fantasies of a religion for the emotionally immature. The waters of the deep shift shape, adapt, flow, and suspend alike the God Who Is and the Gods Who Aren't. There is a both/and dimension to fluidity which, in resisting closure or finality, also fails at fulfilling narcissistic fantasies of protection and revenge. The God Who Does Not Change is the fantasy lover who will never age, never look away, never betray. Facing change, even in divinity, requires courage and emotional maturity. It took emotional maturity for Christians to accept the Copernican idea that the universe was not geocentric (and some still have not done so!), and later, to accept that the known universe is not even heliocentric. Just as a child has to shift its emotional posture in order to transform its primary narcissism into humor and openness toward the world and so grow up, Christian theology has yet to transform its view of divinity away from a narcissistic One into a grown-up, open, worldly encounter with flowing divinity. This takes emotional maturity.[8] Fluidity, fluency, change. As Catherine Keller has so richly traced it, water's flux and fertility is the starting point of a concept of divine multiplicity. But, still, there is more that needs to be said ontologically about divine multiplicity beyond this. In addition to the alliterative play of fluidity, fluency, flux, and fertility that depth and water so richly evoke, there is porosity, heterogeneity, acentered relation and beginning, again. Let us now look at these gestures of description, in turn.

Postures of porosity and interconnection

Once, years ago, in 1972 to be precise, when I seemed to have been another person, related to the person I am now as one is related, tangentially, sometimes embarrassingly, to cousins not seen for decades,—once, when we were living in London, and I was very sick, I had a mystical vision. That is, I "had" a "mystical vision"—the heart sinks: such pretension—or something resembling one. A fever-dream, let's call it. It impressed me enormously and impresses me still, though I've long since lost the capacity to see it with my mind's eye, or even, I suppose, to believe in it. There is a statute of limitations on "mystical visions" as on romantic love.

I was very sick, and I imagined my life as a thread, a thread of breath, or heartbeat, or pulse, or light, yes it was light, radiant light, I was burning with fever and I ascended to that plane of serenity that might be mistaken for (or is, in fact) Nirvana, where I had a waking dream of uncanny lucidity—

My body is a tall column of light and heat.

My body is not "I" but "it."

My body is not one but many.

My body, which "I" inhabit, is inhabited as well by other creatures, unknown to me, imperceptible—the smallest of them mere sparks of light.

My body, which I perceive as substance, is in fact an organization of infinitely complex, overlapping, imbricated structures, radiant light their manifestation, the "body" a tall column of light and blood-heat, a temporary agreement among atoms, like a high-rise building with numberless rooms, corridors, corners, elevator shafts, windows ... In this fantastical structure the "I" is deluded as to its sovereignty, let alone its autonomy in the (outside) world; the most astonishing secret is that the "I" doesn't exist!—but it behaves as if it does, as if it were one and not many.

In any case, without the "I" the tall column of light and heat would die, and the microscopic life-particles would die with it ... will die with it. The "I," which doesn't exist, is everything.

Joyce Carol Oates[9]

What does it mean to betray the secret—ill-disguised and ever more brittle in the imaginary modern worlds of the One—that each of us, human, thing, blue jay, world, or god is actually *porous* and so never singular, never "one"? A person may be intellectually or abstractly aware, for example, that single human bodies are vast tenements of shared life—there are bacteria residing in the digestive system without whose presence a painful death surely results. There are parasites and other squatters who may or may not pay rent in some beneficial way. And there are others, "mere sparks of light" that pass into bodies, constitute them, and pass out of bodies, nomads of galaxies.

Academically speaking, the actual boundaries of bodies are never static, they are in states of constant flux, a "temporary agreement among atoms." The aggregate of flesh that is prosaically and for social and political purposes considered "my body," for example, does not account for the wide swath of body (skin cells, hair, microscopic tissue carried on the winds of breath) that swirls around, away, and sometimes indiscriminately enters neighboring bodies in passing. Are those cells and bits, loaded with DNA, some of which have instructions to reproduce should they land in the right environment, no longer the body they came from because they have traversed some imaginary boundary? If not, and if all bodies are constantly receiving others, then how is anyone's body his or her own to begin with? This process of flux and exchange characterizes bodies from conception, and in this light even start/genesis/origin must come to mean something other than an absolute beginning or end; it must mean that we are always much more than the convention of body-self, and less than it, as well.

Incarnation, divine multiplicity, or *real* divinity, is necessarily characterized by this becoming-porous and interconnected in the world. God-with-us cannot be wholly an abstraction, at least not for those Christians who are willing to take up the doctrine of incarnation in a serious way. The fleshiness of God lies at the heart of the Christian Jesus, at the heart therefore of all that makes the teachings of Christians meaningful and coherent. It is appropriate, therefore, for a Christian dialect of divine multiplicity to start with flesh, with the characteristics of being-and-becoming world. Bodies, whether of humans or of stars, are always in a state of exchange. "Becoming," Rosi Braidotti suggests, "is the actualization of the immanent encounter between subjects, entities, and forces which are apt mutually to affect and exchange parts of each other in a creative and non-invidious manner."[10]

A dialect of porosity is hybrid; it is a divine Spanglish or Camborican. It is powerful Native elders paradoxically named Ishmael and the Lone Ranger; it is water that is wine; it is a pagan poet guide through Christian metaphysics; it is human and divine. Bodies, whether human or not, like cultures and languages, are porously open to each other. Boundaries exist, but they exist temporally and spatially, meaning that they are always in a state of emerging and passing away. Incarnate divine being, therefore, resists univocity just as all bodies resist univocity. Braidotti calls this way of thinking an "eco-logic."[11] The more closely you look at any body, culture, language, or religion, boundaries blur, categories falter between a so-called entity and its environment, between an entity and its past, present, and future, between an entity and the story/stories that enliven it.

Characteristic of and fundamental to a logic of multiplicity, these proposed postures of porosity and interconnection suggest that reality is fundamentally open. Entities are temporal and temporary, always in elemental relation. Human beings are related to every other creature, not only through the texts of DNA that they share with animals and plants, but through the energy that flows into and through them, from mustard seeds to stars. Boundaries between entities are proximal, creative, and temporary. This temporariness is difficult for a humanity bred on fear of flux.

Rilke is right; we live forever taking leave because we live in change, but are unable to accept it, unable to look upon, see, or be what he calls in that same poem, "the Open." From the first lines of the "Eighth Elegy," he contrasts our inability to face the Open to that of "die Kreatur," translated here by Edward Snow as "the animal world":

> With all its eyes the animal world
> beholds the Open. Only our eyes
> are as if inverted and set all around it
> like traps at its portals to freedom.
> What's outside we only know from the animal's
> countenance; for almost from the first we take a child
> and twist him round and force him to gaze
> backwards and take in structure, not the Open
> that lies so deep in an animal's face[12]

It is indeed true that loss, even Heidegger's "being-toward-death," is what a posture of multiplicity entails. But, as Hannah Arendt suspected, "being-toward-death" is not the whole of it, even though it is the passing-away that mesmerized and still mesmerizes the mostly male European philosophers willing to take up and entertain the possibility of a more fluid ontological imagining. Becoming, Arendt proposed all too briefly, is also "the miracle that saves the world," namely, natality.[13] Natality—the "new start"—is open and as inexorable as death. The natal in fact *is* death when reality is One because the natal is the substance of change. Within a logic of the One the natal is incomprehensible, it is a blank. And yet that which comes—the Advent—also forever passes away. In this Heidegger was exactly right. Being is not still. That which *is* is always "toward death." The angst of Eurocentric thought is that it cannot take a still shot of the real, to frame, own, and assess. The philosopher sees only loss here, the theologian a "call to courage."

In terms of divine multiplicity as porosity, however, perhaps we can think of becoming as "death-and" or as "birth-but." Unlike the logic of the One, the logic of multiplicity is an openness that is not blank because it is not mesmerized by possession but is poised for passage, for shape-shifting. Just as porosity is meaningless in a void, multiplicity must be an affirmation of what is, even as the pores of what *is* receive and exchange possibility, and in so doing shift and pass away. A posture of divine multiplicity must not get stuck either in a paralytic stupor over that which is always already inexorably (and heartbreakingly) passing away, or in a naïve embrace of what is always already to-come, an "eternal sunshine of a spotless mind." Both positions resist openness, both oppose the "is" and the "isn't" as if the passing-away does not constitute the coming or as if being does not constitute its own absence. Mary Daly charged Paul Tillich of necrophilia in his favoring—to the point of obsession, perhaps—the angst of existential non-being over wonder at beings that surge all around. She argued, years ago, for a posture of multiplicity that she called "biophilia," charging the theologians of existentialism with too little love of life *lived*, mourning instead what they could not hold on to, or control. The "Verb of verbs," as she described divinity early in her philosophical career, is an ontological expression of existence-in-flux that demands openness to the new even as what is now passes away.[14] And Keller adds, "Let us draw the tehomic inference: the God who is not a Being does not exist over against nonbeing, as the opposite of nothing."[15]

The natal Open is also the porous Deep. Keller names three "capacities"—*implicatio, complicatio, explicatio*—for the tehomic divine that, following Deleuze, she takes from the medieval theologians Giordano Bruno and Nicholas of Cusa. *Implicatio* refers to the creative, interconnected fluidity of the Deep.[16] She discusses the *plis*—fold—at the etymological heart of the three terms, which I take to be more like the folding of batter than the folding of sheets, though I would hate to diminish the potency of such rich language through an overly tedious translation. Porosity, I want to suggest, is related to this provocative suggestion of Keller's—the porousness of the divine is, in the dialect of multiplicity, a kind of open *"implication,"* an unfolding, complicating interconnection that confounds the One–Many divide. It is also suggested by what Thich Nhat Hanh calls "interbeing."

> But before the sun entered me,
> the sun was in me—
> also the cloud and the river.
> Before I entered the river,
> I was already in it.
> There has not been a moment
> When we have not *inter-been*.[17]

As the poet implies, I am only proximally distinct from the sun—I implicate the sun and the sun implicates me as a temporary and vital assemblage (as Deleuze would call it) of its energy and light. The sun folds itself into me, and I radiate it back out, shape-shifting into hot breath, the motor of a muscle, spirit, some new relation. Unities are therefore proximal because they are temporary, porous agreements among atoms, atoms that expand communally into unfinished totalities made up of ever new connections, thereby making possible—implicating—yet new configurations and possibilities. Irigaray writes that "openness permits exchange, ensures movement, prevents saturation in possession or consumption."[18] The more closely and carefully biologists and physicists look with their ever more capable and sensitive tools of observation, the more each "one"—each "I"—emerges as a nexus of exchanges, constituted by those exchanges rather than tolerating or enduring them. This deeply interactive, relational quality of existence undercuts the coherence of the isolatable self—revealing it to be a useful fiction—and makes unlikely even the usefulness of the theological fiction of an absolute, isolatable, and solitary God. But, as we already know, fictions are not the opposite of truth: stories build worlds.

And so there is no absolute impassibility, no categorical distinction between what can be called God and what can be called world. The mistake that most theologians make at this point is to assume that without a categorical, substantive distinction between God and world then nothing is "left" for God but the world, and we face the tired straw man of pantheism, as if a word that literally means "everything-god" makes meaningful distinction between things and between events theologically impossible. But that is the case only within the confines of the logic of the One. Empirical experience demonstrates over and over again constant emergence and so constant differentiation, or what Deleuze more helpfully calls "disjunctive synthesis." When we dispense at last with stasis as a requirement for the divine or for truth, ontology thaws and *flows*, constituted by porous *relation*, and in relation *expressing* time. Such flow and relation, which can only "be" in time (or, as I prefer to put it, which express time) therefore necessitate and implicate real distinction and difference, for the time-being. Events, things, God/s, world/s, occur and so unfold, or *explicate*, difference. But, ontologically speaking, such difference or distinction is never static, never categorical, never forever. "Do not cling to me," the Johannine Jesus says to Mary as she stumbles into his arms in the Bible's most stunning moment of recognition—he was dead! He was the gardener? He said her name!? He is time-being there, as is she (but her time-being is not the point of the story) and will not stay fixed, will not fix the story or, and this is good news, fix her grief. He is about to begin ... again, as is she, and clinging will, well, fix nothing. How did church theology miss this? Baby primates will die if they do not cling to the fur of the parent ... for a time. But, conversely, the time comes when they will die if they do not let go. Theologians have tended to forget that categorical distinctions and absolutes are conveniences; they are not the world, not incarnation.

Multiplicity is a dialect of porous openness, implicating a divinity that is streaming, reforming, responding, flowing, and receding, beginning ... again. Another way to look at this is that God inter-courses ... promiscuously. Divine promiscuity is an economy of "more-than-enough" but it is also a negative gesture. There is no "control" that doctrine can place on divinity, especially in the theory-resistent multiplicity of divine immanence. No amount of caution or puritan restraint will protect from divine trespass, which occurs without regard for scruples in the bump and grind of the world passing through us, taking us along. This is a resolutely dirty conception of God; an imagining of divinity in thoroughly Christian terms of incarnation and solidarity but requiring the maturity not to "cling." The tehomic depth of God, imagined metaphorically in terms of promiscuous intercourse, takes no precautions and precludes no conceptions. This divine multiplicity complicates every relation with an "I am with you" and unfolds, or explicates, every relation with some "new thing."

Divinity, in this sense, comes to *be* in flesh, since in a dialect of multiplicity reality is cosmic intercourse and flow, the everywhere intimate proximity of boundaries constantly give way to touch and trespass. There is always more to be said, more to be given away, more to lose, more to receive—and so, more to become. Here Nancy's notion of being as "being-with" is a way of saying that reality always implicates a relation and there is excess in every relation. To "be" can only mean, he concludes, to "be-with." And, as Catherine LaCugna argues, this is precisely what Christians must mean by the doctrine of the Trinity, at least if we consider that metaphor to be truly reflective of God. The self-sufficiency that classical trinitarian doctrines claim for God cohere, in reality at least, only as a *social* plenitude. World is not separate from that divine sufficiency, indeed it is the very embodiment, the result, of divine being-with.[19]

Jürgen Moltmann goes in much the same direction when he argues that God, for Christian theology anyway, *begins* in the flesh and the pathos of incarnate connection. *This* God, he reasons, is wholly dependent upon the particular enfleshment of Jesus. This is different than what follows from the formulation developed in the Augustinian trajectory through European Reform theology, that enfleshment is wholly dependent on God. The difference lies, perhaps, in Moltmann's own closer relation to Luther than to Calvin. Because he starts with the cross, he cannot work his way to omnipotence as a meaningful expression of *Christian* theology. It is on the cross that divine presence *in the flesh* is revealed. Without that being-flesh of God, he argues, there is no Christian divinity.[20] It is in the irreducible and intimate reality of bodies that God—the Divine—has any reality at all. Without *divine* body, there is only a principle of being or of becoming. Without the depth of interconnection and porosity that makes Jesus of Nazareth a truly human, fleshly reality, *there is no God*, not for Christians anyway. And there is nothing except imperial church fears in the form of later ecclesial doctrines that require a limitation on this incarnation. Indeed, the limitation of incarnation to one man is a product of imperial fears about ecclesial control and more intimate human fears, or jealousies, of divine intercourse with flesh.

Divine multiplicity follows from incarnation. It is a direct result of a theology of the cross, just as it is a direct result of a theology of the manger. The very body, birth, and execution of Jesus, taken seriously as aspects of divine incarnation, are themselves critiques of narrow doctrines that limit divine flesh to a principle of One because bodies always manage to exceed and subvert such rules. Divine multiplicity, in other words, *makes sense*.

12 ... In a world of difference

divine infinity takes *place*; it *materializes*.

Catherine Keller[1]

Then Pilate said to him, "Do you not hear how many accusations they make against you?" But he gave him no answer, not even to a single charge

The Gospel according to Matthew 27:13–14a

Fluidity, porosity, and interconnection, all of which I have argued are characteristics of divine multiplicity, can be only part of the story. Fluidity is slippery, interconnection and porosity blur boundaries—these characteristics swamp all positive claims, all doctrines, in a soup of flux and so revert to oneness. Every statement dissolves the minute you take it up, like water laughing at the grasping fist. Fluidity, porosity, and interconnection are positive claims about divinity. They describe, if partially, some ontological marks of divinity, but they also support the metaphoric exemption, the reminder that whatever we say, proclaim, or describe of the divine is also a deferral, a not-quite-that, a moreless.

And, so, the boundary-blurring slippages of fluidity, porosity, and interconnection do not tell enough of the story. I have said, from the beginning of this book, that God comes, shape-shifts into distinct presences, meets the world in real time, is incarnate, again and again. Fluidity, porosity, and interconnection all help us to get to a place of understanding where such presence can, however you choose to interpret the phrase, *make sense*. And so, in addition to the tehomic complexities and surges that intimately implicate divinity (without exception) in the world, there is also heterogeneity in divinity that, however you choose to interpret the phrase, *makes a difference*.

Heterogeneity, another word for elemental difference, asserts and affirms the positive differences that occur in the world, allowing the basic aspects of space and time to "matter" in real bodies, in their expressive, irreducible, meaning-making comings and goings. Without attention to the heterogeneity and otherness that divine multiplicity requires—that is created in its unfolding articulation of change, its *explicatio*—our concept of divinity will slip its moorings, once again, from the curious scandal of actual embodiment.[2] Without attention to difference, to worlds of difference, any concept of divine multiplicity characterized by fluidity is fully capable of reinventing a sort of Docetism, one that, while allowing a material basis to divinity (which Docetic devotees in the early centuries of Christian theology did not), nevertheless disallows any distinction *in* matter and so achieves the same Docetic, body-denying result. Either way—by flight or flood—actual bodies in all of their irreducible uniqueness and singularity disappear, along with any real hope for incarnational theology.

In several ways now I have indicated that bodies as such have largely gone missing in the history of European and Euro-American theological thought. One of the principle reasons that this is so, despite the nominal claim that dominant Christian theology makes for incarnation, is that bodies as such resist abstraction and so cannot be entirely exchanged with or replace one another. This means that, in their specific occurrence, bodies themselves resist classification in philosophical-ideal, political, or ecclesial systems. In a logic of oneness and stasis, the difference between bodies is negative and can only be named through reference to a standard, or an identity. So only through disappearance into types (male, say, or Roman) can bodies *seem* to appear. The Christian notion of incarnation, to the extent that the term "incarnation" does not get hijacked into another abstraction of real body from divinity, is therefore a pesky and resilient problem within the logic of the One. What to do with the singularity of Jesus' *body?* What to do with the singularity of his *divinity?* How shall we conceive of divinity that becomes particular and momentary, as all bodies do? His silence before Pilate, I will argue a little further on, gives us a clue if we tell the stories right (at least for this time-being).

Gestures of divine heterogeneity, for the time-being

Bodies occur, and so they generate or express space, and time. As physicists have pointed out for generations, matter, space, and time all implicate each other and mean nothing (quite literally) without each other. Space unfolds time out of itself, traced by matter. Or matter rolls space out along its nomadic lines of flight, conjuring time in the gaps. Or time is the story of space stretched into body. "For me," Irigaray writes, "infinity means movement, the mobility of place. Engendering time, yes. Always becoming."[3]

To talk of divinity outside of time and space (and therefore of matter) is to talk of emptiness. Outside of time, space, and matter there is no *via negativa*, no "greater than," there is only *nihil*, nothing. *Real* divinity, real God, matters. And matter without space and time is also nothing, it expresses no difference. Space without body has no place, and so no space. It has no occurrence, and so no time. Space, place, time, occurrence—all the building blocks of matter—constitute bodies by casting the horizons of space through matter and time as the space within space, as distance, for example, or as the intervals of change. And because intervals of change make space and describe matter, incarnation is a revelation of divinity-in-flux. This is an ontology, not of "is" but, as Deleuze and Guattari suggest, of "and."[4] Bodies exceed the "is" in every occurrence *because* of their implication, expression, and movement into and out of place and moment. Outside of bodies, which means outside of space, time and the matter that expresses them, there is no "and," and so, ironically, no "is" either. "Is" by itself contains no change, it is stasis and so *is*-not. This suggests that divinity must matter to be real and to exist, which means it bodily occurs and so is always becoming multiple, excessive, "*and.*"

Divine multiplicity, in other words, comes to body, to being, differently every "time," in every instance of incarnation. Perhaps an example may illustrate what I mean. Let's say that a person is cloned at conception and raised with the clone-twin in identical fashion, even given the same name, "Martha." In the realm of generalizations, there is literally nothing to distinguish the two Marthas apart. In that realm they are exchangeable for one another. Their pictures are identical. Their fingerprints are identical. They are, for all intents and purposes *as clones* exchangeable for each other. So what is their difference? They occupy different places in space. If they increase the spatial distance between them, sit playing in different rooms with different children, say, they must begin to react to different stimuli and begin, imperceptibly, to change. They *are* different, although there is no standard means of generalization that can account for the difference. The difference occurs and forms in each one's bodily connections and travels in the world.

Despite the sameness between them, Martha and Martha *occur* distinctly, and no one could therefore say that they are *completely* the same, able to be wholly exchanged for one another. They differ from one another, change one another even, by the fact of their distinct expressions of space and so of time. Their multiplicity is a differing occurrence in the world. They alter the world, making heterogeneous difference in the world, for all that is technically alike between them. Much the same is true for the two maples growing outside of my library window. And for the river stones on my shelf, rubbed down from the same boulder that once broke across the back of a glacier. All of the similarities between bodies can be compared, but can they be replaced by or *exchanged* for each other, no matter what their internal or external likeness? No.

Writing about grief after an animal's death, Vicki Hearne writes "In over a quarter of a century of [animal] training, I have never met an animal who turned out to be replaceable. Dick Koehler says, 'Hell, even trees are irreplaceable, but we don't know it, and *that* is our loss.'"[5] One crocus blindly muscling itself against the frozen ground in defiance of late winter storms, as crocuses ever have done, is like every other crocus that ever thrust its pretty fist into the cold air. But, at the same time, it is not every other crocus. Its emergence is its own, no other's. And should it lose its gamble against the ice, no other crocus, no matter how lovely or similar, can void the loss.

As I have already argued, the logic of the One cannot abide the difference that bodies make, and so abstracts bodies into classifications, types, and identities. This means that specific, always-differing-and-becoming bodies disappear over and over again in Christian theology and philosophy. Part of the issue has to do with the limitations that oneness places upon bodies which, as bodies, they have a penchant to resist. They don't stay still, unified, or One. Even the stillness of ancient hills is an illusion: they shift and eventually roll into the rivers that trace them. There is difference and differing in what it means to be bodied. As "temporary agreements among atoms," or as events that explicate space and so express time, bodies *become* difference and so create the world. Oneness falters in bodies, and that is the brilliant critique incarnation makes of dominant Christian theology! Right here, at the pulse of space-time explication in matter, the lamp in the One God projector begins to overheat and threatens to break down. There is no depth in that projection, no possibility of difference and so no possibility of creation. Unbodied, this is one hell of stasis. No-body's there. A projected coyote "dream of a big G O D" that cannot *be* any-body, enduring eternally, all hope slowly abandoned.[6]

Divine multiplicity, on the other hand, is all about the difference(s) that incarnation makes. Incarnation, divine becoming which is becoming-flesh, is a material event of distinction, a temporal and so temporary assemblage that *matters* both in the sense of expressing space and time, and in the sense of "making a difference." Every enfleshment, regardless of size or duration, accomplishes these two rather remarkable tasks of mattering. Bodies accomplish difference from other bodies, from the world, and even from themselves in their every particular becomings. Their becomings stretch shape and event and so express space and time in and through relation to other bodies' gravitational attraction. (I was once told by a colleague in physics that gravity is a description, not an explanation. It is the mysterious attraction that *all* bodies, no matter how massive or small, exert on one another.)

Bodies occur and in so doing make difference real. The simultaneous reality of worldly porosity and flux does not in any way diminish the heterogeneity that bodies accomplish now and then, again and again. The heterogeneity that characterizes divine multiplicity is not the neo-orthodox Wholly Other status of God and the world, but the irreducible difference incarnation makes in and of the world, over and over. Is this divine multiplicity then pantheism? It cannot be, for "*pan*," meaning "all," is another One, a totality. Divine multiplicity is not a totalizing All. Its own time-being (which is space-and-matter shaping) cannot be constrained by such a narrow limit as "everything." Divinity in the multiplicity of incarnation occurs with the freedom to come and to go: to fold into the Deep, a brooding implication; to unroll a surface of explicit presence; to strain out of the womb into a homeless, starry night; to weave gravitational complexities that we call communities, or worlds. "Of course," the Ojibwe elder chides, "rocks aren't alive. But some are."[7] Of course, we can remember, the divine is not reducible to *pan,* to the All, even if sometimes it is. For a moment perhaps. Divine multiplicity, in the marvel of incarnation, is not a principle but an occurrence. Occurrences. A distinction. Distinctions. Gravitational pull. Incarnation.

In a discussion of a published series of Kertész photographs that depict various people in various contexts who are reading, Dow Edgerton notes that, while critics complained that Kertész allowed his pictures to "talk too much," the problem may have been that

> the images refused to lose their particularity and pass over into a purely formal beauty ... The child in the doorway sprawled over a pile of torn papers reading the comics does not become 'everychild' but seems more and more *that* child: a presence, not a metaphor; an incarnation, not a form.[8]

Edgerton suggests that the picture, already an abstraction, offended the critics because it somehow resists the further abstractions of formal beauty that art is usually supposed to accomplish. It exposes too much *thereness,* too much particularity. The picture manages to point to something inexchangeable—*this* child—rather than something romantically exchangeable through or away from the child toward some idea, some generality, some "everychild." But even in its particularity, it pulls.

The reading child, Edgerton tells us, is "ripe with untold stories." The child in the photo resists simplification or unity because, he suggests, the untold stories are not intrinsic to the photo or the child but to the viewer: "the silent photograph pulls hard upon stories untold and unknown, stories which were unimagined until this picture came."[9] There is a relation between bodies, in other words, even bodies abstracted in a picture (or a story) and bodies nearby, looking, listening, thinking. To the extent that bodily particularity comes through even a picture or a story, the profound heterogeneity and inexchangeability of it also comes through. But the heterogeneity of bodies, which implies and explicates their irreducible otherness, is not in complete opposition to bodies' gravitational pull on other bodies. Fluid interconnection, including the generalized reductions of difference that language imposes (here is a "child" reading comics like I once read comics, like everychild would read comics if they could, right?) is not an either/or gambit concerning the absolute singularity of *this* child, this incarnational distinction *or* the gravitational pull, the likeness, the language.

Deleuze suggests that "Everywhere the differences between multiplicities and the differences within multiplicities replace schematic and crude oppositions. Instead of the enormous opposition between the one and the many, there is only the variety of multiplicity—in other words, difference."[10] So, the body cannot be generalized in what Heidegger calls its "enownness," in its own incarnation. But generalization—even the generalization that I am undertaking in this very discussion—nevertheless allows for new, hetero-geneous singularities, this time in the viewer, the reader, the listener, the companion, out of whom untold stories are pulled. It is not that bodies shouldn't be spoken of, generalized, and so abstracted (such that other specifics may emerge) but that incarnation resists both generalization and the either/or of body or thought ("language or the kiss" as the Indigo Girls sing it). Bodies incarnationally invite the Deleuzian ontology of "and."

Recently, two young American soldiers were kidnapped, tortured, and killed in the American-led war in Iraq. Their killing was brutal and, unlike the thousands of other soldiers and civilians lost, blown up, shot, and dis-membered in that murky prolonged assault, these two made headline news in the United States for a full week over the course of their disappearance and then reappearance as corpses. Both were soldiers. Both were cogs in a machine that fully anticipates "collateral damage," meaning the loss of human life. Such is the nature of the war mechanism, reflected in its mechanistic language. But, as the days passed, the particularity of each boy, in the form of stories and relations, pulled him from the indistinction of the military machinery. Each became more and more singular, the loss more and more painful even to those who had never met either one. The abstraction of their military identity, having given way to their indivi-duality as soldiers, gave way still further to two boys in their early twen-ties, which in turn gave way to stories of relation that differentiated these boys from all other soldiers, all other boys. Watching the news, it became impossible to regard them as anything but singular, each rolled out of a particular dough of family, neighborhood, deeds, and misdeeds. Over the course of the week they became for the watching millions what each had always been to their families: inexchangable for anyone else. In death, when they had no more function as soldiers, they emerged from the swamp of generality called "American soldier," and became distinct, took on body. Their loss became excruciating, their irreplaceability a hard knot through which the machinery of exchangeable soldiery cannot move.

Soldiers, children, and death, even more than the larger and more banal abstraction of war, bring home the heterogeneity that characterizes exis-tence, the hard and grievous irreplaceability of each instance. The impos-sible grief of a parent who must bury a child is made all the more impossible by the memory of sending off, however many months or years before, that very child into war, a sending off that cannot be exchanged for or completed by the funeral. A boy ripe with untold stories cannot be exchanged for any other boy coming home in a body bag. Only "soldiers" can be so exchanged. Faced with the utter immanence of these two lost individuals, it is their bodies, the fact of their occurrence, that makes a summing up into general terms impossible. The unfinished, untold stories keep multiplying. Their occurrences, their bodies, are unruly multiplicities.

And once a body makes an appearance, really arrives on the scene, there is no retreat or defense, no answer to give in exchange for its life, or its death.

Gilles Deleuze, "philosopher of immanence," realized early on that when he took up the topic of immanence he was talking about multiplicity. "Everything is a multiplicity," he wrote.[11] Thus, the backward pull into generality from real bodies is a pull into new multiplicities. As for the viewer of the pictures of the child reading and of the boy-soldiers, the child and soldiers in the pictures pulls hard on untold and unknown stories in the viewer. The child cannot be exchanged for everychild, the boys cannot be exchanged for soldiers, the viewer cannot but exchange something of each for an inexchangeable something in the viewer. In either case heterogeneity abounds, for particularity in the form of stories and relations, of occurrence in space and time, make the child, the viewer, the boy-soldier utter singularities.

This is a hard thought for one nurtured on monotheistic eschatologies that fantasize the end of all difference in the truth of God. But it is difficult only if difference is understood in transcendent rather than immanent terms.[12] A logic of multiplicity can find no sense in an end to difference just as it can find no sense in an end to porosity, although every body is also already ending, slipping through the open door of its time-being. And so divine multiplicity can make no eschatological promise of an end to difference, as if an end to difference is a promise and not a threat. The exchangeable *idea* of flesh founders on inexchangeable *instances* of flesh, even as bodily becoming is itself in flux, gradually exceeding its boundaries—deterritorializing—and emerging into some new body, some incarnational, ontological "*and.*"

Gestures of ethics and impossible exchange

In the midst of shape-shifting, as a human body ages and leans into gravity, beckoning the earth that will fold it back in, the change of youthful body into aged body into earth is not a transactional exchange of equivalence. The body that was "young" cannot take the place of the body that is now "old." To follow Jean Baudrillard's notion of impossible exchange, exchange entails replacement, like a dollar for a dollar. Nothing lost, nothing gained. Equivalence. "The uncertainty of the world," he points out, "lies in the fact that it has no equivalent anywhere; it cannot be exchanged for anything."[13] *Everything* is lost in bodies as they shift shape, especially the body-that-was. New worlds open up as the territory of youth is exceeded, literally out-grown, and rhizomically deterritorialized into a new country and new embodiments. But the new "age" does not replace the lost "youth" in the sense of exchange—they are not equivalent, and this is Baudrillard's point. This is not a nostalgia for what was, but rather a reflection on the absolute difference that comes from actual embodiment that particularizes space and time. No thing can ever be fully exchanged for or cancel out another thing. Actual bodies, in all of their eccentricity (and uncertainty, Baudrillard notes), are not finally reducible, either to each other or to the generalities that we verbal animals assign them in our own becoming-related and exchanging of stories. Always exceeding the limits of the word, incarnation is a becoming-different deferral of sameness, a multiplicity of heterogeneous, "impossible exchanges."

Jacques Derrida rightly observes that it is here that ethics finally fails. How can we assign value to the utterly unique and unexchangable? Or, in his words,

> what status must be assigned to this exemplarity of re-mark? How do we interpret the history of an example that allows the re-inscription of the structure of a universal law upon the body of an irreplaceable singularity in order to render it thus remarkable?[14]

When ethics is a metric of right and wrong it falls apart on the shores of bodies. There, where right and wrong have no basis of exchange, what is possible is *decision* and *responsibility,* but not any system of ethics. This is because of bodies. The impossibility of exchanging one body for another, one moment for another, one world for another means that each is, quite literally, *in*valuable and so inaccessible to systems, inaccessible to ethics.

Real, uncertain bodies, even those implied in pictures, call out to real, uncertain bodies. There is no exchange in their difference, but there is a pull. This is the mystery of multiplicity and the beauty of gravity. It is only when we forget the messy determinancy and eccentricity of actual bodies that we can indulge in the kind of ethics that presumes systems of comparative value, that can assign status and make exceptions, and that can exchange a not-guilty plea for a life wholly implicated in the complicated world. Assume, like Kant, that exchange is possible between actual bodies on the basis of their likeness and you can go on to assume systems of representation and rationalizations of identity upon which universal laws depend, indeed upon which the idea of the One God depends.

Immanuel Levinas famously argues in his reflection on ethics that it is the vulnerable face of the other which confounds any justification for violence, any universal or "objective" claim that in any way reduces the other to a category of person, or thing. "The face is an irreducible mode in which being can present itself in its identity."[15] The face of the other is irreducible. That face "does not appear in the nominative, but in the vocative"[16] and so is not even subject to naming, to generalization. Yet, the face gives itself away. To be other, to be distinct, itself, uncolonizable and inexchangeable, the face must be real (uncertain); it must be a body, and so gravitationally pull other bodies. The face of the child reading comics and of the smiling boy soldier now mutilated and dead each appear in the vocative; we cannot wholly reduce either to some likeness and so make him disappear again. But, lest heterogeneity sever the pathways of interconnection—cancel gravity—the vocative appearance of the uncolonizable face also lends itself generously to stories untold and unknown in the ones who see (or listen, or read, or attend), and so becomes a body: divine incarnation.

Exchange is impossible, and only a mature theology can acknowledge that and thereby acknowledge the utterly tragic dimension of incarnation, meaning its uncertainty and partiality. Baudrillard notes,

> everything which sets out to exchange itself for something runs up, in the end, against the Impossible Exchange Barrier. The most concerted, most subtle attempts to make the world meaningful in value terms, to endow it with meaning, come to grief on this insuperable obstacle.[17]

Without a logic of exchange—of finding equivalent value or meaning (and so no meaningful difference) between even similar things, between many ones—the world is incalculably more *there,* and so more poignantly sharp and heart-breaking. No one can be exchanged for another both because it is not another, but also because every one has already altered every other. *One* and *other* also fall apart in their own co-constitutiveness, their multiplicity.

Decisions must be made, but none is pure, none ethical. Kant's categorical imperative falls apart on the shores of actual bodies, none of which can in their momentary experience be exchanged for the universal "case" which, in any case, does not exist. Ontology *and* ethics come closer, in a logic of multiplicity, to stories which in turn have seasons. They never conclude, and we never get the telling quite right (though sometimes we do, for the time-being).

The singularity of Jesus

In one of the rare consistencies of the canonical Christian gospels, each includes the detail that, during the trial which led to his execution, Jesus refused to answer for himself. "But he gave ... no answer, not even to a single charge" (Matthew 27:14a). "But Jesus made no further answer" (Mark 15:5a). "He questioned him at some length, but Jesus gave him no answer" (Luke 23:9). Even the later, more voluble Johannine Jesus retains this refusal in Pilate's second round of questioning: "But Jesus gave no answer" (John 19:9b). Among those who measure such things, such consistency is a strong mark in favor of historical authenticity.

Why did Jesus refuse to defend himself? There are a number of possibilities, the simplest of which is that he had no defense, no answer for the charges. Bodies are always hard-pressed to defend themselves because their very existence always exceeds definition, or explanation. "For this I was born," Jesus says enigmatically to Pilate, according to the writer of John (18:37). Through the lens of incarnation, his refusal or inability to defend himself takes on a wonderful richness. Standing silent before Rome and Israel, Jesus effectively challenges all of the legal systems that depend upon a reduction of persons and events to modes of exchange, as if any answer he might give for himself could be exchanged for his deeds (or misdeeds) or especially for his life. His silence lifts up his own irreducibility—*the irreducibility of his embodiment*—to the charges laid against him. Jesus' silence refuses the empire's efforts to measure, dismiss, and cancel him. Having walked the dusty roads of Galilee and Israel, having taught, touched, healed, and loved, there is nothing that Pilate or Herod can do to him that can cancel out, nullify, or constitute an exchange for what he has legally or illegally been and done, for what he is and will be. The divine singularity of Jesus of Nazareth rests in the body, which can be killed, but not cancelled or exchanged.

Sadly, the backward lens of Nicene doctrine, through which we still mostly look at things nominally Christian, does not approach incarnation in such a positive way. Instead, imperial Christian leaders developed in Nicaea and Chalcedon a doctrine that nullifies Jesus' body even as it affirms his humanity. Accordingly, the dominant view passed down from the Church Fathers is that it is Jesus' absolute divinity and not his embodiment that determines his singularity. He alone is divine and human; all others are only human. His body—the human side of the Christological equation—therefore determines his *sameness* with all of humankind, not his utter singularity. This is a rejection of his actual, truly heterogeneous body (which actually constitutes his distinction from all other bodies, all other humans) in favor of a general, ideal, exchangeable body of sameness, which can therefore be only a pseudo-body.

Defined by the logic of the eternal One, the issue of Jesus' body absorbed much of the heat and pressure in the early Christian councils as they formulated what would become the core Christological doctrines of the church. The bishops needed the distinguishing mark of Christian faith—Jesus—to be ontologically different from all other human beings lest other humans attempt to usurp his divine authority. They also needed him to be enough the same to establish his redemptive solidarity with humanity. But to accomplish this, they navigated away from his actual human body, the most logical site of his uniqueness. Why? Heterogeneity is not unique to Jesus because that is what bodies are in their time-being. Any-body can claim absolute distinction since every-body is distinct, irreplaceable, marvelous. What is divine about Jesus, therefore, is not his embodiment. Divinity happens to the body, but body does not happen to divinity, or so the church steeped in the logic of stasis largely seems to have understood it.[18]

Likewise, the bishops agreed (after much quarreling and name-calling) not to locate Jesus' distinctiveness in his divinity alone: all of the gods competing across the Mediterranean world claimed such. No, the bishops instead constructed the *difference* of Jesus *between* his divinity and humanity, in the coexistence of the One God with humanity in Jesus' body. Curiously therefore, while preserving Jesus' body against the various Docetic factions who would deny his bodily existence altogether, this move also displaced the actual body and actual divinity of Jesus into ideal types. His body came to "stand in" for, to speak for all bodies; it lost its inexchangeable heterogeneity in the service of doctrine. His divinity remained the Oneness of the Eternal God. This early theological construction reduced the contradiction his porous, temporary body otherwise posed to the eternity of the One. It abstracted incarnation into a conjunction of types available to eternity: "fully human, fully divine."

But then there is that silent Jesus, refusing or unable to exchange a single word for his own life. The biblical texts report that Pilate never got his answer from Jesus, but it was provided centuries later in Nicaea and Chalcedon by theologians who could not let Jesus' refusals stand. Four times over we are explicitly told by the gospel writers that he gave no answer for himself, neither taking responsibility nor refusing it. Like Pilate and Herod, the church fathers sought an answer, this time not only for his life, but for his death as well. Like their Hellenistic forbears, they sought more than this troublesome silence, they sought an exchange for his body—a body that in simple presence made its mark and its difference on a world that can never *be* the same.

Under pressure to provide an interpretation that could build an imperial church, the bishops wanted an answer that could be exchanged for the irreducibly embodied man, that could convert his silence and the rich, inexchangeable *moment* and divine *presence* of it into the currency of doctrine that would sell Rome to the barbarian hinterlands. Declaring him "fully divine, fully human" at Nicaea, the bishops in effect made an answer for him; they spoke over his silence. They entered him into the very system he had refused to acknowledge, with a plea of "not-guilty by virtue of being God." They deferred his multiple, bodily complicity in order to construct and preserve the un-implicated, non-complicit stasis that they understood his full divinity to be. They also answered for his body, deferring it further by making it a "guilty" surrogate for all of humankind. In the hands of the theologians, the incarnation disappeared, leaving a bill of exchange.

From the post-Nicaean perspective of Jesus' oneness with the eternal, his silence is evidence only of the inscrutable plan of God for Jesus' surrogate death. But from the perspective of the utter singularity of the man who loved riddles, children, and his friends, it is not mysterious at all. There is no exchange that can be made for the fully complicit body that was Jesus' life. His life and death were his own and can be substituted for no others. Jesus' body-self is his divinely multiple uniqueness, and that is the scandal for those who prefer the noisy Coyote dream of the big G O D. The difference-making *occurrence* of Jesus, like the difference-making occurrence of your body-self or mine is what makes for our inexchangeability. This is why incarnation lies at the heart of divine multiplicity, or rather, why divine multiplicity is the revelation of incarnation. God *occurs*.

As a revelation of divinity, Jesus' occurrence is a "mattering" of time, dependent on webs of relation and timely placements that also occur through relation and in relation to other placements, other matters of difference. Divine multiplicity is therefore characterized by the utter singularity of incarnation in its timely occurrence and recurrence. Temporality and spatiality make for singularity. Jesus was a singular divine incarnation, not because he was the One God in a single Everyman coat, but because divinity unfolded in his limbs into utter complicity in the world—as divinity ever does. "Jesus" is a multiplicity, not just because he is a story, but because, as a man, he had a body and so he exceeded the narrow limits of oneness; he himself was legion. As Luce Irigaray asks, "is the body always the same? Can we fix it in one self-same form? Does it not wither when it has to keep to one appearance? Is not mobility its life?"[19] How could he then answer to the charges arrayed against him? How could anyone, really?

"Are you King of the Jews?" Pilate asks him, looking for a jurisdictional frame of reference from which he could proceed with judgment, make some kind of exchange. But the writer of Matthew (and Mark, and Luke, and even John, with a little characteristic elaboration[20]) reports that Jesus only replies with "You have said so."[21] Jesus stands there, divinely multiple and so unable to exchange himself for an answer. The divinity that he incarnates and reveals is therefore not a principle of existence, a "ground of being" or an abstract "lure" or essence of life. It is not an "all," not a system. Divine multiplicity occurs and is guilty of embodiment, guilty, therefore, of difference. It is guilty of the silence that comes from being present, truly *present*.

The Constantinian bishops, bless their hearts, made a lot of errors, but that's what greedy, eager, overconfident Coyote does whenever he tries to tell the story of creation. (But that's how creation happens, according to the Native American keepers of Coyote stories.) In their efforts to construct Christian doctrine they did in fact seek to preserve the incarnation— when they could just as easily have pursued a Manichean or Docetic path and denied outright the humanity of Jesus' divinity. But they did not. Quite the opposite, even though in doing so they processed in heavy clerical solemnity right over Jesus' silence. Even though they displaced the utter singularity of his bodily occurrence with an exchangeable currency of human generality.

Important as the idea of Jesus' body as an exchange for all human guilt is to the doctrine of atonement, this error grounded in the One is not the "pivot" on which divine incarnation rests. Indeed, incarnation fully resists such surrogacy; it is silent and cannot accomplish such an abstraction. Nevertheless, "fully divine and fully human" is in fact a wonderful opening, offered down the centuries from bishops whose quarrels did not completely cancel the possibilities for apprehending the Divine that comes in incarnation. The stories of Jesus pull hard on the untold and unknown stories in us. If one listens to the stories about him again, carefully (and again), he becomes too particular to be Everyman but more and more a body of mucky, intemperate flesh, refusing to disappear into the flattening regime of names, ranks, classifications, and answers to charges. His silences make him a multiplicity of presences that open into the impossible exchange of bodies, of their criminal innocence and polymorphous trespass. If they are told right (or almost right, which is all we humans can do), the stories of Jesus can reveal divinity that still matters.

Gestures of a-centered relationality

> How could movements of deterritorialization and processes of reterritorialization not be relative, always connected, caught up in one another? The orchid deterritorializes by forming an image, a tracing of a wasp; but the wasp reterritorializes on that image. The wasp is nevertheless deterritorialized, becoming a piece in the orchid's reproductive apparatus. But it reterritorializes the orchid by transporting its pollen. Wasp and orchid, as heterogeneous elements, form a rhizome ... At the same time, something else entirely is going on: not imitation at all but a capture of code, surplus value of code, an increase in valence, a veritable becoming, a becoming-wasp of the orchid and a becoming-orchid of the wasp.[22]

The last "proximal mark" of divine multiplicity that I gesture toward in this book (which by no means exhausts the possibilities, and I hope to have encouraged others in this direction) is what I am calling "a-centered relationality." Divine multiplicity, revealed by inexchangeable incarnations and accessible through supple postures of flexibility, openness, humor, and fluency, has no single center, origin, or root. Every point of emergence, or incarnational occurrence, is a center from which ever new migrations occur, generating change, connections, and new centers of emergence. "Origin" in any single sense becomes nonsensical, and certainly not descriptive of creativity, expansion, relation, and becoming. Each center is a margin in relation to other centers. In her wonderful essay on race and cosmos Barbara Holmes asks:

> How can we continue to talk about cultural centers and margins when the new cosmology teaches that the universe is expanding in a very odd way? Rather than a universe that expands from one point, the universe contains multiple centers that are expanding at the same time.[23]

She calls this multiplicity of a-centered relations "omnicentricity." "Omnicentricity means that all centers act as focal points for the activity of expansion and energy" and so move, creating new margins that themselves become centers of becoming. Her use of the Greek prefix "*omni-*" which most often means "all" or "whole" can slant her concept linguistically in a totalizing direction that I do not believe she intends or it is necessary to go.

"*Omni-*" also means "every" or "each," which translate more effectively in this case because the omnicentricity that Holmes describes is rhizomatic and open, rather than totalizing and closed. This "*omni-*" is perforated with incompleteness and partiality precisely because *each* point of intersection or relationship becomes a center that expands outward and inward, disrupting or escaping the claims to totality that other centers may attempt to impose. Indeed, Holmes goes directly to the heart of the political implications of this insight: "Even the most malignant forces of domination cannot hold down a community that is cosmically on the move."[24]

If we follow her insight through Deleuze, communities are on the move if ever there is any life in them at all. He points out that "society is always *en fuite* (leaking, fleeing) and may be understood in terms of the manner in which it deals with its *fuites* (leaks, lines of flight)."[25] Because of rhizomatic omnicentricity, the most malignant forces of domination or "arborescent schema" cannot plug all of the leaks, no matter how brutally or systematically they may succeed at doing for a time. Communities die in controlled conditions of colonization, in other words, if they do not somewhere rhizomatically shift and outgrow the garden plots that would contain them:

> Once a rhizome has been obstructed, arborified, it's all over, no desire stirs: for it is always by rhizome that desire moves and produces. Whenever desire climbs a tree, internal repercussions trip it up and it falls to its death; the rhizome, on the other hand, acts on desire by external, productive outgrowths.[26]

Part of what Holmes offers is a dynamically clear view of the relation between ideas of cosmos, creation, and social configurations like race. Something as deceptively simple as the reorientation toward multiplicity that new cosmological discoveries require (suggesting a shift from the idea of a single point of origin to multiple centers of mutually constituting becomings) shakes the foundations of an entire logical substructure of linear, essential, or evolutionary primacy enacted in social hierarchies. In this light, racism reveals its own continued "fallacy of misplaced concreteness" as Whitehead calls it,[27] when it finds support in evolutionary schemes that assume a single axis (European Heterosexual Man, for example) around which differences circle like so many derivative copies (even among European heterosexual men). Omnicentricity dramatically ruptures the monosyllable of linear progression from an absolute origin and so it directly challenges the grounds upon which social hierarchies like white supremacy stand in their many forms.[28]

Holmes's notion of omnicentricity describes part of the a-centered relationality that marks divine multiplicity. The idea of multiple (and multiplying) centers of origin in the cosmos forces a shift in emphasis: from lines to planes; or genealogical lineages to horizontal connections; or from hierarchies and inheritances to illegal immigrations and emergent relationships. Omnicentricity suggests the spread and mutation of divinity, rather than its singular points. But translation notes aside, omnicentricity can slip from its own marvelous multiplicity in the totalizing direction that All, rather than "every" or "each" implies. In theology especially, omnicentricity runs the risk of drifting back toward a totality, an All, though it need not do so. For this reason only I use "a-centered relationality" instead, to keep in focus the *mode of relation* that Holmes intends for omnicentricity to lift up, a mode (or modes) that operate in divine multiplicity without regard to the propriety of origin, lineage, or *authorized* apostolic succession.

In several of his writings Derrida points out that ideas of origin are always applied after the fact, covering a gap in the subflooring of communal identity. For him they are not so much fictions as cover-ups: stories that pretend to solidity, carving a single surface out of the irreducible and ungraspable multiplicity that turns out to be the questionable genealogy of every assemblage. Because stories that pretend to absolute origins offer a leg to stand on where there is actually none, Derrida playfully calls them "prostheses." Look too closely at any origin and (as Catherine Keller finds in her examination of the doctrinal account of *creatio ex nihilo*) it is *en fuite*. It leaks. The origin turns out to be a middle point of something else. "A becoming is always in the middle; one can only get it by the middle."[29]

And so it is with creation—we can only get it in the middle of the story. "There was a village and their river was drying up" (Penobscot Nation); "Halfway through the story of my life" (Dante); "and the *ruach elohim* vibrating on the face of the waters" (Genesis 1:2).[30] A man named John "appeared in the wilderness" (Mark 1:4). Divine multiplicity is not an origin, or a center. Incarnation—the positive experiential confession of God-with-us—is a rhizome, following lines of occurrence, centering, deterritorializing, decentering, and reterritorializing all that it encounters.

The term "rhizome" comes from botany. It narrowly refers to those plants that propagate by expansion rather than by seed dispersion. They generate new plants "from the middle of the body." As tubers, they "move" across the earth, or through it, actually, by "deterritorializing" and "reterritorializing" underground. Potatoes are rhizomes, as are asparagus, ferns, bamboo, and lilies. They "start" not with seeds that put down roots and come to fruition in a single individual, but by offshoots of an already creeping rootstalk or bulb aggregation that produces nodal "thickenings" in the rootstalk, called tubers and bulbs from which new becomings take flight.

Because rhizomes reproduce in a non-linear fashion distinct lines of origin are unimportant (when you dig up a clot of bulbs, can you identify the "parent"?). Lines of descent go sideways, they do not follow hierarchical pathways of inheritance. Although botanists may scratch their heads at the lines of flight their simple tubers seem to have launched in philosophy, it is this non-linear, a-centered mode of relation that makes the rhizome such a productive metaphor for Deleuze and Guattari, especially in their efforts to articulate ontological multiplicity. "The wisdom of the plants: even when they have roots, there is always an outside where they form a rhizome with something else—with the wind, an animal, human beings."[31]

As an illustration of a mode of relation, rhizomes suggest a heterogeneous, shifty, a-centered connectivity that fully resists the authority of the clear Origin, the pure One and the *ex nihilo* for which the logic of the One endlessly clamors. Rhizomes have no origins, only offshoots, and so they have no ends, or rather their ends are offshoots, which repeat the process. The metaphor here is botanical, but Deleuze and Guattari take this "wisdom of plants" as a launching pad for thinking about ontology. "Being" is best not traced to some prosthetic origin covering up for an offshoot. Better to be honest about the offshoot to begin with. Even Aristotle posits the "Prime Mover" simply because he could not imagine following the domino effect of prior causes back without end! The linear growth of acorn to oak tree (which made that tree into the poster plant of Aristotle's "arborescent scheme" of cause and origin and so of the One) can deceive: forests do drift rhizomorphically.

Deleuze and Guattari argue that everything open even slightly to the outside is rhizomorphic, meaning that its openness is a node of a-centric connection and so of generative migration and deterritorialization. "The outside" may be only a crack in the pavement through which a drop of water draws a line of flight upward from a blindly cast rootstalk to newly emergent plant. Or it may be a virus. Or it may be a picture of a child whose utter particularity "pulls hard on stories untold and unknown" drawing a line of flight outward from memory to story. Rhizomorphic migration occurs sideways and never according to plan, through the gravitational connection that bodies make to each other even as they shift-shape, die, or take flight. Divinity revealed in all of its heart-rending particularity and inexchangeability, gives itself away in this kind of connection. God (Coyote, the Old Ones) rides the lines of flight between points of unexpected, fragile connection, and thereby makes the world, again.

In the middle of a crowded plaza in Jerusalem sometime in the months after Jesus was executed, his followers, who were largely a group of illegals from over the border, found tongues to tell of "the mighty works of God." They apparently overcame their fear of arrest; some of them had even seen Jesus again. They had committed themselves to be "witnesses to the resurrection." In this story, some number of these "witnesses" had gathered for the feast of Pentecost in Jerusalem when a sound burst from the sky, loud enough to draw a crowd. A "mighty wind" and "tongues of fire" swept over the group. "And they were all filled with the Holy Spirit and began to speak in other tongues, as the Spirit gave them utterance" (Acts 2:3). They began to talk, and all the crowd heard them fluently, *in their own tongues*.

Divinity occurs in this marvelous story of a-centered connection in vivid enunciation and disregard for propriety of class and nation. The Parthians, and Medes, the residents of Mesopotamia, Cappadocia, and Asia out on the street that day would hardly have been illiterate day-laborers but persons of enough wealth and status to travel. The followers of Jesus, on the other hand, were recognizable to the crowd as persons of low status from the nearby province of Galilee. "And all were amazed and perplexed, saying to one another, 'What does this mean?'" (Acts 2:1–12). Mother tongues of origin had flared into speech, but not where they belonged. They no longer designated singular identities, but deterritorialized culture and nation, trespassing on mother tongues and signifiers of origin. Understanding came anyway, but as a disorienting surprise. Here was an incarnational migration of fluencies revealing connections that decentered the crowd.

The a-centered relationality here is disclosed in the horizontal concurrence of tongues. Language itself slips sideways in this story, disclosing a nomadic desire,

> like a tuber agglomerating very diverse acts, not only linguistic, but also perceptive, mimetic, gestural, and cognitive: there is no language in itself, nor are there any linguistic universals, only a throng of dialects, patois, slangs, and specialized languages. There is no ideal speaker-listener, any more than there is a homogeneous linguistic community. Language is, in Weinreich's words, "an essentially heterogeneous reality."[32]

Here mother tongues are dislodged from their proper origins. "Are not all these who are speaking *Galileans?*" the Medes, Mesopotamians, Capodocians, and others ask. "And how is it that we hear, each of us in his own native language?" (2:7). In this story, divinity incarnates in the crowd itself. This is not a centered tale but it is one of generative connections coming sideways. New beginnings—indeed, the beginning of a global movement—occurs here rhizomorphically, out of the middle of a feast on a busy street. If we hear this story incarnationally (and how else might we hear it?) this is a queer story of shared tongues and slippages between the nations. God *be*-comes, again.

And so, in addition to its porosity, fluidity, heterogeneity, and impossible exchange, divine multiplicity is marked by a-centered relationality. Like the people on that street in Jerusalem, we may discover through incarnational connections that our relation to one another is rhizomorphically decentering rather than linear, proper, and chaste. Divine relations cannot be traced through inheritance, ownership, racial demarcations, or the political dominance of Mother Tongues or Father Lands. All of these prosthetic markers and origins slip, even as they serve prosthetically to delineate stories of connection and origin through which new lines of flight do take off. Incarnation reveals the world to itself even as it overcomes it in rhizomatic relation. The story, therefore, of incarnation is the becoming-world of divinity, the becoming-divine of world. Not once, not in a single tongue, but heterogenous, shifty, alive.

Rhizomorphic thought expands and contracts from multiple centers. It dispenses with the unitary origin by recognizing the fallacies and restrictions entailed in the Aristotelian (and so Thomistic, and so dominant Christian) stories of ontological root systems that grow from the fully arborified One God. Following the rhizomatic traces and connections of divine multiplicity that is incarnation, promiscuous desire for life has already driven us over the Garden wall. Looking back, we can recognize the prosthesis of origin in the closely pruned hedges. Perhaps God was not there anyway, having climbed the wall to find more clay. Maybe that was just some noisy, doggy, dream of G O D in that prosthetic Garden. As if anything ever stays fully within garden walls once it establishes a relation with the wind and rain! Like potato vines, mint weed, and bamboo—everything migrates in an a-centered fashion. It adapts, climbs the wall, and establishes lines of flight. It makes multiplicity by becoming-body, taking place, and so making both space and time.

The Word is an offshoot, ever becoming, again, the words of this story we will try, again, to tell. It is a story filled with rolling stones; it starts somewhere in the middle: perhaps with water; perhaps with a young woman pregnant with a child of uncertain lineage; perhaps with a knock on the door ...

But we should remember to be careful. Stories make and unmake worlds. "Best not to make mistakes with them,"[33] as Ishmael reminds the Lone Ranger.

Part III

Ethics and postures of multiplicity

13 A turn to ethics
Beyond nationalism

Memorializing unity: a snapshot memoir

When I graduated from college, I traveled to a small town on the Rhine river near Ludwigshafen, in what was then West Germany. I was on my way to a new job in Stockholm and, having never been in Europe before, I felt some inchoate obligation to stop off first at the site in which ancestors of mine had lived and died, and which they had left. My father's father and his parents emigrated from that village to the United States in 1905. At the time of my visit, a few of my grandfather's cousins were still alive and they welcomed me warmly. The sauerkraut factory in which my great grandfather lost his arm and livelihood had burned down, but the small church in which they all had been baptized still stood with its Roman tower and its walled graveyard.

My German language skills were elementary, but I could get by if my elderly, non-English speaking hosts were patient, and used short sentences. They kindly served up a feast of local Wurst und Käse from a sideboard that also sported an old sports trophy with a swastika, and took me on a walking tour of the village. After we left the church and approached the village cemetery, I was mesmerized by a tall black obelisk in the square before the entrance. From where I stood and in the narrowing vision of memory, it looked smooth and unmarked, except for three short lines in plain text. Because of their simplicity I could readily translate them: "Ein Folk—Ein Reich—Ein Gott." One people, one nation, one God.

Perhaps the repugnance I felt for this memorial was the naïve shock I still felt from seeing a swastika in my relatives' home, forty years after the war. Perhaps it was because I assumed that the stone marker was erected by Nazis. I was hesitant to go further, to enter the graveyard. I did not want to see what else, other than names, my ancestors' graves would reveal. Even after learning that the obelisk was a commemoration of Prussian consolidation in the 1870s and not a remnant of Hitler's National Socialist regime, those three stark lines against the smooth black stone limned far more than a yearning for healing after bitter partisan divisions. In memory, they now seem appropriately placed in a public square before a village graveyard in a land that once lost its soul for a dream of unified purity. Oneness, whether of God, nation, or people, held little for them but death.

Nationalism is a name for the fervor of proximal unity in politics, especially in the face of perceived threat. Under the umbrella of monotheism, nationalism is the dream of a seamless, confirming reflection of the divine in the nation, and vice versa: *ein Reich, ein Gott*. It is also the dream of a seamless, confirming reflection of the divine in the people, an ethnosexual mirror of identity: *ein Folk*.[1]

Nationalism is just one of many social dynamics in the modern world that is buttressed by monarchical monotheism and the logic of the One. Its relationship to theology, or its importance for theology, is most evident in those times when political leaders invoke divine right for the very existence of the nation, and for the nation's actions against others. It is also evident when theologians lend support to those efforts, as Karl Barth's German professors did in their declarations of support for the German offensives in what would become World War I.[2] But the relationship of nationalism to theology is also exposed when theologians place themselves in opposition to practices and policies of the state. It is especially evident when they criticize popular and powerful patriotic fervor on theological grounds, even if it leads to imprisonment or death as it did for Martin Niemoller, Paul Schneider or Dietrich Bonhoeffer in Nazi Germany and as it did for Oscar Romero in El Salvador. Theology that concerns itself with ethics and the powers of government deals in the currency of human meaning, authority, tradition, and allegiance, directly threatening contrary political claims or shoring them up, depending on the social and philosophical accommodation the religious community has made to the interests of the state.

Just as the mostly Christian patriots of my ancestors' village in Germany saw clearly a link between one God and one nation when they erected an obelisk dedicated to theo-political unity in the nineteenth century, it is not difficult to see in nationalist feeling everywhere distinct elements of religious feeling, and in definitions of "the nation" ambiguities similar to those inherent in doctrinal explanations. In cultures dominated by monotheism, both the monotheistic idea of "God" and the political idea of "nation" refer to something that is not self-evident; both require explanation just as both demand loyalty. In one of the standard texts on nationalism, Benedict Anderson defines the "nation" as an imagined political community— imagined as both inherently limited (meaning it has finite boundaries, beyond which lie other nations) and as inherently sovereign. Nationalism, then, is the fraternity—the unity—that this imagined community inspires.[3]

Other social theorists define nationalism as an ideology of identity and boundedness that hedge against the porosity and mutability of actual life in and between the social organizations called "nations." Richard Handler, studying the case of Quebec, points out that

> Of course, everyone knows that social life is not neatly integrated: the
> boundaries of nations, states, societies, and cultures are permeable and

even vague. Yet to recognize (and then rationalize) "fuzzy boundaries" does not fundamentally question the epistemology of "entitivity" upon which the notion of boundedness depends.[4]

In addition, the boundedness of nations gets caught up in a certain unboundedness at work in empires, and the idea of the nation becomes conflated with the "world" of empire. Furthermore, while the objective dimension of a group or nation may exist according to the bounded attributes or characteristics observable to outsiders (such as possession of a passport, or specific linguistic patterns, and so forth), nationalism reflects the subjective sense—and ideological force—of a group's self-understanding as such. Czech political theorist Miroslav Hroch argues that this powerful fraternal ideology emerges principally out of constructed "memory" of a shared past that serves powerfully as "destiny."[5]

Memory and destiny working together to give a strong group self-understanding and purpose blurs the somewhat artificial boundaries between nation and religion:

> But you are a chosen race, a royal priesthood, a holy nation, God's own people, in order that you may proclaim the mighty acts of him who called you out of darkness into his marvelous light. Once you were not a people, but now you are God's people; once you had not received mercy, but now you have received mercy.
>
> 1 Peter 2:9–10

Powerful fraternal ideology generated from a common purpose and combined with a constructed memory of a shared past—especially if it is a past filled with trouble and the overcoming of trouble—is a dynamic that theologians with critical consciousness can understand better perhaps than any other kind of scholarly observer. Add to such ideology a density of linguistic or cultural ties enabling in-group communication and recognition, and you have the potency of a nation energized by nationalism (or a religion energized by fundamentalist devotion). It is not coincidental, therefore, that in the late nineteenth century French political theorist Ernest Renan claimed that a "nation is a soul, a spiritual principle."[6]

Although theologians concerned about the robust deployment of religious ideologies in political arenas across the world today may well see that patriotic fervor travels the same nerve pathways as religion and so would not flinch at the association of nation with soul and spirit, few contemporary political scientists follow Renan today in making that claim. Despite his importance in the development of the field of political theory, Renan's romantic and explicitly religious language to discuss the dynamics of nations and nationalism presumes theology and makes dangerously fuzzy the categories of doctrine and of social science for those convinced that the two are separate realms of inquiry.

The logic of the One that undergirds the true/false dualism of much of modern science also undergirds its social scientific offshoots. Because of this, categories of "soul" or "spirit" are problematic for social science; they tend not to fit neatly into true/false dualisms. Objectivity is difficult to maintain in the realm of the spiritual and so social scientists who wish to take such "squishy" notions seriously must entertain conceptual frameworks that diminish objectivity and that implicate the scientists' own categories of belief. At the same time, theology cannot retreat into corners of doctrine, as if there is no porosity and interconnection between religious and national creeds. A more flexible posture, one that does not divide the world into religions and nations, can address the theologies at work in warfare and the politics at work in doctrine. Both theologians and political scientists can then more readily perceive the meta-logic of the One that works to legitimize monotheistic, patriarchal ideologies of nationalism, and perhaps even of key aspects of economic globalization.

There exists in human societies in general a creative, mutually constituting relationship between the images and concepts that obtain for divinity and the social and political arrangements, values, norms, and visions that obtain for the civil society as a whole. As Joane Nagel points out, these arrangements make for a "moral economy of nationalism" that is "gendered, sexualized, and racialized."[7] Nationalism—defined variously as the fraternal energy of imagined community, the ideological construction of shared memory and destiny, or as soul—is fundamentally a category of identity and so a boundary of sameness, unity, and oneness. The theological does not reduce simply to the ethnosexual class system of the polis but the lines of connection do exist and, if we pay attention, the rhetoric of political leaders—particularly in times of war—exposes the nation's dependence on theological structures of meaning just as social stratification systems usually ground their legitimacy in corresponding theological systems. "In other words," Bruce Lerro suggests in his study of the development of monotheism in relation to the development of social class, "just as God becomes a transcendental power beyond the power of human influence, so the upper castes seem to occupy the same unapproachable position relative to the lower classes."[8]

Possessing a latent energy of boundedness not unlike nationalism, monotheism is the metaphor at the heart of the western religious traditions of Christianity, Judaism, and Islam. As the principle theological construct of the nations that currently dominate global politics especially in the western hemisphere, monotheism clearly plays a significant role in global politics precisely because it constitutes a shared and deeply interrelated symbolic system for ultimate reality. What European, American, and Middle Eastern political leaders consider to be within the realm of the possible, in a universe fundamentally made meaningful by exclusive oneness, is in all likelihood quite different than what may be possible in universes conceived otherwise. What operates here is a tautology that is nevertheless illuminating: leaders imagine what is possible based on the parameters of what they assume to be possibly imaginable. The logic of the One, in theology as in the politics of global domination, has not changed since Aristotle quoted Homer: "The rule of the many is not good; let one alone rule."[9] This idea applies as much to systems of governance (like American democracy) as it does to dictators.

As I argued in Chapter Five, since the third century CE Christian theology has largely taken for granted the oneness of God (even in the doctrine of the Trinity). Monotheism has functioned in pride of place in Christian theology as it does in Jewish and in Muslim theology, despite the iconoclasm of the *via negativa* and the metaphoric exemption.[10] Indeed, it is as if theologians forget that monotheism is a metaphor just like all other concepts and images of the divine. Perhaps this forgetting comes from too much at stake in the logic of the One. Too many doctrines have been formulated on the basis of this logic; too many wars have been fought in the name of the One God; too much has been lost or gained; too many rulers justified or toppled. There is a great deal at stake for Christian theology in the constellation of doctrines and theological structures that are built upon the logic of the One, like Dante's *Paradiso* that rests upon the structure of ice in the *Inferno*. Monotheism is not a metaphoric description of the divine, it often *is* divinity, at least in many theologies. This means that there is little basis in Christian thought to temper the often deadly logic of the One among nations.

A full discussion of monotheistic nationalism needs to address the complexities and possibilities for multiplicity in Jewish and Muslim theological traditions as well as those in Christian theology. The scriptural and mystical sources in both Judaism and Islam are rife with such possibilities: fluidity, porosity, a-centered relation, and heterogeneity all flow through and around the strict and dogmatic assertions of divine oneness in those traditions, and it is on the theologians, story-tellers, and poets of those traditions that the burden of such creative reconstruction and recovery must fall. The pressure is on all three religions, in no small part because of the devastation each monotheistic tradition seems incapable of stopping among its own adherents. All three of these patriarchal religious traditions have shaped and energized nations, and all three religious systems appear more like participants than critics in the rhetoric, if not engagement, of war.

Judaism, Christianity, and Islam play a significant role in the ongoing wars that spill over the Middle East. They play a role in the guerilla efforts of insurgents worldwide, and in the defensive tactics of superpowers. It is noteworthy that US President George W. Bush felt obliged to state on many occasions in the months following the first US-led attacks on Iraq that the assaults were not an attack on Islam. He had to do this precisely because the invasion and subsequent war looked very much, both to those in favor and to those opposed to the war, like a Christian and Jewish attack upon Islam rather than a "purely" political invasion of a nation.

Iraqi resisters have found support on religious grounds as well: it is not surprising that Islamic nations have been pressured to support Iraq on theological as well as political grounds. In a moment of historical irony following criticisms of Islamic fundamentalists by the German pope Benedict, outraged Muslims burned effigies of the pope, along with flags of Germany and Israel together. Monotheism structured into political affairs tends toward such violent confusions as have erupted in recent years in the United States against Muslim citizens and in Islamic states against Jews and Christians (and that surfaced in Europe against Jews in the last century, and against Muslims in the Middle Ages) even if it does not always result in open war.

"Monotheism" is an umbrella term for the unitary logic that frames the cultural imagination of global leaders in the first decades of the twenty-first century. Supplying legitimation and weight to the moral economy of nationalism, it is a symbolic force of Ptolemaic proportion that could be said to be (but only with some irony) *the* founding "deep symbol" of our time.[11] Even in the form of Christian trinitarian doctrine, monotheism frames a picture of ultimate reality that passively renders other possibilities false, leading to the very conundrums of opposing Ones that add tinder to the rage of nations today. We have already seen how pervasive the logic of the One is in modern western thought, having contributed heavily to what counts as science, reality, and knowledge. Tethered to this logic, the tragic posturing of the Christian, Jewish, and Muslim nations seems doomed to an endless masquerade of righteous mimicry.

It is of course important to remember that virtually no governmental system can enforce a scientific system that does not *work* in practical terms. The logic of the One has worked well for the expansionist political dreams, particularly of Christians and Muslims. The Ptolemaic solar system, for example, *worked* in the ancient and medieval world until Copernicus altered the solar map. It lasted that long because it served human needs for navigation, agriculture, meaning, and function. It worked well enough for sailors, farmers, match-makers, and those concerned about the place and origin of earthly life in the cosmos. What caused its downfall was not the falsehood of its more or less abstract claim that the heavens revolve around the earth. It stumbled and fell quite simply because the errors in that system began to accumulate among the multitudes who depended upon its use; the geocentric model of reality quite simply began to create more problems than it solved for getting by in the world in practical terms.

The logic of the One, in science as in theology and politics, has *worked* for a very long time. But problems that follow in its wake are becoming evident, especially in the realm of globalization and international politics. Nations are diminishing in importance as coherent descriptors of cultures with large shifts in human populations and the merging of cultural systems through mass communication avenues. Refugees and migrants now alter the demographic landscape on every continent. Warfare in the so-called "age of terror" is intermittent, continual, global, and diffuse rather than regional, bounded, and focused on national boundaries. Like animal and plant bodies, "nations" are "temporary agreements" of porous, inter-connecting and hybrid elements. They describe a putative, rather than essential, unity. The usefulness of the logic of the One in describing nations is diminishing, and the monotheisms that legitimate that logic may be beginning to cause more problems than they solve in establishing peace and stability for the peoples of the earth.

The problem of radical monotheism in neo-orthodox Christian critique

I have argued elsewhere that, as a grounding metaphor, monotheism cannot support both the exclusivist and the universalist meaning that it has come to hold in the history of modern Christian thought.[12] God as the triumphal and exclusive One, against whom all other possibilities for divinity are declared false, is itself falsified by the otherness of the world in all of its multiplicity. And the universal One, within whom all differences fade away, is tenable only from the kind of distance that loses sight of the multiplicity and inexchangability of actual worlds. Both exclusive and inclusive monotheisms require a denial of the real differences that follow embodiment of any kind. Both require a denial of contradiction, flux, and partiality. But that is their effect.

Monotheism has also functioned, in theology if not in politics, as a mode of critique. The nations are relativized by the One God. "Who can stand before His indignation?" the prophet Nahum demands (1:6). The oneness of divinity serves both the cause of political buttress and of political cri-tique: it is the mirror of national authority when the nation is good; it is the source of humiliation when the nation is not good. "Good," of course, begs further questions, but the point here is that monotheism is seldom far away from politics. Indeed, it always tends toward theocracy, Jürgen Moltmann claims.[13] Whether understood as support for theocracy or as a strong criticism of it, the logic of the One, particularly in a context of monotheism mixed with nationalism, forces the issues of allegiance and identity into dualistic gambits of "with us" or "against us."

One of the principal figures in Protestant theology in the twentieth century and a major contributor to the development of what has been called "neo-orthodoxy" in theology, Karl Barth writes in the *Church Dogmatics* that

> No sentence is more dangerous or revolutionary than that God is One and there is no other like Him ... It was on the truth of the sentence that God is One that the "Third Reich" of Adolf Hitler made shipwreck.[14]

He means by this that a truly thorough understanding of the absolute Oneness of God fully demolishes the claims of all tyrants. There is no supreme ruler but God, which puts to shame all human efforts ultimately to rule. Barth's deep iconoclasm makes of radical oneness a divine protection against all allegiances that people may otherwise give to lesser but effective deities, whether they are named King, President, Country, Way of Life, or whatever unifies groups into nations: the fraternal passion of a shared memory that is perceived at the same time as a destiny.

Radical monotheism, the claim that God is beyond all partiality and cannot be invoked for righteousness in any human endeavor, is a last-ditch attempt that Christian theologians make to clean the gore and ash of war from divinity conceived in the logic of the One and stamped on the banners of armies. Such theological efforts may indeed work among Jewish and Muslim theologians who attempt to criticize the contemporary warfare in which Israel and countries dominated by Islam are engaged, but such efforts cannot work among Christians. That is, whether or not the transcendent critique of nations resident in radical monotheism can help to counter the nationalism at work in Jewish or Muslim political endeavors (and it is Jewish and Muslim theologians who must speak to that question), radical monotheism cannot finally get a purchase in Christian theology and so cannot provide the theological critique that Christian-dominated politics so desperately need. Despite the prodigious efforts of mid-century Protestant theologians (like Karl Barth and H. Richard Niebuhr) to reorient Christianity toward the critique embedded in radical monotheism, Christian theology falls into a peculiar and paralysing incoherence when it reduces divinity to the One. As we have already seen, when Christian theology loses sight of the incarnation (or attempts to abstract it into conformity with the One) it denies the revelatory heart of its own understanding of the divine–world relation. Without incarnation there is no Christian theology; within the logic of the One there is no incarnation.

Because of the opening to multiplicity that the theme of incarnation provides, liberation and feminist theologies claim a partiality in the divine; God *chooses* the poor, the vilified, the children, the "least of these." But radical monotheism of the sort expressed by Barth and Niebuhr allows no finitude or partiality in the divine, except in the carefully limited divine–human nexus of Jesus. Like Kant's categorical imperative, radical monotheism is truly universal monotheism; it demands that God stand in categorical distinction from the interests of nations, movements, races, genders, or patriotisms of *any* kind. Universal monotheism, particularly if it is understood iconoclastically in the way that Barth argued, unifies itself in opposition to any and all oppressive powers that claim divine right for themselves. Only in this way is such a God "on" anyone's side—by nature, as it were, rather than in sympathy or in solidarity.

There is great value in this theological approach to monotheism. The only divinity that can truly relativize all the kings and sages of war, truly relativize and expose the petty ideologies of greed disguised as national interest, or of hypocrisy disguised as *realpolitik*, is a divinity that rises above it all, stands in total distinction from the interests of the nations, and judges the oppressors. From this viewpoint one can say with Barth that "No sentence is more dangerous or revolutionary than that God is One and there is no other like Him" and mean that the oneness of God is "His" salvific power. The absolute unity of the divine, understood as oneness (rather than as interconnection) blots out all other powers. But Barth brings this argument to its own logical conclusion and in so doing makes transparent the consequences of radical, universal monotheism by illuminating its close link to the passion of nationalism. He says,

> There is therefore no more room now for what the recent past called toleration. Beside God there are only His creatures or false gods, and beside faith in Him there are religions only as religions of superstition, error and finally irreligion.[15]

The oneness of God, even in the mind of one of the greatest theologians of the twentieth century, slips into fundamentalism and a desire for the utter elimination of difference. This is the logic of the One at work, manifest even in the critique that radical monotheism is supposed to achieve.

Throughout his long theological career, Barth struggled against the capacity of the religions to miss the divinity of the God they seek. True divinity, he argued, must be both one and specific. By "one" he means ultimate, eternal, and simple (undivided). By "specific" he means incarnate in Jesus. Specificity makes God's claim on humanity (or God's "word to humanity") intelligible and real rather than generic and abstract; it is directed to human beings in their specificity. Oneness makes the claim absolute and unchanging. God is one, and so the claim that God makes upon humanity is also one. For specificity to meet the demand of oneness, there can be only one specific revelation. The logic of the One insists that truth is one, and so the one revelation also sets the truth of divinity against all falsehoods.

For Barth and many other Christian theologians, there can be no ambiguity when it comes to the oneness of divinity and the oneness of truth. Therefore, when he cites specificity as the requirement of revelation and in the same breath reaffirms the absolute oneness of divinity he (and all of monotheistic Christian theology) effectively reduces the divine—*all of divinity*—to one revelation and event. In such an explicit move against multiplicity and toleration of multiplicity, Barth exposes the logical conclusion of monotheism as the identity of God and takes up the very tools of those he rails against. Faced with the atrocities of tyrants, Barth did not see his position as faulty, even in the decades following the fall of Nazi Germany. Against the likes of governments that will grasp at the image of the ultimate rule, Barth sets the ultimate rule of God. This approach is and has been a comfort to those who suffer under tyrants. But rather than rail against absolute righteousness, radical monotheism claims absolute righteousness for God, and even Barth cannot keep that claim from slipping to the shoulders of God's righteous defenders. A statement that says there is "no more room now for what the recent past called toleration" is not all that far from statements like those of American president George W. Bush, who asserted his 2002 State of the Union Address that there are only two positions in relation to United States policy on the so-called "war on terror": "Either you are for us or you are with the terrorists." The fact that one applies to theology and the other to nations and political movements seems to make little difference when it comes to real effects or justifications for war.

Barth himself was careful to include, in a self-critical manner, all of Christianity in the realm of "religions of superstition, error, and irreligion" in a way that Bush would not have done regarding the realm of "us." But it doesn't really matter in the end what Barth includes in his logical conclusion of an end to toleration. The thing about logical conclusions is that they show us where proximal claims lead. Monotheism, even as an abstract, universalist "we are fundamentally all one" *proximal* claim reveals a demand that *all* proximal claims either fold into the one or stand against it. A universal One still cannot abide difference outside of it. Outside of the boundary of the absolute One is only that which undoes the One by proving it is not, in the end, either universal or one. And so what is not One must be destroyed. This, as many observers have noted, neatly describes the arrogance of Christian monotheists for centuries.

Multiplicity and the horizon of imagination

The pattern I am tracing here limns a relationship between communal understandings of divinity and lives shared in community. A logic of the One reduces the world to categories and abstractions since actual embodiments confound oneness at every turn. It is in the logic of the One that people can be exchanged for paychecks and bombs can be exchanged for words because the utter inexchangeability of their existence has no place in either universal or exclusive concepts of divine oneness. If Renan is right in suggesting that a nation is a soul or a spiritual principle, and if Hroch is right in suggesting that nationalism depends on communal memory that is treated as a destiny, then a soul that is One, cleaving to one story and memory, can only survive by destroying all other stories and memories, all fuzzy and permeable borders to the soul. A nation spiritualized by monotheism cannot but do this. The nation, like God, is a metaphor—an imagined horizon. But it is no less real for yielding to imaginative flourish.

As nations begin already to dissolve in the contemporary world of porous exchange there is an opening not only for a theology of multiplicity but for a politics of multiplicity as well. There are opportunities here for poets, theologians, and artists to begin imagining a world of interconnecting fluidity beyond nationalism and the powers of empire. But let us not be naïve: the imagining is not easy, and the forces served by exploitive economies of sameness are very strong indeed. Whether the logic of the One is expressed theologically in terms of religious triumphalism or politically in terms of nationalism or in terms of some combination of both, the challenge of imagination—of the courage to see *other* horizons than that proscribed by oneness, and the courage to sin by pointing them out and embarking on travels toward them—is a challenge that faces art and theology together.

Reflecting on Levinas's argument for Jerusalem as the "city of refuge," Jacques Derrida writes about the possibility of cosmopolitan centers, rather than nations, as nodes of possibility for what he calls "democracy-to-come." He reads Levinas's Talmudic discussion of the idea (based on the Levitical story of Moses' establishing three "cities of refuge" for those convicted of unintended murder, or manslaughter) as a vision not only of Jerusalem but of other cities as well. Derrida sees a horizon of possibility for re-imagining the city through its own organic structures of hospitality, in terms not unlike a-centered relationality. It is the place where "the nation" is essentially dissolved in the interconnection of nations. It is a place where art, the very medium of cross-cultural communication, proliferates, and where refugees, illegals, border-crossers, queers, and nomads find shelter and life. In a memorable line from the 1994 movie *The Adventures of Priscilla, Queen of the Desert*, as the three main characters (two drag queens and a transsexual) are leaving Sydney to journey into the outback, one of them quietly remarks,

> It's funny. We all sit around mindlessly slagging that vile stinkhole of a city, but in some strange way it takes care of us. I don't know if that ugly wall of suburbia's been put there to stop them getting in or us getting out.[16]

The idea of "cities of refuge" is not an abstract notion to those who depend upon the complexity of the urban environment to shield them from the normalizing sameness of smaller communities. It is not even utopian in an other-worldly sense. "City of refuge" is an image of a-centered relationality (and even omnicentricity in Holmes's sense) in ethical and practical terms. Derrida simply lifts up what others already know: that it is in the give-and-take of cosmopolitan centers that anything resembling a world beyond totalitarianism might reside.[17]

A philosopher who early schooled himself in the queer art of looking for the unseen in the taken-for-granted, Derrida is famous for turning the obvious over and discerning whole new horizons therein. This is the challenge that a logic of multiplicity sets before political as well as theological imagination. What traces of a logic of multiplicity run through the social realm already—perhaps always have been there—that signal a horizon other than the one of nations in the grip of deadly competition, debt, ethnnosexual cleansing, and terror? What has theology to offer from its own ancient storehouses of imagination, poetry, prophesy, and vision to a re-imagining of the social world into one of peace?

From its inception in the troubled context of Roman expansion and colonial domination, Christian theology and "national" politics have always had something to do with one another. Their co-implication will no doubt continue to be the case, certainly so long as the one seeks legitimation and coherence in—or protest and distinction from—the logic of the other. The eventual probable dissolution of nation-states into some other political form is not likely to change that interconnection. And let us not be any more naïve than the work of imagination requires (and it does require some mature naiveté). The dissolution of nation-states, if that does occur, does not necessarily signal the beginning of peace or an end to the logic of the One. The idea of the nation-state is simply one of many latter doctrines of that logic in the modern political sphere. Peace—understood negatively as the absence of war or positively as the non-violent presence of justice—is a social configuration that must be constructed again and again, in every generation. In the negative sense, peace is certainly possible within the logic of the One. This is what the Constantinian *Pax Romana* was all about, and it is what Gary Dorrien has described as the American "Axis of One."[18] But, to use Bonhoeffer's distinction, peace as the mere absence of war within the logic of the One is more often security in the guise of peace rather than a state of social well-being grounded in just dealings.

> There is no way to peace along the way of safety. For peace must be dared, it is itself the great venture, and can never be safe. Peace is the opposite of security. To demand guarantees is to mistrust, and this mistrust in turn brings forth war.[19]

As long as the logic of the One dominates the horizons of imagination, both churches and nations will remain in the thrall of security rather than in pursuit of peace conceived in concrete and imaginable forms. This is why the work of imagination is so important to theology, but also to politics. Theology, in the form of art such as story, song, film, and even academic discourse can take up the question of the always recurring overlap of nation (as moral ethnosexual economy) and divinity. It can help to puzzle out the enduring dilemma of a world that *will* use concepts of divinity in politics, for good or ill. Theological critique and, perhaps even more importantly, the kind of theological *imagination* that has characterized religious movements throughout the world, can influence the perceptual horizons of possibility when that imagination takes hold in the stories that people tell one another.

Of course, if divinity is understood to be One, and truth is understood to be One, and all the stories support this oneness in science, art, history, and entertainment, then the horizons of imaginative possibilities for politics is influenced by oneness. If, however, divinity begins to show up in terms other than oneness—in terms of incarnation, on the street, at the cross-roads of the peoples—*and* if there are artists and story-tellers enough to build imagination, then the uses to which divinity is put by humans for political purposes, for meaning in the midst of smoke and ash, and for legitimation, especially, of the use of torture, guns, missiles, and embargoes, may actually begin to open up to other possibilities, other endings—which are other beginnings—to the stories of the nations.

14 A turn to ethics
Unity beyond monotheism

Love takes off the masks that we fear we cannot live without and know we cannot live within. I use the word "love" here not merely in the personal sense but as a state of being, or a state of grace—not in the infantile American sense of being made happy but in the tough and universal sense of quest and daring and growth.

James Baldwin[1]

You shall love your neighbor as yourself.
Leviticus 19:18; Matthew 22:39; Mark 12:31; Luke 10:27

A logic of multiplicity is not opposed to unity (the inclusive sense of One) or oneness (the exclusive sense of One), which means that divine multiplicity does not *exclude* either unity or oneness except in their absolute or eternal sense. Oneness and unity are proximal and partial aspects of the divine; they are true in any given space-time occurrence or center, but they are never the "whole" story of divinity and reality. We have discussed how divine multiplicity—and so reality—is rhizomatically adaptive; the Divine is always changing, always beginning, again, and always enfleshing *because divinity exists.* "Always" is therefore a located, context-driven notion rather than some time-and-place busting absolute. It is tied to existence, which occurs in space-defining ways, like breath. And so, always changing, divinity generates space and expresses time *by being.* Put even more starkly, divinity generates space and expresses time *in order to be.* This is the reality of divinity.

   If the line of flight that we have traced here beyond monotheism and the logic of the One is valid, then we can say with some confidence that incarnate divinity is multiple beyond the One–Many divide, opposed neither to oneness nor to unity, but unlimited by both just as the simplest earthworm, in its ever-changing existence from morning till night, is neither an unchanging one nor is it without a certain slant of unity. It goes on about its business with dirt confounding the One at every turn and yet it is an inexchangeable individual, a kind of One-itself that occurs in the specificity of worm-flesh and a patch of soil. The logic of multiplicity, expressed in *this* worm, allows for its own never-the-sameness (from itself and from all other worms) and for its own unity, its interconnection with the world and with other worms, other creatures, other ones. The logic of multiplicity has room for individuals—whether atoms or agreements of atoms—in the place and time that makes them.

So if the logic of multiplicity is not opposed to oneness and unity, why develop this whole argument against the logic of the One, and especially against monotheism? This project is necessary because the logic of multiplicity and the logic of the One are incompatible at least at one point: the logic of the One mistakes the nominal, sanity-producing value of oneness and unity for ontology, for reality. Or, to put it the other way, the logic of multiplicity denies the ontological status of eternity and stasis, upon which the logic of the One depends. Furthermore, as a theological form of the logic of the One, universal monotheism opposes fluidity, change, and partiality. Because universal monotheism is an absolute claim, it theoretically requires strong apophatic assertions of infinity, inconceivability, and eternity to maintain its universality in a world of difference and particularity.

In the logic of the One, anything less than superlative and solitary greatness cannot describe the Divine. And if there is only one God, there is only one truth. Contradictory, finite and unexchangeable bodies undermine both the oneness of God and the oneness of truth. Monotheism ends up protecting divine greatness through denials of the world in its particularity, finitude, conceivability, and temporality, and so cannot avoid denials of multiplicity and therefore of incarnation itself. Monotheism so constructed is incompatible with multiplicity, although the logic of multiplicity remains compatible with individuality in the form of ones that come and go, as they do.

The point here is that oneness and unity are not false; rather they are necessary temporal arrangements. The idea of oneness and of unity is useful. It is this that prompted Ibn Sinna (known in the Latin west as Avicenna), an eleventh-century Muslim doctor and philosopher from Persia to repeat often *"Intellectus in formis agit universalitatem"* ("the universality of our ideas is the result of the activity of the mind itself").[2] The ideas of oneness and unity function in religion, politics, psychology, and history to generate meaning and orientation. And unity actually occurs, in partial and temporal fashion. Without functional unities there would be no groups, no species, no languages, no possibility of societies which, as Deleuze says, can then productively and creatively leak.

Ibn Sinna was profoundly aware of the need that humans have to build habitable structures of meaning out of the vastness of the cosmos. The story of One, especially in the story of monotheism, is a kind of hedge that the Greeks, the Jews, the Egyptians, the Hellenized Christians and the Muslims constructed against all that is changing, unknowable, new. But what most of them could not see, and what strict monotheists of all stripes today generally cannot see, is that both oneness and unity are functional, nominal, and event-based. Both unfold in centers of time/space and, as organizing ideas, serve as a kind of boat on which one can ride the surging waves of fluid, porous, interconnected, and heterogeneous reality.

Oneness and unity, like all abstractions (including the abstraction of divine multiplicity) are vulnerable to the fallacy of misplaced concreteness. Their usefulness makes it easy to forget that they are concepts placed upon reality to sort its ontological multiplicity. No matter how many times we may wish to lift our gaze from the cacophony of embodied existence toward the serenity of unifying concepts in the hope of bringing closure to the world's actual unruly shiftiness, the attempt to construct a summary "after all" fails. As Rajchman summarizes Whitehead's sense of the problem, "the abstract doesn't explain; it must itself be explained by reinsertion into a multiplicity."[3] Whitehead himself cautions, "Have care, here is something that matters! Yes—that is the best phrase—the primary glimmering of consciousness reveals, something that matters."[4] The ethics of unity, therefore, lie inescapably in matter. Or the heart of the matter, in pursuit of unity, is matter. Giorgio Agamben makes this link explicit:

> That the world is, that something can appear and have a face, that there is exteriority and non-latency as the determination and the limit of every thing: this is the good. Thus, precisely its being irreparably in the world is what transcends and exposes every worldly entity. Evil, on the other hand, is the reduction of the taking-place of things to a fact like others, the forgetting of the transcendence inherent in the very taking-place of things.[5]

Without the multiplicity of matter, unity slips into ideology and begins to dream—noisily—of reductions, closures, and totality.

Although unity (even more than oneness) is an ingredient of sanity for human beings, neither idea is adequate to conceptualize divinity, or world. It is out of the logic of the One that Hell's eternity was made, to squash the real multiplicity of divinity and world into a basement closet of ice, and so to pretend that it is "in charge of the world."[6] Because of the dominance of imperial Christian metaphysics in privileging the logic of One, oneness runs amok as a dream of purity, linking Christian, Jewish, and Muslim fundamentalists more closely to each other than to the more moderate of their own faiths. This dream of the One is a denial of incarnation and a serious error in theological reasoning. But even oneness run amok in the noisy "unipolar" dreams of political leaders or in the monotheistic camps of the theologically self-righteous does not negate the necessity and value of proximal ones, and of functional unities, in the work of building peace. Human beings build unities to survive, and to make meaning. "Reason makes use of concepts," Michael Serres writes, "under whose unities are sheltered multiplicities."[7] Without the idea of unity and the differentiation that "ones" provide, the weight and hot breath of the world's worlds would swamp us.

This issue of unity is human—or perhaps mammalian, who can say (until, at last, we can understand the "speech" of flocks, herds, prides, murders, and packs). The idea of unity is not only psychologically useful, it is supported in biology. There is a limit to human capacity to process sensory information. Very low limit thresholds constitute autism, but every human being has limited capacity to receive the world, and so the mind adapts by filtering out the manyness of the world (or by attempting to shout over it). Human adaptation to scent is a good example. In 2001, Randall Reed and Jonathan Bradley, both scientists at Johns Hopkins University School of Medicine, identified a protein with the inglorious name of CNGA4 that effectively stops the brain from sensing scent. According to Randall, "odor adaptation is important in telling whether a scent is getting stronger or going away, and it prevents sensory overload."[8] Probably everyone has experienced encountering a very strong smell, but having the smell diminish or entirely go away in a very short time. This is because the brain has adapted to the sensory overload by diminishing awareness of it. The brain has effectively "reduced" the scent, not by changing the presence of the scent, but by overriding the receptors carrying that information from the nose. To speak figuratively, scent has not changed, but the story that the brain tells about it has.

The brain's "nose plug" is an example of sensory input that the brain recognizes, names, and then minimizes. But the brain does the same thing for countless sensory effects that never make it even to the preliminary cognitive recognition of "What's that?" Most of the world passes through human beings, without recognition, without meaning, without name. The porosity of bodies means that they are never only one. Unity and oneness are cognitive limit thresholds, useful partialities that human minds produce for the purpose of organizing work and life. Without the ability to filter the world in some way, the human mind cannot make sense out of the senses and so cannot survive. There is no reason for divinity—or human concepts of divinity—to be opposed to this very practical need.

A human being, for example, is a meaningful unity as well as a shape-shifting stream of changes. Each person is unique and impossible to exchange *because* of the peculiar unity of elements that occurs and that makes that person distinct: a one. In the Johannine story of Jesus' resurrection, Mary Magdalene is the one who finds Jesus in the garden outside of the tomb. But she does not recognize him; she thinks he is a gardener. In what is arguably one of the most beautiful stories of the New Testament, she weeps and begs the man to tell her "where you have laid him." It is not until he says her name, "Mary," that she turns, and recognizes the gardener as Jesus. Out of the panic and grief of loss, he "remembers her" to herself; he says her name. In that moment, she is a One in her beloved friend's eyes, and so she can in turn recognize him. The fact that everything is changing, at that moment as much as at any other in history, does not negate the importance of her oneness, contained at that moment in the vessel of her name, nor does it negate the unity of their bond with one another, a bond that surges through these few dramatic lines of story. Oneness and unity are parts of multiplicity; *multiplicity makes them.*

People, oceans, epochs, galaxies, murders of crows, and towns of prairie dogs all signify unities but none of them is One in anything but a temporary, proximal sense. Only nothing is One and unified in an ultimate, eternal sense. The unity, the oneness of any real thing, is temporary, but no less true for that fact. The trouble comes in when the temporary gets mistaken for the permanent as, for example, when ice gets mistaken for eternity. The end of change is the end of love.

Love means letting go (of the One)

> One of the first 'deaths' occurring in this kenotic process of omnisexuality is the death of the illusion of limited relationships.
>
> Marcella Althaus-Reid[9]

Divine multiplicity, understood ontologically in postures of fluidity, transience, interconnection, porosity, heterogeneity, and a-centered relationality provides suppleness in conceptualizing divinity such that our thinking about it can actually abide incarnation "now and then."[10] But real engagement entails real consequences. This is particularly clear when we arrive at the possibility of imagining relationships and ethics beyond the logic of the One. Because divine multiplicity is an understanding of change *in* relationship, it is not a disintegration into disconnected manyness. Divine multiplicity, as a concept of God and as an ontological story of reality, implies multiplicity (meaning fluidity, porosity, a-centered relationality, and so forth) in relationships, in fidelity, and in religious commitment as well. What divine multiplicity is *not,* I have argued, is stasis. This means that a faithful approach to ethics must also have sea-legs, capable of navigating a shifting surface without collapse, capable of responding to the velocity and gush of the embodied, real world.

Monotheism, especially in its most exclusive sense, is a freeze-frame on reality, which means that it inhibits the ethical work of love. In *Re-Imagining the Divine,* I suggested that one way to look at the problem of monotheism is through the psychological lens of insecurity: "exclusivity in concepts of the divine provides comfort and protection to the insecure by clearly marking identity and belonging."[11] Furthermore, I suggested a metaphor of jealous lovers "who attempt possession by making their beloved chaste." Although the words recorded in Exodus 20:3 and Deuteronomy 5:7 that "You shall have no other gods before me" comes from the wonderful story of God speaking to Moses on Mt. Sinai, the sentiment of the commandment may reflect the anxiety of a people cast out into uncertainty on a promise of deliverance as much as it reflects divine intention. According to the story, some of the community have begun to worship other deities, invoking the wrath of God and inciting the *Aseret ha-Dvarîm*, the ten commandments.

Typically, the first commandment is interpreted as a claim that *God* makes upon the people, a command to love no other, an indication of divine jealousy and a sign of covenantal fidelity. As such, among Jews, Christians, and Muslims it is often invoked as a declaration of monotheism, despite the fact that the words do not make such an exclusive claim. The people are not told here to worship their God exclusively, but to worship no others *before* "Him." As we have already discussed in Chapter 3, this is a claim of monolatry, but not of monotheism. The *Aseret ha-Dvarîm* is not fully incorporated in the logic of the One; it contains traces of multiplicity and openness.

The logic of the One, however, is what came to dominate Jewish, Christian, Muslim, and even later traditions. For Jews and Christians, at least, it does not even appear to come "from God" but from the forces of anxiety that surrounded the formation and survival of each tradition. Attended over time by doctrines of "final revelations, exclusively disembodied transcendences, exclusively abstracted [pseudo-]embodiments, biblical literalism, and doctrinal certainty," the monotheistic claim that is forced out of this commandment looks more and more queerly to be a claim that the *people* are making on God, rather than the other way around. Placed into the very mouth of God, it "mask[s] the fear and hubris of the insecure lover who wants to know that there is no other in the beloved's heart."[12]

What if the commandment, from within *monotheism* reflects not the jealousy of the Divine, but the jealousy of the people, a jealousy that naturally follows in the wake of the logic of the One? What if it is a jealousy rooted in the trauma of sustained assault and oppression, a dysfunctional corporate anxiety that for varying reasons cannot abide a *God* who loves *indiscriminately, without propriety?* Under the stress of continual attack and exile, for example, or caught in the grip of imperial aspiration, the psychological demands for unity and loyalty are very strong. The logic of the One is efficient (except in its waste of bodies) because it is totalitarian and simple. For those who are exhausted by assault or mesmerized by the promise of absolute power, the logic of the One offers a tempting respite from the plenitude and cacophony of a world that makes no absolute guarantees. And so it is a distinctively queer move to suggest that the *people* are jealous of God; the *people* wish to control God's promiscuous pursuit of lovers—of the world itself—and to somehow contain the very heart of God.

The logic of the One that fuels monotheistic interpretations of the commandments runs up against the ethical demand coursing through the Jewish, Christian, and Muslim texts that understand love in terms of expansion, hospitality, and generosity, rather than jealousy. In the Torah, the law commands Israel to "love the Lord your God with all your heart, and with all your soul, and with all your might" (Deut. 6:5). Elsewhere, the people are also instructed to love one another: "You shall not take vengeance or bear any grudge against the sons of your own people, but you shall love your neighbor as yourself; I am the Lord" (Lev. 19:18). In the New Testament, all three of the synoptic gospels tell of Jesus answering a challenge about the greatest commandment by combining these two legal verses. He answers the scholars' questions by quoting "You shall love the Lord your God with all your heart, and with all your soul, and with all your strength, and with all your mind; and your neighbor as yourself" (Luke 10:27).[13] Jay Stern, among others, has pointed out the similarity of these accounts to a popular Talmudic story of the great rabbi Hillel from the first century before the Christian era:

> Once a heathen came to Shammai and said to him "I'll become a convert if you can teach me the whole Torah while I stand on one foot." Shammai became angry and drove him off with a tool he had in his hand. He came to Hillel with the same proposition. Hillel said to him, "What you dislike, do not do to others. That is the whole Torah. The rest is commentary. Go and learn the commentary!"[14]

While the Qur'an does not quote Leviticus as the synoptic gospels do, it is nevertheless shot through with repetitions on the theme of caring for others as a principle characteristic of what Allah "loves". Indeed, the phrase "Allah loves the doer of good to others" is repeated multiple times throughout the scriptures.[15] In all three traditions, these instructions of openness to others create a tension with the logic of One and suggest openings to the multiplicity that such generosity porously creates. None of these traditions succeeds, really, at monotheism, perhaps because their projected divinity refuses, often, to stay obediently in Heaven or to observe the rules of propriety with regard to intercourse outside of the elect. What leaks out of the monotheistic renderings of Judaism, Christianity, and Islam is a divine love for the world *as it is* (which includes a confounding, improper love for the inhabitants of their fundamentalists' rendering of Hell). Monotheism fails at the heart of these traditions, because it cannot overcome the heartbeat of generosity that will not be stilled no matter how many border guards are deployed, or rockets launched, or soldiers mutilated, or prisoners raped, or villages burned. Monotheism, like all top-heavy constructions, is undone by the witness of "the least of these," the very ones who confound the One, again and again.

And so ethics, in a logic of multiplicity, is not mute. It always comes back to the fluid, transient, and never eternal experience of *being present* in this world—a being-present that is mandated by incarnation. Witness, accompaniment, protest, comfort, solidarity, the "courage to see," and the "courage to sin," all of these are ethical postures suggested by a logic of multiplicity, by the revelation of divine presence in the world's intimate becoming. Ethics, understood from the posture of *being present*, cannot be summed up in simple rules, though it can be characterized, as Hillel characterizes the Torah, as focused on the presence—the gravitational pull—of others. I choose to call this ethical posture of being-present "love."

It is wise, especially in theology, to approach the often abused and overdetermined word "love" with caution. The love that is implied out of a concept of divine multiplicity, from a posture of "being-present" is not nostalgic, simple, or cozy. It is grown-up regard; it is a deep, physically present recognition of actual others in the world; it is a refusal to be dismissed or erased by others; it is courage to see suffering and a courage to sin in witnessing to it; it is a filling out of space and a making of time; it is relinquishment of stasis and openness to strangers, even the dangerous kind. It is an acceptance that love will use up your savings because it is not focused on preservation but on the ethos of generosity and expenditure. This kind of love, in other words, is the *be-ing* of divinity and so it cannot be separated from the question of ethics. To echo Dietrich Bonhoeffer and Immanuel Levinas, the love that follows in the wake of a logic of multiplicity (unlike the jealousy that follows in the wake of the logic of One) is grown-up, and it is not cheap. To be fully present to the bodies of others, to the body of world, the embodied divine shatters illusions and static categories of persons and things, of persons as things. It cuts moorings, and it is a gift that is also always already loss. Love *is* divine presence, as so many sages of the many religions have cried through the millennia. Love is heart-breaking because it is, always, a tehomically true story. It is the possibility of connection and so of becoming, and so it is both coming into intimacy and irretrievable passing away. Is it any wonder that most people anesthetize themselves against the love of God, or, as the Stoic orator Seneca suggested, against living itself?[16]

As the conceptual shape of divinity, multiplicity is therefore the embodiment of love. And love is what divinity is because love cannot *be* One, as Augustine realized. Love, necessitating the existence of others, of difference, gravity, and encounter, is the divine reality of heterogeneity even among those usually classed as "same."[17] And love is the only commandment that is possible in a logic of multiplicity, because at its simplest level, ethical "love" is the actualized recognition of the presence of others, acceptance of the dangerous gift of the world itself. In his search for a Christological phenomenology, Bonhoeffer, like Martin Buber, argued for authentic encounter as the "event" of divine presence. Authentic encounter, he suggested, is a recognition that another is not an "it", not even a "you" but a "Thou", a presence of absolute worth, utterly unexchangeable for another.[18]

Such recognition is only possible in the present, in *presence*. "I" can only encounter another as "Thou" when all of the usual categories by which I regard others are suspended. For example, one cannot meet another in his or her own utter inexchangeability and distinction through the categories normally applied for convenience (friend, co-worker; woman; professional; family member; narrative of expectations, etc.). Those categories compress the other into abstractions and make actual presence impossible to perceive—one misses the meeting entirely. What Bonhoeffer and Buber call the "you" and "it" categories erase what is inexchangeably *present* in favor of scripts about one another. This is not love in a logic of multiplicity, though it may be love in a logic of the One, love that seeks to guard the relationship against change, to guard against loss of possession or control over the meeting. Love that *is presence* is promiscuous, willing to open the door to *whomever* the other is *now* without demand for fidelity to promises made before, without regard for accompanying narratives or expectations. There is no contract. It is not that kind of love. This gestures toward hospitality as Derrida thinks it, which means it is ready for the possibility of death. It is not, however, without return. The return is not a contractual exchange of affections or of "gifts" but the return for such openness is life itself, even life in dying. Bonhoeffer knew *this* kind of love to be the way actually to live.

Put another way, this is love that changes everything, literally. It occurs in bodies. This is love that grasps the fragility of bodies; it sees the loss already imprinted therein but does not turn away from the value and experience of living-in-presence. Love in the logic of multiplicity is temporal, present, embodied, transient, creative, and rarely heroic. It is intimate, partial, responsible, and never nostalgic. But even these are all abstractions. Love is the name of ethics in a logic of multiplicity, but that only means that it is the *result* of the kind of intentional *presence* and *encounter* that Bonhoeffer and Oscar Romero describe. A neighborhood changes, gradually, from a place of despair, pollution, and violence to a place of people, of hope, and of community. What makes changes like this happen? It is clear to me, after years of working for hope in places called hopeless, that change occurs only through the actual presence of people who have the courage to be physically present, to *be* in a place of hunger, violence, or despair, who have the courage really to see, and the courage actually to sin against its prevailing ethos of disrespect and disregard. Such transformations happen only when people "show up" fully, and risk humiliation, or failure, or their lives. Nothing less does it.

And so, finally, if we wish to say that God *is* Love, then we also say that God comes into being specifically, without abstraction. And this is multiplicity because it is presence in the world that is confoundingly multiple. Always in motion, unintelligible in terms of a single, exemplary will but exerting an always specific will to presence, always arriving and passing away, if we but have eyes to see. The multiplicity that is divinity-in-love with the world, acts in what Baudrillard calls "impossible exchange" across the incalculable distance of our otherness. The multiplicity of divinity-in-love with the world speaks directly, in pentacostal fluency across the myriad unities of beings. The paradox of this abstraction—multiplicity—is its very specificity, its incarnation.

The oneness of God in monotheism relieves us of the paradox of love that defies religions, and patriotisms, and identities, upon which wars and their empires depend. Love in a theology of multiplicity cannot turn away from the impossible inexchangeability of the world, cannot assume that missiles are lessons as if what is destroyed can be exchanged for what is gained. If God is love, God cannot be One, an ultimate unity in which the utter inexchangeability of a life for a nation is made not only exchange-able, but coherent. Love is a synonym, therefore, for incarnation just as both are a synonym for divine multiplicity. To follow a God who becomes flesh is to make room for more than One. It is a posture of openness to the world as it comes to us, of loving the discordant, plenipotential worlds more than the desire to overcome, to colonize, or even to "save" them.

Love, the only ethics imaginable in a theology of divine multiplicity, is a promise, not a threat. It is the presence/s of the divine, available for encounter if we leave the scripts aside, if we are prepared to have our hearts broken by beauty, awe, and the redemption of responsibility.

Divine multiplicity, like any construct, is just a concept, metaphor. It is not divinity. "Divinity is, if nothing else, free. And this means that it is also free of theology and doctrine."[19] The stories we tell of it, however, form the fabric of imagination about what is possible for us in this world that God so loves.

Incarnation ... again.

Notes

Preface

1 Excerpt from Nye, 1995, "Telling the Story." Copyright © 1995. Reprinted with the permission of Far Corner Books, Portland, Oregon.
2 Luke 19:40, Revised Standard Version. Verses 39–40 read "And some of the Pharisees in the multitude said to him, 'Teacher, rebuke your disciples.' He answered, 'I tell you, if these were silent, the very stones would cry out,'" (Funk, 1985, p. 420).
3 Hill, 1938, p. 52. Quoted in Gill, 1982, p. 43.
4 Sands, 1994, p. 63.
5 Schneider, R., 2001, pp. 100–108.
6 Keller, 2003, p. xv.

1 Introduction: incarnation ... again

1 Rajchman, 2000, p. 22.
2 I am taking liberties here with the brilliant title of one of Irigaray's (1985) books: *Ce sexe qui n'en est pas un* translated as *This Sex Which Is Not One.*
3 Deleuze and Guattari, 1987, p. 20.
4 Althaus-Reid, 2003, p. 48.
5 Claire Colebrook, 2000a, p. 2.
6 Ania Loomba et al., 2005, p. 1. See also Krishna, 2002, pp. 170–83.
7 Rajchman, 2000, p. 13.
8 For a full discussion of the idea of tehomic theology (derived from the Hebrew term for the Deep in Genesis 1:2, *Tehom*), see Keller, 2003, especially Part I.
9 See Althaus-Reid, 2000 and 2003.
10 Kwok, 2005, and Joh, "In Proximity to the Other: Subjectivity without Sovereignty," talk (not published) delivered at Chicago Theological Seminary, January 11, 2007. See also Joh, 2006, and Perkinson, 2004.
11 Ogbonnaya, 1994; Kathryn Tanner, 2001 and 2005.
12 Williams, 1995; Armour, 1999; Welch, 1990; Deleuze and Guattari, 1987; King, T., 2005.
13 For a fuller discussion of the co-constitutiveness of racism, sexism and heterosexism in particular, see Schneider, L. C., 2004. See also McClintock, 1995.
14 See Daly, 1984, p. 223 and passim. For her first critique of Tillich's notion of the "courage to be", see Daly, 1971, pp. 1108–11.
15 Derrida, 1998 pp. 8ff. On the same idea, and borrowing from Derrida, Althaus-Reid (2003, p. 134) writes, "theological prostheses are the attempt to recover what has been lost in theological language, which is also a language of

origin, written in a dynamics of transplantation, a critical bi-theological language dealing with the incommunicable."

16 Peterson, 1951. For other recent treatments of the Trinity in light of political (and feminist) critiques of monotheism, see also LaCugna, 1991; and Tanner, 2001. For an important contemporary study of the political challenge of liberation theology in the context of empire, see also Sölle, 1974.

17 Boff, 1988; Moltmann, 1981.

18 Jennings, 1985, pp. 24f, 31, 39. Jennings gives a cogent and useful analysis of apologetics that is relevant particularly to theological projects that attempt to give an accounting of divinity that seeks intelligibility outside of canonical sources. He distinguishes between apologetics that function within and between existing religious situations (translating the religious concepts of Christianity into the congenial terms of another religious system) and, in the context of diminished "religious situations" of "reverse apologetics" that require conversion to another philosophical system prior to translation of Christian theological concepts into that system. Using process philosophy as an example, he argues, "The translation of theological categories into the categories of process thought is persuasive and apologetically effective only to the extent to which there is a prior commitment to the persuasiveness of this philosophical system. Otherwise a whole series of other moves must be undertaken – in this case to persuade people to become Whiteheadians. Once again the apologetic task of translating the language of faith into a contemporary idiom is deflected in favor of the new necessity (the reverse apologetic) to propagate process philosophy as an antecedent basis for rendering faith intelligible" (p. 32). Finally, Jennings identifies what he calls "double reverse apologetics" in which the theologian has become convinced that it is secularity itself that provides the point of contact for translation, requiring a rejection of religion altogether in order to "announce the Gospel." The problem with this criticism of reverse and double reverse apologetics, of course, is that many persons raised in the Christian faith, whether within confessional settings or outside of them, are perfectly willing to be introduced to new antecedent philosophies, cosmologies, and anthropologies if doing so will help them to make better sense both of current life as they experience it and of divinity in relation to that life. His own project in *Beyond Theism* is heavily dependent upon the explanatory task of presenting a linguistic phenomenology that is antecedent to understanding what he means by "God-language." Despite the fact that I think the apologetic dimension of contemporary theological work to be far more complex and inextricably "involved" with antecedent philosophies of various metaphysical or anti-metaphysical stripes than he seems to allow, the value of his analysis, especially of reverse apologetics, is its reminder that the agenda in constructive theology is often both impure and multi-intentional.

19 Moltmann (1999, p. 5) has suggested "it is simple but true. Theology has only one problem: *God*." He goes on to explain: "We are theologians *for God's sake*. God is our dignity. God is our suffering. God is our hope." God, in other words, is for Moltmann the *point* of theology since "God is not in *our* religion, our culture or *our* church. God is in *his own* presence and in *his own* kingdom." This recentering reminder, reminiscent of Barth's (1960) reminder to liberal theology that human flourishing and happiness (progress) is not the point of theology but that only God is the point, for nothing but God makes progress possible, while a dogmatically circular argument is effective in limning the hubris both of liberal scientific claims to reality and to fundamentalist claims to God.

20 Keller, 2003, p. 44. In her introduction she writes (p. xvi), "Christian theology, I argue, created this *ex nihilo* at the cost of its own depth. It systematically and symbolically sought to erase the chaos of creation."

21 Ibid., p. 44
22 Sands, 1994, p. 63.
23 In her criticism of the limits of Saussurean structuralism that presumed too much closure to written texts, Julia Kristeva (1980, p. 69) introduced the idea of inter-textuality to get at the wider matrix of influence and interaction that "composes" any text, even long after it has been written. With Derrida, text has come also to signify far more than the written word. Cf. Derrida, 1997, esp. pp. 158ff.
24 Joan Osborne's recording of the song "What if God Was One of Us?" (*Relish*, Blue Gorilla/Mercury Records, 1995) was a hit on rock and roll radio stations for several years after it came out in 1995. Written by Eric Bazilian.
25 Jordan, 2005, p. 121.
26 Keller, 2003, p. 229.
27 Rather than humor, Althaus-Reid (2003, p. 22) suggests dance toward a creative mode of uncertainty: "Tangoing may be a way to get into the rhythm of a theology in movement which does not care for sitting even if offered a chair. It may disclose the fundamental differences between the critical Bisexual theologian and the mono-loving one. Basically, the call to do theology is different, because it disrupts certainty. The eschatology is different, as bisexuality disconfirms in the future what the present verifies."
28 Jean Baudrillard, 2001, p. 8.
29 Not to be confused, though it often is so (especially in recent years by philosophers and theologians), with the Heisenberg Uncertainty Principle, which measures changes in velocity and position of certain particles relative to the observer.
30 Gebara, 1999.
31 Pierre Bourdieu (2001) develops the notion of "habitus" particularly in relation to bodily postures, an idea that I take in a slightly different direction here, though the emphasis and allusion to embodiment that Bourdieu intends will be my point as well.
32 See my book *Re-Imagining the Divine* (Schneider, L. C., 1999) for a fuller discussion of the tension between experiential confession and metaphoric exemption. One way that the metaphoric exemption has been expressed in historical Christian theology is through what Pseudo-Dionysius called the *via negativa*. The classic expression of this "negative way" comes from the theologian Anselm (1986, p. 246) in the eleventh century of the Christian era. He wrote "et quidem credimus te esse aliquid pro nihil maius cogitari possit" which means that God is "that than which nothing greater can be conceived." In the twentieth century, Paul Tillich referred to the deep iconoclasm of Christian theology after the Reformations in particular as the "Protestant Principle."
33 DeHart, 2002, p. 96.
34 Schneider, L. C., 1999, p. 134.

2 Then came the word: the invention of monotheism

1 Jaffee, 2001, p. 754.
2 Deleuze and Guattari, 1987, p. 3.
3 In 144 CE, the Gnostic Christian Marcion was excommunicated for his claim that the Creator God of the Hebrew scriptures was another deity altogether from the God proclaimed by Jesus. In 382 Pope Damascus presided over the council that listed the canonical books of the Old and New Testaments, codifying in scripture the unity of the God of Israel and of Jesus and Paul. Cf. Chadwick, 1990, and Markus, 1990.
4 Throughout this book, "Christian Era" (CE) will refer to the common Christian calendar that marks the putative birth of Jesus as its zero point. "Before the Christian Era" (BCE) will refer to the years before that zero point.

5 Smith, M., 2001, p. 12.

6 Wigoder, et al., 2002, p. 47.

7 The Oxford English Dictionary records the first use of monotheism in 1660, in Henry More's treatise entitled *An Explanation of the Grand Mystery of Godliness, or, A true and faithfull representation of the everlasting Gospel of our Lord and Saviour Jesus Christ, the only begotten Son of God and sovereign over men and angels.* More writes, "But thus to make the World God, is to make all; and therefore this kinde of Monotheisme of the Heathen is as rank Atheisme as their Polytheisme was proved before." (III, ii. 62). The second recorded use of "monotheism" occurs in Henry Rowlands' 1723 *Mona Antiqua Restaurata,* referring to the Druids of Anglesey, whereas it is not until 1812 that T. Cogan deploys the term in reference to Judaism. (T. Cogan, *Jewish Dispensation* ii, paragraph 7.322). Quoted in the OED, Dec. 2002 online edition.

8 Smith, M., 2001, p. 11.

9 Mach, 1999, p. 24.

10 Peterson, D., 1988, p. 97.

11 Ibid.

12 See, for example, James C. Livingston's (1998, pp. 3–22) introduction for a helpful overview of the difficulties that face contemporary scholars regarding the term "religion". Native American scholars in particular have raised this issue, as have anthropologists dealing with native traditions in Asia, South America, and Africa. The modern concept of "religion" tends to sever important connections between, for example, work (hunting, agriculture, study, etc.) and so-called "ritual" or "religion". Cf. Gill, 1982, but, better yet, look for almost anything by Native writers, like M. Scott Momaday, Leslie Marmon Silko, Thomas King, Joy Harjo, and others for evidence of the problematic in story and poetry as well as academic essay.

13 Smith, M., 2001, p. 11.

14 Pakkala, 1999, p. 15, n. 77. Pakkala also quotes Oswald Loretz (1999): "Die neuzeitliche Problem – und Frontstellung 'Monotheismus – Polytheismus' erweist sich für viele modernen Autoren beim Studium der mesopotamischen, westsemitischen und biblischen Quellen auf weite Strecken hin als hinderlich für ein wirkliches Verständnis des Beweisverfahrens der altorientalischen Theologie über die Einzigkeit eines Gottes."

15 Smith, M., 1990, p. xxx.

16 Pakkala, 1999, p. 16.

17 Jennings, 1985, p. 114.

18 For example, in many of the Pueblo traditions of the American Southwest, worldly forces such as rain, sun, snow, birth, corn, and death are capable of becoming "beings" who interact with humans in ritual or in daily life. This does not mean that these divine "persons" remain beings all of the time or are present all of the time. There is a fluidity to their existence that, on the other hand, is not idiosyncratic or chaotic. The fact that European systems of thought, circumscribed by Pythagorean notions of existence and ontological categories shaped by Aristotelian notions of substance and form, are largely unable to grasp these other understandings of divinity in relation to world does not mean that they are ungraspable according to other systems of ontological logic.

19 The development of process theology reflects this shift among liberal and feminist theologians, while the emergence of "Open Theism" among more conservative contemporary Christian theologians suggests shifts along these lines as well. For introduction to the former, see Cobb and Griffin, 1976, and Suchocki, 1992. For introduction to the latter, see Pinnock et al., 1994.

20 West, 1999, p. 21.

21 Pettazoni, 1965, p. 37.

22 Smith, M., 2001, p. 12.
23 Ibid., p. 11.
24 Halperin, 2000, p. 196.
25 Reynolds, 1637, p. 163.
26 A great deal of attention has been given to the idea of Christian supremacy as a tool of cultural expansion in which Christian faith is conflated with notions of civilization and improvement. The arguments for colonization from the 1500s through the 1900s are full of this idea. Excellent examples of this approach can be found in the accounts of conquistadors in the Americas: for example, Schneider, P., 2006, or the journals of Christopher Columbus, or of Bartolomé de las Casas (Sullivan, 1995) and a fine essay by Howard L. Harrod (1984).
27 Hume, 1956, p. 23.
28 Rousseau, 1979, p. 256.
29 Robert Bellah (1965, pp. 73–5), for example, proposed a progressive sequence of "five ideal typical stages of development" for anthropological approaches to the study of comparative religion: "primitive, archaic, historic, early modern, and modern" based on the presupposition that "religious symbolization ... tends to change over time ... in the direction of more differentiated, comprehensive, and in Weber's sense, more rationalized formulations." While monotheism in any doctrinal sense may not be proposed in later twentieth century progressive schemes (the parochial hubris of such Euro- and Christo-centric assumptions having been identified) there remains a strong residual set of assumptions privileging monotheism in the progressive project itself, which places western culture by default at a kind of developmental pinnacle.
30 Gnuse, 1997, p. 63.
31 Petersen, D., 1988, p. 94. Gnuse (1997, p. 63) puts it this way: "Late 19th century scholars, influenced by ... notions of scientific evolution, began to describe the Israelite religious development as a passage through several natural stages of evolution toward increased intellectual sophistication until they attained monotheism and an ethical view of reality ... Hence, Israel's religious odyssey was described with the successive stages of animism, totemism, polytheism, henotheism or monolatry, and finally monotheism."
32 Troeltsch, 1991, p. 82.
33 Pakkala, 1999, p. 15.
34 Moltmann, 1985, p. 50.
35 It is of course interesting to note that the proverbial emperor of "new clothes" fame in children's literature is fooled into thinking he is wearing a fancy new robe (our metaphor for the Trinity, in this case) when in fact he is not. Clothed or unclothed, however, he is still the emperor. Nothing regarding his *rule,* so the story goes, has changed.
36 Ruggieri, 1985, p. 21.

3 "No god but me": the roots of monotheism in Israel

1 Except where noted, all quotations from the Bible are taken from the New Revised Standard Version.
2 Robert Gnuse, 1997, p. 64, notes that the most well-known proponent of the Mosaic revolution viewpoint was William Foxwell Albright. Albright's (1940) text, *From the Stone Age to Christianity,* exemplifies a scholarly Christian apologetic for monotheism. Albright openly opposes the evolutionism favored by other scholars such as Julius Wellhausen, not on the grounds that an evolutionary theory betrayed the unscholarly prejudice toward monotheistic supremacy that it often did, but because it diminished the uniqueness of the

revelatory claim of monotheism for Israel and therefore for Christianity. Contemporary biblical scholars, for the most part, reject both approaches.

3 The Sh'ma Yisrael comes from Deuteronomy 6:4–9: *Sh'ma Yisrael Adonai Elohaynu Adonai Echad* (Hear, Israel, the Lord is our God, the Lord is One); *Barukh Shem k'vod malkhuto l'olam va-ed* (Blessed be the Name of His glorious kingdom for ever and ever); *V-ahavta et Adonai Elohecha b-chol l'vavcha u-v-chol naf'sh'cha u-v-chol m'odecha* (And you shall love the Lord your God with all your heart and with all your soul and with all your might); *V-hayu ha-d'varim ha-ayleh asher anochi m'tzav'cha ha-yom al l'vavecha* (And these words that I command you today shall be in your heart); *V-shinantam l-vanecha, v-dibarta bam b-shivt'cha b-vaytecha, u-v-lecht'cha ba-derech, u-v-shachb'cha u-v-kumecha* (And you shall teach them diligently to children, and you shall speak of them when you sit at home, and when you walk along the way, and when you lie down and when you rise up); *U-k'shartam l'ot al yadecha, v-hayu l-totafot bayn aynecha* (And you shall bind them as a sign on your hand, and they shall be for frontlets between your eyes); *U-chtavtam al m'zuzot baytecha u-vi-sharecha* (And you shall write them on the doorposts of your house and on your gates).

4 The Nicene Creed that is most often recited in Christian communities today was revised from the original adopted in Nicaea at the First Ecumenical Council, called by the Emperor Constantine in 325. This revised version was adopted by the Second Ecumenical Council that convened in Constantinople in 381 CE It reads: "We believe in one God, the Father, the Almighty, maker of heaven and earth, of all that is, seen and unseen. We believe in one Lord, Jesus Christ, the only Son of God, eternally begotten of the Father, God from God, Light from Light, true God from true God, begotten, not made, of one Being with the Father. Through him all things were made. For us and for our salvation he came down from heaven by the power of the Holy Spirit he became incarnate from the Virgin Mary, and was made man. For our sake he was crucified under Pontius Pilate; he suffered death and was buried. On the third day he rose again in accordance with the Scriptures; he ascended into heaven and is seated at the right hand of the Father. He will come again in glory to judge the living and the dead, and his kingdom will have no end. We believe in the Holy Spirit, the Lord, the giver of life, who proceeds from the Father and the Son. With the Father and the Son he is worshiped and glorified. He has spoken through the Prophets. We believe in one holy catholic and apostolic Church. We acknowledge one baptism for the forgiveness of sins. We look for the resurrection of the dead, and the life of the world to come. Amen."

5 The Shahadah is the most basic, and universal Sunni declaration of faith: "I bear witness that there is no god except God and I bear witness that Muhammad is the Messenger of God." (The Arabic transliteration is: "Ash hadu anlaa ilaaha illallaahu wa ash hadu anna muhammadar-rasulallah." The Qur'anic text most closely associated with this primary confession is Sura 3:18: God bears witness that there is no god except He, and so do the angels and those who possess knowledge. Truthfully and equitably, He is the absolute God; there is no God but He, the Almighty, Most Wise.

6 Halperin, 1987, p. 77.

7 Gnuse, 1997, p. 62.

8 Unlike Chapters 1–39, which are traditionally attributed to Israelite authorship of the late eighth century BCE, Chapters 40–55 of Isaiah are believed to be a collection of speeches of the mid sixth century BCE, "delivered to the Jews who had been deported to Babylon from their native Judah a half century earlier." (Clifford, 1984, p. 3).

9 Mach, 1999, p. 25.

10 See, for example, Genesis 1:26, 11:7, 31:19ff., and elsewhere.

11 Juha Pakkala, 1999, p. 238, notes the strict intolerance toward other gods takes place in advance of the articulation of monotheism as a concept.

12 Halperin, 1987, p. 84.

13 The literature concerning the development of pre-Israelite monotheism in Egypt is extensive. The most famous example is the short-lived anti-polytheistic Aten revolution of King Akhenaten, though Jan Assmann (1997, p. 193) points out that "time and again the [traditional] Egyptian sources predicate the oneness/ singleness/uniqueness of a god. Amun-Re in particular is regarded as a solar deity who develops his all-embracing creative and life-giving efficiency in the form of the sun."

14 The Persian One-God, called Ahura Mazda or Aramazd, is itself the product of a more ancient, Aryan concept of a single purifying fire at the heart (and birth) of the unified cosmos. Cf. Boyce, 1992.

15 Halperin, 2000, p. 198.

16 "In sum, the Israelites may have perceived themselves as a people different from the Canaanites. Separate religious traditions of Yahweh, separate traditions of origins in Egypt for at least some component of Israel, and separate geographical holdings in the hill country contributed to the Israelites' sense of difference from their Canaanite neighbors inhabiting the coast and valleys. Nonetheless, Israelite and Canaanite cultures shared a good deal in common, and religion was no exception. Deities and their cults in Iron Age Israel represented aspects of the cultural continuity with the indigenous Late Bronze Age culture and the contemporary urban culture on the coast and in the valleys. The examples of El, Baal, and the symbol of the asherah illustrate this continuity for the period of the Judges." Smith, M., 1990, p. 7.

17 Smith, M., 1990, p. 154.

18 West, 1999, p. 24.

19 West (1999, p. 27) points out that "according to normal Semitic idiom, 'sons of gods' means 'members of the class "god"', not individually distinguished', just as 'sons of craftsmen' means 'craftsmen'. In the 29th Psalm these lesser deities are actually addressed directly: 'Render to Yahweh, O sons of gods, render to Yahweh glory and strength; render to Yahweh the glory of his name, worship Yahweh in the splendor of holiness.'"

20 Halperin, 1987, p. 78.

21 Mach, 1999, p. 23, n. 11.

22 Thompson, 1996, p. 119, n. 13. What is more, Halperin (1987, p. 80) writes, "early Israel was somehow not quite monotheistic, despite its concentration of YHWH as the special deity of the people and the supreme causal force in the cosmos. On the other hand, Israel's neighbors were not fully polytheistic, for their cults centered around particular higher gods."

23 Smith, M., 1990, p. 166.

24 Halperin, 1987, p. 79. Not all, of course, agree in the details. "Albright speaks of a Mosaic age of monotheism deriving from the Sinai experience. H. Gottlieb, M. Smith, B. Lang, and P. K. McCarter note the role of the monarchy in the development of monotheism. Smith, followed by Lang, stresses the importance of the development of the 'Yahweh-only party' in the ninth century and afterward. Lang especially emphasizes the 'prophetic minority' that provided initial support for this religious posture in the northern kingdom before its fall and later in the southern kingdom. Many commentators attach great importance to the Exile as the formative period for the emergence of Israelite monotheism" (Smith, M., 1990, p. 154).

25 Smith, M., 2001, p. 179.

26 Mach, 1999, pp. 22ff.

27 Ibid., p. 25.
28 Ibid.
29 2 Kings 5:15ff. See also Lang, 1983, p. 22.
30 Cf. Durkheim, 1965, pp. 322ff.
31 Mach, 1999, p. 25.
32 Isaiah 40:15.
33 Isaiah 42:10.

4 The end of the many: the roots of monotheism in Greek philosophy

1 Aristotle, 1941, "Metaphysics" 986:18–21, p. 698.
2 Frede, 1999, p. 47.
3 Guthrie, 1955, p. 258: "The religion of Homer, with its class-distinctions and elementary morality, is a mirror of the social conditions of his times. Xenophanes shows up no less the character and prevalence of Greek polytheism by his tirades against it."
4 Theophilus of Antioch, 1970, 1.10, p. 15.
5 Aeschylus, *The Daughters of Helios,* Fragment 70, quoted in Ferguson, 1980, p. 95.
6 See Proclus, 1939, Chapter 4.
7 Plutarch, 1880, p. 129.
8 Iamblichus, 1989.
9 "In the absence of written records before Philolaus in the late 5th century, it is impossible to tell how much of the Pythagorean tradition in mathematics, music, and astronomy can be traced back to the founder and his early followers. Since the fundamental work of Walter Burkert, it has been generally recognized that the conception of Pythagorean philosophy preserved in later antiquity was the creation of Plato and his school, and that the only reliable pre-Platonic account of Pythagorean thought is the system of Philolaus." Price and Kearns, 2003, p. 461. Cf. Burkert, 1985.
10 See Lesher, 1992.
11 As Lesher, 1992, reminds us, there is too little of Xenophanes' writing left to allow us to conclude with confidence that *he* was making an argument for one god alone. In fact it is Lesher's opinion that Xenophanes does not do so, although others have argued differently. But the number of gods is less important at this stage in Greek thought than the character of divinity itself as immutable, transcendent, and whole, and it is this ball that the sixth-century Greeks clearly send rolling down the centuries.
12 Plato, *The Republic* (1961, p. 832), 10.606e-607a: "when you meet encomiasts of Homer who tell us that this poet has been the educator of all Hellas, and that for the conduct and refinement of human life he is worthy of our study and devotion, and that we should order our entire lives by the guidance of this poet, we must love and salute them as *doing the best they can,* and concede to them that Homer is the most poetic of the poets and the first of tragedians, *but we must know the truth,* and that we can admit no poetry into our city save only hymns to the gods and the praises of good men. For if you grant admission to the honeyed Muse in lyric or epic, pleasure and pain will be lords of your city instead of law and that which shall from time to time have approved itself to the general reason as best [my emphasis]."
13 Xenophanes, 1992, p. 82 "Fragment 11."
14 According to Lesher (Xenophanes, 1992, p. 81), "Xenophanes shows his displeasure not only with beliefs about the gods in mortal form (fragment 14), and with attributions to the gods of improper conduct (fragments 11–12), but also with the impact on personal virtue and the social fabric of the city of ancient poetic fictions about divine battles and conflicts, (fragment 1)."

15 Xenophanes, 1992, fragments 15–16, pp. 89–90. It is important to note Lesher's caution in interpretation of this famous set of fragments. It is probable that Xenophanes indeed meant to ridicule the anthropomorphizing tendency in Greek religious thought by suggesting that animals would also construct gods in their images. It is Clement who adds the implied moral: "The Greeks suppose that the gods have human shapes and feelings, and each paints their forms exactly like their own, as Xenophanes says: 'Ethiopians say ...'"

16 Tillich, 1951, p. 241.

17 Baldwin, 1963, p. 44.

18 Daly, 1973, p. 19.

19 Xenophanes, 1992, fragment 1, p. 13.

20 Ibid., pp. 31–3.

21 Plato, 1961, pp. 747–72, spells this theory out in his famous allegory of the cave in *The Republic,* Book VII.

22 Kenney, 1991, p. 33.

23 Ibid.

24 See Aristotle's *Nichomachean Ethics* 1:6 (1941, pp. 935ff). See also Plato's *Parmenides* (1961, pp. 920ff.) for a thinly disguised jab at a character named Aristoteles who lifts weights, struts, and dares to take on Parmenides himself.

25 Aristotle's *Physics,* 11:3 (1941, pp. 218ff.).

26 Ibid., II.

27 For a discussion of Cicero's contributions to the expansion of the Latin language from the Greek, see Powell, 1995.

5 "I am because we are": an opening of multiplicity in Africa

1 Mwoleka, 1975, p. 203.

2 Osborn, 1997, p. 5.

3 For a helpful discussion of the influence of Greek thought on Roman cultural development, see Griffin, 1988, pp. 76–100.

4 For a good overview of Philo's influence in early Christian thought, see Runia, 1993.

5 VanderKam, 2001, p. 138.

6 Moltmann, 1981, p. 131.

7 Philo (1929a) of Alexandria, *Quod Omnis Probus Liber Sit,* 5.

8 Philo (1929b), *De Opificio Mundi,* 8. Interestingly, as I noted in Chapter 4, there is a tradition recorded by Iamblichus (1989) that claims Pythagoras studied in Egypt and it was there that he developed his more advanced and more mystical view of mathematics.

9 Surburg, 1975, p. 156.

10 It is important to note that one Gospel records Jesus' paternal reference to God with the linguistic hybrid of "ἀββά ὁ πατρρ" or "Abba, Father" (Mark 14:36). Some scholars translate the Aramaic "Abba" by the more intimate and domestic term of "daddy". There is some evidence that the tradition of this use passed into the worship practices of the pre-Nicaean church communities, reflected in the two epistolary repetitions of the phrase in Romans 8:15 and Galatians 4:5–7. For the first treatment of this idea, see Jeremias, 1966, pp. 15–67. For a helpful criticism of this use, see D'Angelo, 1992.

11 Even the account of Jesus' conception and birth in Matthew and Luke is clouded by the possible variances in interpretation. Just what the first writers meant by "conceived of the Holy Spirit" cannot be fully known. Later, when the Holy Spirit was doctrinally understood to be the same as God the Father in the Trinity, the idea of Jesus' divine *paternity* rather than his honor brought about by

God's blessing on his conception is clarified, but not before then. The very fact
of the centuries' long battles over this very question is evidence of the lack of
clarity provided by the first storytellers.

12 Theissen, 1999, p. 48.
13 Ibid. p. 47.
14 Aristotle, 1941, *Metaphysics*, Book 12, 1074a.
15 Davila, 1999, p. 3.
16 Rusch, 1980, p. 2.
17 Cf. Kee, 1977; Smith, J. Z., 1975; King, 2000, pp. 12–16.
18 Rusch, 1980, p. 6.
19 Moltmann, 1981, p. 130.
20 Geffré and Jossua, 1985, p. ix.
21 Bauckham, 1998, p. 28.
22 Porter, 1980, p. 530.
23 Osborn (1997, p. 2) is quoting Jerome *vir. Illust.* 57.
24 My thanks to Brandee Mimitzraiem of Drew University for suggesting the term
"creole".
25 Evans (Tertullianus, 1948, pp. 184f) suggests that the name "Praxeas", which
means "busybody" could be a nickname for some notable person, probably
Noetus of Smyrna.
26 Quintus Septimii Florentis Tertulliani, *Adversus Praxean Liber*, 2. Tertullianus,
1948, p. 91 (Latin) p. 132 (English trans.). See also Rusch, 1980, p. 10.
27 Tertullianus, 1948, p. 3.
28 Ibid., p. 6.
29 Jan Assman (1997, p. 153) claims that "The concept of a universal god as the
religious counterpart of political imperialism originated in Heliopolis. The
pharaohs of the 18th Dynasty transcended not only the political borders but
also the mental boundaries of the Egyptian world. While ruling over a multi-
national empire which they deemed universal, they formed the concept of a
universal deity as the creator and preserver of all. While the Egyptian armies
were conquering the world, the Heliopolitan priests were drawing the con-
comitant conclusions." Also, Smith, M. (2001, p. 147) writes of the pre-exilic
monarchy in Israel: "The monarchy was equally a political and religious institution, and, under royal influence, religion combined powerful expressions of
state and religious ideology. When the prestige of the national deity was
increased, the prestige of the dynasty in turn was enhanced. See also Fowden,
(1993), Ruggieri (1985), Kirsch (2004) and Halperin, (1987).
30 It is interesting to note that the Greek text uses the specifically Latin name
"legion" (appearing in transliteration as λεγιών in the Greek text) rather than
the Greek term for "many" (πλῆθος, for example). This supports the possibility
that the Gospel writers fully intended to implicate the Roman military system in
a story of demonic possession and exorcism.
31 Of course, this focus on the pastoral may have been deliberate on the part of
the Gospel writers, whose cultural context of Jewish messianism was strongly
focused on the political; the Messiah would restore the kingdom of Israel in all
of its glory and power. Any analogy or parable based on political rule might
have been precisely what the Jesus movement wished to avoid, either because
they strongly opposed a political messianism in favor of an apocalyptic and
eschatological one, or because they saw analogies in the pastoral motifs that are
opaque to contemporary listeners, or because in the aftermath of crucifixion the
Gospel communities could not make sense of such sayings and did not repeat
them. There is, of course, no documentary evidence for the latter hypothesis,
only the fact that all of the sayings attributed to Jesus are second-hand, filtered
through communities struggling to make sense of his execution.

32 Moltmann (1981, p. 193) points out, for example, that "it was all-important for the Christian apologists to present their faith as the truly reasonable religion, and hence as the divine worship which really sustained the state. Following Josephus, they linked biblical tradition of the one rule of the one God with philosophical monotheism."

33 Ibid., p. 194.

34 Tertullianus, 1948, Section 3.

35 Ibid.

36 Ibid., Section 8., pp. 139–40.

37 Ogbonnaya (1994), among others, has made a persuasive argument that the facility Tertullian shows for a trinitarian concept of divinity is most effectively explained by his African context rather than the circuitous routes scholars have attempted to take to avoid any attribution to African cultural origins. Such racist historicizing is evident even among those who grant to Tertullian the appellation "African" but take pains to define the name such that most of the continent and its cultures is left out. Cf. Tertullianus, 1948, p. 1, n. 1. Like Augustine, Tertullian was raised in Carthage, a Creole city at the crossroads of African, Mediterranean, and Asian cultures. To exempt Tertullian from African influence is without geographic or historical basis, as Ogbonnaya demonstrates.

38 Mbiti, 1990, p. 107.

39 See especially Ogbonnaya, 1994.

40 Vähäkangas, 2002, p. 71. Cf. Raymond Mosha, "The Trinity in the African Context" in *Africa Theological Journal* 9:1, pp. 40–7; and Oduyoye, 1986.

41 Tertullianus, 1948, n. 1, p. 1.

42 Ngong, 2003.

43 Vähäkangas (2002, p. 69) notes that there is tension in contemporary African theological circles regarding the trinity which casts positions like Ogbonnaya's (1994) in the minority even among Africans. He writes, "The Holy Trinity has not gained much attention among African academic theologians. Even in those cases when it has been discussed, it has sometimes been briefly mentioned almost as if it were a necessary evil or in other cases the Trinitarian dogma, or at least its traditional form, has been rejected. This is done on the grounds that the vocabulary of the doctrine of the Trinity is based on Hellenistic metaphysical thinking and that the entire idea of three persons in one God is totally incomprehensible according to African patterns of thought. On the other side there are those African theologians who have been eager to find *vestigial trinitatis* in African traditional cultures."

44 Ogbonnaya, 1994, p. xiii.

45 Tertullianus, 1948, p. 138, 7.

46 Ogbonnaya, 1994, p. 1.

47 Quoted in MacMullen, 1997, p. 130.

48 Tertullianus, 1956, 4:36–37, "*sed circumspice, Marcion, sit amen non delesti: Stulta mundi elegit dues, ut confundat sapientia.*" Paul's own argument for the apparent foolishness of God (1 Cor. 1:27) is a weapon in Tertullian's hand.

49 Osborn, 1997, p. 121, n. 17.

50 Rev. Karen Mosby-Avery, personal correspondence, July 13, 2006.

51 Jennings, 1985, p. 13.

52 LaCugna, 1991, p. 391.

53 Wilson, 1997, p. 9. Jonathan Kirsch (2004) develops this notion further, especially with reference to the elaborate state spying system and institution of secret police that Constantine established.

54 Ruggieri, 1985, pp. 18–19.

55 Moltmann, 1981, p. 200. See also p. 250 n. 24.

56 Fowden, 1993, pp. 100–101.

57 Alföldi, 1948, p. 11.
58 Moltmann, 1981, p. 195.
59 Ruggieri, 1985, p. 17.
60 I am grateful to Pat Schneider for this important insight.
61 Augustine, *De Trinitate*, VIII:14, 8.12.14.
62 See Tanner, 2005.
63 Augustine, *De Trinitate*, 9.5.8.
64 LaCugna, 1991, p. 94;
65 Ibid.
66 Ogbonnaya, 1994, p. 20.
67 See Keller's (2003) discussion of the "drying up" of Christian theology from Augustine to Barth.
68 The full text of the 1648 Westminster Confession is available at www.reformed. org/documents/wcf_with_proofs/.

6 Monotheism, western science, and the theory of everything

1 Copernicus, 1989, p. 40.
2 Nietzsche, 1975, 110, p. 170.
3 Ibid., 92, p. 145.
4 Nietzsche, 1954, 19, p. 586.
5 See, for example, Aquinas' (1969, p. 164) argument for the unity of God in relation to the unity of the world, "Question 11, Article 3" of the *Summa Theologica*. He defends the oneness of God with three arguments, the third of which is: "Thirdly, because the world is one. For we find all existent things in mutual order, certain of them subserving others. Now divers things only combine in a single order where there is a single cause of order. For unity and order is introduced into a plurality of things more perfectly by a single cause than by many, unity only incidentally in so far as they too are somehow one. So the primary source of unity and order in the universe, namely God, must be one himself, for the primary is always most perfect and not incidental but essential." See also his discussion of the necessary unity of the cosmos in his discussion of resurrection and renovation in "First Treatise on Faith", Chapters 141–83, in Aquinas, 1958, pp. 150–85.
6 Descartes, 1993, pp. 14ff.
7 I have discussed this dynamic at length in Schneider, L. C., 1999, especially in the final chapter, "Beyond Monotheism."
8 I base this claim on the result of linguistic theory in anthropology and sociology. Cf. Geertz, 1973, or Berger and Luckmann, 1966.
9 See Plato's (1961) *Dialogues,* especially *Meno, Theaetetus,* and *Apology* for a discussion of the necessity that the true, the good, and the real be conflated, thus instituting a contradiction between truth and imagination, for example. Socrates also adds the category of eternity to the true and the real, thereby ensuring the abstraction of both "true" and "real" from the realms of flesh, flux, and sensation.
10 Bacon, 1887, pp. 392–6.
11 Hawking, 1988, p. 10.
12 Bacon, 1901, "Aphorisms 39–46" pp. 428–34.
13 I am indebted to my teachers, Michael Dorris and Howard Harrod, for this insight. For a useful discussion of dreams, particularly in Native North American traditions, see Irwin, 1994, and Tooker, 1979.
14 Two statements in William of Occam's fourteenth-century writings apply to the concept known as "Occam's razor". One is *Frustra fit per plura quod potest fieri per pauciora* (It is vain to do with more what can be done with less) and

the other is *Numquam ponenda est pluralitas sine necessitate* (Plurality should not be posited without necessity). Thomas Aquinas (1945) later wrote, "If a thing can be done adequately by means of one, it is superfluous to do it by means of several; for we observe that nature does not employ two instruments where one suffices."

15 Newton, 1989, p. 146.

16 Hawking, 1988, p. 55.

17 Victor Stenger (1990, p. 25) insists that the simplicity demanded by the principle of Occam's razor not be mistaken for a denial. He argues that the "use of Occam's razor, along with the related critical, skeptical view toward any speculations about the unknown, is perhaps the most misunderstood aspect of the scientific method. People confuse doubt with denial. Science doesn't deny anything, but it doubts everything not required by the data. Note, however, that doubt does not necessarily mean rejection, just an attitude of disbelief that can be changed when the facts require it." I am arguing, of course, that science does deny some things. It denies complexity when simplicity will do, and it denies contradiction. Both of these denials have far-reaching effects on our openness toward experience.

18 This perspective could fit well into Milton Bennett's (1998) developmental theory of intercultural awareness. In intercultural theory, this is a developmental stage called "minimization." In brief, "minimization refers to the stage of intercultural awareness development in which significant aspects of one's own cultural worldview are seen, experienced, or thought of as universal. Doing so obscures cultural differences, by trivializing or romanticizing them." Thanks to Kathryn Lyndes for this insight.

19 Hallowell, 1960, p. 24 (essay pp. 19–52).

20 Native American ontologies have generally been treated by academic scholars in terms of "culture" rather than either "religion" or "science." Where "science" refers to the methodologies and results of empiricism as outlined by the early modern Europeans, the category of the religious has until recently been reserved—via anthropological presuppositions—to those traditions and practices that reproduce the modern religious–secular divide. Native American religious beliefs and practices regularly do not do so, particularly among the eastern woodland, plains, and southwestern nations. As cultural critiques of western science mount, and as the cultural link between the theological heritage of monotheism and the logic of the one that governs science mounts, so Native American and other non-European understandings of reality tend to dissolve the opposition altogether. For further reading on this topic, see for example Vine Deloria Jr., 1999.

21 Welch, 1990, p. 156. Also, there is a current debate in psychology concerning the status of truth in a patient's psychosis. See, for example, Szasz, 1971.

22 Gleiser, 2005, p. 24. See also Gleiser, 1997.

23 Cf. Lacan, 2002, pp. 271–80.

24 Irigaray, 1985.

25 Process theology has developed a notion of becoming that is focused on an Aristotelian framework of change and motion that is fundamentally linear (cf. Whitehead, 1960). Another philosophical understanding of becoming can be found in both Nietzsche (1967) and Kierkegaard, 1992.

7 When hell freezes over

1 Althaus-Reid, 2003, p. 36.

2 Bighorse, quoted in Martin, C. L., 1999, p. 179.

3 Carson, 2002, p. xiii.

4 Dante, 2002, p. 1, Canto I:1–2. All quotations from *The Inferno* come from Carson's translation.
5 Erdoes and Ortiz (1984). Also Dana Barry, *Penobscot: The People and Their River,* a production of the Penobscot Indian Nation, 12 Wabanaki Way, Indian Island, ME 04468. The video is available as part of the Penobscot Nation Cultural and Historic Preservation Curriculum Packet at www.penobscotnation.org.
6 Dante, 2002, p. 6, 115–17.
7 Martin, C. L., 1999, p. 195.
8 Tertullianus, 1956, *De Carne Christi* 5.
9 Brown, 2003.
10 Dante, 2002, Canto III:7–9, p. 15.
11 Kierkegaard, 1992, p. 308.
12 Dante, 2002, Canto XXXII:22–4, p. 223.
13 Ibid., Canto XXXIV:22, p. 238.
14 Ibid., 10–15, p. 237.
15 Ibid., 18.
16 Ibid., 73–81, p. 240.
17 Ibid., 136–8, p. 243.
18 Ibid., 103–11, pp. 241–2.
19 Sedgwick, 1990, p. 68.
20 www.kristinreisinger.com/training/heavenandhell.html.
21 Deleuze and Guattari, 1994, p. 206
22 Conway, 1911, Chapter 8.

8 Starting the story again

1 Tohe, 1997, p. 41.
2 Alice Walker, 1984, excerpt from "I Said to Poetry" in *Horses Make a Landscape Look More Beautiful: Poems by Alice Walker,* copyright © 1984 by Alice Walker, reprinted by permission of Harcourt, Inc.
3 Even contemporary astrophysics, as Sallie McFague (1993) has often pointed out, is hard at work on various stories of cosmic beginnings.
4 Bultmann, 1958, p. 19.
5 Ibid., p. 20.
6 Ibid., p. 21.
7 Ibid.
8 Edward Farley, 1996, pp. 4ff.
9 Ibid., p. 4.
10 For a discussion of the metaphoric exemption as a critical tool in theological method, see my discussion of it in Schneider, L. C., 1999.
11 Paul Tillich (1956, pp. 128–47), for example, complicates the possibility of separating myth and truth in his meditations on enchanted art, like Picasso's harrowing *Guernica.* Mary Daly (1984) refuses the separation altogether in her deadly serious play with Verbs and in her ontological spirals of Be-ing. And in various ways, Gianni Vattimo's (2002) notion of hermeneutic ontology, Hans Frei's (1980) notion of narrative traditioning, and Alfred North Whitehead's (1960) notion of actualization attempt to bridge the misty gap of connection between the rationalizing effort of interpretation and the concrete worlds that come into being in response.
12 C. S. Song (1999) has made clear that story is essential to any grasp of Asian theological claims, as has Ada-Maria Isasi-Diaz (1996) in reference to Cuban and other Latina approaches to theology.
13 Of course, the inseparability of fact and fiction is also vividly illustrated through the centuries in the Midrash of rabbinical writings like those of Hillel, as it also is in the Hadith of poets and interpreters of the Qur'an.

14 Suspicion here may take the form of fear or of satisfaction, all depending on the believer's own sense of righteousness and interest in punishment for others. Certainly, a three-storey universe serves the retributive desires of many, if they are convinced that they themselves are destined for the gated community of heaven.

15 McFague, 1975, 1982 and 1987.

16 Keller, 2003, p. 177.

17 Farley, 1990, pp. 106–8.

18 Keller, 2003, pp. 6, 15.

19 Ibid., p. 177.

20 Ibid., p. 4.

21 Actual calculations of the percentage of water in human bodies are complex, making 50 percent overall a relatively safe number, despite the fact that individual cells contain 75–80 percent water. "The percent water in the entire body by weight varies with age, sex, and physical conditioning. Heart and lung contain the most water, about 80%. Fat (about 20%) and bone (about 43%) are among the lowest. Therefore, the total body is an average of all organs, blood, and extracellular fluids. Several physiology texts place average young men at 60% water, and young women at 50% water, the difference due to relatively more fat in females. Thus, a 70 kg young man has about 42 kg (or 42 liters) or water. With age fat increases and muscle decreases, so that in old age the body may contain only 45% water. Infants, by contrast, average 73% or more." John Morris, responding to an Oregon school child on the *Science Education Partnership* website sponsored by the Covallis School District 509J, Oregon State University, and Hewlett Packard Corp, www.seps.org/oracle/oracle.archive/Life_Science.Biochem/2001.06/000991410254.7589.html.

22 I am grateful to my students Sharon Ellis Davis and Kathryn Lyndes for pointing out that those readers like themselves who have not grown up around boats may not know the meaning of the phrase "sea legs," which refers to the body's ability to learn to stand and walk around the moving deck of a ship; to function when the surface is quite literally always shifting. Those who adapt to the motion of the sea on board ships often suffer a temporary disorientation when they walk again on land.

23 Translations of passages from John 4 are my own.

24 John 4:17 makes note of the historic enmity between Samaritans and Jews: "the Samaritan woman said to him, 'how is it that you, a Jew, ask a drink of me, a woman of Samaria?' (Jews do not share things in common with Samaritans)". Little is known about the rift, except that both claimed to be the true descendants of Israel, and disagreed over the center of worship (Jerusalem for the Jews, Mt. Gerizim in the North for the Samaritans). In 128 BCE, the Jews destroyed the temple at Mt. Gerizim, which undoubtedly ensured the enmity of the Samaritans well into the lifetime of Jesus.

25 Gingrich and Danker, 1979.

26 "The term ζωήν appears as a synonym for God, as does αἰώνιον in a variety of Greek sources. *A Greek-English Lexicon* (Gingrich and Danker, 1979), reports many examples of God as ζωή in extra canonical sources. "f Dg 9: 6b; cf. Philo, Fug. 198 God is the πρεσβυτάτη πηγή ζωής; Herm. Wr. 11, 13; 14; 12, 15 God the πλήρωμα τό ζωής; PGM 3, 602 [cf. Rtzst., Mysteriienrel. 286, 1.11]; the deity called Νοῦς as ζωή Herm. Wr. 1, 9; 12; 17; 21; 32; 13,9; 18; 19. Cf. also Ps 35:10; 55:14; Sib. Or. Fgm. 3, 34".

27 My thanks to Dr. Holly Toensing of Xavier University for pointing this out.

28 It is important to note, however, that this is not really a foreign well to a Jew. It is Jacob's well, Jacob being the common ancestor of Israelites and Samaritans (see n. 23). But Samaritans and Jews were rivals, and she claims this well for her community, not for Jews, and, at least according to this story, Jesus does not contest the claim.

29 Trickster is "a name referring to a complex character type known for his trickery, buffoonery, and crude behavior, but also as a creator, culture hero, and teacher. The trickster is commonly found in stories throughout native North America and is similar to figures in traditional cultures the world over." ("Trickster" in Gill and Sullivan, 1992, p. 308.) A classic source on the topic is Radin, 1956. For a good collection of native North American accounts of Trickster, see Erdoes and Ortiz, 1984.

30 King, T., 1993, p. 11. Excerpts from *Green Grass, Running Water* by Thomas King. Copyright © 1993 by Thomas King. Reprinted by permission of Houghton Mifflin Company. All rights reserved.

31 Ibid., pp. 38–9.

32 Ibid., pp. 1–3.

33 Lopez, 1981, pp. 58–63. Quoted in Martin, C. L., 1999, pp. 211–12.

34 King, T., 1993, p. 11.

35 Ibid., p. 468.

9 Thinking being? Or why we need ontology ... again

1 Holmes, 2002, p. 81.

2 Irigaray, 1985, p. 29.

3 Althaus-Reid, 2003, p. 8.

4 See Irigaray, 1985, "This Sex Which Is Not One" and "The Power of Discourse and the Subordination of the Feminine."

5 Deleuze and Guattari, 1987, p. 22.

6 I am unable to quote from these songs for the purpose of illustrating my point because the publishers of popular music lyrics attach prohibitively high fees on individual lines, despite the small run of publication and the lack of profit therein. I apologize to all of those readers and students who have suggested that I include more references to popular culture in the form of lyrics, movies, and other popular art forms.

7 For example, Regina Schwartz (1998) discusses the logic of scarcity that, she argues, shapes the beginning of monotheistic images in the Hebrew Bible.

8 Deleuze and Guattari, 1987, pp. 25, 98.

9 Deborah Creamer (2004) makes the point that creativity occurs in frustration of ability and that this should cause rethinking in relation to divine creativity, especially in terms of omnipotence.

10 Thinking multiplicity

1 Whitman, 1983, p. 72.

2 Kenyon, 1978, p. 33. Copyright ©1978 by Jane Kenyon. Reprinted with the permission of Alice James Books.

3 I am particularly grateful to Catherine Keller for lifting up this caution in her reading of the manuscript.

4 See especially early books by Rosemary Radford Ruether, 1975, and Mary Daly, 1973. For more recent discussions, see Melanie May, 1995; Lisa Isherwood and Elizabeth Stuart, 1998.

5 Jantzen, 1999, p. 17.

6 I am thinking here particularly of the creative efforts of theologians like Rita Nakashima Brock (1988) in thinking about the notion of "Christic" love, Elizabeth Johnson's (1992) notion of Jesus-Sophia and Marjorie Suchocki's (1992) process notion of Christ.

7 See Boff, 1978; Cone, 1975; Gutierrez, 1973. Joanne M. Terrell (1998) looks at this dynamic and addresses it critically; see also Jürgen Moltmann's (1974) discussion.

8 Ivone Gebara's (1999) move into ecofeminism has resulted in a Latin American liberation theology that is also a celebration of earth and so engages critique through the fullness of the body, not just its suffering. Althaus-Reid (2003) focuses on the significance of pleasure as a liberative critique of "T-theology", particularly in terms of orgiastic and voyeuristic pleasure implied in Trinity. Likewise, Karen Baker-Fletcher (1998) writes of the revolutionary and liberative dimensions of celebration (she focuses on dance) that cannot be contained, domesticated, or monitored by oppressive classes, and sees Black culture in America as rich with these sorts of critiques that are also resources for Womanist theology; see also Baker-Fletcher, 2007. Finally, Anne Joh (2006, p. xxi) challenges Asian liberation theologians to incorporate *"jeong"* as well as *"han"* in their understanding of critique and of liberation. *"Jeong"* refers to the connectivity between beings, it is "a Korean way of conceiving an often complex constellation of relationality of the self with the other that is deeply associated with compassion, love, vulnerability, and acceptance of heterogeneity as essential to life ... the power embodied in redemptive relationships." All of these approaches begin to break the silence that more traditional liberation theologies have imposed on understanding incarnation in terms that are broader than suffering alone.
9 Whitehead, 1960, p. 522.
10 Whitehead, 1966, p. 186.
11 Whitehead, 1960, p. 523.
12 Keller, 2003, p. 177.
13 de Spinoza, 1981, p. 95. He continues: "For no one has hitherto known the body so accurately as to be able to explain all its functions; not to mention that many things may be observed in brutes which far transcend human sagacity, and that somnambules do many things in sleep which they would not venture on awake; a sufficient proof that the body itself, from the laws of its nature alone, can do many things at which the mind is astonished."
14 Serres, 1995, p. 6. Quoted in Keller, 2003, p. 176.
15 Braidotti, 2002, p. 1.
16 Serres, 1995, p. 3.
17 Braidotti, 2002, p. 1
18 Nancy, 2000, p. 39.
19 Ibid., p. 40.
20 Hanh, 1988.
21 For the example of a desk, see Hanh, 1976, pp. 47–8; for the piece of paper, see Hanh, 1988; for the chair, see Hanh, 2001, pp. 59–60.
22 Nancy, 2000, p. 40; de Beistegui, 2005, p. 56; Deleuze and Guattari, 1987, p. 6.
23 Braidotti, 2002, p. 2.
24 Keller, (2003) suggests the "manyone," a related idea.
25 Badiou, 2005.
26 I am indebted to John Thatamanil (2006) for this excellent insight.
27 Deleuze and Guattari, 1987. See also Rajchman, 2000, p. 7.
28 de Beistegui, 2005, p. 49.
29 Ibid., 45.
30 Paul Tillich's (1951) existential theory of divine being ("the Ground of Being" or "Being Itself") or Bonhoeffer's (1966) theory of Christ as event can be seen as examples of the latter.
31 It is important to remember that the particular notion of "becoming" that traces itself through existentialism to Kierkegaard and Nietzsche should not be confused with Whiteheadian theories of "becoming" in process thought.
32 Martin, C. L. 1999, 26.
33 Barker, 2002, p. 4.

34 For example, Jean Baudrillard (2001, p. 3) claims that "Everything starts from impossible exchange. The uncertainty of the world lies in the fact that it has no equivalent anywhere; it cannot be exchanged for anything. The uncertainty of thought lies in the fact that it cannot be exchanged either for truth or for reality. It is thought which tips the world over into uncertainty, or the other way round? This in itself is part of the uncertainty."

35 Rilke, 2000, pp. 50–51.

36 A few notable exceptions among white feminist theologians include Ellen Armour, 1999, Sharon Welch, 2004, and Susan B. Thistlethwaite, 1989.

37 See, for example, Chandra T. Mohanty, 2003, Evelynn Hammonds, 1997, Katie Geneva Cannon, 1988, and Seyla Benhabib, 1992.

38 Schneider, L. C., 2004.

39 Colebrook, 2000b, p. 125.

40 Keller, 2003, 171.

41 I am grateful to Dow Edgerton (1992) for this insight. The writer of Matthew claims that the parables are "given to know the secrets of the kingdom of heaven" (Matthew 13:11).

11 Divine multiplicity ...

1 Irigaray, 1992, p. 21.

2 Sweet, 1995, fragment 36, pp. 16–17.

3 Schneider, L. C., 1999.

4 Althaus-Reid (2003, p. 26) writes, "In a time when Third World theologians have made contextuality a hermeneutical key, it is sad to notice how contextuality has remained linked to the geographical more than the epistemological. By epistemological contexts we mean the fact that *ways of knowing relate to each other* [my emphasis]."

5 Levinas (1990, pp. 11–23), "A Religion for Adults."

6 Stockton, 1994, pp. 277–315.

7 Walker, 1983, p. 1.

8 I am grateful to Sharon Ellis Davis and Kathryn Lyndes for this insight.

9 Oates, 1986. This excerpt is reprinted courtesy of Daniel Halpern, founding editor of *Antaeus*, New York.

10 Braidotti, 2002, p. 68.

11 Ibid., pp. 99ff.

12 Rilke, 2000, p. 47.

13 Arendt, 1958, pp. 247ff.

14 See Daly, 1973 and 1984. I also discuss this aspect of Daly's "elemental feminist philosophy" in Schneider, L. C., 2000.

15 Keller, 2003, p. 202.

16 Ibid., pp. 231–2; Deleuze, 1994, pp. 122ff.

17 Hanh, 1999, p. 150.

18 Irigaray, 1992, p. 63.

19 LaCugna, 1991. Kathryn Tanner (2005) also gets at this point. See especially the section entitled "Economy of Grace", pp. 62ff.

20 Moltmann, 1974 and 1984. He begins this argument in *The Crucified God* and makes the claim even more explicit in *God In Creation*.

12 ... In a world of difference

1 Keller, 2003, p. 207.

2 I say curious because, with Gilles Deleuze I am mystified by Christian theology's historic phobia of immanence, a phobia that has so structured European

philosophy that as Daniel W. Smith (2003, pp. 61–2) suggests, "Deleuze and Guattari more or less ask: What *is* it with immanence? It should be the natural acquisition and milieu of philosophy, yet such is not always the case. Moreover, arguments brought to bear against immanence are almost always *moral* arguments. Without transcendence, we are warned, we will fall into a dark of chaos, reduced to a pure 'subjectivism' or 'relativism', living in a world without hope, with no vision of an alternate future."

3   Irigaray, 1992, p. 71.
4   Deleuze and Guattari, 1987, p. 14
5   Hearne, 1994, p. 96.
6   See Chapter 7 for discussions of hell as stasis and Chapter 8 for Coyote's dream of God.
7   Hallowell, 1960, p. 24.
8   Edgerton, 1992, p. 116.
9   Ibid., p. 117.
10   Deleuze, 1994, p. 182.
11   Ibid.
12   See Smith, D. W., 2003, for a good discussion of Deleuze's understanding and use of "transcendence."
13   Baudrillard, 2001.
14   Derrida, 1998, p. 26.
15   Levinas, 1990, p. 5.
16   Ibid., p. 7.
17   Baudrillard, 2001, p. 6.
18   Otherwise, Moltmann's (1984, p. 287) claim that "without body there is no God" as an interpretation of the incarnation would not be so radical. But it is radical. He has to argue against the Pythagorean logic of stasis to make that claim.
19   Irigaray, 1992, p. 33.
20   John, again, is slightly different and more wordy: "Are you King of the Jews?" Jesus answered, "Do you say this of your own accord, or did others say it to you about me?" Pilate answered, "Am I a Jew? Your own nation and the chief priests have handed you over to me; what have you done?" Jesus answered, "My kingship is not of this world; if my kingship were of this world, my servants would fight, that I might not be handed over to the Jews; but my kingship is not from the world." Pilate said to him, "So you are a king?" Jesus answered, "You say that I am a king" (John 18:33b-37a).
21   It is interesting to note that Jesus is also asked a similar question from the religious leaders, and chooses to answer them in the affirmative. One implication here is that at the time the gospels were written there was a greater perceived distance between the Christian communities and Roman authority than between those communities and Jewish authorities. Conversely, an argument can be made here through rhetorical criticism that the story tradition of Jesus' self-revelation to Caiaphas and deferral before Pilate emphasizes a growing rift between the largely Gentile Christian communities (who "understand and accept" Jesus' claim to be the Messiah) and the traditional Jewish authorities (who are depicted as refusing to accept Jesus' claims).
22   Deleuze and Guattari, 1987, p. 11
23   Holmes, 2002, p. 110.
24   Ibid.
25   Rajchman, 2000, p. 12. See also Deleuze and Guattari, 1987, pp. 88–9
26   Deleuze and Guattari, 1987, p. 14 and esp. p. 293. They discuss arborescent schema as those systems that focus on originary points rather than "lines of flight" between them, thus betraying the originary claim of the origin.

27 Whitehead, 1932, pp. 64, 72.
28 See Holmes, 2002. Also Schneider, L. C., 2004, for more on the entailments of gender and sexuality in relation to white supremacy.
29 Deleuze and Guattari, 1987, p. 293.
30 These references come from, in order of appearance: Barry Dana relating the story of the origin of the Penobscot Nation in *Penobscot: A People and Their River*; Dante, 2002, Canto I in *Inferno,* and Keller, 2003, p. xv.
31 Deleuze and Guattari, 1987, p. 11.
32 Ibid., p. 7.
33 King, T., 1993, p. 11.

13 A turn to ethics: beyond nationalism

1 For a complete discussion of the ethnosexual aspects of nationalism, see the excellent essay "Sex and Nationalism" by Joane Nagel (2003, pp. 140–76).
2 Barth, 1960, p. 40.
3 Anderson, 1991, pp. 5–7.
4 Handler, 1988, pp. 6–8.
5 Hroch, 1996, pp. 78–9.
6 Renan, 1996, p. 41.
7 Nagel, 2003, p. 146.
8 Lerro, 2000, p. 303.
9 Aristotle (1941) *Metaphysics, Book l* (12), 1074a. See also Homer, 1933.
10 See Schneider, L. C., 1999, for a full discussion of the metaphoric exemption.
11 See Farley, 1996, for a discussion of this very useful concept.
12 Schneider, L. C., 1999, pp. 154–78.
13 See Moltmann's (1981) discussion of political and clerical monotheism (Chapter 6, pp. 191–202).
14 Barth, 1976, pp. 443f.
15 Ibid..
16 *The Adventures of Priscilla, Queen of the Desert*, written and directed by Stephan Elliott (Australian Film Finance Corporation, 1994). Quoted in Harmon, 2003.
17 See, especially, Derrida, 2001. For an interesting discussion of both, see Eisenstadt, 2003, pp. 474–82.
18 Dorrien, 2003.
19 Bonhoeffer, 1995, pp. 404–8.

14 A turn to ethics: unity beyond monotheism

1 Baldwin, 1963, p. 128.
2 Quoted in Prantl, 2005, p. 348.
3 Rajchman, 2000, p. 53.
4 Whitehead, 1968, p. 116.
5 Agamben, 1993, p. 14.5.
6 These are gestural references to Chapters 7 and 8, in particular to my discussion of Dante's (2002) *Inferno* and Thomas King's (1993) *Green Grass, Running Water.*
7 Serres, 1995, p. 3.
8 Downer, 2001.
9 Althaus-Reid, 2003, p. 58.
10 Along with many others, I am forever grateful to Catherine Keller (1997) for her use of "now and then" in the title of her second book, *Apocalypse Now and Then.* The wonderful double entendre suggested by that title has become a

regular part of my own thinking regarding the temporality of divine multiplicity. It is elegant *and* funny, a lovely combination for insight.

11 Schneider, L. C., 1999, p. 162.

12 Ibid.

13 See also Matthew 22:38–9 and Mark 12:29–31

14 Babylonian Talmud, Sabbath 31a. Quoted in Stern, 1966, p. 313.

15 See, for example, the Qur'an, Surahs 2:177; 2:195; 3:134; 3:148; 5:13; 5:93;
19:96; 30:21; and 60:8.

16 For a brilliant critique of the anesthetic of projection that most people use to
shorten their actual living see Seneca, 1997, *On the Shortness of Life.*

17 Biddy Martin (1997, pp. 109–35) makes the provocative argument that homo-
sexuality is erroneously categorized as the attraction of "same;" that among
lesbians in particular the "maternal swamp of sameness" is a death-sentence for
relationships.

18 See Bonhoeffer, 1966, and Buber, 1959.

19 Schneider, L. C., 1999, p. 150.

Bibliography

Agamben, G. (1993) "Taking Place" in *The Coming Community,* trans. M. Hardt, Minneapolis: University of Minnesota Press

Albright, W. F. (1940) *From the Stone Age to Christianity: Monotheism and the Historical Process,* Baltimore: Johns Hopkins Press

Alföldi, A. (1948) *The Conversion of Constantine and Pagan Rome,* trans. H. Mattingly, Oxford: Clarendon Press

Althaus-Reid, M. (2000) *Indecent Theology: Theological Perversions in Sex, Gender, and Politics,* London: Routledge

——(2003) *The Queer God,* London: Routledge

Anderson, B. (1991) *Imagined Communities: Reflections on the Origin and Spread of Nationalism,* revised edn., New York: Verso

Anselm, Archbishop of Canterbury (1986) *Monologion; Proslogion: Capitulum II,* Paris: CERF

Aquinas, T. (1945) *Basic Writings of St. Thomas Aquinas,* ed. A. Pegis, New York: Random House

——(1958) *Compendium of Theology,* trans. C. Vollert, London: B. Herder

——(1969) *Summa Theologica,* Vol. 1, Blackfriars edn., ed. T. Gilby, New York: Doubleday

Arendt, H. (1958) *The Human Condition,* Chicago: University of Chicago Press

Aristotle (1941) *The Basic Works of Aristotle,* ed. R. McKeon, New York: Random House

Armour, E. (1999) *Deconstruction, Feminist Theology, and the Problem of Difference: Subverting the Race/Gender Divide,* Chicago: University of Chicago Press

Assmann, J. (1997) *Moses the Egyptian: The Memory of Egypt in Western Monotheism,* Cambridge, MA: Harvard University Press

Augustine, St. (1968) *De Trinitate,* Turholti: Brepolis

Bacon, F. (1887) "The Advancement of Learning" in Spedding, J., R. L. Ellis, and D. D. Heath (eds.) *The Works,* Vol. 3, London: Longman

——(1901) *The New Organon (1620),* in Spedding, J., R. L. Ellis, and D. D. Heath (eds.) *The Works,* Vol. 4, London: Longman

Badiou, A. (2005) *Being and Event,* trans. O. Feltham, New York: Continuum

Baker-Fletcher, K. (1998) *Sisters of Dust, Sisters of Spirit: Womanist Wordings on God and Creation,* Minneapolis: Augsburg Fortress Press

——(2007) *Dancing with God: The Trinity from a Womanist Perspective,* St. Louis: Chalice Press

Baldwin, J. (1963) *The Fire Next Time,* New York: Dell Publishing Company

Barker, J. (2002) *Alain Badiou: A Critical Introduction,* Modern European Thinkers Series, London: Pluto Books

Barth, K. (1960) *The Humanity of God,* Richmond: John Knox Press

——(1976) *Church Dogmatics,* Vol. 2, Pt. 1, *The Doctrine of God,* trans. T. H. L. Parker, W. B. Johnston, H. Knight, and J. L. M. Haire, Edinburgh: T & T Clark

Bauckham, R. (1998) *God Crucified: Monotheism and Christology in the New Testament,* Grand Rapids: William B. Eerdmans

Baudrillard, J. (2001) *Impossible Exchange,* trans. Chris Turner, New York: Verso

Bellah, R. N. (1965) "Religious Evolution" in Lessa, N. and E. Vogt (eds.) *Reader in Comparative Religion: An Anthropological Approach,* New York: Harper & Row

Benhabib, S. (1992) *Situating the Self: Gender, Community, and Postmodernism in Contemporary Ethics,* London: Routledge

Bennett, M. (1998) *Basic Concepts of Intercultural Communication: Selected Readings,* Yarmouth: Intercultural Press

Berger, P. and T. Luckmann (1966) *The Social Construction of Reality,* New York: Anchor Books

Boff, L. (1978) *Jesus Christ Liberator: A Critical Christology for our Time,* Maryknoll: Orbis Books

——(1988) *Trinity and Society,* trans. P. Burns, New York: Orbis Books

Bonhoeffer, D. (1966) *Christ the Center,* lectures delivered in 1933, ed. E. Bethge, trans. J. Bowden, New York: Harper and Row

——(1995) "Address to Ecumenical Council, Fäno, Denmark, August 1934" in Kelly, G. B. and E. B. Nelson (eds.) *A Testament to Freedom: Essential Writings of Dietrich Bonhoeffer,* San Francisco: HarperSanFrancisco

Bourdieu, P. (2001) *Masculine Domination,* Cambridge: Polity

Boyce, M. (1992) *Zoroastrianism: Its Antiquity and Constant Vigour,* New York: Mazda Publishers

Braidotti, R. (2002) *Metamorphoses: Towards a Materialist Theory of Becoming,* Cambridge: Polity

Brock, R. N. (1988) *Journeys by Heart: A Christology of Erotic Power,* New York: Crossroad Publishing

Brown, D. (2003) *The Da Vinci Code,* New York: Doubleday

Buber, M. (1959) *I and Thou,* trans. R. G. Smith, Edinburgh: T&T Clark

Bultmann, R. (1958) *Jesus Christ and Mythology,* New York: Charles Scribner's Sons

Burkert, W. (1985) *Greek Religion: Archaic and Classical,* Oxford: Oxford University Press

Cannon, K. G. (1988) *Black Womanist Ethics,* Atlanta: Scholars Press

Carson, C. (2002) "Introduction" in *The Inferno of Dante Alighieri,* trans. C. Carson, London: Granta Books

Chadwick, H. (1990) "The Early Christian Community" in McManners, J. (ed.) *The Oxford History of Christianity,* Oxford: Oxford University Press

Clifford, R. J. (1984) *Fair Spoken and Persuading: An Interpretation of Second Isaiah,* New York: Paulist Press

Cobb, J. B. and D. R. Griffin (1976) *Process Theology: An Introductory Exposition,* Philadelphia: Westminster Press

Colebrook, C. (2000a) "Introduction" in Buchanan, I. and C. Colebrook (eds.) *Deleuze and Feminist Theory,* Edinburgh: Edinburgh University Press

Colebrook, C. (2000b) "Is Sexual Difference a Problem?" in Buchanan, I. and C. Colebrook (eds.) *Deleuze and Feminist Theory,* Edinburgh: Edinburgh University Press

Cone, J. (1975) *God of the Oppressed,* New York: Seabury

Conway, Fr. P. (1911) *Saint Thomas Aquinas,* London: Longmans, Green and Co

Copernicus, N. (1989) "Dedication of the Revolutions of the Heavenly Spheres to Pope Paul III" in *De Revolutionisbus* (1543), in Matthews, M. R. (ed.) *The Scientific Background to Modern Philosophy: Selected Readings,* Indianapolis: Hackett Publishers

Creamer, D. (2004) *The Withered Hand of God: Disability and Theological Reflection,* doctoral dissertation, Iliff Theological Seminary

Daly, M. (1971) "The Courage to See," *The Christian Century,* No. 88 (September 22, 1971), 1108–11

——(1973) *Beyond God the Father: Toward a Philosophy of Women's Liberation,* Boston: Beacon Press

——(1984) *Pure Lust: Elemental Feminist Philosophy,* Boston: Beacon Press

D'Angelo, M. R. (1992) "'Abba' and 'Father': Imperial Theology and the Jesus Traditions," *Journal of Biblical Literature* 3:4, 611–30

Dante, Alighieri (2002) *The Inferno of Dante Alighieri,* trans. C. Carson, London: Granta Books

Davila, J. R. (1999) "Of Methodology, Monotheism and Metatron: Introductory Reflections on Divine Mediators and the Origins of the Worship of Jesus" in Newman, C. C., J. R. Davila, and G. S. Lewis (eds.) *The Jewish Roots of Christological Monotheism,* Leiden: Brill

de Beistegui, M. (2005) "The Ontological Dispute: Badiou, Heidegger, and Deleuze" in Riera, G., (ed.) *Alain Badiou: Philosophy and Its Conditions,* Albany: SUNY Press

DeHart, P. (2002) "The Ambiguous Infinite: Jüngel, Marion, and the God of Descartes," *Journal of Religion* 82:1, 75–96

Deleuze, G. (1994) *Difference and Repetition,* trans. P. Patton, New York: Columbia University Press

Deleuze, G. and F. Guattari (1987) *A Thousand Plateaus: Capitalism and Schizophrenia,* trans. B. Massumi, Minneapolis: University of Minnesota Press

——(1994) *What is Philosophy?* trans. H. Tomlinson and G. Burchell, New York: Columbia University Press

Deloria, V., Jr. (1999) *Spirit and Reason: The Vine Deloria Jr. Reader,* Golden: Fulcrum Press

Derrida, J. (1997) *Of Grammatology,* trans. G. C. Spivak, Baltimore: Johns Hopkins University Press

——(1998) *Monolingualism of the Other or the Prosthesis of Origin,* trans. P. Mensah, La Jolla: Stanford University Press

——(2001) "On Cosmopolitanism" in *On Cosmopolitanism and Forgiveness,* trans. M. Dooley and M. Hughes, London: Routledge

Descartes, R. (1993) *Meditations on First Philosophy in which the Existence of God and the Distinction Between the Soul and the Body are Demonstrated,* trans. D. A. Cress: Hackett Publishing

Dorrien, G. (2003) "Axis of One: The 'Unipolarist' Agenda," *The Christian Century,* March 8, 2003, 30–35

Downer, J. (2001) "Johns Hopkins Scientists Find Brain's Nose Plug" (Baltimore: JHMI Office of Communications and Public Affairs, Dec. 7, 2001), available at www.hopkinsmedicine.org/press/2001/DECEMBER/011207.htm

Durkheim, E. (1965) *Elementary Forms of the Religious Life,* trans. J. W. Swain, New York: The Free Press

Edgerton, W. D. (1992) *The Passion of Interpretation,* Literary Currents in Biblical Interpretation, Louisville: Westminster John Knox Press

Eisenstadt, O. (2003) "The Problem of the Promise: Derrida on Levinas on the Cities of Refuge," *CrossCurrents* 52:4, 474–82

Erdoes, R. and A. Oritz (eds.) (1984) *American Indian Myths and Legends,* New York: Pantheon Books

Farley, E. (1990) *Good and Evil: Interpreting a Human Condition,* Minneapolis: Fortress Press

——(1996) *Deep Symbols: Their Postmodern Effacement and Reclamation,* Valley Forge: Trinity Press International

Ferguson, J. (1980) *Greek and Roman Religion: A Source Book,* Park Ridge: Noyes Press

Fowden, G. (1993) "Empire to Commonwealth: Consequences of Monotheism in Late Antiquity" in Siebers, T. (ed.) *Religion and the Authority of the Past,* Ann Arbor: University of Michigan Press

Frede, M. (1999) "Monotheism and Pagan Philosophy in Later Antiquity" in P. Athanassaidi and Michael Frede (eds.) *Pagan Monotheism in Late Antiquity,* Oxford: Clarendon Press

Frei, H. (1980) *The Eclipse of Biblical Narrative: A Study in Eighteenth and Nineteenth Century Hermeneutics,* New Haven: Yale University Press

Funk, R. W. (ed.) (1985) *New Gospel Parallels: Volume One, The Synoptic Gospels,* Philadelphia: Fortress Press

Gebara, I. (1999) *Longing for Running Water,* Minneapolis: Fortress Press

Geertz, C. (1973) *The Interpretation of Cultures,* New York: Basic Books

Geffré, C. and J.-P. Jossua (1985) "Editorial" in Geffré, C. and J.-P. Jossua (eds.) *Monotheism,* trans. R. Nowell, Edinburgh: Concilium and T&T Clark

Gill, S. D. (1982) *Native American Religions: An Introduction,* The Religious Life of Man Series, Belmont: Wadsworth Publishing Company

Gill, S. D. and I. F. Sullivan (1992) *Dictionary of Native American Mythology,* Oxford: Oxford University Press

Gingrich, W. and F. W. Danker (1979) *A Greek-English Lexicon of the New Testament and Other Early Christian Literature,* 2nd edn. (rev. and aug. from Walter Bauer's 5th edn., 1958) Chicago: The University of Chicago Press

Gleiser, M. (1997) *The Dancing Universe: From Creation Myths to the Big Bang,* New York: Dutton

——(2005) "Cosmic Birth: Must Modern-Day Cosmologists Be Mythmakers to Explain Creation?" *Harvard Divinity Bulletin* 33:1, pp. 20–30

Gnuse, R. K. (1997) *No Other Gods: Emergent Monotheism in Israel,* Supplement Series 241, *Journal for the Study of the Old Testament,* Sheffield: Sheffield Academic Press

Griffin, M. (1988) "Cicero and Rome" in Boardman, J., J. Griffin and O. Murray (eds.) *The Roman World,* Oxford: Oxford University Press

Guthrie, W. K. C. (1955) *The Greeks and Their Gods,* Boston: Beacon Press

Gutierrez, G. (1973) *A Theology of Liberation,* Maryknoll: Orbis Books

Hallowell, A. I. (1960) "Ojibwa Ontology, Behavior, and World View," in Diamond, S. (ed.) *Culture in History: Essays in Honor of Paul Radin,* New York: Columbia University Press

Halperin, B. (1987) "'Brisker Pipes Than Poetry': The Development of Israelite Monotheism" in Neusner, J., B. A. Levine, and E. S. Frerichs (eds.) *Judaic Perspectives on Ancient Israel*, Philadelphia: Fortress Press

——(2000) "YHWH the Revolutionary: Reflections on the Rhetoric of Redistribution in the Social Context of Dawning Monotheism" in Bellis, A. O. and J. S. Kaminsky (eds.) *Jews, Christians, and the Theology of the Hebrew Scriptures*, Atlanta: Society of Biblical Literature

Hammonds, E. (1997) "Black (W)holes and the Geometry of Black Female Sexuality" in *Feminism Meets Queer Theory*, Bloomington: Indiana University Press

Handler, R. (1988) *Nationalism and the Politics of Culture in Quebec*, New Directions in Anthropological Writing: History, Poetics, Cultural Criticism, ed. C. E. George, Madison: University of Wisconsin Press

Hanh, T. N. (1976) *The Miracle of Mindfulness: A Manual on Meditation*, Boston: Beacon Press

——(1988) *The Heart of Understanding: Commentaries on the Prajnaparamita Heart Sutra*, Berkeley: Parallax Press

——(1999) "Interbeing" in *Call Me by My True Names: The Collected Poems of Thich Nhat Hanh*, Berkeley: Parallax Press

——(2001) *Essential Writings*, ed. R. Ellsberg, Modern Spiritual Masters Series, Maryknoll: Orbis Books

Harmon, C. (2003) "The Suburbs as Havens for Difference," *The Next American City* 1, available at www.americancity.org/article.php?id_article=76

Harrod, H. L. (1984) "Missionary Life-World and Native Response: Jesuits in New France," *Studies in Religion* 13:2, 179–92

Hawking, S. (1988) *A Brief History of Time: From the Big Bang to Black Holes*, New York: Bantam Books

Hearne, V. (1994) "Oyez à Beaumont" in Hearne, V. *Animal Happiness*, New York: HarperCollins Publishers

Hill, W. W. (1938) "The Agricultural and Hunting Methods of the Navajo Indians," *Yale University Publications in Anthropology* 18:3, 1–194

Holmes, B. A. (2002) *Race and the Cosmos: An Invitation to View the World Differently*, Valley Forge: Trinity Press International

Homer (1933) *The Illiad of Homer*, trans. A. Lang and W. B. Moffett, New York: Macmillan

Hroch, M. (1996) "From National Movement to the Fully Formed Nation: The Nation-building Process in Europe," in Balakrishnan, G. (ed.) *Mapping the Nation*, New York: Verso

Hume, D. (1956) *The Natural History of Religion*, Stanford: Stanford University Press

Iamblichus (1989) *On the Pythagorean Life*, trans. G. Clark, Liverpool: Liverpool University Press

Irigaray, L. (1985) *This Sex Which Is Not One*, trans. C. Porter and C. Burke, Ithaca: Cornell University Press

——(1992) *Elemental Passions*, trans. J. Collie and J. Still, New York: Routledge

Irwin, L. (1994) *The Dream Seekers: Native American Visionary Traditions of the Great Plains*, Tulsa: University of Oklahoma Press

Isasi-Diaz, A. M. (1996) *Mujerista Theology for the Twenty-First Century*, New York: Orbis Books

Isherwood, L. and E. Stuart (1998) *Introducing Body Theology*, Sheffield: Sheffield Academic Press

Jaffee, M. S. (2001) "One God, One Revelation, One People: On The Symbolic Structure of Elective Monotheism," *Journal of the American Academy of Religion,* 69:4, 753–76

Jantzen, G. (1999) *Becoming Divine: Towards a Feminist Philosophy of Religion,* Bloomington: Indiana University Press

Jennings, T. W. (1985) *Beyond Theism: A Grammar of God-Language,* New York: Oxford University Press

Jeremias, J. (1966) *Abba: Studien zur neutestamentlichen Theologies und Zeitgeschichte,* Göttingen: Vandenhoek and Ruprecht

Joh, W. A. (2006) *Heart of the Cross: A Postcolonial Christology,* Louisville: Westminster John Knox Press

Johnson, E. (1992) *She Who Is: The Mystery of God in a Feminist Theological Discourse,* New York: Crossroad

Jordan, M. (2005) *Blessing Same Sex Unions: The Perils of Queer Romance and the Confusions of Christian Marriage,* Chicago: University of Chicago Press

Kee, H. C. (1977) *Community of the New Age,* Philadelphia: Westminster Press

Keller, C. (1997) *Apocalypse Now and Then,* Boston: Beacon Press

——(2003) *Face of the Deep: A Theology of Becoming,* London: Routledge

Kenney, J. P. (1991) *Mystical Monotheism: A Study in Ancient Platonic Theology,* Providence: Brown University Press

Kenyon, J. (1978) "Cages" in *From Room to Room: Poems by Jane Kenyon,* Farmington: Alice James Press

Kierkegaard, S. (1992) *Concluding Unscientific Postscript,* trans. H. V. Hong and E. Hong, Princeton: Princeton University Press

King, K. (2000) "Sacred Texts and Social Contexts," *Harvard Divinity Bulletin* 29:1, 12–16

King, T. (1993) *Green Grass, Running Water,* New York: Bantam

——(2005) *The Truth About Stories: A Native Narrative,* Minneapolis: University of Minnesota Press

Kirsch, J. (2004) *God Against the Gods: The History of the War Between Monotheism and Polytheism,* New York: Penguin

Krishna, S. (2002) "In One Inning: National Identity in Postcolonial Times" in Chowdhry, G. and S. Nair (eds.) *Power, Postcolonialism and International Relations: Reading Race, Gender and Class,* London: Routledge

Kristeva, J. (1980) *Desire in Language: A Semiotic Approach to Literature and Art,* New York: Columbia University Press

Kwok, P. (2005) *Postcolonial Imagination and Feminist Theology,* Louisville: Westminster John Knox Press

Lacan, J. (2002) "The Signification of the Phallus" in *Ecrits: A Selection,* trans.-Bruce Fink, New York: W. W. Norton

LaCugna, C. M. (1991) *God For Us: The Trinity and Christian Life,* San Francisco: HarperSanFrancisco

Lang, B. (1983) *Monotheism and the Prophetic Minority: An Essay in Biblical History and Sociology,* The Social World of Biblical Antiquity Series, Vol. 1, Sheffield: Almond Press

Lerro, B. (2000) *From Earth Spirits to Sky Gods: The Socioecological Origins of Monotheism, Individualism, and Hyperabstract Reasoning from the Stone Age to the Axial Iron Age,* Lanham: Lexington Books

Lesher, J. H. (1992) "Introduction" in Lesher, J. H. (trans.) *Xenophanes of Colophon: Fragments,* Toronto: University of Toronto Press

Levinas, I. (1990) *Difficult Freedom: Essays on Judaism,* trans. S. Hand, Baltimore: Johns Hopkins University Press

Livingston, J. C. (1998) *Anatomy of the Sacred: An Introduction to Religion,* 3rd edn., Upper Saddle River: Prentice Hall

Loomba, A., S. Kaul, M. Bunzi, A. Burton and J. Esty (2005) "Beyond What? An Introduction" in A. Loomba, S. Kaul, M. Bunzl, A. Burton and J. Esty (eds.) *Postcolonial Studies and Beyond,* Chapel Hill: Duke University Press

Lopez, B. H. (1981) "Winter Count 1973: Geese, They Flew Over in a Storm" in Lopez, B. H. *Winter Count,* New York: Avon Books

Loretz, O. (1999) *Des Gottes Einzigkeit: Ein altorientalisches Argumentationsmodell zum "Schma Jisrael",* Darmstadt: Wissenschaftliche Buchgesellschaft

McClintock, A. (1995) *Imperial Leather: Race, Gender and Sexuality in the Colonial Context,* London: Routledge

McFague, S. (1975) *Speaking in Parables: A Study in Metaphor and Theology,* Philadelphia: Fortress Press

——(1982) *Metaphorical Theology: Models of God in Religious Language,* Philadelphia: Fortress Press

——(1987) *Models of God: Theology for an Ecological, Nuclear Age,* Philadelphia: Fortress Press

——(1993) *The Body of God: An Ecological Theology,* Minneapolis: Fortress Press

Mach, M. (1999) "Concepts of Jewish Monotheism During the Hellenistic Period" in Newman, C. C., J. R. Davila and G. S. Lewis (eds.) *The Jewish Roots of Christological Monotheism: Papers from the St. Andrews Conference on the Historical Origins of the Worship of Jesus,* Leiden: Brill

MacMullen, R. (1997) *Christianity and Paganism in the 4th–8th Centuries,* New Haven: Yale University Press

Markus, R. A. (1990) "From Rome to the Barbarian Kingdoms" in McManners, J. (ed.) *The Oxford History of Christianity,* Oxford: Oxford University Press

Martin, B. (1997) "Extraordinary Homosexuals and the Fear of Being Ordinary" in Weed, E. and N. Schor (eds.) *Feminism Meets Queer Theory,* Books from *Differences,* Indianapolis: Indiana University Press

Martin, C. L. (1999) *The Way of the Human Being,* New Haven: Yale University Press

May, M. (1995) *A Body Knows: A Theopoetics of Death and Resurrection,* New York: Continuum

Mbiti, J. (1990) *African Religion and Philosophy,* 2nd edn., Oxford: Heinemann

Mohanty, C. T. (2003) *Feminism Without Borders: Decolonizing Theory, Practicing Solidarity,* Durham: Duke University Press

Moltmann, J. (1974) *The Crucified God: The Cross of Christ as the Foundation and Criticism of Christian Theology,* London: SCM Press

——(1981) *Trinity and the Kingdom: The Doctrine of God,* trans. M. Kohl, San Francisco: Harper and Row

——(1984) *God In Creation: An Ecological Doctrine of Creation,* trans. M. Kohl, London: SCM Press

——(1985) "The Inviting Unity of the Triune God" in Geffré, C. and J.-P. Jossua (eds.) *Monotheism,* trans. Robert Nowell, Edinburgh: Concilium and T&T Clark

——(1999) *God for a Secular Society: The Public Relevance of Theology,* trans. M. Kohl, Minneapolis: Fortress Press

Mosha, R. (1980) "The Trinity in the African Context," *African Theological Journal* 9:1, 40–7

Mwoleka, C. (1975) "Trinity and Community," *African Ecclesiological Review* 17:4, 203–6

Nagel, J. (2003) *Race, Ethnicity, and Sexuality: Intimate Intersections, Forbidden Frontiers*, New York: Oxford University Press

Nancy, J.-L. (2000) *Being Singular Plural*, trans. R. D. Richardson and A. E. O'Byrne, Stanford: Stanford University Press

Newton, I. (1989) "Rules of Reasoning in Philosophy" in Matthews, M. R. (ed.) *The Scientific Background to Modern Philosophy: Selected Readings*, Indianapolis: Hackett Publishers

Ngong, D. T. (2003) "Review of *On Communitarian Divinity*," *Review & Expositor* 100:4, 730–32

Nietzsche, F. (1954) *The Antichrist* in W. Kaufman (ed. and trans.) *The Portable Nietzsche*, New York: Viking Press

——(1967) *Genealogy of Morals and Ecce Homo*, trans. W. Kaufmann, New York: Vintage Books

——(1975) *The Gay Science*, trans. W. Kaufman, New York: Random House

Nye, N. S. (1995) "Telling the Story" in Nye, N. S. *Words Under the Words: Selected Poems*, A Far Corner Book, Portland: Eighth Mountain Press

Oates, J. C. (1986) "Against Nature," *Antaeus* 57, 242–43

Oduyoye, M. A. (1986) *Hearing and Knowing: Reflections on Christianity in Africa*, Maryknoll: Orbis Books

Ogbonnaya, A. O. (1994) *On Communitarian Divinity: An African Interpretation of the Trinity*, New York: Paragon House

Osborn, E. (1997) *Tertullian: First Theologian of the West*, Cambridge: Cambridge University Press

Pakkala, J. (1999) *Intolerant Monolatry in the Deuteronomic History*, The Finnish Exegetical Society, 76, Göttingen: Vandenhoeck & Ruprecht

Perkinson, J. W. (2004) *White Theology: Outing Supremacy in Modernity*, New York: Palgrave Macmillan

Peterson, D. (1988) "Israel and Monotheism: The Unfinished Agenda" in Tucker, G. M., D. L. Peterson and R. R. Wilson (eds.) *Canon, Theology, and Old Testament Interpretation: Essays in Honor of Brevard Childs*, Philadelphia: Fortress Press

Peterson, E. (1951) "Monotheismus als Politisches Problem" in Peterson, E. *Theologische Traktate*, Munich: Kösel-Verlag

Pettazoni, R. (1965) "The Formation of Monotheism" in Lessa, N. and E. Vogt (eds.) *Reader in Comparative Religion: An Anthropological Approach*, New York: Harper & Row

Philo (1929a) *Quod Omnis Probus Liber Sit*, Loeb Classical Library, Cambridge: Harvard University Press

——(1929b) *De Opificio Mundi*, Loeb Classical Library, Cambridge: Harvard University Press

Pinnock, C., R. Rice, J. Sanders, W. Hasker and D. Basinger (eds.) (1994) *The Openness of God: A Biblical Challenge to the Traditional Understanding of God*, Downers Grove: InterVarsity Press

Plato (1961) *Plato: The Collected Dialogues*, trans. P. Shorey, E. Hamilton and H. Cairns (eds.) Princeton: Princeton University Press

Plutarch (1880) *Solon* in Dryden, J., et al. (trans.) *Plutarch's Lives of Illustrious Men*, New York: T. Y. Crowell

Porter, L. B. (1980) "On Keeping 'Persons' in the Trinity: A Linguistic Approach to Trinitarian Thought," *Theological Studies* 41:3, 530–48

Powell, J. G. F. (1995) "Cicero's translations from the Greek" in Powell, J. G. F. (ed. and intro.) *Cicero the Philosopher: 12 Papers*, Oxford: Clarendon Press

Prantl, C. (2005) *Geschichte der Logik im Abendlande: Band II*, Elibron Classics Series, Leipzig: Adamant Media

Price, S. and E. Kearns (eds.) (2003) *The Oxford Dictionary of Classical Myth and Religion*, Oxford: Oxford University Press

Proclus (1939) "Summary," in Thomas, I. (ed. and trans.) *Greek Mathematical Works I: From Thales to Euclid*, Loeb Classical Library, Cambridge, MA: Harvard University Press

Radin, P. (1956) *The Trickster: A Study in American Indian Mythology*, New York: Schocken Books

Rajchman, J. (2000) *The Deleuze Connections*, Cambridge MA: The MIT Press

Renan, E. (1996) "What is a Nation?" in Eley, G. and R. G. Suny (eds.) *Becoming National: A Reader*, New York: Oxford University Press

Reynolds, E. (1637) *The Vanitie of the Creature and Vexation of the Spirit*, London: Printed by Felix Kyngston for Robert Bostocke, at the Kingshead in Pauls Church-yard

Rilke, R. M. (2000) "Die Achte Elegie" in *Duino Elegies*, bilingual edn., trans. E. Snow, New York: North Point Press

Rousseau, J.-J. (1979) *Emile or On Education*, trans. A. Bloom, New York: Basic Books

Ruether, R. R. (1975) *New Woman/New Earth: Sexist Ideologies and Human Liberation*, New York: Seabury Press

Ruggieri, G. (1985) "God and Power: A Political Function of Monotheism?" in Geffré, C. and J.-P. Jossua (eds.) *Monotheism*, trans. Robert Nowell, Edinburgh: Concilium and T&T Clark

Runia, D. T. (1993) *Philo in Early Christian Literature: A Survey*, Minneapolis: Fortress Press

Rusch, W. G. (trans. and ed.) (1980) *The Trinitarian Controversy*, Philadelphia: Fortress Press

Sands, K. (1994) *Escape From Paradise: Evil and Tragedy in Feminist Theology*, Minneapolis: Augsburg Fortress Press

Schneider, L. C. (1999) *Re-Imagining the Divine: Confronting the Backlash Against Feminist Theology*, Cleveland: Pilgrim Press

——(2000) "The Courage to See and to Sin: Mary Daly's Elemental Transformation of Paul Tillich's Ontology" in Frye, M. and S. L. Hoagland (eds.) *Feminist Interpretations of Mary Daly*, Re-Reading the Canon Series, Philadelphia: Pennsylvania State University Press

——(2004) "What Race is Your Sex?" in Harvey, J., K. A. Case and R. Hawley Gorsline (eds.) *Disrupting White Supremacy From Within: White People On What We Need to Do*, Cleveland: Pilgrim Press

Schneider, P. (2006) *Brutal Journey: Cabeza de Vaca and the Epic First Crossing of North America*, New York: Henry Holt

Schneider, R. (2001) "Performance Remains," *Performance Research* 6:2, 100–108

Schwartz, R. (1998) *The Curse of Cain: The Violent Legacy of Monotheism*, Chicago: University of Chicago

Sedgwick, E. K. (1990) *Epistemology of the Closet*, Berkeley: University of California Press

Seneca, L. A. (1997) *On the Shortness of Life*, trans. C. D. N. Costa, New York: Penguin Books

Serres, M. (1995) *Genesis*, trans. G. James and J. Nelson, Ann Arbor: University of Michigan Press

Smith, D. W. (2003) "Deleuze and Derrida" in Patton, P. and J. Protevi (eds.) *Between Deleuze and Derrida*, New York: Continuum

Smith, M. (1990) *The Early History of God: Yahweh and Other Deities in Ancient Israel*, New York: Harper & Row

——(2001) *The Origins of Biblical Monotheism: Israel's Polytheistic Background and the Ugaritic Texts*, Oxford: Oxford University Press

Smith, J. Z. (1975) "The Social Description of Early Christianity," *Religious Studies Review* 1, 19–25

Sölle, D. (1974) *Political Theology*, trans. J. Shelley, Philadelphia: Fortress Press

Song, C. S. (1999) *The Believing Heart: An Invitation to Story Theology*, Minneapolis: Augsburg Fortress Press

de Spinoza, B. (1981) *Ethics*, trans. G. Eliot, T. Deegan (ed.) Salzburg, Austria: Institut für Anglistik und Amerkanistik Universität Salzburg

Stenger, V. J. (1990) *Physics and Psychics: The Search for a World Beyond the Senses*, New York: Prometheus Books

Stern, J. B. (1966) "Jesus' Citation of Dt 6:5 and Lv 19:18 in the Light of Jewish Tradition," *The Catholic Biblical Quarterly* 27:3, 312–16

Stockton, K. B. (1994) "Growing Sideways, or Versions of the Queer Child: The Ghost, the Homosexual, the Freudian, the Innocent, and the Interval of Animal" in Bruhm, S. and N. Hurley (eds.) *Curiouser: On the Queerness of Children*, Minneapolis: University of Minnesota Press

Suchocki, M. (1992) *God Christ Church: A Practical Guide to Process Theology*, New York: Crossroad

Sullivan, F. P. (1995) *Indian Freedom: The Cause of Bartolomé de las Casas 1484–1566*, Kansas City: Sheed & Ward

Surburg, R. F. (1975) *Introduction to the Intertestamental Period*, St. Louis: Concordia Publishing

Sweet, D. (ed.) (1995) *Heraclitus: Translation and Analysis*, Lanham: University Press of America

Szasz, T. S. (1971) *The Manufacture of Madness: A Comparative Study of the Inquisition and the Mental Health Movement*, London: Routledge & Kegan Paul

Tanner, K. (2001) *Jesus, Humanity and Trinity: A Brief Systematic Theology*, Minneapolis: Fortress

——(2005) *Economy of Grace*, Minneapolis: Fortress Press

Terrell, J. M. (1998) *Power in the Blood? The Cross in the African American Experience*, Maryknoll: Orbis Books

Tertullianus, Q. S. F. (1948) *Tertullian's Treatise against Praxeas*, trans. and ed. E. Evans, London: SPCK

——(1956) *De Carne Christi liber. Treatise on the Incarnation*, trans. and ed. E. Evans, London: SPCK

Thatamanil, J. (2006) *The Immanent Divine: God, Creation And the Human Predicament*, Minneapolis: Fortress

Theissen, G. (1999) *The Religion of the Earliest Christians: Creating a Symbolic World*, trans. J. Bowden, Minneapolis: Fortress Press

Theophilus of Antioch (1970) *Ad Autolycum*, R. M. Grant (ed. and trans.) Oxford: Clarendon Press

Thistlethwaite, S. B. (1989) *Race, Sex, and God: Christian Feminism in Black and White*, New York: Crossroad

Thompson, T. L. (1996) "The Intellectual Matrix of Early Biblical Narrative: Inclusive Monotheism in Persian Period Palestine" in Edelman, D. V. (ed.) *The Triumph of Elohim: From Yahwisms to Judaisms*, Grand Rapids: William B. Eerdman

Tillich, P. (1951) *Systematic Theology*, Vol. I, Chicago: University of Chicago Press

——(1956) "Existentialist Aspects of Modern Art" in C. Michalson (ed.) *Christianity and the Existentialists*, New York: Charles Scriber's Sons

Tohe, L. (1997) Introduction to "She Was Telling It This Way" in Harjo, J. and G. Bird (eds.) *Reinventing the Enemy's Language: Contemporary Native Women's Writings of North America*, New York: W. W. Norton

Tooker, E. (ed.) (1979) *Native North American Spirituality of the Eastern Woodlands*, Mahwah: Paulist Press

Troeltsch, E. (1991) "Christianity and the History of Religions" in *Religion in History: Essays* trans. J. L. Adams and W. F. Bense, Minneapolis: Fortress Press

Vähäkangas, M. (2002) "African Approaches to the Trinity" in Katongole, I. (ed.) *African Theology Today*, Scranton: University of Scranton Press

VanderKam, J. C. (2001) *An Introduction to Early Judaism*, Grand Rapids, MI: William B. Eerdmans

Vattimo, G. (2002) *After Christianity*, trans. L. D'Isanto, New York: Columbia University Press

Walker, A. (1983) *In Search of Our Mothers' Gardens: Womanist Prose*, San Diego: Harcourt Brace Jovanovich

——(1984) "I Said to Poetry" in *Horses Make a Landscape Look More Beautiful: Poems by Alice Walker*, San Diego: Harcourt Brace Jovanovich

Welch, S. (1990) *A Feminist Ethic of Risk*, Minneapolis: Fortress Press

——(2004) *After Empire: The Art and Ethos of Enduring Peace*, Minneapolis: Fortress Press

West, M. L. (1999) "Towards Monotheism" in Athanassaidi, P. and M. Frede (eds.) *Pagan Monotheism in Late Antiquity*, Oxford: Clarendon Press

Whitehead, A. N. (1932) *Science and the Modern World*, Cambridge: Cambridge University Press

——(1960) *Process and Reality*, New York: Macmillan Press

——(1966) *A Key to Whitehead's Process and Reality*, Sherburne, D. (ed.) New York: Macmillan Company

——(1968) *Modes of Thought*, New York: Free Press

Whitman, W. (1983) *Song of Myself*, New York: Bantam

Wigoder, G., F. Skolnik, and S. Himelstein (eds.) (2002) *The New Encyclopedia of Judaism*, New York: New York University Press

Williams, D. (1995) *Sisters in the Wilderness: The Challenge of Womanist God-Talk* Maryknoll: Orbis Books

Wilson, A. N. (1997) *Paul: The Mind of the Apostle*, New York: W. W. Norton

Xenophanes (1992) *Xenophanes of Colophon: Fragments*, trans. J. H. Lesher, Toronto: University of Toronto Press

Index of names and subjects

Aeschylus 41
Agamben, Giorgio 200
Akhenaten ix, 1, 30, 214 n. 13
Albright, William 27, 212 n. 2; 214
  n. 24
Alexander the Great 35, 39, 40, 46,
  51–52
Althaus-Reid, Marcella 2–3, 91, 127,
  133, 140, 156, 202, 208 n. 15, 210
  n. 27, 224 n. 8, 225 n. 4
Aquinas, St. Thomas 46, 52, 76–77,
  101, 108, 111, 132, 219 n. 5, 219–20
  n. 14
Anderson, Benedict 186
Arendt, Hannah 160
Aristotle 39, 46; 50–54; 58, 111; prime
  mover 51, 58, 77, 179; rule of one
  58, 63, 189
Armour, Ellen xiii, 3, 225 n. 36
Assmann, Jan 32, 214 n. 13
Augustine 99; African roots 61, 65–66,
  70, 218 n. 37; empire 70; love 71,
  205; idea of trinity 71–72

Bacon, Sir Francis 78, 80–81, 93
Badiou, Alain 144–46, 150
Baker-Fletcher, Karen 140, 224 n. 8
Baldwin, James 44, 198
Barker, Jason 148
Barth, Karl 186, 191–94, 209, 211 n.
  19
Bauckham, Richard 60
Baudrillard, Jean 8, 146; impossible
  exchange 149, 170–72, 206, 225 n.
  34
becoming 4, 89, 98, 135, 146, 149,
  151, 159–60, 163, 165–67, 170–71,
  176–81, 204–5, 220 n. 25, 224 n.
  31; becoming-fluent 152, 155–56;

becoming-other xi, 89; concretion
  116, 127, 140–41, 159, 167
de Beistegui, Miguel 145
Boff, Leonardo 4, 223 (chapter 10) n.
  7
Bodies ix, 13–14, 30, 44–45, 81, 113,
  116, 120, 125–26, 138, 170, 178,
  200, 224 n. 13; feminism 2, 88, 116,
  139–40, 149–50; hell 95–104, 127;
  heterogeneity/impossible exchange
  5, 150–51, 164–71, 170–76, 199;
  incarnation 2–5, 10–14, 67, 93,
  115–17, 127, 139–42, 155, 159,
  163–65, 176, 205–6, 226 n. 18;
  interconnection 157–61; love 71,
  205–6; making sense ix, 6, 111, 150,
  163–64, 201; opposition to the logic
  of the one ix, 3, 5, 13–14, 49–52,
  57–59, 67, 72, 88–90, 91–104, 127;
  queerness 5, 10, 91–93 96–99,
  102–4, 127; race/postcolonialism/
  liberation theology 100–103, 140,
  149–50, 224 n. 8; sources for logic
  of multiplicity ix–xi, 13–14, 111–20,
  128, 139–42, 145, 149–53, 163–70,
  181, 191–94, 201–2, 210 n.31, 222
  n.21; see also incarnation
Bonhoeffer, Dietrich 186, 196, 205–6,
  224 n. 30, 228 n. 18
Braidotti, Rosi 10, 142–46, 159
Brock, Rita Nakashima 223 (chapter
  10) n. 6
Brown, Dan 7, 93–94
Buber, Martin 205–6
Bultmann, Rudolph 108–10, 113

Cicero, Marcus Tullius 52–54, 216 n.
  27
Colebrook, Claire 2, 150,

Gleiser, Marcelo 88
Gnuse, Robert 28, 212 n. 31, 212 n. 2
God: Aten 214 n. 13; black 132–33;
images 5–6, 11–14, 18, 44–45,
63–64, 71, 107–14, 189, 216 n. 15;
male/patriarchal 7, 35–38, 44,
54–56, 63–64, 76, 132, 139–40,
154; prime mover/cosmic principle
30, 34–38, 50–52, 58, 62, 67, 77–79,
147, 179; language/terminology
11–14, 44; warrior king 32, 35–38,
105; Yahweh 26–37, 214 n. 16–24;
Xenophanes 43–44, 215 n. 11 & 14,
216 n. 15; *see also* divine
multiplicity; *see also* incarnation; *see
also* Jesus; *see also* monotheism; *see
also* trinity
Hanh, Thich Nhat 121, 224 n. 21
Halperin, Baruch 22, 27, 29, 32, 37,
214 n. 22, n. 24, 217 n. 29
Hallowell, A.I. 86
Handler, Richard 86–87
Harrod, Howard 212 n. 26, 219 n. 12
Hawking, Stephen 80, 88; theory of
everything/TOE 79, 82, 88–90, 136,
144, 156
Hearne, Vicki 166
Heidegger, Martin 132, 144–46, 160,
169
hell 9–10, 92–104, 108–9, 112, 127,
138, 152, 167, 200; *see also* Satan
hellenism 6, 18–20, 25–26, 34, 39–40,
47, 51–62, 67–72, 119, 139, 174,
199, 218 n. 43
Hill, Willard W. x
Hillel 204–5, 221 (chapter 8) n. 13
Holmes, Barbara 113, 127, 176–78,
195, 227 n. 28
Homer 44–45, 48, 52, 189, 215 n. 3,
215 n. 12, 227 (chapter 13) n. 9
Hroch, Miroslav 187, 194
Hume, David 23–24, 108
humor xii, 3, 6, 8–9, 94–95, 100–102,
111, 114–15, 120–23, 126, 135,
147, 157, 176, 210 n. 27, 227–28
(chapter 14) n. 10

Ibn Sinna (Avicenna) 78, 199
ice 91–92, 96–104, 107, 115, 137,
147–48, 155, 167, 189, 200;
metaphysical 10, 90–91, 97, 100–103,
112–13, 117, 126, 202; *see also*
logic of the One; *see also* water
Ignatius of Antioch, 68–69

immanence/presence 1, 4–12, 37,
114–16, 146, 151–74, 201–7, 209 n.
19, 225–26 (chapter 12) n. 2
incarnation ix, 1–14, 139–45, 154–81,
199–207; challenge to monotheism
58–62, 139, 154, 165–67, 199–202;
embodiment 2, 5, 14, 67, 128,
140–42, 155, 159, 163–67, 170–75,
194, 205, 210 n. 31; Jesus 6–9,
58–62, 139, 172–75; particularity
168–76; suppressed/limited 13, 72,
115, 139–40, 163, 173–74, 192,
199–200; trinity 61–62, 67; *see also*
bodies; *see also* immanence/presence
Irigaray, Luce 1, 88, 113, 127, 139,
146–47, 149, 153, 161, 165, 175,
208 (chapter 1) n. 2
Islam 6, 23–24, 27, 36, 188–90, 192,
199, 204; Qu'ran 7, 204, 213 n. 5,
221 (chapter 8) n. 13, 228 n. 15;
monotheism 6, 23–27, 36, 39,
188–90, 192, 199, 204; multiplicity
189, 204; political tensions with
Christianity 189–90; *see also*
Shahadah

Jaffee, Martin 17
Jantzen, Grace 139
Jennings, Theodore 4–5, 68, 71, 209 n.
18
Jesus 6–7, 10, 13–14, 17–18, 39, 55–56,
61–62, 67, 111–13, 117–20, 162,
179–80, 201–2, 217 n. 10, 217–18
n. 11; Christ 9, 23, 55–56, 60,
67–69, 93, 117, 223 (chapter 10) n.
6, 224 n. 30; divinity 5–10, 23,
55–65, 115, 139–40, 159, 163, 165,
173–75, 193, 213 n. 4; humanity 62,
67, 115, 159, 163, 173–75, 213 n.
4; Jewish identity 17–18, 52, 55,
115, 117, 119; movement 7, 18, 51,
55–57, 59, 63; Pontius Pilate 164,
172–75, 226 n. 20–21; teachings
151–52, 204, 217 n. 31
Joh, Wohnee Anne 3, 140, 208 n. 10,
224 n. 8
Johnson, Elizabeth 211 n. 19, 223
(chapter 10) n. 6
Jordan, Mark 8
Josiah, King ix, 28–29
Judaism 6, 17–20, 26–28, 39, 56–60,
76, 121, 156, 189, 192, 200, 203;
ancient Israel 17–20, 28–34;
hellenized 54–55; relationship to

early Christianity 54–58, 117–19,
217 n. 31, 226 n. 21; Torah 17, 37,
39, 54, 203–5

Kaul, Suvir 2
Keller, Catherine xi, xii-xiii, 3, 6, 8,
112–16, 133, 141, 151, 157, 161,
164, 178, 209 n. 20, 219 n. 67, 223
(chapter 10) n. 3, 224 n. 24, 227
(chapter 14) n. 10; *see also* tehom
Kenney, John 50
Kierkegaard, Søren 95, 145, 149, 220
n. 25, 224 n. 31
King, Thomas xii, 3, 117, 120–26,
146, 211 n. 12
Kristeva, Julia 147, 210 n. 23
Kwok Pui-lan 3

Lacan, Jacques 88, 147
LaCugna, Catherine Mowry 4, 68, 71,
163, 209 n. 16
Lerro, Bruce 188
Levinas, Immanuel 156–57, 171, 195,
205
logic of multiplicity x, 2, 5, 8, 10,
138–52, 154–63, 164–81, 195–207;
a-centered relationality 176–81,
202; fluency, 140, 155–57, 206;
fluidity 100–102, 107–8, 116–26,
154–57, 161–65, 194, 211 n. 18;
heterogeneity 164–81; impossible
exchange 149, 165–79, 194, 198–207
interconnection 67, 116, 123, 157–63,
168–72, 188, 194–202; porosity 93,
156–63, 188–201; shape-shifting 18,
87, 91 101–2, 137, 157–70, 179, 201;
see also incarnation; *see also* bodies
logic of the One ix, 1–2, 9, 45–60,
69–73, 99, 110–11, 138–49, 160–67,
173–75, 179, 189–94, 199–204;
certainty 8, 113–15, 123, 138, 156;
immutability 40–50; in western
science 74–90, 188; non-
contradiction 83–86, 99; one-minus
143–44; simplicity 43–52, 59, 75,
82–83, 88, 220, n. 17; stasis/eternity
1–2, 5, 49, 68, 72, 78, 91–104,
111–16, 140, 144–47, 154–55,
165–67, 226 n. 18; *see also*
monotheism; *see also* dualism
Loomba, Ania 2
Lopez, Barry 125
love 3, 10, 12, 17, 25, 110, 133, 152,
158, 199, 202–7, 213 n. 3; model of

trinity 71; lovers 71, 82, 94–95, 125,
157, 202–3

Mach, Michael 20, 32–34, 36
Martin, Biddy 228 n. 17
Martin, Calvin Luther 93, 146–47
Mbiti, John 65
McFague, Sallie 113, 221 n. 3
metaphoric exemption 153–55, 164,
189, 210 n. 32, 221 (chapter 8) n.
10, 227 (chapter 13) n. 10
Moltmann, Jürgen 4, 25, 59, 63, 71,
163, 191, 209 n. 19, 218 n. 32, 223
(chapter 10) n. 7, 225 n. 20, 225 n.
18, 227 n. 13
monotheism 5, 72, 136, 140, 186–94,
199, 202–7, 212 n. 29, 214 n. 11 &
13; Christian/trinitarian 4, 17–18,
56–82, 91, 99–102, 191–94, 209 n.
16, 218 n. 32, 227 n. 13; exclusive
28–37, 56, 79–80, 188–94; Greek
monism 42–55, 218 n. 32; history of
the term 19–26, 211 n. 7 & 14;
inclusive 41, 79–80, 85, 89, 191–94;
Jewish 17–18, 20, 27–38, 40, 42,
54–57, 189, 212 n. 31, 212–13 n.
2, 214 n. 24; monolatry 21, 32–33,
42, 203, 212 n. 31;
monotonotheism 76
moreless 144, 164
Mosby-Avery, Karen 68, 218 n. 50
Mosha, Raymond 65

Nagel, Joane 188, 227 n. 13
Nancy, Jean Luc 142–44, 146, 163
natality ix, 160–61
nationalism 3, 185–97; ethnosexual
186–88, 227 (chapter 13) n. 1;
Nazism 185, 193; theory 187–89
Newton, Sir Isaac 25, 78–79, 82–83,
94, 124
Ngong, D. T. 66
Niemoller, Martin 186
Nietzsche, Friedrich 74–76, 115, 127,
133, 145–49, 220 n. 25, 224 n. 31
Nye, Naomi Shihab ix, xiii

Occam's razor 82–83, 88, 219–20 n.
14, 220 n. 17
Ogbonnaya, A. Okechukwu 3, 65–67,
72, 218 n. 37, n. 43
omnicentricity 176–78, 195
oneness/the One: *see also* monotheism;
see also logic of the One

Index of biblical references

Genesis

1	116
1:2	178, 115–16, 208 n. 8
1:26	214 n. 10
11:17	214 n. 10
31:19ff	30, 214 n. 10

Exodus

20:2	27, 30
20:3	202

Leviticus

19:18	198, 204

Deuteronomy

4:19–20	30
4:35–39	30
5:7	30, 202
6:4–9	17, 213 n. 3
6:5	203
32:8–9	30

Psalms

29	30, 214 n. 19
82	30

Isaiah

40–55	28–29, 31–36, 42, 58, 208 n. 8
40:15	37
42:10	36
44:6–8	32
44: 24–28	27
45:18	32
49:6	32

Related titles from Routledge

Feminist Philosophy of Religion

Critical Readings

Edited by Pamela Sue Anderson and Beverley Clack

Feminist philosophy of religion has developed in recent years because of the exposure of explicit sexism in much traditional philosophical thinking about religion. The struggle with a discipline shaped almost exclusively by men has led feminist philosophers to redress the problematic biases of gender, race, class and sexual orientation in the traditional subject.

Feminist Philosophy of Religion: Critical Readings brings together key new writings in this growing field. Part one of the reader explores important approaches to the feminist philosophy of religion, including psychoanalytic, poststructualist, postmetaphysical and epistemological frameworks. In part two, the contributors survey significant topics including questions of divinity, embodiment, spirituality and religious practice. Supported by explanatory prefaces and an extensive bibliography, *Feminist Philosophy of Religion: Critical Readings* is an important resource for this new area of study.

ISBN10: 0-415-25749-2 (hbk)
ISBN10: 0-415-25750-6 (pbk)

Available at all good bookshops
For ordering and further information please visit:
www.routledge.com

Related titles from Routledge

The Face of the Deep

A theology of becoming

Catherine Keller

'*Face of the Deep* challenges one of the oldest of orthodox beliefs: that God created the world out of nothing. Remaining close to the Bible, and encompassing Augustine and Barth, Genesis and Moby Dick in a single, lucid gaze, Catherine Keller develops a compelling theology of creation that is also a profound theology of living.'
Kevin Hart, University of Notre Dame

'Biblical hermeneutics, postmodern science, feminist process theology – and so much more – roil the deep waters of this profound new creation theology. A wonderful display of erudition, wisdom and playfulness from Catherine Keller at her engaging best.'
Kathryn Tanner, University of Chicago Divinity School

The idea that an omnipotent God created our complicated world from nothing dominates Western religious discourse, but no biblical text actually teaches this. The ancient texts imagine a messier beginning with no unambiguous point of origin and no final end. In an increasingly crowded and heterogeneous postmodernity *The Face of the Deep* finds this biblical chaos more resonant that the classical erasure and offers the first fully theology of creation from the primal oceanic chaos-creatio ex profundis. The author draws on poststructuralist, feminist and chaos theory to present an alternative representation of the cosmic creative process which doesn't celebrate chaos but proposes in form and content an order of self-organizing complexity.

ISBN13: 978-0-415-25648-3 (hbk)
ISBN13: 978-0-415-25649-0 (pbk)

Available at all good bookshops
For ordering and further information please visit:
www.routledge.com

Related titles from Routledge

Indecent Theology
Marcella Althaus-Reid

'I believe that this may be the best feminist theology (and I am not exaggerating) in the last decade.'
Robert Goss, Webster University

'It is absolutely unique in the field, well written and provocative ... groundbreaking and wild.'
Mary Hunt, author of Women Alliance in Theology

- All theology is sexual theology.
- Indecent Theology is sexier than most.
- What can sexual stories from fetishism and sadomasochism tell us about our relationship with God, Jesus and Mary?
- Isn't it time the Christian heterosexuals came out of their closets too?

By examining the dialectics of decency and indecency and exploring a theology of sexual stories from the margins, this book brings together for the first time Liberation Theology, Queer Theory, post-Marxism and Postcolonial analysis in an explosive mixture. Indecent Theology is an out of the closet style of doing theology and shows how we can reflect on the Virgin Mary and on Christology from sexual stories taken from Fetishism, Leather lifestyles and Transvestism.

Indecent Theology is based on the sexual experiences of the poor, using economic and political analysis while unveiling the sexual ideology of systematic theology. Theology is a sexual act and Indecent Theologians are called to be sexual performers of a committed praxis of social justice and transformation of the structures of economic and sexual oppression in their societies.

ISBN13: 978-0-415-23603-4 (hbk)
ISBN13: 978-0-415-23604-1 (pbk)

Available at all good bookshops
For ordering and further information please visit:
www.routledge.com

Related titles from Routledge

The Queer God
Marcella Althaus-Reid

'First class: an exciting, original work.'
Alistair Kee, University of Edinburgh

There are those who go to gay bars and salsa clubs with rosaries in their pockets, and who make camp chapels of their living rooms. Others enter churches with love letters hidden in their bags, because their need for God and their need for love refuse to fit into different compartments. But what goodness and righteousness can prevail if you are in love with someone whom you are ecclesiastically not supposed to love? Where is God in a salsa bar?

The Queer God introduces a new theology from the margins of sexual deviance and economic exclusion. Its chapters on Bisexual Theology, Sadean holiness, gay worship in Brazil and Queer sainthood mark the search for a different face of God – the Queer God who challenges the oppressive powers of heterosexual orthodoxy, whiteness and global capitalism. Inspired by the transgressive spaces of Latin American spirituality, where the experiences of slum children merge with Queer interpretations of grace and holiness, *The Queer God* seeks to liberate God from the closet of traditional Christian thought, and to embrace God's part in the lives of gays, lesbians and the poor.

Only a theology that dares to be radical can show us the presence of God in our times. *The Queer God* creates a concept of holiness that overcomes sexual and colonial prejudices and shows how Queer Theology is ultimately the search for God's own deliverance. Using Liberation Theology and Queer Theory, it exposes the sexual roots that underlie all theology, and takes the search for God to new depths of social and sexual exclusion.

ISBN13: 978-0-415-32323-9 (hbk)
ISBN13: 978-0-415-32324-6 (pbk)

Available at all good bookshops
For ordering and further information please visit:
www.routledge.com

Related titles from Routledge

Theology Goes to the Movies
Clive Marsh

'By starting from issues explored in particular films, the book helps to ground theological debates in relation to human questions and experience. This really helps to bring the discipline of theology alive, and I wish this book had been available when I was a theology student.'
Gordon Lynch, Senior Lecturer in Religion and Culture, University of Birmingham, UK

'Marsh is correct! Theology is not just cognitive, but affective, aesthetic and ethical. And film has become a primary resource. Here is a helpful work-book for culturally-savy theology students and theologically-interested film-lovers.'
Robert K. Johnston, author of Reel Spirituality: Theology and Film in Dialogue

'Marsh never reduces the theological analysis of culture to an imposition of theological concepts onto culture; rather, theology is developed in critical engagement with popular culture, within "peaceful mutual critique." He accomplishes this task with clarity, open-mindedness, and grace.'
John Lyden, Professor and Chair of Religion, Dana College

Theology Goes to the Movies is an introduction to understanding theology through film. Clive Marsh, an experienced teacher in the field, uses a range of contemporary films including *Touching the Void*, *Bruce Almighty*, *Notting Hill*, *21 Grams*, *Legally Blond*, and *The Piano* to explain key theological concepts such as ideas of God, the church, eschatology, redemption, humanity and spirit.

Starting from the premise that film watching is a religion-like activity, the book explores the ways in which films require the viewer to engage at many levels (cognitive, affective, aesthetic and ethical) and argues that the social practice of cinema going has a religious dimension. This stimulating and entertaining book shows how theology through film can be both a method of reading the dialogue between film and Western culture, as well as a relevant and contemporary practical theology.

ISBN13: 978-0-415-38011-9 (hbk)
ISBN13: 978-0-415-38012-6 (pbk)

Available at all good bookshops
For ordering and further information please visit:
www.routledge.com

eBooks – at www.eBookstore.tandf.co.uk

A library at your fingertips!

eBooks are electronic versions of printed books. You can store them on your PC/laptop or browse them online.

They have advantages for anyone needing rapid access to a wide variety of published, copyright information.

eBooks can help your research by enabling you to bookmark chapters, annotate text and use instant searches to find specific words or phrases. Several eBook files would fit on even a small laptop or PDA.

NEW: Save money by eSubscribing: cheap, online access to any eBook for as long as you need it.

Annual subscription packages

We now offer special low-cost bulk subscriptions to packages of eBooks in certain subject areas. These are available to libraries or to individuals.

For more information please contact webmaster.ebooks@tandf.co.uk

We're continually developing the eBook concept, so keep up to date by visiting the website.

www.eBookstore.tandf.co.uk